THE VOICES OF GEMMA GALGANI

The Voices of Gemma Galgani

THE LIFE AND AFTERLIFE OF A MODERN SAINT

* * *

RUDOLPH M. BELL AND CRISTINA MAZZONI

The University of Chicago Press
Chicago and London

RUDOLPH M. BELL is professor of history at Rutgers University. He is the author of several books, including *Holy Anorexia* and *How to Do It: Guides to Good Living for Renaissance Italians,* both published by the University of Chicago Press.

CRISTINA MAZZONI is associate professor of Romance languages at the University of Vermont. She is the author of *Saint Hysteria: Neurosis, Mysticism, and Gender in European Culture* and *Maternal Impressions: Pregnancy and Childbirth in Literature and Theory.*

The University of Chicago Press, Chicago 60637
The University of Chicago Press, Ltd., London
© 2003 by Rudolph M. Bell and Cristina Mazzoni
All rights reserved. Published 2003
Printed in the United States of America

12 11 10 09 08 07 06 05 04 03   1 2 3 4 5

ISBN: 0-226-04196-4 (cloth)

Library of Congress Cataloging-in-Publication Data

Bell, Rudolph M.
    The voices of Gemma Galgani : the life and afterlife of a modern saint /
Rudolph M. Bell and Cristina Mazzoni.
        p. cm.
    Includes bibliographical references and index.
    ISBN 0-226-04196-4 (alk. paper)
        1. Galgani, Gemma, Saint, 1878–1903.   2. Christian saints—Italy—
Biography.   1. Galgani, Gemma, Saint, 1878–1903.   II. Mazzoni, Cristina,
1965–   III. Title.

BX4700.G22 B45 2003
282′.092—dc21

                                                                        2002007141

PER KATIA, DA NONNO RUDY
E
PER GEMMA, DA MAMMA CRISTINA

CONTENTS

We are pleased to thank the two anonymous readers for the University of Chicago Press who gave such careful attention to earlier versions of this book. Two additional readers for the press chose to make themselves known to us, and so we are able to thank them more specifically. Robert Orsi for a time considered contributing an essay to part 2 of this book and, although that did not work out, we remain in his debt for early suggestions for revisions of other parts of the work and for sharing with us his deeply personal reflection on Gemma Galgani. William A. Christian Jr provided an extraordinarily detailed critique of our study, which is stronger for his advice. At the press itself, Doug Mitchell and Robert Devens believed in the project from the outset and supported us not merely as editors but as friends. Some other acknowledgments are better said individually.

At the Biblioteca di Spiritualità A. Levasti in Florence, on virtually every Thursday morning from September 1981 until June 1983, the late Padre Innocenzo Colosio freely shared documents and first explored with me various ways of understanding the mystical experiences of Gemma Galgani and her many Italian predecessors. Laura Tomici Bell, my wife, aided me in a variety of scholarly chores during those years and was instrumental in obtaining access to materials at the Santa Gemma Monastery outside Lucca. She also inspired me to take up the project again in 1998, providing both sound advice and encouragement. Tara Cristina Giovannetti and Alessia Tamara Bell, my daughters, took time out of their busy lives to read and critique various drafts and managed to get past the father/daughter thing to tell me where my thinking was muddled or my expression garbled. Members of the Gender Studies group at Rutgers University, led by Bonnie Smith, invited me to talk about my work at an informal seminar in the fall of 1999, and I thank them for their lively responses and suggestions. My colleagues Phyllis Mack, Nicole Postel-Pellegrin, and Bonnie Smith read major portions of the work-in-progress and offered many useful comments. Samantha Kelly, also a colleague, cheerfully tracked down materials in Rome. Rutgers University provided funds to assist in carrying out the research, and it also has been a great place to work. Colleagues at the university's Alexander Library have been unfailingly effective in acquiring materials specific to the project as well as in supporting my scholarly and teaching endeavors more generally. At the Passionist Center in Chicago, the late Father Roger Mercurio and Sister Loretta Ciesielski, S.S.J.-tosf were especially gracious in assisting my research there. *Rudolph M. Bell*

I am grateful as always to the staff at the Interlibrary Loan Office of the Bailey-Howe Library here at the University of Vermont, without whose courteous and efficient labor none of my research would be possible. In the medieval village of the Celio hill in Rome, a haven from traffic, tourists, and pollution, Father Juan Llorente, of the Casa Generalizia dei Padri Passionisti, was kind enough to give me access to Gemma's letters and autobiography. The Dean's Office of the College of Arts and Sciences at the University of Vermont provided me with funds to make the trip to Rome. Less tangibly but no less effectively, during the writing of this book two spiritual retreats offered here in Burlington by Miriam Therese Winter and Catherine Joanne helped me to think, feel, and pray through some of its issues. Heartfelt thanks are due to all those who work and pray so that our Church may protect and nourish all of her members. More personally, I myself could not have worked and prayed through and on this book without the prayer and work of my family: my parents, Stefania and Giuseppe, my children, Paul, Gemma, and Sophia, and especially my husband John Cirignano. *Cristina Mazzoni*

It is I, Jesus, who speaks with you . . . in a few years by my doing you will be a
saint. You will perform miracles and you will receive the highest honors of the altar.
JESUS CHRIST TO GEMMA GALGANI, *March 1901*

Gemma Galgani is a compelling saint in so many ways: confident, grandiose, manipulative, childish, abandoned, loved, complicated, simple-minded, admired, forgotten. She is a modern saint, at least in the narrowly chronological sense, since she is the first person who lived into the twentieth century to receive the Catholic Church's highest honors, beatification in 1933 and canonization just seven years later on May 2, 1940. Yet she is also a timeless saint. During her brief life (March 12, 1878, to April 11, 1903) Gemma experienced all five of Christ's wounds in her hands, feet, and side. She bled as she wore her savior's crown of thorns, and while in rapture she received numerous celestial consolations. Jesus appeared as her spiritual lover, the Virgin Mary as her affectionate Mom, and Saint-to-be Gabriel Possenti as her playful friend. She also enjoyed on a daily basis the companionship and caring advice of her guardian angel, who took on additional tasks such as delivery of her letters across the hundreds of miles from her home in the Tuscan city of Lucca to Father Germano Ruoppolo di San Stanislao, her spiritual advisor, who lived at a monastery near Rome. In life, Gemma Galgani fasted prodigiously, mortified her flesh, fought the devil in physical combat, nursed the sick, and engaged in extended prayer vigils.

When Gemma died peacefully on the Saturday before Easter, crowds flocked to her humble bier, eager to touch her corpse one last time. Father Germano, also her biographer, wrote that the nuns keeping vigil at the wake barely succeeded in restraining the relic-seeking faithful from pulling every last hair out of her head. Shortly after the burial, convinced that Gemma was a saint-to-be, he hurried to Lucca and, countermanding her explicit wishes, exhumed her body from its initial resting place. He then ordered the removal of her heart, which upon examination appeared fresh, supple, and rubicund, exactly like a live heart. The local secular official who supervised the autopsy reported a noted curvature of her rib to accommodate her enlarged heart; when an attending physician sliced it open, this official saw blood flowing freely to inundate the marble slab on which they worked, as did an attending nun.

After her death, the documents tell us, Gemma Galgani's reputation grew rapidly. Above all, she interceded to cure the faithful of their crippling illnesses, paving the way to her formal designation as a blessed and then as a saint. Also, between the First and Second World Wars, missionaries carried her photograph, affectionately captioned as the "Lily of Lucca," to the farthest reaches of China. And in the 1920s, young visionaries in Spain, mostly female, took inspiration from her, although this fact was dropped from her hagiology when their apparitions failed to obtain recognition and formal approval. In the words of the *Bibliotheca Sanctorum,* a recent twelve-volume encyclopedia of saints' lives published under Vatican auspices, Gemma Galgani is "worthy to be placed next to Francis of Assisi and Catherine of Siena."[1]

Hyperbole aside, setting Gemma in the company of Saints Francis of Assisi and Catherine of Siena appropriately captures the transhistorical quality of her holiness. Stigmata, visions, ecstasy, deep contemplation, ascetic practices, pain, mortification, uncorrupted corpse, odor of sanctity, miraculous intercessions—the signs and circumstances for a Catholic saint abound. And there is more. Gemma Galgani wrote an autobiographical confession, kept a diary for a time, had her ecstatic words copied down by scribes, and penned hundreds of letters, an oeuvre of sufficient scope to warrant a place for her in the venerable tradition of Christian mysticism.[2]

And yet, notwithstanding her early miraculous intercessions and the vigorous promotion of her cult by the Passionist Order, Saint Gemma Galgani is not widely known today, just one century after her death. To be sure, her memory has not vanished entirely. A church in Detroit is dedicated to her; girls continue to be named after her, especially in Spain and Italy but also among Irish and Korean Catholics; starting in March 1924 and continuing throughout the 1930s, the Gemma League ran full-page advertisements for support of Passionist missionary activity in the Far East; and a motor boat, christened the *S. Gemma,* in 1963 began plying the Huallaga and Marañon rivers to bring medicines and the sacrament to remote villages in Peru.[3]

More recently, an internet search for "St. Gemma" landed upon www.st-gemma.co.uk, a web-page welcoming the seeker to St. Gemma's Hospice in Leeds, England, where the terminally ill may find refuge and

support. And a variant of that search string then brought up www.stgemma
.com for a hyperlinked biography. Also in our own time and less high-tech,
at Montes Belos in Brazil, a group of religious women dedicated to Passionist ideals continues to support their male counterparts in spreading the
word in that region. Closer to Gemma's native land, visitors to the environs
of Lucca are welcome to pray at the Monastero-Santuario "Santa Gemma,"
where her corpse was translated. The faithful also may buy various memo-
rabilia there, or perhaps sign on to receive the sanctuary's monthly bulletin,
published regularly from 1932 until the present.[4]

Still, there is no evidence of intense, widespread devotion to Saint
Gemma such as one finds, for example, among Italian Americans for Saint
Gerard Maiella, guardian of tens of thousands of Newark's babies, not to
mention the designated protector of one of New Jersey's finest neo-natal
hospital facilities. Nor do organized pilgrimages stop at Lucca; instead, they
make their way to remote San Giovanni Rotondo, where favors may be
sought by invoking a far more popular modern stigmatic, Padre Pio. A visit
on December 20, 2001, to http://saints.catholic.org/patron.html failed to
find Gemma as the patron of any of the hundreds of places, groups, or
specific needs it includes (although old-fashioned scholarly searching turns
up the fact that she is a celestial guardian of pharmacists, orphans, hospitals,
a diocese in Tanzania, parachutists, and an Italian organization opposed to
blasphemy).[5] And while a single "first class bone relic" of Saint Gemma
resides in relative obscurity at the Regina Caeli Chapel in Fargo, North Dakota, it was the wonderworking remains of Saint Thérèse of Lisieux that
spent the spring of 2000 in a four-month pilgrimage across the United
States, with major stops in New York City and Los Angeles. Even the Passionist Order itself, by championing the cause of the martyr Maria Goretti
(1890–1902), who died in defending her chastity, contributed significantly
to removing Gemma Galgani's complex, even ambiguous, religious messages from popular view, leaving her life and writings to the perusal of a relatively small number of devotees and scholars.[6]

Why, then, is Gemma a hidden treasure worth knowing about, a woman
whose spirituality holds such fascination for the authors of this book, someone we think you will want to know better? Before turning to her, allow us
to tell you a bit more about ourselves, about how we came together for this
endeavor. Rudolph Bell encountered the life of Gemma Galgani while doing research in the early 1980s for what became his book, *Holy Anorexia*.[7] He
read the saint's writings and studied the printed canonization proceedings

concerning Gemma Galgani, which are extremely rare; these and other materials were made available through the kindness of the late Padre Innocenzo Colosio at the Biblioteca di Spiritualità A. Levasti of the Convento San Marco in Florence, where several Dominican scholars had undertaken the research that resulted in a series of articles on Gemma Galgani that appeared in the 1978 issues of *Rivista di ascetica e mistica*.

Gemma Galgani, as much as any holy woman, experienced the key characteristics of "holy anorexia," and this combined term emphatically insists on "holy" and excludes "nervous" or "neurotic" anorexia. Nonetheless, when it came to fashioning *Holy Anorexia*, Bell had not resolved to his own satisfaction the problem of bridging the historical gap separating her from the "living saints" of the late fifteenth and early sixteenth centuries whose religious impulses seem so clearly akin to hers.[8] What of the Reformation that intervened, and the traditions of the saintly female teacher and the missionary healer so valued by the modern Catholic Church? Mother Elizabeth Ann Bayley Seton, Katherine Drexel, and Mother Teresa are closer in time to Gemma Galgani, yet her sanctity shares little with theirs, harking back instead to the harsh asceticism and intensely personal piety of late-medieval mystics like Columba of Rieti, Osanna Andreasi, Catherine of Genoa, Catherine of Racconigi, and Maria Maddalena de' Pazzi. Even her French contemporary, Thérèse of Lisieux, so similar to her in many ways, initially seems far more accessible to our modern religious sensibilities than does Gemma Galgani.

Fifteen years and some experience later, Bell returned to Gemma and decided upon a different approach than he had taken earlier. Let the woman speak for herself, not be cast into one or another socio-historical category of religious experience. To shine on her a spotlight less refracted through the prism of secular scholarly analysis, and to recover for her a script adulterated as little as possible by promoters of her cult, he chose to devote major sections of his planned book to making Gemma Galgani's writings readily available to an English-reading public. He selected for translation the complete autobiography and diary, as well as all letters and ecstasies dated between June and September of 1902. He decided to deal with the male-dominated, official canonization process as a separate essay, cast in a more traditional mode of historical analysis.

In picking up a project left fallow for so long, Bell necessarily wondered whether other writers in the meantime had come upon the terrain. As it turned out, Gemma had indeed exerted her charms on another scholar, this time a literary critic fascinated by the connection between mysticism and the hysteria diagnosis at the turn of the century. In the stacks of Yale University's Sterling Library, Cristina Mazzoni came upon books on and by Gemma Galgani. After working on Gemma in *Saint Hysteria* and elsewhere,[9] Mazzoni knew she wanted to return to this saint, though her personal and professional circumstances had in the meantime led her in different directions. But when, thanks to the modern miracle of email (one that Gemma would certainly have liked, given her troubles with the Italian postal system), Bell invited Mazzoni to participate in a book project on this saint, she was overjoyed. Gemma had finally returned to her—and she to Gemma. A decision to collaborate soon followed, with Mazzoni contributing the contemporary reflection on Saint Gemma's spiritual journey that appears in part 2. Moreover, she brought her expertise as a native speaker of Italian to her full participation with Bell in the translations found in part 1.

Gemma Galgani's writings beckoned our spiritual sensibilities, her fortitude in illness commanded our admiration, her childhood peevishness awoke our nostalgic recollections, her embrace of pain struck a chord. How, then, to structure a book about this somewhat forgotten saint? Fifteen years ago Bell had not seen how to place Gemma Galgani within a study of her pious kin from the late Middle Ages primarily because he failed to appreciate adequately the timelessness of her spiritual journey. The setting matters, for the modern context in which Gemma lived inevitably shaped the meaning of her individual religiosity, for herself as for others; but the limits of historical analysis also deserve candid acknowledgment. The *trans*cendency of Gemma's life calls for a *trans*disciplinary strategy, and that is our approach in this collective work.

Chapter 1, written by Bell, addresses the historical contexts that seem especially relevant to understanding Gemma's world. It examines the conflict between church and state in late-nineteenth-century Italy as it played itself out in the Tuscan city of Lucca, where Gemma spent virtually her entire life. It also explores Gemma's childhood and adolescence for evidence about the path of her early spiritual development, before she came under the direct influence of the Passionist Order.[10]

Part 1 gives primacy to Gemma Galgani's voice, to her own words, translated by us from her Italian into contemporary American English. We devote a chapter each to three major works: her written general confession covering her life until 1899, her diary for the summer of 1900, and her original letters and transcribed ecstasies for the summer of 1902. In each chapter, Bell provides introductory information on how Gemma's writings came down to us and gives some background on the daily events and people she refers to in them. The intent is to convey enough so that you, the reader, have a comfortable sense of the cast of characters and what is going on, but not to intervene so forcefully in the texts that they become bits of evidence in a narrative constructed by us as secular scholars rather than by Gemma herself. You will be reading the life of Gemma Galgani, when she was not yet Saint Gemma.

Finally, part 2 shifts to our readings of Gemma's words, with a focus on her afterlife. In chapter 5, Bell, the historian, examines the process of canonization and explores in depth how the Church confronted a thoroughly "medieval" holy woman who lived in a profoundly "modern" world, although the contradiction was more in the prelates' heads and hearts than it ever had been in hers. Powerful churchmen used her, as they do all saints.

In chapter 6, Mazzoni, the literary critic, employs the device of a spiritual alphabet to suggest contemporary feminist theological reflections drawn from Gemma's writings.

Our hopes for this book go unabashedly beyond the scholar's usual aims. We challenge teachers to rethink the assumption that modern times are monolithically secular, even though we present only one case and eschew any attempt to chart the specific course of that rethinking. We encourage students to consider Gemma Galgani not as a quaint exception to major developments in post-eighteenth-century Western European and American religious history but rather as a vibrant, heretofore neglected, alternative expression, one worthy of further exploration. We invite feminists to apply theoretical constructs in ways that might enable us to understand more fully the aspirations and accomplishments of young women like Gemma Galgani. Finally, we welcome readers who may be inspired by Gemma's words and deeds to reach deeper levels of individual spirituality.

THE VOICES OF GEMMA GALGANI

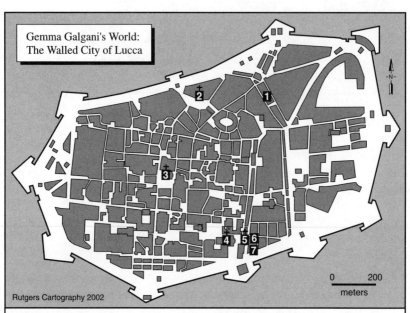

Gemma Galgani's World:
The Walled City of Lucca

Rutgers Cartography 2002

0   200
meters

1 The Galgani family's home in Lucca, on Via del Biscione (since renamed via Santa Gemma Galgani)
2 San Frediano, where Gemma made her first communion
3 San Michele, where Gemma went daily to confession with Monsignor Volpi
4 San Martino, where Gemma first heard Passionist missionaries preach in June, 1899
5 Santa Maria della Rosa, frequented by Gemma after she moved to the Giannini home in the fall of 1900
6 The room where Gemma was isolated during her last illness in the winter and spring of 1902-1903
7 The Giannini home

The Historical Setting

Sometime in the early 1940s the renowned Florentine anti-clerical, Gaetano Salvemini, by then a professor at Harvard University who for two decades had lived in exile from Mussolini's Fascist regime, delivered what have come to be known as his "Harvard Lessons." Seeing before him a Protestant, male, mostly young audience with little appreciation of his native land, he felt the need to explain as clearly as possible a world completely alien to them: Italian Catholicism. He knew the Church firsthand, and in his lecture he would attack the venerable institution and its current adherents with his usual verve. But in his opening words he adopted instead a somewhat apologetic style, asking students to give up the misconception that all Italians were Catholic and therefore obedient to the pope and the clergy. By his reckoning, only a minority should be counted as such, a conclusion he reached by dividing Italians into five groups.

First, he identified 10,000 Jews and 125,000 Protestants as non-Catholics; to them he added 1.5 million "indifferent" folks (from the 1911 census) who, although baptized, married, and buried by the Church, are otherwise irreligious. Then he singled out a third group, the "idolaters," comprising the "mass of the lower classes in southern Italy, the Papal States, and a good part of Tuscany," who seek after liquified holy blood, heap abuse on the neighboring village's favorite saint, lick the ground as they grovel toward magical icons, and generally are beyond the teachings of the clergy.

Turning next to "Catholics proper," he measured their strength by results from the last free national election, in 1919, based on universal suffrage, in which the Populists, clearly perceived as the "Catholic party," polled about one-fifth of the vote. In a necessarily rushed treatment that nonetheless was good enough for his undergraduate audience, he concluded that most of these "Catholics proper live in rural areas, especially in northern Italy."

Whatever the merits of Salvemini's statistical analysis thus far, our interest is in his fifth and final category, a group he labeled "mystics." He provided no estimate of their numbers, instead giving free rein to spontaneous and effusive admiration. Theirs is the Italy of Saint Francis, Saint Catherine of Siena, Girolamo Savonarola, and Don Bosco. These mystics take no interest in dogma, only in the sacraments as the means to their salvation; their prayers are not for favors but for the souls of sinful humanity; in accord with their means, they perform infinite good works. They worship the pope but seek not a word about what is happening in Rome. "They are possessed of great moral beauty, but politically they are inert." In a sweeping gesture of inclusion, Salvemini declared none other than Dante Alighieri to be among the "great race of mystics." [1]

With ironic prescience, the unabashedly secular teacher Salvemini now, after more than half a century, provides a lesson for us as well, a reminder that the mystic tradition in Italy, dare one say in the world more generally, while it harks back to the Middle Ages of Saint Francis and Dante Alighieri, remains vital in modern times. It is among the "great race of mystics" that Gemma Galgani finds her place.

GEMMA'S EARLIEST YEARS

She was born in the hamlet of Borgo Nuovo in the provincial town of Capannori, about four miles from Lucca, the first daughter of Enrico Galgani and Aurelia Landi, after four sons. Another boy and two girls followed before Aurelia died of tuberculosis in 1885, when Gemma was seven. Within a month after Gemma's birth, her father, the son of a physician and himself a trained chemist/pharmacist, moved the family from their comfortable village home to substantial quarters in the city of Lucca. Many years later, during the initial gathering of evidence in his sister's canonization proceedings, Gemma's brother Guido, who followed his father's path and became a pharmacist, recalled that the move had been undertaken to facilitate the children's education. While his sons' schooling must have been Enrico's primary concern, other testimony in the same hearings reveals that in 1880, when she was just two-and-a-half years old, Gemma began to attend a private nursery school run by the unmarried sisters Elena and Ersilia Vallini. Reports have it that Gemma's mother, a woman of "illustrious" but not noble heritage, suffered greatly for at least five years from the tuberculosis that caused her death in 1885, and her poor health no doubt contributed to the decision to send Gemma to nursery school at such a young age. At home, also at a very young age, she received catechism lessons from a friendly neighbor, Isabella Bastiani, who later testified formally to this fact. Gemma excelled at her lessons: "at five years she read the breviary for the Office of the Blessed Virgin Mary and for the dead with the same facility and ease that an experienced person was able to read them."[2]

In her autobiography, Gemma tells about how her family became destitute, but for the early years their financial situation, unlike their physical health, was good; they were educated, professional, and property-owning. Even when her natal family literally disintegrated, an extended network of aunts and uncles came to the rescue, allowing the children to be reared in some semblance of bourgeois security and even material comfort until they were old enough to go their own ways.

Gemma's family was deeply Christian, although not entirely exempt from the secularization and scientific rationalism that permeated the educated classes in nineteenth-century Europe. Her mother Aurelia worried that Gemma's very name, which had been selected by the infant's uncle, did not appear among the lists of Christian saints she knew, and that the child therefore would be denied admission to Heaven. Neither the parish priest's assurances that this "gem" would find a place in Heaven anyway, nor adding the names Umberta and Pia to her baptismal record, assuaged all doubts, and years later the adult Gemma was greatly relieved to learn from a Passionist priest that in fact there was a Saint Gemma (of Goriano Sicoli, near Sulmona in the Abruzzi). Whether this priest also told Gemma Galgani about the heroic penitential mortifications and mystical consolations of her fourteenth-century namesake is not recorded. On her paternal side, although Enrico's piety may have been more conventional, Gemma's reports about how he accepted his own death from throat cancer suggest that he too was a person of deep faith. Finally, the fact that he allowed one of his sons, Gino, to study for the priesthood indicates that he was not an implacable foe of the Church.

CHURCH AND STATE IN LUCCA

The life and afterlife of Gemma Galgani, climaxed by her canonization, can be appreciated fully only by understanding their wider contexts, both the political and the ideological. Lucca's citizenry experienced not only the secular impulses that, according to the papacy, threatened all of Christendom, but also felt intensely the conflict between church and state raging in the years after Italy's unification, achieved over the Vatican's unrelenting opposition. While Salvemini's remark—the "great race of mystics" are people of "moral beauty" who care not a whit for papal politics—rings true, and certainly there is no evidence that such matters ever concerned Gemma Galgani, it remains the case that several of the clerics she interacted with most directly during her lifetime were thoroughly caught up in the conflict.

In the Lucchese countryside, where Gemma's forebears had made their home and lived in comfort though not luxury, a very restricted number of ecclesiastical institutions, along with no more than a few hundred aristocratic clans, ran everything. This elite class, notwithstanding its defects, by and large acted with enough benevolence to render grinding poverty virtually unknown among working families. According to local historian Mirena Stanghellini,[3] even late into the nineteenth century "certain bonds of affection were not yet lost" between the peasantry and the landowners. Within Lucca's walls, however, by mid-century pauperism had become a major problem, as it had throughout urban Europe. The specter of socialist agitation was real in a city where children were "walking cadavers" and "mothers were ruined by hunger." Country-based ecclesiastical institutions, no doubt looking at least in part to defend their riches against possible government incursions, extended their beneficence to city folk, but too little and too late. Artisanal production of figurines, for which the Lucchese were justly famed throughout the world, remained bottled up in the city, blocked by poor transportation, inadequate marketing facilities, and a shortage of cash or credit. Late in the century a few of the more entrepreneurial men headed off for the New World, often with no more than a sack of statuettes to barter, but even this outlet required money to pay for passage, and in any event left the city to cope with those residents who were even less able to support themselves.[4]

In her autobiography, Gemma describes with childlike ease the antics she employed to aid the poor, once she had thoroughly exceeded her father's considerable tolerance for such good deeds. In these innocent gestures one may see not only the pathetic futility of a little girl, but also a metaphoric comment on the harsh realities of life in the wake of modern capitalist industrialization.

Faced with intractable problems created by depths of urban poverty threatening to overwhelm completely the traditions of benign charity that had functioned well for centuries, especially in the countryside, Lucca's churchmen found their sphere of activity further restricted by papal insistence on the doctrine known generally as "Catholic intransigence." Secular Italy had formed a nation by seizing what belonged to the pope, and if his armies were no longer capable of defending God's turf, then at least the Holy See would refuse any cooperation with the enemy. What traitors like Camillo Benso, Count of Cavour, and brigands like Giuseppe Garibaldi had stolen in worldly possessions would be recovered by priests and bishops in the spiritual realm: no baptism, no communion, and no last rites for the infidels. And without question there was to be no cooperation with the secular government in easing even the most pressing social tensions. Nor, for those nearest to Gemma Galgani, were these merely the remote events of history books; among the thousands who fled in 1870 from Rome, to Belgium and then France, was none other than her future spiritual director and biographer, Father Germano, then a twenty-year-old Passionist studying for the priesthood. The six-year exile left an indelible impression on him, and to that experience he ascribed the "cerebral anemia" that plagued him for years.[5]

Papal extremism did not go unchallenged locally, even though the more secular, liberal political leadership of Tuscany as a whole ridiculed the Lucchese for their continued devotion to the Vatican. The pope's self-declaration of his imprisonment in August 1870 fired popular outrage for some years, but as the decade passed, concerns raised by the *Syllabus of Errors* (1864)[6] and similar documents condemning modern liberalism became less heated, more a set of abstract intellectual issues than an emotional and psychological powder keg. The local Catholic broadsheet, *Fedele,* gradually resorted less frequently to publishing selected extracts from Garibaldi's violently anticlerical diatribes as a means of fanning popular fears that the upheavals convulsing Paris would reach the quiet streets of Lucca. Carnivalesque parades mocking people of faith waned in popularity, and while secret Masonic lodges and liberal intellectual clubs continued to meet behind closed doors, they less often reached out to bring their secular messages to the citizenry at large.[7] Even the subjugation of ecclesiastical property and privilege to governmental control, once done, aroused less passion than had the clergy's fears that all would be lost to the godless. The years between the capture of Rome in 1870 and Pope Pius IX's death in 1878 may rightly be seen as a period of mutual intransigence by Catholics and liberals. The climate during Leo XIII's reign, 1878–1903 (coinciding precisely with Gemma Galgani's life span), however, is better understood as a time of distrustful accommodation. Leo XIII, no less than his predecessor Pius IX, unflinchingly condemned all of modernity, yet his weapons were discourse more than action and his venue the confessional rather than the street.[8]

Despite the continuation of profound ideological disagreement, in Lucca, as elsewhere in Italy, political intransigence inexorably gave way to mutually beneficial accords. When things went well, the self-congratulators spoke of benign compromise, and when they did not, the recriminators decried the consequences of crass opportunism, but less often did Heaven and Hell enter the debate. A distinction between "thesis" and "hypothesis" soothed more than one conscience on either side, as did differentiating greater from lesser evils, and principles from practices. The earlier papal admonition against voting in national elections (*non-expedit,* 1867), as well as the recent prohibition on electoral participation (*non-licet,* 1886), could not be ignored completely, but the time had come to join local elites of all political persuasions in meeting the twin challenges at hand: maintaining the status quo among rural folk while exterminating the infectious peril of socialist agitation aimed at Lucca's urban poor.[9]

GEMMA'S CHILDHOOD

Such was the hotly contested political and social context in which the Galganis reared their children. Surviving records about the family, which come mostly from zealous supporters of Gemma's canonization, portray an upbringing of great piety, with the mother's religiosity painted in particularly vivid hues. Nonetheless, there are troubling dark spots. Consider more fully Gemma's baptismal names. Adding the name Pia (directly after the recently deceased Pope Pius IX) may have assuaged the mother's fears about her daughter's place in Heaven, but it did not sit well with someone. The civic register of Capannori (as opposed to the parish baptismal record) lists the infant's name as Maria Gemma Umberta. The name "Pia" disappears, replaced by the ubiquitous "Maria" to accompany the secular "Gemma" and the royal "Umberta," surely no scribe's error. The explanation offered by the Passionist Enrico Zoffoli, Gemma's most careful biographer, rings true: "It is very probable that in those years of misguided patriotism, either the parents of the saint thought it imprudent to impose the name of the hated Pius IX, dead that same year, on the newborn, or else the officer of vital records, owing to his sectarian spirit, refused to do so, or maybe just advised against it." A trivial issue, perhaps, but throughout her life Maria Gemma Umberta [Pia] Galgani never referred to herself as anything beyond "Gemma." Moreover, Eufemia Giannini, Gemma's "adopted sister," upon her vestition as a nun chose as her name in religion "Maria Gemma Maddalena," adding the penitential "Maddalena" to the official, civic name "Maria Gemma" and again leaving out "Pia."[10]

Then there is the matter of Gemma's schooling. From the enthusiastic autobiographical description of her days with the nuns at Santa Zita, one would think, as her biographer mistakenly did, that she began her formal education there. But according to classmates who wrote lovingly yet assertively from as far away as Buenos Aires to correct the impression conveyed in Gemma's posthumously published autobiography and in Father Germano's biography, she and they together had attended the Mencacci (public) school until she was seven, and at the age of ten or eleven her fourth-grade teacher was Barbara Poli, obviously a secular person.

Gemma's father, of course, and not Gemma, chose the secular path of her first four or five years of formal schooling, and he surely understood the political meaning of his decision. Only thereafter, at a point when public education options for girls were few, or may have been limited by this father's lack of ambition for his daughter, did this bright child enter school with the nuns for the first time.[11] Thus, I suggest that his religiosity was conventional, trimmed to accord with his professional needs. Certainly that is what Gemma thought about her paternal aunts' piety, as she states in no uncertain terms in her autobiography.

Relevant also is evidence about Gemma's siblings. Among her surviving older brothers (the firstborn, Carlo, died in early childhood, before Gemma's birth), her beloved Gino had been studying for the priesthood before he came down with a fatal case of tuberculosis, and among her sisters, all younger than she, little Giulia was so good that even Gemma did not worry for her soul when she died. The others, by contrast, were far from splendid examples of pious childrearing. The eldest, Guido, did well enough in school to continue in his father's profession but, as shown in the canonization proceedings for his sister, he knew so little about basic Catholic doctrine that some of his testimony, already bearing clear signs of having been coached, required casuistic apologies to keep it from compromising the desired result of portraying Gemma's childhood as worthy of a saint. The brother next in line, Ettore, lost touch with the family after he emigrated to Brazil, and promoters of his sister's canonization apparently dropped their efforts to bring him home to testify when word surfaced that he was living in squalid circumstances with a woman to whom he was not married. One of these two, Guido or Ettore, must be the unnamed brother that Gemma tells in her autobiography "hit me many times" because she pestered him to accompany her to church every morning. Her younger brother, Antonio, who studied for a career in pharmacy until his death from tuberculosis on October 21, 1902, was likable but rather irascible, indeed, "un po' scapestratello" (a bit of a rascal) according to one acquaintance.[12] Gemma reported him to her aunts and to her confessor for the great distress he caused her with his frequent blasphemies.[13] The worst Galgani sibling, at least in the eyes of the saint's promoters, was her sister Angelina, who on several occasions brought her teenage friends over to the house to giggle and ridicule Gemma as they watched her in ecstasy, and who later would be smeared as a woman of ill repute.

As a young adult, Gemma became painfully aware of her family's derision. In a letter to her confessor dated August 10, 1900, she begged in vain for his help:

> Listen to this: I'm almost disheartened. She [Angelina] knows all about my things. This morning she was talking about my things like they were no big deal; and my brother was making fun of them together with her. I'm not afraid of their jokes, you know? I'm afraid of many other things. [Angelina] from 11 this morning until 3:00 never left me alone; she says she wants to see everything, almost like a little devil. My aunts laugh about it, and I have a desire to cry, and cry a lot, you know? But I wait to cry until tonight with Jesus. But now he also has gone away! I find myself alone. . . .
>
> I'm not asking to leave this house in order to not suffer, only because I'm afraid that [Angelina] . . . She even brought her classmates to the house, and she tells them this, just to make fun of me: "Come, let's go see Gemma go in ecstasy." And they repeat these words constantly, loudly, even at the portico in the evening.[14]

What might one make of these bits of evidence—so ordinary—seemingly reflective less of the supernatural master-plan later imposed by her biographer than of human foibles, mundane parental failings, and youthful hypersensitivity? Admittedly the markers are fragile, but they do contain a message: Gemma was a girl brought up in the modern world, one where secular concerns and institutions intruded everywhere. Her name, her school, her friends and siblings, all reflected the realities of well-to-do, educated, bourgeois life in Europe's western, Catholic, urban regions outside the great cities.

GEMMA'S FIRST CONFESSOR

In Lucca, among those who spoke authoritatively for the Church was Gemma's local confessor, Monsignor Giovanni Volpi, Auxiliary Bishop of Lucca. The chapters that follow portray him through Gemma's eyes: an occasionally uncomprehending male authority figure so absorbed with the Church's worldly affairs that he sometimes failed to appreciate the spiritual travails she poured out to him in almost daily visits to the confessional for nearly fifteen years. Never mind that one might ask how a bishop found time to offer so much guidance to this singular young penitent, or wonder whether he actually read the more than seventy letters she wrote to him, or doubt how much care he gave to pondering entries in the diary he ordered her to keep. For Gemma, he was a first-and-only trusted spiritual counselor. She made her initial general confession with him at the age of nine, a self-inquiry that required three sessions occurring over several days. She continued as his penitent until the fall of 1900, when as a young woman of twenty-two she found a more supportive guide in Father Germano, the Passionist priest who took it upon himself to make her a saint. Even then, however, Monsignor Volpi continued to hear her confessions regularly, since Father Germano lived far away and came to Lucca only rarely.

The auxiliary bishop no doubt found himself amply occupied with other matters that to him seemed more pressing than the confessional secrets he was wont to dismiss as little Gemma's imaginings. One of his notable duties was to be the archbishop of Tuscany's personal liaison to the region's Catholic political action steering committee (Comitato Regionale Toscano— CRT). In that role, he necessarily played a crucial part in nurturing the CRT's movement toward a politics of "practical transigence," away from the sterile confrontations of the 1870s. In an age and place where heritage still counted, Monsignor Volpi was an obvious choice for this delicate position. Undoubtedly, he had been recommended by his uncle Giuseppe Toniolo, the renowned jurist and professor at the University of Pisa who was among the nation's leading theoretical architects of the sacralization of modern Italian politics. For nearly two decades, then, until his promotion to Bishop of Arezzo in 1904, the prelate worked assiduously at his assigned tasks in and around Lucca. These necessarily kept him deeply mired in the secular world.[15]

Gemma recounts in her autobiography how the monsignor did not always have as much time for her as she wished. He had said he hoped to instruct her personally during her stay with the Salesian nuns (known in English as Nuns of the Visitation) preparatory to being considered for a novitiate. But during this trial period, which turned out very badly for Gemma, he never came, and instead sent along a book for her to read. Alas, Gemma does not provide the title of the book, nor any sense of how she responded to this poor substitute for her confessor's personal attention, and about this incident as about so much else in her religious formation, one is left to construct cautiously and incompletely. Details from her early years are too sparse and ambiguous to reach any conclusion beyond a general affirmation that she imbibed the symbols and forms of pious expression popularized by Tridentine and Reformation Catholicism. Her concerns with bodily purity, her charitable impulses, and her eagerness to confess, attend mass, and receive communion certainly set her apart from the majority of girls her age, and are consistent with her desire to become a nun, but they do not delineate clearly anything more lofty.

GEMMA AND THE NUNS

Gemma's formal religious education at Santa Zita also fails to provide solid clues about her future path. The joy she recalls in her autobiography upon entering school with the nuns finds little confirmation among her teachers. Their testimony at the canonization proceedings, to be considered in depth in part 2 below, actually allowed the defender of the faith, whose role it is to protect the Church against false claimants, to raise doubts about young Gemma's heroic virtue. According to them, it seems she sometimes answered back, behaved spitefully, and was disobedient—exactly as Gemma describes herself—although that sort of conduct is hardly what anyone anticipated would be documented by the nuns.

Another tantalizing but ultimately frustrating bit of information comes from one of Gemma's favorite teachers, Sister Giulia, who recalled that her young pupil, upon hearing a feast-day sermon preached at Santa Zita on the virtues of Venerable Bartolomea Capitanio (1807–33), resolved that she too would become a saint, just like her new heroine. One cannot know with certainty how much Gemma learned about this saint-to-be, who before her death at the age of twenty-six had engaged in prodigious feats of private austerity while pursuing a public career as a holy teacher who radiated love for her pupils. Did Gemma think Venerable Bartolomea, known for absolutely never striking her students, was like the nuns at Santa Zita, or did she perhaps wish them to be more like her? Perhaps she hoped she too would be such a beloved teacher in the future, or possibly she was fascinated instead with the stories of Bartolomea's self-denial, her compulsive licking of the floor in a pattern of crosses until her tongue bled, and her specific imitation of the fierce mortifications attributed to her male role model, the Jesuit Aloysius Gonzaga. While it is impossible to recapture the details of one unrecorded feast-day sermon, Gemma's schooling surely included regular introductions not only to the lives of the major saints noted in daily masses for all Catholics but also to stories about less prominent women of heroic virtue whose hagiographies were being nurtured primarily in convents rather than among the lay faithful. What the canonization testimony does record is that Sister Giulia had to remind Gemma frequently about her resolve to be more like Bartolomea Capitanio.[16]

In retrospect, the most surprising wisp of evidence to be drawn from Gemma's years at Santa Zita is no more than a telling silence. The school's founder, Elena Guerra, herself beatified in 1959 and currently a pending candidate for canonization, never testified publicly about the putative saint who during several of the years from 1889 to 1893 had sat before her, eye-to-eye for six mornings each week, as teacher and pupil, separated only by their respective desks. Owing to a bitter conflict among the nuns at Santa Zita, Sister Elena had been dismissed as mother superior in 1906, a year before initial formal inquiries concerning Gemma Galgani, but she remained at the convent school as "the most humble and obedient of the sisters," so presumably she could have been asked to testify.[17] Father Germano, the chief architect of these proceedings, must have considered the possibilities, for his biography relates that in a letter written sometime in 1905, Sister Elena had exulted in the proposed glories to be bestowed upon her "holy former student," recalling Gemma as follows: "For about two years she was in the classes I then taught, and I can attest that she never gave occasion for me to lament about her conduct. She was very reserved and always obedient."

How does one explain why a knowledgeable former headmistress, who obviously thought well of her star pupil and who herself would come to be honored as a blessed, was not invited to testify? There is a report that the Council of Teachers at the school voted to reject Gemma's application to be admitted as a "probationary" among the Oblates of the Holy Spirit, as they were properly called. The record is silent about why, but headmistress Elena Guerra must have played a key role, as she defensively recalled years later: "It was I who said those words. . . . Were these the words which impeded that beautiful soul from coming to us? My God, if I am at fault, have mercy upon me."[18] Whatever the realities of the decision, Father Germano must have learned from someone or else merely sensed that Elena Guerra's memories might not be entirely helpful in a possible canonization process, and so she was not invited to testify.

Continuing in this speculative mode, one may examine Gemma's report cards, thanks to the efforts of Father Enrico Zoffoli, since such documents were not introduced into the formal canonization record. These exist for the period when she attended the Institute of Santa Zita, from the ages of eleven to fifteen, and they show grades for the seven subjects on which students were evaluated (see table 1).[19]

Father Zoffoli's search of the school's files concluded that Gemma's teachers were not especially strict graders overall, and that Gemma's marks generally were among the worst in the class. Even in her best subject, religion, she attained a perfect "ten" only in one year, something Gemma's autobiography tells more about, and her marks in "civility" (*civiltà*) seem almost punitive. Moreover, her grades each year tended to decline as fall gave way to winter and spring, which as every teacher knows, is a pattern disappointing no less to the instructor than the student. Overall, it is hard to find much in her academic record that might predict what lay in store for her in the years ahead.[20]

DEVOTION TO THE SACRED HEART OF JESUS

The key to understanding Gemma Galgani's spiritual development prior to her encounter with the Passionist Order is not with her family, nor her schooling, nor her confessor. Instead, it comes from within herself, her personal response to a life-threatening illness. Specifically, on February 19, 1899, with her twenty-first birthday approaching in exactly three weeks, Gemma appealed to Margaret Mary Alacoque for recovery from the paralysis that had kept her bedridden for many months.[21] Why to her? Blessed Margaret (1647–90), beatified in 1864, would be canonized only in 1920, after verification of two additional miracles attributed to her. Such reports can occur and then be validated, of course, only if the faithful pray for divine assistance through the intercession of that specific blessed, whether by invoking her name in prayer, making a pilgrimage to her shrine, or touching her relics. In short, Margaret Mary Alacoque, although dead for over two hundred years, was still a saint-in-the-making. Her tomb, upon its canonical opening in 1830, had been the site of two miraculous cures, and throughout the nineteenth century pilgrims from all over the world sought her favors as they flocked to the altar at Paray-le-Monial in France where her body had been translated. Veneration of her, and the seeking of favor through her, meant that men and women, numbering in the thousands if not tens of thousands, put their faith explicitly in her, making a choice from among a myriad of opportunities available—many of them actively promoted—for appeals to the sacred realm in resolving secular needs. Gemma might have obtained holy water from the springs at Lourdes,[22] or she might have sought a miraculous cure at Knock, La Salette, Marpingen, or Pont-

TABLE I. *Gemma Galgani's Report Cards*

Date	Study	Religion	Penmanship	Conduct	Work	Civility	Precision
1889–90							
Fall	8¼	10	6½	9	7¾	7½	7
Winter	7½	9½	6½	8½	7½	7½	7
Spring	7½	9½	7	8	7½	7½	7
1890–91							
Fall	7½	10	6	9	8	7	6
Winter	6½	10	7½	8¼	7¾	7	6
Spring	7	10	7½	8	7½	7	6
1891–92							
Fall	7	8	7	8¼	8½	8	7½
Winter	6½	9	6½	8	7½	7	7
Spring				not found			
1982–93							
Fall	7½	9	8	9	8	8	7
			no longer at school due to illness				

main.[23] Closer to home, she might have joined the throngs who set their hopes on Rita of Cascia, in that very decade being hailed anew as "the saint of the impossible,"[24] or she might have arranged to have her paralyzed body transported to any of dozens of holy sites in the environs of Lucca.[25]

But there is no evidence that the bedridden and impoverished Gemma Galgani ever considered the possibility of making a pilgrimage or seeking out physical contact with a wonderworking relic. Instead, she turned her life itself into a spiritual journey, one inspired by Margaret Mary Alacoque's *vita*. Gemma, like Margaret, always recalled with deep regret even her most trivial childish faults, whether the wearing of ostentatious jewelry or the donning of a mask at carnival time; both girls made their first communion at a precocious age and both yearned from their tender years to pledge their virginity to Jesus; as teenagers, both publicly expressed intense love of the blessed sacrament and privately engaged in severe bodily mortifications; as young women, both were plunged suddenly into poverty at the deaths of their fathers; both experienced direct consolations from Jesus, who frequently appeared in the bloodied form of Christ Crucified, *Ecce Homo;* at the behest of their respective spiritual directors, both wrote autobiographical sketches they intended to burn, and both were prolific letter-writers.[26]

More than two centuries earlier, Margaret had been confined to her bed for four years by a childhood paralysis, just as Gemma now found herself. Margaret, upon vowing to the Blessed Virgin that she would become a nun should she recover, was healed instantly. Now Gemma would make a similar promise, and through the intercession of Blessed Margaret she too would be restored to perfect health. The deeper parallels in their subsequent spiritual quests, enriched by synergy with their bouts of anorexia and pica, at least according to their own telling, challenged their contemporaries' aversion to pain and suffering, just as it does our own, and both women relished the challenge.[27]

Gemma tells us why she initially directed her prayers to Margaret Mary Alacoque. On Sunday, February 19, 1899, Monsignor Volpi promised her "absolutely" that she would arise from her bed, fully healed, if she made a novena to Blessed Margaret. His advice apparently had only limited impact until it was reinforced by a mysterious visitor. On that day and the next she said her prayers as suggested, but the following Tuesday she forgot. During that night a voice reminded her to say the novena immediately, but she felt sleepy and the following day she could not remember whether she had completed her prayers. The next evening, Wednesday, when Gemma again forgot, a voice once more whispered to her, this time into her normally deaf left ear, scolding her for such forgetfulness and asking her if this was how she expected to receive a miracle.

Thoroughly frightened—all the more so because the night-light suddenly went out—Gemma tried to cry out for help, but no words came out. Then a hand reassuringly touched the left side of her forehead, and another moved the sheet to clasp her left hand. The visitor's hands were "very hot," especially the one on her forehead. Gradually Gemma became calm and she no longer felt any pain. Then the voice admonished her that Blessed Margaret wanted to heal her but could not: the Heart of Jesus was holding back because Gemma so sorely lacked devotion to prayer. Gemma wanted to ask whether Jesus would heal her if she improved her ways and recommenced the novena, but once again she could not speak. After about two minutes the voice resumed, proposing a double novena. Together they would offer one to the Most Sacred Heart of Jesus and then Gemma would do another on her own to Blessed Margaret, both to consist of nine recitations each of the Our Father, the Hail Mary, and the Glory be.

And so it happened, for that night and the next eight—the room dark, Gemma clutching her crucifix between her hands, the visitor placing one hand on the left side of her forehead while the other lifted the sheet and held her left hand, the two of them jointly reciting the prayers, Gemma falling asleep before the end of the nine Our Fathers, Gemma awakening some time later and offering her own novena to Blessed Margaret. On the fifth night, out of curiosity, Gemma listened for the clock and recalled that when 11:15 struck the visitor had not yet arrived, but that when she heard the sound of midnight both novenas had been completed. During this time, as each evening approached, Gemma came to look forward to receiving her mysterious guest and insisted on being alone, but in the daytime she felt frightened by all she was experiencing and constantly wanted someone at her sickbed.

Among her daytime callers was her former teacher at Santa Zita, Sister Giulia Sestini, who came on Thursday, February 23, the first day after the warm-blooded evening visitor had directed Gemma to initiate a double novena. Sister Giulia told Gemma that during Lent the nuns added to their usual prayers a "Holy Hour," in honor of the hour that Jesus had asked of Margaret Mary Alacoque, so that she might share his agony in the Garden of Olives when his disciples abandoned him. One cannot know whether Sister Giulia explained to Gemma that this devotional exercise, instituted by Blessed Margaret in 1674, when she was twenty-seven (just six years older than Gemma), traditionally took the form of an hour of prayer while lying prostrate with face to the ground from eleven until midnight on the eve of the first Friday of each month. Whatever the information exchanged, Gemma decided to promise Jesus that if he made her well she would do a Holy Hour every Thursday evening. She was ready to begin immediately until she learned that Sister Giulia had not brought along a copy of the special prayers the nuns offered, written by their founder Elena Guerra, but Gemma's resolve remained firm and the following Thursday evening at 10:00 she began the practice she would continue for the remaining four years of her life: on the floor face downward when her health permitted, otherwise in bed, as she did that night, making four meditations on the Passion, followed by orations and offerings of the self.

Immediately after her first Holy Hour, Gemma commenced the prayers that would terminate her double novena, for this was the ninth and last night, only this time she did not fall asleep during the first half. At their conclusion, the mysterious visitor assured her that both Jesus and Blessed Margaret were pleased with her and that Blessed Margaret had obtained permission from the Heart of Jesus to heal her, but first Gemma would have to promise to become a Salesian nun, the same order to which Margaret had belonged. Gemma eagerly agreed, and the following morning she was healed. Weakened by such a protracted paralysis, initially she needed a bit of assistance in arising from bed, but in no time at all she was ready to fly to wherever Blessed Margaret wished, preferably straight to the Salesian convent.

This version of Gemma's miraculous cure comes directly from the account she wrote just a few days after the event itself.[28] Although it generally conforms with her autobiographical recollection written down two years later in the spring of 1901 and translated in the next chapter, a few telling details differ and in these there are instructive hints about Gemma's spiritual growth. In the earlier version, which cannot have been influenced by Father Germano or his fellow Passionists, the commitment to join the Salesian Order is unequivocal. There is absolutely no suggestion that the mysterious nighttime visitor is Gabriel of Our Lady of Sorrows (Francis Possenti), the Passionist saint-in-the-making identified clearly in the autobiographical version. In fact, nothing is revealed about the visitor—male or female (not even a telltale gendered pronoun), young or old, angel or saint—except that it had warm hands and exuded a detectable mouth odor. Moreover, in the later recollection the visitor gives much less homage to Blessed Margaret (who, after all, was not a Passionist), so much so that Gemma's prayers to her seem like something of an afterthought. Finally, Sister Giulia's daytime visit and her key role in inspiring Gemma to undertake the Holy Hour prayer disappear completely in the later version, replaced by a promise Gemma made to the Sacred Heart of Jesus (sewn symbolically on the vestments of all Passionists), for which no further explanation is given.[29]

News events of the day provide further nuggets of evidence concerning the formative background of Gemma Galgani's religiosity prior to the period when she clearly came under the influence of the Passionists. She could read, she went to church daily, sometimes twice daily, she spoke with Monsignor Volpi almost as often, and now was herself spoken about by pious townswomen who had heard of her miraculous cure. It is not unreasonable to imagine, then, that she knew of the May 25, 1899, papal letter consecrating the entire human race (not just Catholic believers) to the Sacred Heart of Jesus.[30] In this gesture of openness to the secular world, Pope Leo XIII looked forward to the Jubilee Year of 1900; indeed the missions that the Passionists came to Lucca to preach in June 1899, which Gemma attended, were authorized explicitly to highlight the forthcoming festivities, and there is ample evidence that Gemma too was swept up in the excitement, for the

Sacred Heart had been especially dear to her long before she knew anything of the Passionists.[31]

Finally, there are her stigmata, that most exquisite sign of mystical union, which Gemma Galgani received on the eve of June 8, 1899, the Feast of the Sacred Heart of Jesus. This grace, too, preceded any direct contact with her future director extraordinary, Father Germano, and must be considered essentially independent of clerical influence, especially since her regular confessor, the eminently practical Monsignor Volpi, was deeply suspicious about any such manifestations of supernatural favor. All this is to suggest that the critical juncture in Gemma Galgani's spiritual development, one clearly not predicted by anything that came before, occurred in her twenty-first year, while she suffered a paralyzing illness and then suddenly recovered, a miracle she attributed directly to the intercession of Blessed Margaret. The contemporary world of Lucca and of her two families, the Galganis of her birth and the Gianninis who would adopt her, along with other people among whom she lived and who upon her death would make their judgments about her, shaped Gemma's piety, to be sure. But Gemma also drew from the past, patterning herself in the mold of Margaret Mary Alacoque's religiosity, gaining inspiration from her predecessor's love of the Sacred Heart and of Christ Crucified, and even surpassing her as Christ's beloved by experiencing the grace of stigmata. In her afterlife, men would make Gemma a saint, but as an adolescent she forged her own spiritual path.

PART ONE

Her Words: Gemma Galgani's Life

CHAPTER TWO

Autobiography ✳ *Until Fall 1899*

Sometime in the winter of 1900–1901, Father Germano Ruoppolo di San Stanislao (1850–1909) decided that he needed to learn more about Gemma Galgani, the young woman he believed God had chosen to receive an abundance of spiritual graces. The priest must have been quite sure about her, for on rather scant and mostly secondhand evidence, during the preceding September, while on a short visit to Lucca, he had intervened directly with Monsignor Volpi, the powerful local prelate who had served as Gemma's confessor since her girlhood, to take over primary responsibility for her spiritual direction. By that point in his clerical career, having overcome bouts of "nervous disturbance" and "mental exhaustion" lasting for several years in the 1880s, Father Germano in 1890 had risen to the position of postulate general for the entire Passionist Order, a post he held until his death. Also in the 1890s, he began to devote less time to amateur archeology (at which he had been highly successful) and more to saint-making. But all these experiences, while useful, afforded him little opportunity to learn about Lucca and none at all about Gemma Galgani or her family. Effectiveness in his role as this obscure penitent's new director required that he repair this gap in his knowledge. And if, as seems likely, he thought of Gemma from the very outset as a potential saint-to-be, then he had to learn everything possible about her experiences in the twenty-two years from her birth until he first met her. As he understood so well from his ongoing labors since 1891 as a key promoter of the cause of Francis Possenti, soon to be Blessed Gabriel, establishing that a candidate for sainthood lived a life of heroic virtue is the essential first step in the journey toward canonization. Above all else, there must be no unwelcome surprises along the way.

Father Germano worked energetically at his new task. Based on the materials assembled in his biography of Gemma Galgani, first published in

1907, just four years after her death, he must have talked with many people during his admittedly infrequent but busy visits to Lucca. He corresponded regularly with at least one local person, Cecilia Giannini, who served as his eyes and ears, for his account contains numerous details found nowhere else in the documentary record so carefully preserved at the Passionist Order's General House in Rome and at the Saint Gemma Monastery outside Lucca. He also encouraged Don Lorenzo Agrimonti, a priest who lived with Gemma's adopted family, to surreptitiously gather information from daughters Annetta and Eufemia Giannini, always exhorting him to "write everything down."[1] But all his biographical assertions pale in significance (and credibility) when set against Gemma's own words in the autobiographical confession he encouraged her to write and which you are about to read. No one knew more about Gemma than Gemma, and her appraisal is wonderfully candid and self-revealing, quite intentionally. To be sure, she was influenced in the telling by what she thought her new director wanted to hear, and in the preceding chapter I made much of the changes in her recollections about her miraculous healing that consistently give the Passionists a major part, when in fact the order is entirely absent in an earlier account written a few days after the event. As I also previously pointed out, her exuberant memories of school with the nuns at Santa Zita give no hint of her earlier public education. Finally, a small number of notes to the translation indicate other "errors" worthy of mention or correction. But, overall, the misstatements and discrepancies are negligible and, if anything, give a sense of verisimilitude to the whole.

When initially asked by Father Germano for a written general confession—on the flimsy pretext that he did not have time to come to Lucca and hear of her sins in person—Gemma protested that she did not wish to put anything on paper, seeing in the possible endeavor an occasion for sinful self-aggrandizement. "I have no desire, my dear Dad, to write a general confession. An idea presents itself—all the sins that can be committed on this earth, I have committed them, every kind: lies, disobediences; the biggest you already know: breaking fasts, in short all the sins of the world, I have done them all."[2] Earlier, in the account of her miraculous healing presented in the previous chapter, Gemma had closed by writing:

> Jesus, I have written these pages for the greater glory of Blessed Margaret [Mary Alacoque] but if the day should arrive when some thought of pride or vainglory should come over me, Jesus, just make me die.
>
> I have nothing else to say.
> Gemma Galgani[3]

There could be no possible use in writing about her life, she believed, unless the recollection of her sins in general confession served as a means of further self-abnegation. But it was not about Gemma's sins that Father Germano wished to know more. To put his investigation in competent hands he turned to the substitute mother with whom Gemma had been staying for the past six months, after she finally had extricated herself from the hostile home environment described in her letter of August 10, 1900, to Monsignor Volpi, quoted in chapter 1 ("I'm not asking to leave this house in order to not suffer, only because I'm afraid that . . ."). Much remains to be said about the haven that Gemma found with the Giannini family, and this will be taken up in introductions to the next two chapters, but for now I shall simply state flatly that Mrs. Cecilia (as Gemma respectfully referred to her substitute mother, the unmarried Cecilia Giannini) always acted as Father Germano's alter ego in giving Gemma spiritual direction, often by deceptive means. On February 8, 1901, he wrote to his confidante: "Think about how to induce Gemma to write what I call *a general confession* of her entire life. She also calls it like this: *general confession of sins;* but make her do it so that, while she believes she is recounting sins and imperfections, I will end up having a complete history of her life, which will serve me in its own time. Proceed, therefore, with *maximum* prudence."[4]

Gemma may have sensed the collusion, one that she came to learn also involved Monsignor Volpi, because in response to Father Germano's letter prodding her to get on with the writing by taking advantage of the long hours she spent at Mrs. Cecilia's bedside, Gemma shot back: "In Mom's bedroom I will not write, because I am too distracted." And then she added a pointed and thoroughly pragmatic observation about Mom: "She's a lot better, but really, these people I don't know what else they want; maybe they want perfect health. That, by now, is impossible."[5]

Somewhere in the Giannini house, perhaps in Don Lorenzo Agrimonti's study, but certainly not in her own room since she did not have one, Gemma must have found the necessary moments of privacy, and she began to write copiously. In the same February 23, 1901, letter quoted above, six days after she had started in earnest, she reported to Father Germano that his guardian angel was bringing everything to mind, on occasion even suggesting specific words, so that the task was not at all tiring. Indeed, by April 16, 1901, she happily proclaimed that she soon hoped to send the little book with her confession terminated, since already she had reached the point in her story when Father Germano had come into her life. A letter to him from Cecilia Giannini dated May 18, 1901, states that Gemma had just completed the work; then no further word comes about the confessional autobiography until July, when several letters refer to a diabolic attack on the manuscript, which for several months had been placed for safe-keeping in a drawer at the Giannini house.

According to Gemma, during a recent visit, Father Pietro Paolo dell'Immacolata (Moreschini), the provincial head of the Passionist Order, had prohibited the devil from physically assaulting Gemma, but this left the door open for verbal abuse, and on July 8 she wrote to Father Germano about how the evil one had screamed at her: "War, war, on your Dad! Your manuscript is in my hands." Then she added rather coyly that the devil "seems more angry with you than with me." In his biography of Gemma, Father Germano proudly reports how upon hearing this terrible news he got the stolen treasure back by exorcizing the devil, using a ritual stole and holy water, as he prayed at the tomb of saint-to-be Brother Gabriel in the Gran Sasso, a feat all the more remarkable in his eyes because it occurred over a distance of nearly 400 miles. Finally, there is Gemma's July 27 letter to Father Germano consoling him on the return via Father Pietro Paolo of the precious copybook, now thoroughly charred. "To me, it seemed impossible that the enemy would not want to vindicate himself! But, thank God, it is not so ruined as to be unintelligible, and it does not need to be written anew."[6] All these reports of diabolic troubles are especially ironic because on the opening page of the autobiography itself, Gemma ordered Father Germano alone to read her work and then to burn it. Perhaps she had second thoughts about the matter, or at the very least did not want the devil to be doing her bidding.

In her desire to leave no autobiographical record, Gemma Galgani once again followed in the footsteps of Blessed Margaret Mary Alacoque, who on her deathbed begged her attending nun to write to "Father Rolin [her confessor] and ask him to burn my letters and to keep inviolably the secret which I have so often asked of him." Then she remembered an even more telling legacy of her vainglory, her unfinished and unread "life written by herself." She pleaded with her nurse to assist her in a final, disobedient act: "To burn the copybook which you will find in the cupboard and which was written by order of my confessor, Father Rolin of the Society of Jesus, who forbade me to destroy it myself before he had examined it."[7]

The humility of a saint and the hubris of autobiography did not cohabit easily in Gemma's conscience. Certainly she was never the eager participant in recounting her life that her near contemporary, Thérèse of Lisieux, had been just four years earlier, when the French nun compared herself and the act of writing to the wild flower that, if it could, would talk freely of God's gifts.[8] But once Gemma undertook her task, out of obedience and with the help of her guardian angel, she completed it in a remarkably fresh and unaffected style. Her precedents for writing a confession were many, although she does not mention them. Nonetheless, while she did not have a reputation for being an assiduous reader,[9] Gemma reportedly had been a good student of French, and it is plausible that she at least knew something of Margaret Mary Alacoque's autobiography in its original language. One can only speculate about whether she read the autobiographical writings of her saintly Italian predecessors such as Maddalena Gabriella di Canossa (d. 1835), Bartolomea Capitanio (d. 1833), Maria Luisa Maurizi (d. 1831), Maria Maddalena Martinengo (d. 1737), Maria Allegri (d. 1677), Giacinta Marescotti (d. 1640), Maria Vittoria Fornari Strata (d. 1617), Maria Maddalena de' Pazzi (d. 1607), Caterina de' Ricci (d. 1590), and above all Veronica Giuliani (d. 1727), who wrote her autobiography five times as each revised version caused new and unacceptable discomforts for her confessors. With good reason, Father Germano urged Cecilia Giannini to oversee Gemma's work with "*maximum* prudence" (emphasis in the original). My best judgment, based on close comparison of these and other more distant autobiographical texts in the corpus of saints' lives, is that Gemma Galgani may have been familiar with the genre, and surely she had access to derivative hagiographies commonly found in convent libraries, but she did not write her confession in a way consciously modeled upon any specific antecedent.

Technical notes pertaining to the translation of the autobiography that follows:

The source is Galgani, *Estasi, Diario, Autobiografia, Scritti vari, Versi,* 221–69. All ellipses (. . .) are as in this source.

Abbreviations used by Gemma (and these are infrequent) are spelled out in their English equivalents, for example, M.S. [Maria Santissima] = Most Holy Mary.

The subtitles in the autobiography are not in the original manuscript and were added beginning with the first printed edition (1943).

The opening words of the text—"Al babbo mio che lo bruci subito" ("To my Dad, who should burn it immediately")—appeared on the cover of the copybook.

"Babbo" is translated as "Dad" whether Gemma is referring to her biological father or to her confessor, Father Germano. There is a major, widely known precedent for use of the familial and endearing word "Babbo" in addressing a cleric, which may be found in most of Saint Catherine of Siena's letters to Pope Gregory IX. "Mamma" is translated as "Mom" whether Gemma is referring to her biological mother or to her adopted second Mom, Cecilia Giannini, or to Mary, the mother of Jesus.

* * *

TO MY DAD,
WHO SHOULD BURN IT IMMEDIATELY

My dear Dad,

Listen to this; I had in mind to make my general confession of sins without adding anything else, but your guardian angel scolded me, telling me to be obedient and to do something like a summary of everything that has happened in my life, good and bad.

How tiring, dear Dad, to obey in this matter! However, take care: you can read and re-read as much as you wish, but no one else, only you, and then burn it immediately. Do you understand?

The angel has promised to help me and make me remember everything; because, let me say openly, I also cried, because I did not want to do this: it dismayed me to recall everything, but the angel assured me of his help.

And I think also, dear Dad, when you have read this letter and listened to my sins, you'll get angry and no longer want to be my Dad; in that case . . . but I hope you will always want to. So, prepare to hear every sort of thing and sins of all kinds.

And you, dear Dad, do you approve of what the angel said, to talk about my whole life? It's his command, and anyway, what the angel says I realize are things that you, dear Dad, already have in your head and your heart. If I write everything, good and bad, you will understand better how bad I have been and how good everyone else has been with me; how much I have shown ingratitude toward Jesus, and how much I have resisted listening to the good counsel of my parents and teachers.

Here I am, ready to work, dear Dad. Long live Jesus!

First memories—Mom

*

The first thing I remember is that when I was little (less than seven), Mom regularly took me in her arms, and very often as she did so, she cried and said over and over: "I prayed so much that Jesus would give me a girl; I was consoled, it is true, but too late." "I am sick, and facing death," she repeated; "I have to leave you. If only I could bring you with me! Would you come?"

I understood very little and cried, because I saw Mom crying. "And where would we go?" I would ask. "To Heaven, with Jesus, with the angels . . ."

It was Mom, dear Dad, who instilled in me from infancy a desire for Heaven, and when I still desire Heaven and wish to go there, I get scolded and promptly hear a loud "No" in response.

I answered "yes" to Mom, and I remember that after repeating these things to me many times, that is to take me to Heaven, I never wanted to be without her, and I no longer left her room. [She even put me to sleep with my eight-year-old little brother (now he is in Heaven) so that I would not cry and be far away from her; this way I was happy. (You see, Dad, when I was less than seven years old I began to disobey, and I used to sleep many times with my brother, as a whim.)][10]

The doctor himself prohibited us from even approaching her bedside, but for me every order was useless; I did not obey. Each evening, before going to bed, I went to her to say my prayers; I kneeled at her bedside and we prayed.

One evening, to my usual prayers she made me add a De profundis ["Out of the depths," Psalm 130] for the souls in Purgatory and five Glory be's for Christ's wounds. I did say them; as usual I mouthed the words with little care and feeling (in all my life I have never been attentive to prayer). I made a big fuss, complaining to Mom that this was too many prayers and I didn't feel like saying them all. Mom, always indulgent, kept things briefer on other evenings.

Confirmation (1885)
Mom in Heaven (1886)

✳

The time was drawing close for making my confirmation. She thought I should get some instruction, because I knew nothing; but I was so bad I wouldn't leave her room and so the catechism teacher had to come to the house every evening, always under Mom's eyes. One day in May 1888 I made my confirmation,[11] crying the whole time because after the ceremony I had to stay for mass and I was always afraid that Mom would go away (die) without taking me with her.

I heard mass as well as I could, praying for her, when all of a sudden a voice in my heart said: "Do you want to give me your Mom?" "Yes," I answered, "but only if you also take me." "No," the usual voice repeated, "give me your Mom freely. For now you must remain with your Dad. I'll bring her to Heaven, you know? Will you freely give her to me?" I was forced to answer yes; once the mass was over I ran home. My God! I looked at Mom and cried; I could not stop.

Two more months went by and I never left her side. Finally Dad, who was afraid I would die before Mom, took me away by force and brought me to Mom's brother's house, no longer at Lucca.

Dad, dear Dad, that's when . . . What torment! Not seeing anyone, not

Dad, not my brothers and sisters; I learned later that Mom died on September 17th of that year.

At S. Gennaro with her uncle

*

My life changed completely when I went to my uncle; I also found an aunt there who did not resemble Mom at all; she was good and religious but wanted to be involved in the church only to a certain point. How much I came to miss the time Mom made me spend saying so many prayers! But the whole time I stayed with my aunt, I could not go to confession (something I very much desired to do); I had only gone to confession seven times and after Mom died I would have wanted to go every day (after my confirmation, Mom brought me to confession every week).

My aunt decided to keep me as a daughter, but when my brother who is now dead found out, there was no way he would agree and on Christmas day I returned to my family, with Dad, my brothers, and two little sisters (one of whom I did not know, because she was taken away at birth), and two servants.

What a consolation it was to return home and get out of my aunt's hands. She loved me enormously, but I did not love her at all, at all. Dad then put me in school at the Institute of S. Zita (they were nuns).

All the time I was with my aunt I was always bad. She had a son who teased me and put his hands on me; one day he was horseback riding (he was fifteen), and my aunt ordered me to bring him something, I don't remember what, to cover himself. I brought it and he pinched me; so I gave him a shove and he fell off and hurt his head. My aunt tied my hands behind my back for an entire day. I was vexed, and got mad; I answered back and made faces at him and vowed to get even, but I didn't.

At school with the S. Zita nuns
First communion (1887)

*

I started school with the nuns; I was in Heaven. I showed a desire to make my first communion immediately, but they found me so bad and ignorant that they were appalled. They began to instruct me and to give me much good advice, but I got worse and worse, thinking only of my desire to receive communion as soon as possible and making my wishes known so strongly that they soon gave in.

The nuns usually held first communion in June, and as that time was approaching I had to ask Dad for permission to stay at the convent for a while. Dad was irritated and granted me nothing; but I knew a good trick to bend him into giving me anything, so I put it into effect and immediately got what I wanted. (Every time Dad saw me crying, he did whatever I asked.) I cried, otherwise I got nothing. That evening I got permission and the next morning I went to the convent to stay for two weeks. All that time I saw no one from my family. But how good I felt! What heaven, dear Dad!

[I must say something, Dad, about the time that I was with the family; I am afraid that in this writing there are some accusations, but I intend to say everything. Among the servants there was one who seemed to me not very good. One evening, at night, she called me, took an oil lamp and a plate of water and . . . I don't know anything else, she accused me as if I had done it and it seems to me a bad thing. Other times I remember very well this woman used to take me into a closed room and undress me . . . and this is enough . . . I could have accused her to my Dad, but I didn't do it because it would have been useless, I loved her very much. At times I even remember very well that one day my brother and I tattled on her and we were seriously punished, and Dad even hit us, but this happened because I was disobedient and talked back and played tricks on her.] [12]

As soon as I was in convent and found myself so happy, I ran to the little church to thank Jesus and I prayed fervently that he prepare me for holy communion.

I had another desire beyond this; when I was little, Mom would make me look at the crucifix and she would say that Jesus died on the cross for the sake of humanity; later I heard the same thing from the teachers but I had never understood anything. I wanted to know in detail the entire life of Jesus and his Passion. I expressed this desire to my teacher and she began day by day to explain some things to me, and for this she chose an hour when the other children were in bed, and she taught me, hidden from the mother superior, I believe.

One evening she was explaining something about the crucifixion and the crowning with thorns, about all of Jesus' sufferings; she explained so well, like something alive, that I felt so much pain and compassion that I instantly developed such a high fever that for all the next day I had to stay in bed. That day the teacher stopped all further explanations.

Those nuns also made me upset; they wanted to tell Dad that I had a fever but they paid dearly for it as well, for there were reproaches for them, for me, and for everyone in the convent. This happened especially during the ten days of retreat.

So, one day in March I began with eleven other children the period of spiritual retreat, which was led by Mr. Raffaele Cianetti.[13] All the children were eager to prepare well to receive Jesus; I alone among the many was the most negligent and the most distracted, but I gave no thought to changing my life; I listened to the homilies but quickly forgot them.

Often, every day actually, that good preacher said: "Whoever eats of the life of Jesus will live of his life." These words filled me with great consolation, and this is how I reasoned: so, when Jesus will be with me, I will no longer live in me, because Jesus will live in me. And I was dying with desire to soon be able to say these words. Sometimes, in meditating on these words I spent entire nights, consumed with desire.

Finally the long-awaited day arrived. The previous day I had written a few words to Dad:

Dear Dad,
We are on the eve of the day of first communion, for me a day of infinite happiness. I write you this line only to assure you of my affection and ask you to pray Jesus that when he comes to me for the first time, he will find me disposed to receive all the graces he has prepared.

I ask you to forgive all the repugnant and disobedient things I have done, and I pray this evening that you will want to forget them. Asking your blessing, I am
        Your affectionate daughter, Gemma

With those good nuns I prepared my general confession with such tirelessness that it required three sittings with Monsignor Volpi; I finished on Saturday, the eve of the happy day.

When Sunday morning finally came I got up early and ran to Jesus for the first time. My hopes were finally realized. I understood then for the first time Jesus' promise: "Whoever eats of me will live of my life."

Dear Dad, I don't know how to express what took place between me and Jesus in that moment. Jesus made himself felt in a very strong way to my wretched soul. In that moment I understood that the delights of Heaven are not like those of earth. I felt captured by the desire to make permanent this union with my God. I felt increasingly detached from this world, and increasingly disposed to contemplation. On that same morning Jesus gave me the great desire to be a nun.

First communion resolves

✳

Before leaving the convent I proposed for myself certain resolves to regulate my life:

1. I will confess and receive communion as if each time were my last.
2. I will go frequently to adore Jesus in the Blessed Sacrament, especially when I am afflicted.
3. I will prepare for every feast in honor of Mary with some mortification, and every evening I will ask for my Heavenly Mother's blessing.
4. I want always to stay in the presence of God.
5. Every time the clock chimes, I will say three times: my Jesus, have mercy.

I wanted to add others but the teacher wouldn't let me; and she was right because once I returned to my family, within a year I forgot my resolves and all the good advice and became worse than ever. I continued to go to school with the nuns and for a while they were happy. I received communion two or three times a week; Jesus increasingly made his presence felt and many times he let me taste great consolations, but as I soon abandoned him, I began to become proud, more disobedient than before, a bad example to my companions, and a scandal to all.

At school not a day went by when I was not punished; I did not know my lessons, and I was nearly thrown out. At home I let no one find peace; every day I wanted to go out strolling, always in new dresses, and poor Dad indulged me for a long time. I omitted to say my usual prayers every morning and evening; but even among all these sins I never forgot to say three Hail Mary's a day with my hands under my knees (something my mother taught me, so that Jesus would liberate me every day from sins against holy purity).

Toward the poor—a new conversion

✳

It was also in this period of time, which lasted nearly a full year, that the only thing left to me was my charity toward the poor. Every time I left the house I asked Dad for money and if on occasion he denied it to me, I took the household bread, flour, and other items; and God truly wished that I should frequently meet the poor because there were three or four every time I left the house. And to those who came to the door, I gave linens and anything I had.

Then came the prohibition from my confessor, and so I stopped; and by this means Jesus worked a new conversion in me. Dad no longer gave me any money and I could not take things from the house, yet every time I went out I encountered nothing but poor people and they all ran to me. I couldn't give them anything and this grieved me so that I cried continuously; so I did not go out any more except for dire necessity and in the end I got tired of dresses and all such things.

I tried to make a new general confession but my confessor refused; I confessed to everything anyway and Jesus gave me such a deep sense of remorse that I feel it still. I begged forgiveness from my teachers, whom I disgusted more than anyone.

My father and my brothers, however, did not like this change in me; one brother in particular hit me many times because I wanted to go to church on time every morning. But Jesus from then on helped me more than ever.

In the family with her aunts

*

At this time, my grandfather and uncle having died, two aunts on my father's side came to stay with us. They were good, religious, affectionate aunts but never like Mom's tender affection. They took us to church almost every day and did not fail to give us religious instruction.

Among us brothers and sisters some were better and others worse; the oldest, the fourth to die, and the youngest, Giulia, were the best and so my aunts loved them the most; but the others, who had followed my bad example, were much livelier and so were more neglected, but not that for this they lacked the necessities.

The worst one of all was always me, and who knows how I will have to answer the Lord for the bad example I set for my brothers and sisters and friends. My aunts did not neglect to correct me in all my failings but I responded to them only with arrogance and from me they got back only sharp answers.

Nonetheless, as I said, Jesus used this means of not letting me give charity to convert me. I began to think about the great offense my sins gave Jesus; I began to study and to work, and the teachers continued to love me; the only defect for which I kept receiving strong scoldings and punishments was my pride. The teacher frequently called me "Miss Pride."

Yes, unfortunately I had this sin, but Jesus knows whether I was aware of it or not. Many times I went on my knees in front of the teacher, and all the students, and the mother superior to beg forgiveness for this sin. Then in the evening and for many nights I cried by myself; this sin I did not know, and many times during the day I fell and re-fell into it without realizing it.

The good teacher
✳

The teacher who during the preparations for first communion had explained the Passion to me, one day (perhaps because she saw a change in me) tried again to explain it to me; she went very slowly however, and even frequently repeated: "My Gemma," she would say, "you belong to Jesus and you must be entirely his. Be good: Jesus is happy with you, but you are in need of great help. Meditation on his Passion must be the most precious thing you do. Oh, if I could always have you with me . . ."

That good teacher had guessed my thoughts well. Other times she repeated: "Gemma, how many things Jesus has given you!" I understood nothing of all this, and remained like a mute, but on occasion I had so much need for a word, (and I admit) for a caress from my dear teacher, that I ran to find her. Sometimes she had a stern look and when I saw her like that I cried and eventually she took me in her arms (even though I was eleven years old) and caressed me, and in the end I was so attached to her and loved her so much that I called her Mom.

Retreat, 1891
✳

Every two years the nuns regularly organize a retreat for external students; I was unspeakably happy that I could commune so deeply again with Jesus. This time, however, I was alone with no help: the nuns did their own retreat and the children theirs.

I understood well that Jesus gave me this opportunity to know myself better, to purify myself better and be more pleasing to him.

Retreat done in the year 1891, in which Gemma must change and give herself entirely to Jesus.[14]

I remember that the good priest repeated: "Let's remember that we are nothing, God is everything. God is our Creator, and everything we have, we have from God."

I remember that after a few days the preacher made us do a meditation on sin. Then I truly understood, dear Dad, that I deserved everyone's contempt; I saw myself so ungrateful to my God and I saw myself covered in many sins.

Then we did a meditation on Hell, which I recognized I deserved, and in this meditation I made a resolve: I will make Acts of Contrition, within the very day, especially if I have committed some omission.

In the closing days of the retreat we considered [Jesus'] examples of humility, gentleness, obedience, and patience, and from this meditation I drew two resolves:

1. Every day to visit Jesus in the Blessed Sacrament, and to talk more with my heart than with my tongue.
2. I shall try as much as I can not to engage in trivial talk but to speak of heavenly things.

The retreat ended and then I obtained permission from my confessor to receive communion three times each week and also to go to confession three times, which lasted about three or four years, until 1895.

Meditating on Jesus' Passion

*

I continued to go to school every day, but the desire to receive Jesus and to know his Passion grew in me to the point that I got permission from the teacher that every time I earned a 10 in work and in study, she would teach me for a full hour. I could not wish for more; every day I received a 10 and every day I got an explanation about some aspect of the Passion. Many times, reflecting on my sins and my ingratitude toward Jesus, we began to cry together.

It was during the course of these four years that this good teacher also taught me to do little penances for Jesus: the first was to wear a little cord around my waist, and many others; but as much as I tried, I never got permission from my confessor. Then she taught me to mortify my eyes and my tongue; she managed to make me better, but only with great effort.

This good teacher died after keeping me under her guidance for six years; so I passed under the direction of another, good just like the first, but she also had much to complain about me for my ugly sin of pride.

I began under her direction to have much more desire to pray. Every evening, as soon as I left school, I went home and closed myself in my room to recite the entire rosary on my knees, and many times during the night I would get up for fifteen minutes and commend my poor soul to Jesus.

Dad's favorite daughter—her brother Gino

✻

My aunts and my brothers had little concern for me; they let me do whatever I wanted because they already knew how bad I was. Dad, especially, always gave in to me; he frequently said (and it made me cry so many times): "I have only two children, Gino and Gemma."

He talked like this in front of everyone else and to tell the truth we were disliked by everyone else in the house.

I too loved Gino more than the rest; we were always together; on vacation we had fun making little altars, preparing feasts, and the like; we were always alone. He expressed the desire, when he got a little bigger, to become a priest, so he was put in seminary, and he was initiated, but a few years later he died.

During the time he was bedridden, he did not want me to leave him. The doctor had given up on him, and I so hated to see my brother die that in order to die with him I used all his stuff; and only barely did I not actually die, because a month after his death, I myself became gravely ill.

I cannot fully convey all the care that everyone had for me, especially Dad; many times I saw him crying and asking Jesus to let him die in my place. He tried every remedy, and after three months I was healed.

Goodbye to school—the jewels of a bride of the Crucified

✻

The doctor forbade me to study, and I left school. Very often the mother superior and the teachers sent for me to return, but Dad no longer wished to send me. Each day he took me out; anything I wanted he gave me, and I started once again to take advantage. Still, I went to communion three or four times a week and, even though I was so bad, Jesus came, stayed with me, and said many things to me.

One time, I remember very well, I was given a gold watch with a chain; I, show-off that I was, couldn't wait to put it on and go out (that is when, dear Dad, my imagination began to work on me). In fact I went out; when

I returned and started undressing, I saw an angel (who I now know was my guardian angel) who sternly said to me: "Remember that the precious jewels which adorn a bride of Christ Crucified cannot be other than thorns and the cross."

These words I did not even tell my confessor, I'm saying them now for the first time. Those words frightened me, like that angel frightened me; but then upon reflecting on these words, without understanding anything, I made this resolution: I resolve for love of Jesus and to please him, not to wear and not even to talk about vain things.

I also had a ring on my finger; I took that off too and from that day I have had nothing.

So I resolved (because Jesus then gave me clear signs that I should become a nun) to change my life, and I was offered a great opportunity, because the new year 1897 was soon to begin.[15] In a little book I wrote:

> In this new year I resolve to begin a new life. What will happen in this new year I do not know. I abandon myself in you, my God. All my hopes, all my affections shall be toward you. I feel weak, oh Jesus, but with your help I hope and resolve to live in another way, one that is closer to you.

The desire for Heaven
✳

From the moment that Mom had inspired in me the desire for Heaven, I always (even in the midst of such sinfulness) desired it ardently, and if God had left the choice to me, I would have preferred to free myself from my body and fly to Heaven. Every time I had a fever and felt ill, for me it was a consolation; but when, after whatever illness, I felt my strength returning, for me it was painful. Indeed, one day after communion I asked Jesus why he didn't take me to Heaven. He answered: "Daughter, because during your life I shall give you many opportunities to achieve yet greater merit, redoubling in you the desire for Heaven, while at the same time you must accept with patience your life."

These words in no way diminished this desire; indeed, every day I saw it increasing more.

To love Jesus and suffer with him
✳

In this same year of 1896 another desire grew in me; I felt growing in me a desire to love totally Jesus Crucified and together with this a desire to suffer and to assist Jesus in his sufferings.

One day I was overcome with such pain in gazing, that is in staring at the cross, that I fainted and fell to the floor. It just happened that Dad was home and he began to reproach me, saying that it was bad for me to always stay home and only to go outside early in the morning (it had been two mornings that he had not let me go to mass). I answered crossly: "It is bad for me to stay away from Jesus in the Blessed Sacrament."

This answer so angered him that he yelled at me; I hid in my room and then it was that for the first time I gave vent to my suffering with Jesus alone.

My dear Dad, I do not remember my words, but my angel is here, dictating to me word for word. These are the words: "I want to follow you at the cost of whatever pain and I want to follow you fervidly; no, Jesus, I don't want to sicken you with my lukewarm doings like I have done thus far; that would be coming to you and causing you disgust. Therefore, I resolve: more devout prayers, more frequent communion. Jesus, I want to suffer, and suffer a lot for you. Prayer always on my lips. The one who resolves often, falls often. What then will happen to someone who resolves seldom?"

My dear Dad, these words were dictated to me by my heart in that moment of pain and of hope, alone with my Jesus.

I had made lots of resolves but never observed any of them. Every day, in the midst of my many sins of every kind, I asked Jesus to let me suffer and to suffer a lot.

Sickness of the foot
*

After so much, Jesus consoled me; he sent me an infirmity in one of my feet. I kept it secret for quite a while but the pain became sharp; the doctor came and said I should be operated if time still allowed, otherwise cut off the foot. Everyone in the family was very upset, only I remained indifferent. I remember that while being operated upon, I cried, screamed; but afterward, gazing at Jesus, I prayed him to forgive my outburst. Jesus sent me other tribulations and I can truly say that ever since Mom died, I have not spent a single day without suffering some little thing for Jesus.

At this time I never stopped committing sins; every day it became worse; I was full of every fault and I don't know how Jesus managed never to show anger. One time only did I see Jesus angry with me, and I would desire to suffer the pains of Hell a thousand times in this life rather than find myself in front of an angry Jesus and see before my eyes the horrible portrait of my soul, like it happened at that time I'll tell you about later.

Her first vow

✳

On Christmas day of the same year I was allowed to go to mass and receive holy communion. I was nearly fifteen years old,[16] and for some time I had begged my confessor to allow me to make a vow of virginity (I had been asking for many years, but without knowing what it meant; but to my mind it seemed the most beautiful gift that Jesus could hold dear). It was not possible for me to do this, but instead of vowing my virginity he let me vow my chastity and on Christmas night I made my first vow to Jesus. I remember that Jesus was very pleased, that he himself, after communion, said to me that to this vow I should add the offer of myself, of my feelings, and of my submission to his will. I made the vow with such joy that I spent that night and the next day in Heaven.

The year of great pain (1897)—Dad's death

✳

That year ended, we enter into 1897, a year of great sadness for the entire family. I alone, heartless, remained indifferent to all these tragedies. The thing that most afflicted the others was that we became completely impoverished, and furthermore the gravity of Dad's illness.

I understood one morning after communion how great a sacrifice Jesus would soon ask; I cried a lot but in those days of pain Jesus made himself more felt than ever to my soul, and also I saw that Dad was resigned to death, giving me an inner strength so I could tolerate the premature tragedy with much tranquility. And the day he died, Jesus prohibited me from losing myself in useless screams and tears, and so I spent the time in prayer, resigned fully to God's wish, so that in this moment he took the place of Heavenly Father and Earthly Father.[17]

With her aunt in Camaiore
Return to Lucca (1898)

✳

After Dad's death we found ourselves with nothing; we had no means to live on. An aunt, learning of this, helped us in every way, and did not want me to stay with my family any more. The day after Dad's death she sent for me and she kept me with her for several months. (This was not the aunt after Mom's death, it was another one.)

Every morning she took me to mass; I received communion very rarely because I did not find a way to confess to anyone but Monsignor [Volpi]. At this time, unfortunately, I began to forget Jesus, I began to leave prayer aside, and I began once again to love amusements.

Another niece for whom my aunt provided a home became my friend, and we were a perfect pair for doing bad things. My aunt frequently sent us out alone; I realized well that (had Jesus not taken pity on my weakness) I would have fallen into grave sin; love of worldly things began very slowly to take over my heart. Then Jesus once again came forward: suddenly my back bent over with sharp pains. For a time I resisted but seeing that things were getting worse, I asked my aunt to bring me back to Lucca. Without wasting any time, she had someone take me back.

But, dear Dad, the recollection of those months spent in sin made me tremble; I had committed all kinds: even impure thoughts floated in my head; I had listened to evil conversations rather than fleeing; I told lies to my aunt to protect my friend; in short, I saw Hell open before me.

Mortal illness (1898–99)

※

Once back in Lucca, I remained ill for some time; I did not want to obey and let a doctor visit me (because I never wanted anyone to put his hands on me and see me). One evening suddenly the doctor came to the house and by force examined me, and found an abscess on my body that he feared was serious because he believed the abscess would affect my back.

Already for quite a while I had felt pain there but I myself did not wish to touch or to look, and this was because from childhood I had heard a homily and listened to these words: "Our body is the temple of the Holy Spirit." These words struck me and as much as possible I guarded my body carefully.

The doctor, after visiting me, called for a consultation. What distress, dear Dad, to have to let myself be undressed. Each time I felt the doctor I cried. After the consultation things became steadily worse and I was forced to stay in bed, unable to move. They tried every remedy but instead of making me better they made me worse. In bed I was restless, annoying everyone.

The second day that I was bedridden I found no peace and I wrote to Monsignor that I wanted to see him. He came immediately and heard my general confession; not because I was ill but so I might find a peaceful conscience, which I had lost. After confession I returned to peace with Jesus, and to show me a sign that same evening he gave me again a strong sense of pain for my sins.

Oh, dear Dad, now yes! The pain became steadily sharper and the doctors decided to operate (on the area I already spoke about). Three of them came (my suffering from the illness was nothing in comparison); the pain, the distress was only when I had to stay in their presence almost completely naked . . . My dear Dad . . . how much better to die! In the end the doctors saw that every cure was useless and they completely abandoned me; they only came occasionally, out of duty I would almost say.

This illness, which nearly all the doctors said was spinal meningitis, only one insisted in saying it was hysteria. I stayed in bed always in one position; it was impossible to move by myself. To have a little relief once in a while, I had to beg those in the house to assist me to lift first an arm, then a leg; they took every care for me, but I to the contrary had nothing for them but bad ways and back-talk.

The comfort of her guardian angel
✴

One evening, more restless than usual, I complained to Jesus, saying I would not pray any more unless he made me better and asking him why he was making me stay so ill. My angel answered as follows: "If Jesus afflicts you bodily, he does it to purify your soul. Be good." Oh how many times in my long illness I heard in my heart such words of consolation! But I never paid heed.

What afflicted me most about being bedridden was that I wanted to do what the others were doing; every day I would have been happy to go to confession, every morning to mass. Then one morning, when they brought me holy communion at home, Jesus made himself felt strongly, and he reprimanded me sharply, saying to me that I was a weak soul. "It is your misplaced self-esteem which resents not being able to do what others do," he said, "and causes the confusion you feel in needing help from others; if you were truly dead to yourself, you would not be so agitated."

These words of Jesus did me good, and for a while I was always in cheerful spirits.

S. Gabriel of Our Lady of Sorrows
✴

During this time my family prayed triduums and novenas,[18] and had others pray them for my recovery, but nothing happened. I myself remained indifferent; the words of Jesus had fortified me, but not converted me.

One day a lady, who regularly came to visit, brought me a book to read (the Life of Venerable Gabriel).[19] I took it almost with disdain and put it under my pillow; she asked me to commend myself to him, but I gave the matter no thought. At home each evening we began to offer him three Our Father's, three Hail Mary's, and three Glory be's.

One day I was alone, it was past noon; I felt a strong temptation and said to myself that I was bored, being bedridden had become tiresome. The devil took advantage of these thoughts and began to tempt me, saying that had I paid attention to him I would have been healed and he would have done everything I wished. My dear Dad, I was on the verge of caving in; I was agitated and I was about to give up. Suddenly I had an idea; I ran mentally to Brother Gabriel and shouted: "First my soul and then my body!"

Nonetheless the devil continued with even stronger assaults; a thousand ugly thoughts floated in my head. Once again I appealed to Brother Gabriel and with his help I won; regaining my self-control, I made the sign of the cross and in about fifteen minutes I returned to union with my God, whom I had disdained. I remember how that same evening I started reading the life of Brother Gabriel. I read it several times: I never got enough of re-reading it and admiring his virtues and his examples. Alas, my resolves were many but my deeds none.

From the day that my new protector, Venerable Gabriel, saved my soul, I became particularly devoted to him; in the evening I could not sleep if I did not have his picture under my pillow and I began from then on to see him nearby (here, dear Dad, I don't know how to explain myself: I felt his presence). In every deed, in every bad action I might have taken, Brother Gabriel returned to my mind and I desisted. I did not forget to pray to him every day with these words: "Soul first, then body."

Then one day the lady came to take back the book about Venerable Brother Gabriel. In taking it from under my pillow and returning it to the lady I could not hold back my tears; she, seeing how unhappy I was about giving it up, promised to come back for it only after the person who had lent it to her asked for it. She returned a few days later and now, crying or not, I had to give her the book. What a great pain.

But that saint of God wanted to reward quickly the little sacrifice and in a night-dream he appeared dressed in white; my dear Dad, I did not recognize him. He realized that I did not recognize him and he opened his white habit to show me his Passionist cassock; then I quickly recognized him. I remained in silence before him. He asked me why I had cried about giving up the book about him; I do not know what I answered but he said to me: "See how much I am pleased by your sacrifice, so pleased that I have come myself to see you. Do you love me?" I did not answer. He caressed me several times and repeated to me: "Be good, because I will return to see you." He told me to kiss his habit and his rosary, and he went away.

The work of my imagination kept increasing. I then wished to await another visit, but it didn't come for many, many months.

Here is how it happened. It was the feast of the Immaculate Conception; on that occasion the Barbantine nuns, Sisters of Charity, came to change my bedding and attend to me; among them one came frequently who had not yet taken the habit and would not for another two years because she was too young. On the vigil of this feast the nuns arrived as usual and this inspiration came to me; if tomorrow, I thought to myself, which is Mom's feast, I should promise that, if she made me better, I would become a Sister of Charity, what would happen? . . .

This thought consoled me; I shared it with Sister Leonilda and she promised me that if I recovered, she would allow me to take the habit together with that novice of whom I just spoke. We agreed that in the morning I would make this promise to Jesus after communion. Monsignor came to hear my confession and from him I immediately gained permission. Further, he gave me another consolation: the vow of virginity that he never had been willing to let me make, that same evening we made together in perpetuity. He renewed his and I made mine for the first and last time. What tremendous graces, such as I have never repaid.

That evening I was perfectly calm. Night came and I fell asleep. All of a sudden I saw my protector standing before me and he said: "Gemma, go ahead and freely make a vow to become a religious, but do not add anything else." "Why?" I asked. And he answered, caressing my forehead. "My sister!" he said looking at me and smiling. I understood nothing of this; to thank him I kissed his habit. He took his heart, the one of wood [worn by the Passionists], let me kiss it, and placed it on the bedcovers, over my heart, and again he repeated: "My sister!" Then he disappeared.

The next morning on the bedcovers there was nothing; I received communion and made my vow, but added nothing else. I didn't talk with the nuns about all this nor with my confessor; at that time however, and many times later, those nuns reminded me of my vow, because they thought I had promised to become a Sister of Charity, and one time they said to me that the Blessed Virgin could make me ill again. Jesus was very pleased with this situation and he rejoiced in my poor heart.

Miraculous recovery (March 3, 1899)

✳

Months passed and I did not improve at all. The 4th of January the doctors made one last try; they put twelve studs of fire along my spine. Enough, I began to get worse. Beyond these pains, on the 28th of January was added an unbearable headache. The physician called in for consultation declared that the illness was dangerous (a brain tumor); no operation was possible because of my extreme weakness; I was getting worse every day and on February 2 I received the last rites. I made my confession and awaited the moment to go with Jesus. But slow down! The doctors, thinking I could no longer understand, said among themselves that I wouldn't make it to midnight. Long live Jesus!

My teacher from school (the one I already spoke about earlier) came to see me and also to say goodbye and that we'll see each other in Heaven. She begged me nonetheless to offer a novena to Blessed Margaret Mary Alacoque, saying that without doubt she would do me the grace either of recovering fully or else of flying straight to Heaven as soon as I died.

The teacher, before leaving my bedside, made me promise to begin the novena that very evening, which was February 18th; in fact I began it; I did the first one that same evening but the next day I forgot. The day of the 20th I started once again, but again I forgot. What kind of attention is this to prayer, eh, Dad?

On the 23rd I began for the third time (that is, I had the intention of beginning) but a few minutes before midnight I heard a rosary clicking and felt a hand on my forehead; I heard the start of an Our Father, a Hail Mary, and a Glory be, for nine consecutive times. I barely responded because I was worn out with illness. That same voice, which had led the Our Father, asked me: "Do you want to recover?" "It is all the same to me," I answered. "Yes," he added, "you will recover; pray with faith to the Heart of Jesus; every evening, until the novena is completed, I will come here to you, and we will pray together to the Heart of Jesus." "And Blessed Margaret?" I asked him. "Go ahead and add three Glory be's in her honor."

This happened for nine consecutive evenings: the same person came every evening and put a hand on my forehead; together we recited the Our Father to the Heart of Jesus and then he had me add three Glory be's to Blessed Margaret.

It was the second-to-last day of the novena and at the end I wanted to receive holy communion; in fact the novena ended on the first Friday of

March. I sent for my confessor; he heard my confession, and early the next morning I received communion. What happy moments I spent with Jesus. He repeated: "Gemma, do you want to get better?" I was so deeply moved that I could not answer. Poor Jesus. The grace was done. I was healed.

Jesus' caresses

✳

"Daughter," Jesus said as he embraced me, "I give myself entirely to you, and will you be entirely mine?" I saw clearly that Jesus had taken away my parents and sometimes I was in despair, believing I had been abandoned. That morning I complained to Jesus and Jesus, increasingly good, increasingly tender, repeated to me: "I, daughter, shall be with you always. I am your father, your mother will be . . ." and he pointed to Most Holy Mary, Our Lady of Sorrows. "Whoever stays in my hands can never lack paternal care, so you will lack nothing, even though I have taken from you every consolation and support on this earth. Come, come closer . . . you are my daughter . . . Aren't you happy to be the daughter of Jesus and of Mary?" The total love that Jesus inspired in my heart kept me from answering.

Barely two hours went by and I got up. My family cried with happiness; I too was happy, not because I had regained my health but because Jesus had chosen me to be his daughter. Jesus said to me before leaving that morning: "My daughter, to the grace I have given you this morning others will follow, much greater." And this turned out to be true, because Jesus has always protected me in a special way: for him I have had only coldness and indifference, which he has exchanged with infinite signs of love.

Hunger for the eucharist

✳

From then on I was unable to resist unless I went to Jesus every morning, but I couldn't; I had permission from my confessor but I was so weak that I could barely stand on my feet. On the second Friday of March 1899 I went out for the first time to receive communion and since then I've not abandoned the practice, except a few times because my many sins rendered me unworthy or if my confessor punished me.

At the Salesians [Nuns of the Visitation]

✳

That same morning of the second Friday [in March] the Salesian nuns wanted to see me; so I went to them and they promised that in the month of May they would take me in for a retreat and then in June, if it should be my desire and true vocation, they would let me enter the convent for always. Yes, I felt happy with their offer, more so because I knew Monsignor was truly in accord.

Holy Week, 1899

✳

In the meantime, I spent the month of March going to communion every morning and Jesus filled me with ineffable consolations. Then came Holy Week, which I greatly desired so that I might assist at the sacred functions, but Jesus had decided otherwise; in that week Jesus wanted a big sacrifice from me. Holy Wednesday came (no sign ever manifested itself in me, except that when I received communion Jesus made himself known in a huge way).

The guardian angel, teacher and guide

✳

From the moment I recovered, my guardian angel began to be my teacher and guide; he chastised me every time I did something wrong, he taught me to speak little and only when asked. One time when my family was talking about a person, and not saying anything very nice, I wanted to speak up but my angel reproached me sharply. He taught me to keep my eyes cast downward and even in church he sharply reproached me, saying: "Is this how you behave in the presence of God?" And other times he yelled at me like this: "If you are not good, I will not let you see me anymore." He taught me many times how one should be in the presence of God: to adore him in his infinite goodness, in his infinite majesty, in his mercy and in all his attributes.

The first Holy Hour—Jesus crucified

✳

So we were, like I said, in Holy Week and it was Wednesday; my confessor finally decided to let me make a general confession, as I had wished for so long; he chose exactly this Wednesday evening, at a rather late hour. Jesus in his infinite mercy gave me a deep sense of pain for my sins, and this is how. Thursday evening I began for the first time to pray a Holy Hour (I had promised the Sacred Heart of Jesus that, if I recovered, every Thursday without exception I would pray a Holy Hour). This was the first one I did on my feet; indeed, the other Thursdays I did it, but in bed, because my confessor did not allow me to get up due to my extreme weakness. But after my confession he let me do everything.

So I set forth to pray the Holy Hour but I felt so full of pain for my sins that I spent days of continuous martyrdom. In the midst of this infinite pain only one comfort remained: that of tears, comfort and relief at once. So I spent the whole hour praying and crying until, tired as I was, I sat down; the pain continued. Soon thereafter I felt fully collected and a little later, almost in an instant, I lost all my strength (only haltingly was I able to get up and lock the door of my room). Where was I? My dear Dad, there I was in front of Jesus, who had just been crucified. He bled from everywhere. I instantly lowered my eyes but that sight disturbed me greatly; I made the sign of the cross and turbulence quickly gave way to a tranquility of spirit. But I felt pain for my sins ever more acutely; I never lifted my eyes to look at Jesus: I didn't have the courage; I lay with my forehead to the ground and stayed that way for several hours. "Daughter" he said, "look, you opened all these wounds with your sins; but now be consoled as you have closed them with your pain. Do not offend me again. Love me, as I have always loved you." Again and again, he repeated: "Love me."

That dream vanished and I returned to my senses; from then on I began to have a great horror of sin (the biggest grace Jesus gave me). The wounds of Jesus remained so clearly in my mind that they were never erased.

Good Friday (March 31, 1899)

*

The morning of Good Friday I received communion, and during the day I wanted to attend the Three Hours of Agony but my family wouldn't let me, even though I cried, and only with great effort did I make this first sacrifice for Jesus. Jesus, always so generous, even though I had sacrificed only reluctantly, wanted to reward me; so I shut myself in my room to pray the Three Hours, but not alone; my guardian angel came and we prayed together: we assisted Jesus in all his suffering and comforted our Mom in her sorrows. Nevertheless, my angel did give me a gentle reproach, saying that I should not cry when I had to make some sacrifice for Jesus but instead I should thank those who had given me the opportunity to do so.

This was the first time and also the first Friday that Jesus made himself felt so strongly in my soul; even though I did not receive the true Jesus from the hands of a priest, because it was impossible, still Jesus came on his own and gave me communion. But this union of ours was so strong that I remained like stupid.

But Jesus spoke in a strong voice: "What are you doing?" he said. "What do you say? Aren't you even moved?" Unable to resist further, it was then that I forced myself to speak: "Oh, Jesus, how can this be: you—the most perfect, the most holy—how can you love someone who shows nothing but coldness and imperfection toward you?" "I am burning with desire to unite with you," Jesus repeated; "run to me every morning. But you know," he said, "I am a jealous father and bridegroom; will you be my faithful daughter and bride?"

I made a thousand promises to Jesus that morning, but oh my God! how quickly I forgot them. I always felt the horror of my sins and yet I always committed them. And no, Jesus was not pleased, yet he always consoled me, sending my guardian angel to be my guide in everything.

After this happened, I ought first to have revealed everything to my confessor; I went to confession but I did not have the courage and I left without saying anything. I went home and upon entering my room I realized that my angel was crying; I was not bold enough to ask him anything, but on his own he addressed these words to me: "So, you don't want to see me any more? You are bad: hiding things from your confessor. Remember this," he said, "which I shall repeat for the last time: if you ever again keep something from your confessor, I will not show myself to you again. Never again, never again." I knelt down and he ordered me to say an Act of Contrition and he made me promise to reveal everything to my confessor; then he pardoned me in the name of Jesus.

A severe reproach from Jesus

✳

It was the month of April and I waited impatiently for the moment when I could go to the Salesians for the retreat, as they had promised. One time, actually one morning after communion, Jesus let me know about something that displeased him greatly; I had done it the previous evening.

Two of my sister's girlfriends used to come to my house regularly and we spoke of things that were not bad, merely mundane; I took part in the conversation and had my say just like the others; but in the morning Jesus reproached me very sharply and I was so terrified that I wanted never to speak and never to see anyone again.

Jesus made himself felt more fully every day in my soul and filled me with consolation, but I to the contrary turned my back on him and offended him with no remorse.

Thirst for love and for suffering

❋

Two feelings and two thoughts arose jointly in my heart after Jesus first made himself felt and seen dripping with blood. One was to love him and to love him to the point of sacrifice; but since I did not know how to truly love him, I begged my confessor to teach me, and he answered like this: "Well, how does one learn to read and write? We practice continuously reading and writing and eventually we learn." This answer did not convince me: in fact I understood nothing. Many times I begged him to teach me but always I got the same response.

The other thing that arose in my heart after seeing Jesus was a great desire to suffer something for him, seeing that he had suffered so much for me. At that time I procured a thick cord by cutting a piece from the well-rope without anyone knowing; I made several knots and tied it around my waist. But I wasn't even able to wear it for fifteen minutes when my guardian angel reprimanded me to take it off because I had not asked permission of my confessor; a little later I asked and he granted me permission. But what really afflicted me was being unable to love Jesus as I would have wished; I took care not to offend him but my bad inclinations toward evil were so strong that without a special grace from God I would have fallen into Hell.

"Learn how to love"

❋

This not knowing how to love him troubled me, but Jesus, who in his infinite goodness was not ashamed to humiliate himself even to the point of being my teacher, one day in order to calm me, while I was saying my evening prayers, made me internally collected, and I found myself for the second time before Jesus Crucified and he said these words to me: "Watch, daughter, and learn how to love," and he showed me his five open wounds. "See this cross, these thorns, this blood? They are all works of love, of infinite love. Now do you see to what lengths I have loved you? Do you want to truly love me? First learn to suffer. Suffering teaches one how to love."

At this sight I felt a new pain; thinking about Jesus' infinite love for us and about the agonies he suffered for our salvation, I fainted, fell to the ground, and revived only after several hours. All this happened to me during these prayers, and it was such a great consolation that even if it had continued many more hours, I would never have gotten tired.

Every Thursday I continued to pray the Holy Hour, but it sometimes happened that this hour lasted until around 2:00 because I was staying with Jesus and almost always he let me participate in the sadness he felt in the garden upon seeing my many sins and those of the entire world; a sadness such that it could rightly be compared to the agony of death. After all this such a sweet calm and sense of consolation remained in me that I burst into tears and these tears let me taste an incomprehensible love and increased the desire in me to love Jesus and to suffer for him.

In the convent of the Salesians [Nuns of the Visitation]
✳

The time for the retreat that I so desired was approaching, and on May 1, 1899, I entered the convent at 3:00. I thought I was entering Heaven. What consolation! The first thing I did was to prohibit my family ever to come and see me during this time because those days were all for Jesus. The monsignor came to see me the same evening I entered and granted me permission (as the mother superior wished) not to make the retreat in private, but rather, as a test, I should do everything the nuns did. This consoled me in one way but also displeased me because I would not be able to collect myself completely; but I wanted to obey without answering back. The mother superior handed me over to the mistress of novices, who gave me a schedule to follow for the days I was to spend there.

I had to arise at 5:00, go to choir at 5:30, receive communion and then recite prime and sext with the nuns; then breakfast and after half an hour back to my cell; at 9:00 again in the choir-loft to hear the community mass and recite nones; then at 9:30, had the monsignor been able he would have come for instruction, but instead he gave me a book so at that hour I could meditate, and he came later to say something. At 10:15, when meditation ended, I was to join the nuns in the adoration of Jesus and then at 10:30 to lunch, until 11:30; from this hour until 12:30 recess (I obtained permission from the monsignor to have recess only once a day with the nuns, because in the evening I preferred to stay in the choir-loft with Jesus). At 12:30 I went to the novitiate until 3:00 and worked; at 3:00 again to recite vespers and then once more the entire community gathered and mother superior gave some instruction until 5:00. At 5:00 again in church to say compline and meditate for an hour, each as most pleased her; after meditation again to the refectory and then recess, but that time I spent either with the mother superior, in her room, or else in the choir-loft. The community gathered at 8:30 for about half an hour and at 9:00 recited matins, and then to bed.[20]

My dear Dad, I felt that this life was too easy on the nuns and rather than get attached to them I began to find no pleasure at all in that mode of living. The novices, who all showed some special concern for me, from time to time gave me advice and told me what the community would like best, but I gave no thought to this; what afflicted me was that I had to return to the outside world. I would have preferred to remain there (even though I did not feel drawn) rather than return once again to places where there were so many opportunities to offend Jesus; and I begged the monsignor to give me permission to never leave the convent again.

With the approval of mother superior and the entire community he asked permission from the archbishop, but he refused, saying I was still in too poor health and because I wore a metal corset to straighten my spine. (I honestly don't know who spied for the archbishop.) Mother superior then ordered me to take off the corset out of obedience; I cried at this order because I knew I wouldn't be able to stand; I ran to the novitiate's quarters and prayed to my beloved Infant Jesus, and then I ran to my room; I took it off and now almost two years have gone by without my wearing it and I am perfectly well.

Mother superior learned of this and went off immediately to inform the monsignor so that he in turn would inform the archbishop. One day was left before the end of the retreat when Monsignor Volpi came to hear my confession and asked me if I would like to stay in the convent for another twelve days because on May 21 several of the novices were to be professed and he would have liked me to be present.

I was infinitely happy to remain with them but one thought was fixed in my mind: that life was too easy for me. I had sinned so much and I had to do more penance. I revealed my fears to Jesus after communion and Jesus, never looking in judgment at my wretchedness, consoled me and made himself felt even more fully in my soul, and he calmed me, always saying consoling words. I was present, as the monsignor wished, at the profession of the four novices; that morning I cried, and I cried a lot. Jesus moved me more than usual, and several nuns, who saw me, surrounded me and asked me if I needed something because I was on the verge of losing my senses. (It was true; the nuns had forgotten to give me breakfast and also forgot to give me lunch, so that day I didn't eat until after 1:00.)

I was, however, reprimanded, as I fully deserved; I should have gone by myself to the refectory after the bell rang but I was ashamed (listen, Dad, to the extent of my badness and lack of respect for others). The mother superior usually kept me at her side wherever I was but on that day of profession, the nuns who profess stay next to their mother superior. So I remained excluded and out of pride I did not join the others, and thus I remained without eating.

I deserved worse, my God! But Jesus again put up with me; he gave me a punishment: to not make himself felt for several days. I cried a lot about this but Jesus once again sent my guardian angel who said to me: "Be happy, oh daughter, to merit such a just punishment! . . ." I understood nothing of these words but I felt that they consoled my heart.

Return home—nostalgia for the cloister and disappointed hopes

*

My God! Behold, a new pain; the next day I had to leave the convent to return home; I hoped that day would never come, but it arrived. It was at 5:00 in the evening on May 21, 1899, that I had to leave; in tears, I asked the mother superior's blessing, bade farewell to the nuns, and left. My God! What pain!

But an even greater pain was soon to follow this one. I returned home but no longer could I fit in; already my mind and my heart were fixed on the idea of becoming a religious and no one could tear this away; to leave the world behind I decided absolutely to become a Salesian nun. Almost every day I ran to the monastery and the sisters promised me that in the month of June, on the feast of the Sacred Heart of Jesus, they would take me in with them.

I must say however that in my heart I did not feel fully content, still because the Salesian life was too easy. And many times Jesus on different occasions repeated in my heart: "Daughter, you need a more austere rule." I almost never listened to these words and continued to be firm in my resolve.

We entered the month of June and I realized that the nuns had changed somewhat; I was not disturbed at all; every time I went to see mother superior they told me she couldn't come and she sent someone or other instead. They began to give me lectures, telling me that unless I could get at least four medical certificates they would not accept me. Even this I attempted but every effort was in vain: the doctors wanted to do nothing and then one day the nuns said when I should get the certificates they would admit me immediately, otherwise absolutely not. This outcome never upset me because Jesus did not fail to console me with many graces.

An enormous grace: stigmata

*

The day of June 8, after communion, Jesus informed me he would give me an enormous grace that evening. I went that same day to confession and I told the monsignor and he answered that I should take great care to refer everything back to him afterward.

It was evening and all of a sudden, earlier than usual, I felt an internal pain for my sins, so strong that I never again felt it to such an extent; that pain reduced me, I would almost say, to the point of death. After this I felt all the forces of my soul collecting: my intellect knew only my sins and the offense toward God; my memory recalled all of them and made me see all the torments Jesus had suffered to save me; my will made me detest them all and promise to want to suffer totally to expiate them. A bunch of thoughts all danced in my head; they were thoughts of pain, of love, of fear, of hope, and of comfort.

My internal collection was quickly followed by the rapture of my senses and I found myself before my Heavenly Mom, who had at her right side my guardian angel, who first commanded me to recite the Act of Contrition.

This done, Mom addressed me in these words: "Daughter, in the name of Jesus may all your sins be forgiven." Then she added: "My son Jesus loves you so much that he wants to give you a grace: will you know how to be worthy?" My wretched self did not know how to respond. She added: "I shall be your mother, will you show yourself to be my true daughter?" She opened her cloak and covered me with it.

In this instant Jesus appeared with all his wounds open, but blood was no longer flowing from the wounds; flames of fire flowed instead and in an instant the flames touched my hands, my feet, and my heart. I felt myself dying and I would have fallen to the ground, but Mom sustained me, still covering me with her cloak. For several hours I had to stay in that position. Then, Mom kissed me on the forehead, and everything vanished; I found myself on my knees and I still felt an intense pain in my hands, feet, and heart.

I got up to go to bed and realized that blood flowed from those parts where I hurt. I covered those parts as well as I could and then, helped by my angel, I was able to climb into bed. The pains, the suffering, instead of afflicting me, gave me perfect peace. In the morning I could barely go to communion and I put on a pair of gloves, at least to hide my hands. I could not stand on my feet and every moment I thought I would die. These pains lasted until 3:00 on Friday, the solemn feast of the Sacred Heart of Jesus.

I ought to have told my confessor first about this event but instead I went to confession several times without ever saying anything; several times he asked me and always I answered no.

Stigmata repeated
✳

Quite a while passed and every Thursday around 8:00 or earlier, I felt the usual pains; however, each time this happened, I first felt such deep and intense pain for my sins that this caused more suffering than the pains in my hands and feet and in my head and heart; this pain for my sins reduced me to a state of such sadness as to die. But even with this great grace of God I did not improve at all; each day I committed innumerable sins and acts of disobedience; with my confessor I was never sincere at all and I was always hiding something. The angel many times warned me, telling me he would leave and never let me see him again if I continued in this way; I did not obey and he did go, or rather he hid for a while.

Ardent desire for the cloister
Comforts and reproaches of Jesus
✳

During this time, however, my desire to become a nun increased constantly; I revealed it to my confessor but his answers almost always gave me little consolation; I discussed the idea with Jesus, and one morning when I felt this desire strongly, more strongly than usual, Jesus said to me: "Oh daughter, what are you afraid of? Hide this desire in my heart and from my heart no one will be able to snatch it away." Jesus spoke to me this way because my yearning to enter the convent, so I might be ever more united with him, was so strong that I feared someone would be able to take it away; but Jesus promptly consoled me with these words, that I never forgot.

Jesus never failed to make himself seen and felt, especially when I was

afflicted. One day (that I particularly remember) was when one of my brothers yelled at me, as always deservedly, because I went out early to go to
church. Beyond the quarrel there were also some small blows, which I certainly deserved, and I complained about it; my Jesus remained displeased and
reproached me with certain words, which truly hurt me. "Daughter," he
said, "do you also contribute to increasing the sufferings in my heart? I exalted you with being my daughter, honored you with the title of my servant, and now this is how you behave? Arrogant daughter, unfaithful servant. Bad girl!"

Those words made such an impression on my heart that when Jesus afterward added new crosses he always gave me the strength to thank him and
not to complain any more.

Jesus reproached me sharply one time with these words, which later I realized were the truth, but at that moment I did not understand. "Daughter,"
he said, "you complain too much about adversity, you are perplexed by
temptations, and too timid in governing your sentiments. From you I want
only love: love in adversity, love in prayers, love in affronts, love in everything. And tell me, daughter, can you deny me such a just satisfaction and
such a small repayment?" I had no words to answer Jesus and my heart was
bursting with pain; I did pronounce a few words that I remember well: "My
heart," I said, "oh Jesus, is ready to do everything; it is ready to burst with
pain if you wish. My God! and . . ."

The Holy Missions at the Church of San Martino
❉

June passed and toward the end of that month the Holy Missions had begun
at the Church of San Martino. I always preferred to skip the Missions rather
than not participate in the prayers to the Sacred Heart; but once they were
over, I began to go each evening to the homilies at San Martino. What my
impression was in seeing those priests preaching I cannot describe. It was a
very big impression because I recognized that they wore the same kind of
habit I had first seen worn by Brother Gabriel. I was taken with a special affection for them, such that from that day onward I never missed a homily.

We were at the last day of Holy Missions and all the people were gathered in church to make a general holy communion; among the many, I also
took part, and Jesus, who I could see was pleased with this, made himself
clearly felt in my soul and asked me: "Gemma, do you like the habit that
priest is wearing?" (And he pointed toward a Passionist who was a short dis-

tance from me.) There was no need for me to answer Jesus with words; more than anything, my heart spoke with its palpitations. "Would you like," (Jesus added) "to be clothed in the same habit?" "My God!" I exclaimed. "Yes," Jesus continued, "you shall be a daughter of my Passion and a favored daughter. One of these sons shall be your father. Go and reveal everything . . ." And I recognized the one indicated by Jesus to be Father Ignazio.

In fact I obeyed; in the afternoon (which was the last of the Missions) I went, but for all that I forced myself, I could not speak about my experiences; instead of Father Ignazio, I ran to Father Gaetano,[21] with whom I forced myself to reveal all of what had happened, what I have just related here. He listened with infinite patience and promised me that on Monday after the Holy Missions he would return to Lucca and do everything to hear my confession. We agreed on this. A week passed and again I was able to confess before him, and this continued for a while.

At this time and at the introduction of this priest, I made the acquaintance of a lady whom from then on I loved as a mother and whom I always regarded as such.[22]

Triple vows

*

The reason I went to that priest for confession was one only; my ordinary confessor [Monsignor Volpi] several times had prohibited me from making the three vows of chastity, obedience, and poverty, because as long as I stayed in the world it would be impossible for me to observe them. I, who always had a great desire to make these vows, took this opportunity to ask it first thing; immediately he let me make them, from July 5th until the holy day of September 8th, after which I could renew them. I was very pleased with this outcome, which for me was among my greatest consolations.

With this confessor's great effort, and to my great shame, I revealed everything: all the particular graces the Lord had granted me, the frequent visits from my guardian angel, the presence of Jesus, and the various penances I did every day without anyone's permission and solely because they were in my head. First he ordered me to stop everything; further, he wanted me to turn in the penitential instruments I used; finally, this priest told me clearly that he was not able to direct me by himself and that I had to talk with my ordinary confessor.

I did not want to agree on this matter because I already foresaw a big argument and the danger of being abandoned by the monsignor because of my lack of sincerity and trust in him; there was no way I was going to reveal the name of my confessor; I said I did not know his name and I don't remember for sure if I even invented a false name. But this trick didn't get very far and to my shame I was found out. Father Gaetano learned that my confessor was Monsignor [Volpi] but he was not allowed to speak to him unless I gave permission; finally, after giving Father Gaetano a lot of trouble, I consented, and both of them were in complete accord. From the monsignor I got permission to go for confession to that priest and he didn't yell at me, as I fully deserved; then I spoke of the vows already made and he too approved them and to the three already made he had me add another: sincerity with my confessor. The confessor then commanded me to keep my experiences hidden and not to speak of them with anyone, only with him.

A doctor's visit in vain
Complaints and Jesus' reproaches

*

The happenings of Friday continued and the monsignor thought it best to have a doctor visit me without my knowledge, but Jesus himself informed me of it and said: "Tell your confessor that in the presence of a doctor I will do nothing of what he desires." On Jesus' orders I so informed my confessor, but he did as he wished anyway and things went as Jesus had said they would, as you already know.

My dear Dad, from that day a new life began for me and here I would have so much to say, but if Jesus wishes, I will say it only to you (in confession).

Here it is, the first and most beautiful humiliation that my beloved Jesus gave me; nonetheless my great pride and love of myself took offense, and Jesus in his infinite charity continued to grant me his graces and his favors. One day he said lovingly to me (why Jesus addressed me with these words, my Dad, I will tell you alone but maybe you will understand without my explaining): "Daughter, what should I say when in your uncertainties, in your afflictions, and in your adversities you turn to everyone but me; why do you run for some relief and comfort to everyone but me?"

My dear Dad, did you understand? A just reproach from Jesus which I understood I deserved; but nonetheless I continued in the usual way. Jesus once again reproached me, saying: "Gemma, do you think I am not offended when in your greatest needs you turn to things which cannot bring you consolation? I suffer, daughter," he said, "when I see that you forget me." This last reproach was enough and served to detach me completely from every living creature in order to turn all of myself toward my Creator.

Father Germano

*

Once again my confessor prohibited all the extraordinary experiences of Fridays and Thursdays, and for a while Jesus obeyed, but then I returned to my usual experiences, and even more than before. I was no longer afraid to reveal everything to my confessor, and he emphatically told me that unless Jesus let him see things clearly, he would not believe in such reveries. Not wasting any time, the same day I made a special prayer to Jesus in the sacrament for this purpose, and behold, as happened often to me, I felt internally collected and quickly my senses were enraptured. I found myself before Jesus, but he was not alone; he had with him a man with white hair; from his habit I knew he was a Passionist priest; he had his hands folded as he prayed, prayed fervently. As I looked at him Jesus pronounced these words: "Daughter, do you know him?" I answered no, which was true. "You see," he added: "that priest will be your director and he will be the one who will know in you, wretched creature, the infinite works of my mercy."

After this happened I thought no further about it. Then one day I chanced to see a small portrait and it was in fact that priest whom I had seen with Jesus; but the portrait bore only a slight resemblance. My intimate union in prayer with you, dear Dad, began then, from the first time I saw you with Jesus in a dream. I wished from then on always to have you with me, but the more I desired it, the more impossible it seemed to be. I prayed, and I began ever since then to pray several times each day, and after a few months Jesus consoled me and made you come. Now I shall stop speaking, because from then until now you have been acquainted with me and so you know everything.

CHAPTER THREE

Diary ✳ *Summer 1900*

Monsignor Giovanni Volpi, Gemma Galgani's regular confessor, did not accept the divine origin of her recent, potentially controversial, spiritual graces.
This she knew, as her autobiographical confession makes abundantly clear.
His response to reports of her frequent raptures, which in part came to him
secondhand from confessors in whom she had recently felt greater confidence (however misplaced, given that they uniformly consulted with him),
was to order his young penitent to desist from allowing herself to go in ecstasy. A very revealing brief letter, undated but surely written in late August
or early September 1899, illuminates several aspects of their relationship.

> Monsignor,
> Yesterday I spoke with Father Gaetano and he told me that you wanted me
> to pray to Jesus that he remove all raptures from me. I told Jesus; he re-
> sponded that he will remove everything, everything, once I enter a convent.
> But as long as I remain outside, he will make things stay as they are, so that
> you will have more urgency to shelter me. Jesus told me to tell you that you
> could place me as what the nuns call a lay sister, but Jesus did not use the
> word lay sister, ready to do the most humble tasks, like a servant, but in the
> convent, in which case the expenses would be very small; then he will take
> care of the rest.
>   Bless me and pray so much to Jesus for your poor,
>   Gemma[1]

I suspect that Monsignor Volpi did not take kindly to a young woman
who told him so confidently what Jesus wanted, nor to her brazen threats to
use his consternation over her behavior to blackmail him into approving
what she so desperately desired, nor to her very sensible suggestions about
how to overcome whatever financial obstacles might stand in her way. He

chose to ignore Gemma's advice and instead to put into action a most earthly plan of his own, one he must have known carried the certainty—whatever its outcome—that this extremely private, shy, frail girl would instantly be exposed to public scrutiny. Eschewing a quiet and private inquiry, perhaps in the company of a sympathetic cleric such as Father Gaetano, the monsignor instead called on a prominent and by no means neutral member of the Lucchese medical community, Dr. Pietro Pfanner, to accompany him in conducting a surreptitious examination, from a secular, scientific perspective, of Gemma's reported experiences. The risk that she might be exposed as self-deluded or fraudulent is immediately obvious, no less now than it surely was a century ago. On the other hand, were her graces to be deemed gifts from God, she would be exposed instantly to an onslaught of miracle-seekers. Ignoring such considerations, and leaving aside the difficult question of frequent raptures, the men went directly to Gemma's most vulnerable sign, her stigmata.

Dr. Pfanner had known Gemma since her childhood.[2] At the Lucca, 1907, Ordinary Proceedings to assess Gemma's sanctity, he testified that he had been called in to see Gemma when the family was living on Via degli Angeli, some time after 1887, so that Gemma would have been about ten. Examining her in the company of the family's regular physician, Dr. Lorenzo Del Prete, he had observed that although she manifested an irritable cough, her lungs were not infected, leading him to diagnose her condition as a "hysterical cough." Calling in a second physician for consultation about a childhood cough may seem unusual, but less so if one recalls that Gemma's mother had died only a few years earlier, a victim of tuberculosis. Further, her father was a pharmacist who no doubt maintained good relationships throughout Lucca's medical community. More may have been amiss. Dr. Pfanner probed other parts of Gemma's body and noted a total anesthesia of her palms, which he could prick freely without her reporting any pain. He judged that she might be suffering from some sort of neurosis, an opinion he maintained steadfastly in the years ahead.

Dr. Pfanner was summoned on a second occasion (about which he also testified at the Lucca proceedings), during the illness recounted by Gemma in her general confession, the one from which she reported a miraculous recovery on March 3, 1899, after completing her novena to Blessed Margaret Mary Alacoque. He recalled that because Dr. Del Prete had been out of town, he, Pfanner, had served as primary physician. Gemma presented an abscess from her upper hip bone, which he drained several times with a lance. He diagnosed the abscess as a symptom of Pott's disease (TB spondylitis), yet he noted as well a paralysis of her right leg for which there was no good clinical explanation, because if it was the result of spinal compression resulting from Pott's disease, she should have been completely paralyzed. Perhaps it was a more limited lesion of the spinal cord, he speculated. Even as she recovered from the Pott's disease, this paralysis continued and spread to her left leg. Then Dr. Pfanner learned from an aunt that when Gemma had to go to the bathroom she ordered everyone out of the room and somehow managed to drag herself to the toilet. This fact led him to reach a diagnosis of "hysterical paralysis," which made sense, he reasoned, given his earlier findings of hysterical cough and anesthesia of the palms. Pressed by Gemma's defenders during the canonization hearings to concede his own fallibility, Dr. Pfanner agreed that he could not exclude entirely the possibility that the force of Gemma's will, driven by her great sense of modesty, somehow might have enabled her to use her upper limbs to drag herself to the toilet on her own. Yet he remained highly skeptical and stuck to his opinion that hysteria had been involved in both the illness and its cure.

Dr. Pfanner next recounted his treatment approach. If the paralysis was due to hysteria, as he suspected, and since he had heard that Gemma was such a good and pious girl, it should be easy to heal her via the following regimen:

> Monsignor Volpi was her spiritual advisor and I went to see him; I explained the case and proposed that he should have the family pray a triduum or a novena, instilling in her the idea that for this supplication surely she would obtain the grace of being made well.
>
> Monsignor Volpi accepted and in fact at the end of the triduum and the novena, the patient suddenly was healed.

One additional encounter before the visit of September 8, 1899, seems likely. While there is no direct testimony from Dr. Pfanner, surely he was among the four physicians who had refused to give Gemma the certificates of good health that she desperately needed in order to enter the Salesian convent the previous June. Moreover, the collaboration between him and Monsignor Volpi initiated during her March illness suggests that Gemma's suspicions about a collusion resulting in the Salesian mother superior's sudden change of heart were well founded. At first the monsignor may have thought the convent would be suitable for Gemma, but then he apparently changed his mind. It would seem that, rather than telling her straight out, he sent her chasing hopelessly after four separate medical certificates from physicians of good standing, with whom no doubt he was in steady contact about the perplexing behavior of his young charge.

Thus, when Dr. Pfanner came at Monsignor Volpi's invitation to conduct a secret examination of Gemma's stigmata, he had some preconceptions about what would face him. In her autobiographical account of the fateful day, Gemma wrote about how Jesus had told her of the plan and that he would withhold all his graces: "Tell your confessor that in the presence of a doctor I will do nothing of what he desires." Gemma did as she was told, and in a written note delivered on that very morning she warned: "Monsignor, if you want to come, come alone, otherwise Jesus will not be happy and will not make his presence known." Ever dutiful and humble, she added: "I am happy whatever you do, whether you come in company or alone. Bless me, your poor Gemma."[3]

When the all-knowing doctor and the powerful confessor arrived at the Giannini house, where the orphaned Gemma was staying in the daytime, on Friday, September 8, at around 2:00 in the afternoon, she was in ecstasy and oblivious to their presence. They found her semi-seated, her eyes partially opened so that they could not see her pupils; her entire body was in convulsions as if she were the victim of a nervous attack. As Dr. Pfanner testified years later, he noted spots of blood on the palms of her hands and on her forehead but he observed that these were not in the form of droplets, as happens with bleeding from a subcutaneous cut. Further, the spots were irregular in shape and several showed fingerprints. He had the impression they had been made artificially with her fingers, which he immediately examined and found to be full of short blackish streaks at the extremities, like one sees in people who on their jobs habitually cut their fingertips, he explained. Then he ordered a wet towel and wiped away the bloody spots; immediately it became clear—indisputably, scientifically—that there were no wounds and no flow of blood. Dr. Pfanner instantly suspected simulation on Gemma's part, a judgment confirmed for him when Cecilia Giannini, Gemma's substitute Mom, spotted a telltale sewing needle on the floor next to Gemma. Monsignor Volpi knew the girl better and simply could not share his professional friend's conclusion about Gemma's fakery, but he readily conceded, according to those gathered at the scene, that hysteria could well have entered here. The two agreed. Said Dr. Pfanner: "Didn't I tell you this was all hysteria? In my opinion it is abundantly evident that in fact we are dealing not with a miracle but with a case of hysteria, and not a very refined one at that. And the monsignor didn't want to hear anything more about those signs." As Cecilia Giannini testified during the canonization proceedings: "Everyone remained mortified, starting with Monsignor Volpi."

Fifteen years after his initial testimony in 1907 at Lucca, Dr. Pfanner softened his judgment a bit, affirming in the Apostolic Proceedings held at Pisa (opened on January 20, 1922) that science could only go so far and that as a physician he could be more certain about what he had observed than about its cause and meaning. He conceded that shortly after this moment when "everyone remained mortified" he had left, because he sensed that the others present did not fully share in his opinions. Once he had dashed the family's hopes for a miracle in progress, he felt unwelcome and did not stay to do a more thorough examination.

Elsewhere, the promoter general of the faith recounted that whereas Dr. Del Prete's testimony had been nebulous, even forgetting that it was he who had performed the operation on Gemma's foot, and Dr. Giulio Tadini's had been obstinately hostile, insinuating that the mystical aura of the Giannini household had influenced the impressionable young Gemma and testifying that his autopsy of her heart found absolutely nothing unusual about it, Dr. Pfanner seemed truly to support recognition of Gemma's sanctity, even though he did not believe he could affirm the supernatural origin of her signs. Nonetheless, the eminent Cardinal Pietro Maffi, in summarizing the Apostolic Proceedings at Pisa, concluded that all three physicians were infected with materialism and scientific positivism. For good measure, detailed scientific refutations of the hysteria charges by expert professors Joseph Antonelli and August Friedrich Ludwig, replete with citations of Jean-Martin Charcot, Paul Richer, Henri Huchard, and Adolf von Strümpell, were referenced as part of the official record.[4]

Whatever the high churchmen finally came to judge decades later, as of September 8, 1899, the damage had been done. Gemma responded initially with innocent confidence that her beloved Jesus somehow would come to her rescue. In an ecstasy that very evening, she asked Jesus: "Do you love me more now or before, when everyone thought I was holy? Now, right? Go console the monsignor, he is so unhappy." And on the following Tuesday she implored again:

> You know, I'm not asking on my behalf, but for my confessor; you, Jesus, see inside me. With you I want to get serious, with you; do you know when I'll laugh again with you? When you have done me this favor. Until then, when you call me I won't answer. You wanted to draw me to you and I was unable to resist but from now on I'll find excuses. You think about it, Jesus, make me happy, because I want to do everything to make you happy . . . Let my

confessor know about all this; otherwise, I will no longer laugh with you, you know: I will remain very serious and I will not embrace you.[5]

But these girlish charms had no apparent effect, and in three letters to Monsignor Volpi dated September 8, 12, and 13, Gemma pursued more traditional arguments and appeals. The fiasco had been intended all along by Jesus as a lesson in humiliation, she wrote, a just punishment for her vainglory, a sacrifice necessary to prepare her for even more difficult spiritual tests ahead. "Oh, how much more I welcome you now, so scorned, than before, when everyone believed you were a saint," is how Gemma reports Jesus' comforts. "Tell your confessor I will provide whatever sign he wishes, as long as he comes alone, since only he needs to know for sure that this is not some illness." Alternatively, Gemma tried defiance: "I told Jesus that if it is truly him, he should reveal everything; but if it is the devil, chase him away." Lastly, Gemma attempted a written version of the ecstatic, playful exchange recorded above ("I will no longer laugh with you, you know: I will remain very serious and I will not embrace you"), explaining how in rapture Jesus had appeared in her arms as a happy infant and how she had understood him to promise he would soon set things right with her confessor.[6] Alas, nothing worked to restore Monsignor Volpi's trust in Gemma, not in her brief lifetime and not for decades thereafter. Indeed, the powerful prelate ordered Gemma to make the horn sign and spit upon the face of Jesus when he visited her, apotropaic gestures sure to ward against a diabolic trick. This too she did: "Poor Jesus, sometimes I made the cuckold sign and spit in his face (because this is what my confessor ordered), and he stayed good, so good; he watched me, laughed, and caressed me."[7]

Only after much searching during a year of self-doubt and agony did Gemma find her way to a new spiritual director in whom she had more trust. It was he, Father Germano, "my dear Dad" (*Babbo mio*) as Gemma quickly and confidently came to address him, who took on the task of weaving a satisfactory explanation of the events of September 8, 1899. In his biography of Gemma, as in his fervid promotion of her cult and her proposed canonization, Father Germano accepted that the day had been one of humiliation for Gemma. In an instant her reputation among Lucca's faithful for innocence and piety had given way to disgrace, involving charges of hysteria and possibly even simulation. A key obstacle to redeeming Gemma's reputation was her ordinary confessor, Monsignor Volpi, Auxiliary Bishop of Lucca, and on his way to becoming Bishop of Arezzo.[8] A more politically attuned churchman would be hard to find, one skilled in the art of compromise and burned by experience to know better than to become entangled in fights about modernity. While he personally remained skeptical to the very end, at least the monsignor allowed others to continue to look for proof that Gemma's spiritual graces were genuine. And in an ironic way, his doubts may have contributed to the care and the ultimate success with which Father Germano built a case for her sanctity.

The very reports that caused Monsignor Volpi such consternation were of the utmost interest to Passionist missionaries who arrived in Lucca to exhort the faithful about the upcoming Jubilee Year of 1900, less than a month after Gemma Galgani initially experienced stigmata on June 8, 1899. As its name states, the order is inspired by the Passion; its members focus above all else on Jesus' sacrifice in accepting crucifixion, the central event that gives meaning to his life. They treat the Passion not merely as an event to be recalled and commemorated in devotional activities but as a living memory to be enacted in their daily existence. They value pain, austerity, mortification, and sacrifice positively as ways to expiate for the sins of humanity, as paths to self-realization, as the imitation of Christ. Controversies over how best to keep the "living" memory of Christ's crucifixion marked the order from its very founding (witness the softening of language in the proposed Rule of 1736 before the papacy accepted the 1741 version) and continue even in our own time, as expressed in Superior General José Agustín Orbegozo's commentary in 1991, for a rescript of the regulations on the 250th anniversary of their approval.[9]

From a very different perspective, a contemporary student of medieval culture, Mary Carruthers, identifies the secular milieu in which this living view of the crucifixion was embedded: "Few features of medieval scholarship are so distinctive as an utter indifference to the pastness of the past, to its uniqueness and its integrity 'on its own terms,' as we would say." Or, to take a cue from David Hume, eighteenth-century enlightened contemporary of the order's founder: "All belief of matter of fact or real existence is derived merely from some object, present to the memory or senses."[10] For Passionists, that object is the cross; its existence is real, present tense intended, and its meaning is suffering.[11] The wounds of stigmata, then, are not some embarrassing psychosomatic medical condition but an exquisite expression of the highest ideals of re-living Jesus' commitment to mankind. So it is for Gemma.

Passionist Father Gaetano, to whom she had initially confessed her special relationship with Jesus at a time when she was holding back her experiences from Monsignor Volpi, believed her. He instantly allowed her to make the triple vows of chastity, obedience, and poverty that the monsignor had denied. Upon his return to Lucca in the fall of 1899, shortly after the day of disgrace, he obtained permission to visit Gemma, whereupon he ordered her to wash her wounds three or four times in his presence; not only did they remain, but the flow of blood quickly recommenced. Among the ways the devil reportedly tormented Gemma was to call Father Gaetano a liar and to threaten to strangle him, a likely indication of how much she had come to depend on his counsel.[12]

Father Germano's biography next recounts an even more thorough investigation by another Passionist, also undertaken with the blessing of Monsignor Volpi. Then known simply as Father Pietro Paolo dell'Immacolata, he went on as Monsignor Camillo Moreschini to become superior general of the entire Congregation of Passionists and the Archbishop of Camerino, a sign of his probity approvingly emphasized by Father Germano. Having heard that Gemma experienced on her body not only stigmata but also Jesus' flagellation and his crown of thorns, Father Pietro Paolo determined to "see with his own eyes when blood should issue from the girl's head." His report continues as follows:

> After a brief while, together with Mr. Don Lorenzo Agrimonti [the priest who resided with the Giannini family] I went to the room where Gemma had retired shortly before and I saw her alienated from her senses and already the victim of a cruel martyrdom. I stayed in that room for more than two and a half hours, resolved not to leave until after I had seen the blood with my own eyes. The girl was in the grip of a heart palpitation so terrible and violent as to heave up the blanket of the bed on which she was lying in the direction of her heart. The attack was so strong that the whole bed shook and I confess that I felt sentiments of terror and of devotion at the same time. After an hour or a little more, the palpitation calmed and then blood began to flow from the girl's head, in such great quantity that the pillow remained wet and also the sheet. In certain parts of her head, especially her upper forehead, the blood was so much that as it coagulated you could see clots in several places. When the flow of blood from her head finally stopped (it was 11:30 at night) the girl, who earlier had been stirring slightly, from that moment onward, that is until about 3:00 A.M., remained totally rigid; her face had the look of an actual cadaver and seeing her in that state, with that coloration of a corpse, her head all imbued with live blood, anyone would have thought she was dead; her breathing was barely perceptible. Thus passed fully three hours. In her lodging, toward 6:00, I saw her again as she was already dressed to go and receive communion in church; and already the natural color had returned to her visage, as if she had suffered nothing.[13]

Father Germano continued his defense with a reminder to readers of his biography about all the other witnesses who could testify to the veracity of Gemma's stigmata: from among the Giannini clan there were Cavalier Matteo and his wife Giustina, their eldest son Giuseppe, and most centrally Matteo's sister, Cecilia, not to mention, of course, Father Germano himself. None of them had ever lost faith in Gemma. Finally, as a capstone to his treatment of the physical evidence, he provided an informed discourse on the remarkable parallels between the shape, size, depth, texture, appearance, and disappearance of Gemma's wounds and those of her remarkable predecessors, some of them saints and others saints-in-the-making, including Diomira Allegri, Francis of Assisi, Veronica Giuliani, Catherine of Siena, John of the Cross, and Louise Lateau. At first the crescent-shaped wound in Gemma's side had puzzled Father Germano, until he read of the similar shape of Diomira Allegri's stigmata, all the more convincing since he believed it unlikely that such phenomena could occur after three centuries by chance alone.[14]

As to the fiasco of September 8 itself, was it not proof of supernatural grace that Gemma knew of the secret visit in advance and that Jesus had told her what would happen? Or so the priest reasoned. Gemma was an extremely private person, devoted entirely to Jesus, and had word of her stigmata gotten out and about in Lucca, she would have been swamped with curiosity-seekers, hounded by skeptics and well-wishers alike, and subjected to immodest medical examinations. Humble servant of God that she was, she kept her treasure secret. Moreover, her prudence, sagacity, doctrine, and the esteem in which she was held should have been sufficient proof of her sanctity, even to Monsignor Volpi, without resorting to a medical test. Science cannot pretend to explain the supernatural, it can only ascertain facts, he protested. Nor were Gemma's experiences at all consistent with either hysteria or hypnotic suggestion, Father Germano affirmed, a judgment he documented in three lengthy dissertations produced of his own labor and initially published as an appendix to his biography, although dropped in posthumous editions.

Father Pietro Paolo's firsthand verification of Gemma's supernatural physical experiences, along with his later written appraisal of her virtuous character, manifestly assisted the Church in coming to its eventual conclusion that Gemma was a saint, not a fraud or a hysteric. But for Gemma herself, the doubts of those she had most relied upon were not overcome so easily. The pages of the diary she kept in the summer of 1900 at the explicit command of Monsignor Volpi put a spotlight on her internalization of these haunting uncertainties. Recall that although Gemma had already begun to correspond with Father Germano in January 1900, she had never met him, and her sole spiritual director was still Monsignor Volpi. Perhaps he hoped his assigned exercise might allow her, and possibly himself, to make some sense of her supernatural encounters, especially as the devil came to torment her. Some of the trouble, he clearly suspected, arose from Gemma's own inclination to engage in dalliances with supernatural forces of evil.[15] He explicitly ordered her not to stop and talk with the devil, no matter what the temptation. But according to testimony by the pious spinster Cecilia Giannini, who already has appeared fleetingly in our story and about whom more shall be said further along, Gemma enjoyed the thrill of doing battle with the eternal enemy. She told Mrs. Cecilia of this pleasure openly, even though clearly she understood that such behavior violated Monsignor Volpi's dictates and required her to go to confession before receiving communion.[16]

As if matters were not already thoroughly confused, Gemma reports that the devil tried to trick her by appearing in the guise of none other than the monsignor himself:

> I had from Monsignor an absolute prohibition to leave the house alone; that day my aunt was away from Lucca and so no one could spy on me, and I left to go to the Forty Hours. I had just made a visit and upon leaving I saw a man who began to follow me; I began to walk without knowing where I was going; after I don't know how much time I found myself in the Church of San Michele. That man also entered the church and then he disappeared. I went to confess myself, I entered, and Monsignor was there. The first thing I accused myself of was having almost run away from home and he did not yell at me like always, indeed, he said I had done well. I continued to confess myself and he approved of everything I was saying. I exited and again the same man behind continued to follow me all the way to the Church of SS. Trinità. I ran to the nuns to liberate myself from him and begged them to accompany me home, because I was afraid; but they did not want to take me right away and they had me stay a while. I felt very topsy-turvy, restless, agitated; the nuns did so much, said so much, that they succeeded in making my head take off. A crucifix appeared before me, and I, without even thinking, as I usually did, made the sign of the cross and to disparage what I saw, began to talk to it, and I don't know how long I continued. It was all a devilish day; Monsignor, then, was the devil and he even came with the miter on his head.[17]

Nor were Gemma's uncertainties played out in supernatural encounters alone. Consider her letter to Monsignor Volpi written during August 1900, at the very time that she kept, at his command and for his review, the diary you are about to read:

Then yesterday evening Jesus let me know about lots of people who thought badly: one even thought I might be a somnambulist; others believe I am sick; others that the signs in my hands and feet are me scratching myself. Jesus told me these are all things that he allows; he will allow even worse but at least he has assured me that by means of Father Germano he will thoroughly convince my confessor. The other people Jesus wants to stay as they are.[18]

Given the powerless circumstances in which Gemma now found herself, mocked by family and townspeople and doubted by her regular confessor, these defiant words confirm her continued ability to give positive meaning to both her earthly and her supernatural experiences, including the setbacks.

No matter that the monsignor's order to write everything down might be a trap, or a subterfuge to keep her occupied with mundane tasks, she would obey in dutiful fashion. Apart from the usual school exercises and a few letters, Gemma's prior experience as a writer had included only two items that are preserved for us. The first is the brief report, considered earlier, about her miraculous healing, done to document Blessed Margaret Mary Alacoque's intercession. The second consists of dated thoughts done intermittently on individual sheets of paper, mostly in the spring of 1899, at Monsignor Volpi's command. These were collected for a printed edition of her writings, edited by the Passionists and first published in 1943,[19] but it is unclear whether anyone other than the monsignor (and maybe not even he) read these snippets carefully at the time, or in the years that followed. Gemma reports how sorely she was troubled upon learning from the devil that Monsignor Volpi was keeping everything "because one day they will serve for many things,"[20] but however one assesses that threat, it is clear that the words she had written up to that point in her life had not constituted an integrated piece of work.

Thus, the diary she kept in the summer of 1900 is Gemma's first attempt at sustained writing of this kind. Inexperienced and racked by doubt, she resisted and threatened and begged, but in the end she obeyed her confessors' commands to reveal herself to them. First it was Monsignor Volpi's command to keep this diary and next it would be Father Germano's insistence on a written autobiographical confession (completed in the spring of 1901 but placed earlier in our translation since it recounts events that preceded the time of the diary). My sense about both efforts is that Gemma knew her words might be kept for the eyes of posterity, but this can only be suggested, not proved. Whether driven by obedience, pride, or both, she continued the anguishing process of remembering and recording—each day for over six weeks with only a few failures—until Father Germano arrived at Lucca in person. The first thing he did was to order her to desist immediately from a routine that seemed to this experienced spiritual director only to deepen Gemma's uncertainties, while in an ironic way breaking her dependency on clerical direction. With the same order, he also put an end to what had become for Gemma a deeply painful exercise, evidently a sensible and fruitful way to begin his relationship as her new spiritual director. Only after he had returned to his home monastery at Corneto, near Rome, did he inform, in deferential but firm language, Monsignor Volpi of what he had done.[21]

Technical notes pertaining to the translation of the diary that follows:

The source is Galgani, *Estasi, Diario, Autobiografia, Scritti vari, Versi,* 163 – 217. All ellipses (. . .) are as in this source.

The date of the first entry, July 19, was written by Gemma and followed by a symbol of the cross. Subsequent dates are in the original manuscript only sporadically, and many were added beginning with the first printed edition (1943). They should be taken as good approximations, since it is not always possible to determine precisely when one day's entry ended and another began. Apparent confusion about "today" and "yesterday" results from the insertion of dates into text that Gemma often wrote on the day following the day when the described events occurred. The terminal date of September 3, 1900, is certain since that is when Father Germano ordered Gemma to desist from keeping the diary.

Spelling out of abbreviations is as for the autobiography.

✳ ✳ ✳

Thursday, July 19 [1900]

✳

This evening, finally, after six days of suffering for Jesus' absence, I could collect myself. I began to pray, as I usually do every Thursday; I would have wished to be on my knees but for obedience I had to stay in bed, so I did. I started to focus on Jesus' crucifixion. At first I felt nothing but after a few minutes I could collect myself better: Jesus was near. With collection, it happened like other times: my head took off and I found myself with Jesus, who was suffering terrible pains.

How could I see Jesus suffer and not help him? I felt a great desire to suffer and asked Jesus to grant me this grace. Immediately he agreed to it, and as he had done other times, he came near and took the crown of thorns from his head and put it on mine, and then he let me be. But he saw that I was watching him, quietly, very quietly and right away he understood a thought that came to me just then. I thought: maybe Jesus doesn't love me anymore because usually when Jesus wants me to know how much he loves me, he presses the crown firmly down on my head and into my forehead. Jesus understood, and with his hands he pressed the crown into my temples. They were painful moments, but happy moments. I stayed this way for an hour, suffering with Jesus. I would have wanted to stay the whole night, but Jesus loves obedience so much that he submitted himself in obedience even to my confessor and so after an hour he left. I mean, he did not show himself to me further, but something occurred that had never happened before. Normally each time Jesus puts his crown on my head, when he leaves me he takes it off and places it once again on his head; but yesterday he let me keep it until about 4:00 the next afternoon.

To tell the truth I suffered a bit but I managed to complain only once. Jesus will forgive me if on occasion a lament comes out, because it is truly involuntary. I suffered greatly with any movement I made: but this was all my imagination.

Friday, July 20

✳

Yesterday [Friday] around 4:00 a desire came upon me to unite a little more with Jesus; I tried and immediately united with him. To tell the truth I was very reluctant because I felt tired and without strength; I found myself once again before Jesus. He came to my side but he was no longer sad like the night before, he was happier; he caressed me a little and then happily, very happily he lifted the crown from my head (I still suffered a little, but less) and put it back on his head, and I no longer felt any pain. My strength immediately returned and I felt better than before I had suffered.

Then Jesus questioned me about various things and I told him not to send me to confess with Father Vallini,[22] to whom I do not want to go; then Jesus got serious and a little mad and told me that as soon as I needed, I should go. I promised, and I shall go willingly.

I always had so many things to tell Jesus and I felt that little by little he was leaving me, so he promised to return a bit later, during evening prayers. Then he was even happier than usual; he opened his heart where I saw two words written that I did not understand. I asked him what they said and Jesus answered: "I love you so much because you resemble me so." "In what way, oh Jesus," I said, "since I see myself so different from you?" "In accepting humiliation," he answered.

Then I understood everything well and my past life returned to mind. A big fault had always been my passion, pride. When I was little, wherever I went everyone said that I was full of pride. But what methods Jesus used to humiliate me, especially this year! Finally I understood who I truly am. Jesus be thanked always.

Then my God added that in time he would make me a saint (here I don't say anything because it is impossible that what God said could happen to me).[23]

He gave me various cautions to tell my confessor and blessed me. I understood, as always, that he would be away for a few days. But how good Jesus is! As soon as he departs he leaves me with my guardian angel who assists me with his constant charity, vigilance, and patience.

Oh Jesus, I promised always to obey you and this I affirm anew. Even if this be entirely my imagination, or if it be the work of the devil, I want to obey anyway.

Saturday, July 21

✳

Today, Saturday July 21, I thought there was no way I could achieve contemplation. But as soon as I was able to be alone and I tried to say the Sorrowful Mysteries of the Rosary, I'm not sure exactly when, I felt my head take off. My beloved Mom, Most Holy Mary, Our Lady of Sorrows, wanted to pay me a little visit (I had forgotten it was Saturday, which is the day she usually shows herself to me).

She was afflicted; I'm not sure but I think she was crying. I called her several times with the sweet name of Mom; she did not answer but when she heard the name Mom she smiled; I repeated it several times, as much as I could, and she smiled each time. Finally she said: "Gemma, would you like to come and rest a while at my breast?" I moved as if to get up and kneel and get closer to her; she also arose and kissed me on the forehead and then she vanished.

I am alone again, but certain that my Mom still loves me even though she is deeply offended. After all these things I feel, yes, always afflicted, but much more resigned.

This evening, as I had promised Jesus, I went to Father Vallini for confession. But who knows why, after leaving confession I immediately felt agitated and disturbed; it was a sign the devil was nearby.

Unfortunately, he was indeed nearby! I realized it later, for sure, when I began to say my prayers. Already, as I said, I was internally and externally very unsettled; I would have preferred to go to bed and sleep rather than pray, but no, I wanted to try. I began to say the three invocations to the Sacred Heart of Mary that I usually say every evening; as soon as I went on my knees the enemy, who for several hours had been there hiding, made himself seen in the form of a little, very little man; but so ugly that I was completely terrified.

My mind was contemplating Jesus and I paid no attention to the devil; I continued to pray but all of a sudden he began to hit me on my shoulders and even further down; he hit me a lot. I was in that turmoil for about half an hour and I realized that what most bothered the devil were my ecstasies, which Jesus very frequently let me experience. I commended myself to Jesus, but to no avail! Anyway, the hour was approaching when for obedience I had to go to bed; going in this state displeased me: I had not yet made my examination of conscience. I prayed to my guardian angel and he truly helped me, in a way I must say was strange.

As soon as he appeared, I prayed wholeheartedly that he not leave me alone. He asked what was troubling me: I showed him the devil, who had moved away but still threatened me constantly. I prayed that he stay with me the entire night and he said: "But I'm sleepy." "But no," I kept repeating, "the angels of Jesus don't sleep." "But really," he added, "I have to rest (then I realized he was kidding); where will you put me?" I wanted to tell him he could have my bed and I would stay in prayer, but that would have been disobedient. I told him to stay near me and this he promised to do.

I went to bed; then it seemed to me he spread his wings and came above my head. I fell asleep and this morning he was still there. I left him and when I returned from mass, he was gone.

Sunday, July 22
✳

I received communion but Jesus did not make his presence felt at all; nevertheless I am quite calm now.

Then today, when I believed I had been liberated from that ugly beast, instead he gave me a hard beating. I had retired with the intention of going to sleep; instead, just the opposite: he began with blows that I really feared would cause my death. He came in the form of a huge black dog and he put his legs on my shoulders; he hurt me a lot, with pain in all my bones. At times I felt he would break them; one time, a while back, in taking holy water, he twisted my arm so sharply that I fell to the floor in great agony and in fact he dislocated my bone; but it returned to its proper place right away, because Jesus touched it and everything was healed.

After that time I remembered that around my neck I wore a relic of the holy cross, and when I made the sign of the cross with it, my calm returned instantly. I immediately thanked Jesus, who made himself visible, but only briefly: he encouraged me again to suffer and to struggle and then he left. From then on I have not been able to collect myself completely; may God be blessed anyway.

During the day, yesterday, however, I should repeat a few warnings my holy angel said. The first came to me during dinner. He came near me, and I must admit that again in that moment I thought . . . It was clear he understood, saying: "Daughter, do you really want me to go and not come back any more?" I was ashamed and came back to my senses. He said these words so loudly, I wondered whether the others also heard.

A second time yesterday was during the day, in church; he approached me then too, and said: "The greatness of Jesus and the place where you are deserve a different way of behaving yourself." At that moment I had raised my eyes to see how two little girls were dressed.

The last was tonight; I was in bed in a somewhat immodest posture; he reproached me, saying that instead of progressing in his teaching I was constantly getting worse, always slack about doing good.

All of these things happen when I am awake.

In my opinion, instead of being good and preparing myself for the visits of Mary, Our Lady of Sorrows, and Brother Gabriel, as much as I try, I will not succeed.

Monday, July 23

❋

Today Jesus showed me again that he always continues to care for me, not in the way he first did, with union in him and contemplation, but in another way. I went to bed and fell asleep, and how well I slept; after about fifteen minutes (because my sleep is always brief) I saw at the foot of the bed, on the floor, the usual little man, black, very black, little, very little. I realized who he was and immediately I got very upset; I said: "What now, you've taken up again this habit of not letting me sleep?" "What! Sleep?" he answered, "why aren't you praying?"

"I'll pray later," I said, "now I'm sleeping." "It's two days, you know, that you're not able to collect yourself; fine, leave me to take care of things." He began to hit me, so I took the cross in my hand, but it was useless. He was about to climb on top of me and hit me as much as he could; I don't know what happened next; I saw him rise up in a rage and roll on the floor.

I laughed; today I seemed not to feel afraid. He said: "Today I can't do anything to you, but I'll take revenge another time." I asked him: "But why can't you? If other times you could, you certainly still can; I am the same, I just have Jesus around my neck."

Then he said to me: "That woman in your room, what did she do to you? Take off that thing wrapped around you and then you'll see."

I insisted that I had nothing, because I was sleeping, but I knew about whom he was talking. After these words I stayed happily in bed and laughed, watching the ugly faces he made and the rage that devoured him.

He said if I prayed any more he would make me suffer more. "I don't care," I said, "I shall suffer for Jesus."

In short, today I had a lot of fun with him: I saw him so angry; but he promised to take his revenge.

He waited until evening, but thank God he was not able to last for long; he knocked me down three times, so sharply that afterward it took me a long time to get to bed. At certain moments he runs around with such frenzy that I don't know what possesses him. He hurt me so much I could barely move.

How much I called Jesus! Not at all, he never came; I also prayed to my guardian angel that he should bring me to Jesus, but every effort was useless.

He stayed with me a bit and then said: "Tonight Jesus is not even coming to bless you, and tonight I won't bless you either."

I was very alarmed because without the strength of Jesus' blessing I could not get up: there would be nothing in me. He realized that I was about to cry and said: "But, you know, Jesus will send someone. And if you knew whom he is sending this evening, how happy you would be."

My mind flew immediately to Brother Gabriel. I asked him, but he gave no answer; he left me to stay a while in suspense and filled with curiosity. Finally he said: "But if Jesus truly sends Brother Gabriel to bless you, what will you do? Don't talk to him, otherwise you would be disobeying your confessor." "No, I won't talk," I answered impatiently, "but how can Brother Gabriel bless me?" "It is Jesus who sends him; anyway, Jesus sent him other times to bless you. But will you be able to stay silent and obey?" "Yes, yes, I will obey; have him come."

After a few minutes he came. What frenzy overtook me! I would have wished . . . but I was good and kept myself in check. He blessed me with some Latin words which I remember well, and then he immediately got ready to leave.

Then I couldn't resist saying: "Brother Gabriel, beg our Mom that Saturday she will bring you to me and let you stay a long time." He turned around and said, laughingly: "You be good," and in so saying he took a black belt from his waist and said: "Would you like it?" Sure, I truly wanted it: "It's very good for me, so give it to me now." He made a sign of no, that he would give it to me on Saturday, and he left. He told me that the belt was the one which had liberated me from the devil the other night.

Tuesday, July 24
✻

Yesterday the usual happened: I had gone to sleep, and in fact had fallen asleep, but not the devil, who seemed to want otherwise. He made himself visible in a filthy way, tempted me, but I was strong. I commended myself internally to Jesus, that he should take my life rather than have me offend him.

What horrible temptations those are. They all displease me but the ones against holy purity how they hurt me!

Afterward my guardian angel came to re-establish my peace of mind and he assured me that I had done no wrong. At times I complain, because I would like him to come and help me at certain moments but he says that whether I see him or not, he always stays on top of my head; indeed, yesterday, because Mary, Our Lady of Sorrows, truly helped me and I was really strong, he promised that Jesus would come that evening to see me.

When evening arrived I waited impatiently for the moment to go to my room; I took the crucifix and went to bed. My guardian angel also was happy that I went to bed, because . . .

I felt at the point of being fully collected; my Jesus came, even though he stayed quite far away from me. What beautiful moments those are!

I asked him immediately if he would love me always, and he answered with these words: "My daughter, I have enriched you with so many beautiful things, without any merit of yours, and you ask me if I love you? I worry so much about you." "Why?" I said. "Oh daughter, on the days when you most enjoyed my presence you were full of fervor, you didn't get tired saying prayers; now instead, prayer bores you; a bit of negligence in your obligations is insinuating itself in your heart. Oh daughter, why do you get discouraged like this? Tell me: in earlier times, did your prayers seem as long as they now do? You do some little penance, but how long you wait to make resolves!"

How I responded to that sweet reproach I don't know; I was speechless. Then I continued to talk about the convent and in that I found much consolation. I told him that if he loved me he should grant me the grace of entering the convent; I begged him again to tell me something about the new convent, and he answered: "Soon the words of Brother Gabriel will be put into effect." "All of them, all?" I asked, almost beside myself. "Everything, do not be afraid: soon. When your confessor returns, I will explain things even better."

Finally I commended my poor sinner[24] to him. He blessed me and in going away said: "Remember that I created you for Heaven; you have nothing to do with earthly concerns."

Wednesday, July 25

✳

And what about today? What shall I say today?

I find no peace; pride predominates over me more than in earlier times. I suffered much to complete even a small act of humiliation.

July 25. About what happened to me yesterday I shall speak very little; my tongue is too long and for this reason I cause other people to suffer.

For obedience to my confessor I must speak very little and never with people who know about my experiences. A few days ago when Father Norberto[25] came, I hid instantly; another time he came and I did the same; I was ready, truth be said, to be obedient, but then what happened to me? After a few days I chanced to be speaking to another friar about this and I invented a big lie, saying that it was Mrs. Cecilia who had made me hide; but that was not true, it was I who did it on my own.

I don't know how Father Norberto came to learn of this, but instantly he referred the matter to Mrs. Cecilia, who was very hurt. But I was no less hurt. She interrogated me about whether I had really spoken and I answered no, because I had completely forgotten about it; but there's always the one who makes me remember everything; my guardian angel came and reproached me, saying: "Gemma, what's this, even lying? Don't you remember a few days ago, when as punishment for telling Brother Famiano[26] about your experiences, I made you stay half an hour . . . ?"

I then recalled everything well (I must say that my guardian angel, every time I do a bad thing, punishes me; not an evening passes that I do not have some punishment) and he commanded me to go to Mrs. Cecilia and tell everything and beg her in his name to forgive me.

I promised to do this, sure! The day passed, then the evening and I never made that little act of humility. My angel reminded me again, saying that if I didn't go to her and tell her everything, that night the devil would come.

Well, that threat I could not ignore and so I went to her room. She was in bed and the lamp was out; I couldn't believe it: this way she would not see me. As well as I could I told her everything, but in a forced way; it was a great shame, my being unable to humiliate myself. Finally, after she said all would be forgotten, I went to my room. Yes, of course! She said all was forgotten but it was impossible. I asked Jesus many times for forgiveness and also my beloved angel, and I went to bed. What a horrible night! My angel, because of the great resistance I had put up before accepting my humiliation left me alone, and with a few visits by the enemy. I could not sleep because my conscience was ill at ease; how I was troubled!

Thursday, July 26

✳

In the morning my guardian angel finally came and he reproached me harshly, very harshly and left me once again alone and afflicted. I received communion but, my God, in what a state! Jesus did not make himself felt. When after all this I was able to be alone, then I let out my feelings freely; I was at fault, I realize that; but if I can say one thing, I did not wish to cause certain displeasures to certain persons, but my evil inclinations are so bad that I often fall into these things. For more than an hour Jesus made me stay in that state; I cried and I was afflicted. Then Jesus had pity on me and he came; he caressed me and made me promise not to do these things again, and he blessed me.

I have to say that in what happened yesterday I told three lies, I had angry thoughts, and I had the idea of avenging myself against whoever had tattled on me, but Jesus prohibited me from speaking with Brother Famiano and with others. I quickly became calm, and to be even more so, I ran to confession.

Then in the evening, after saying my prayers, I set out to do the usual Holy Hour prayer. Jesus stayed with me throughout; I was in bed, as usual, because otherwise I would not have been able to remain with my beloved Jesus and suffer with him. I suffered a lot; he proved anew his love toward me by giving me his crown of thorns until the following day; Jesus loves me most on Friday. That evening he took back the crown, saying he was happy with me and as he caressed me he said: "Daughter, if I add other crosses, do not be afflicted." I promised, and he left me.

Friday, July 27
✳

This Friday I suffered even more, because I had to do some chores and at every movement I thought I would die. Indeed, my aunt had commanded me to fetch water: I felt so exhausted I thought the thorns went into my brain (but this was all my imagination), and a drop of blood began to appear at my temple. I hurriedly cleaned up so she barely noticed it. She asked me if maybe I had fallen and cut my head; I told her I had scratched myself with the well-chain. Then I went to the nuns, it was 10:00 and I stayed with them until about 5:00. Then I returned home, but Jesus already had removed the crown.

Saturday, July 28
✳

The night passed very well; in the morning my guardian angel came: he was happy and he told me to take a piece of paper and write what he would dictate:

Here it is:

"Remember, my daughter, that whoever truly loves Jesus speaks little and bears everything."

"I order you, on behalf of Jesus, not to give your opinion unless you are asked; never to hold to your wishes but to submit immediately."

"Obey promptly your confessor and others he designates, without answering back; when it is necessary, make only one reply, and be sincere with your confessor and with others."

"When you have committed some fault of omission, accuse yourself instantly, without waiting to be asked."

"Finally, remember to guard your eyes, and think, eyes that have been mortified will see the beauty of Heaven."

After saying these things he blessed me and said I should go to communion. I ran there right away; it was the first time in nearly a month that Jesus had made himself felt.

I told him all of what was happening and he kept me with him a long while, because I received communion at 8:30 and when I returned to my senses it was much later. I ran home and on the way the clock struck 10:15. I was good and found myself in the same position I had been in for communion, and as I got up I saw that my guardian angel was above my head with his wings spread. He accompanied me home himself and warned me not to pray during the day, not until nightfall, because I could not be safe. In fact I realized that I was safe from the others in the household, but not from my sister, because she had stuffed the keyhole and it was impossible to lock myself in; then my aunts intervened and in the evening I could close the door.

Toward evening, I went to the Fifteen Saturdays at S. Maria Bianca [the parish church of the Giannini family]; the Blessed Virgin told me she would not be paying me her usual little visit because in the past few days I had disgusted Jesus. I said to her that Jesus had forgiven me, but she said: "I don't forgive my daughters so easily; I absolutely want you to become perfect: we'll see if Saturday I can come and bring Brother Gabriel." Nonetheless, she blessed me and I resigned myself.

But I do not lack for temptation; one, a strong one, was Saturday evening: the devil came and said to me: "Good, good girl! Sure, go and write everything: don't you know that everything there is my work and if you are discovered, think about the scandal! Where will you go to hide? I pass you off as a saint, but you are deluded."

I felt so badly that out of desperation I swore that when Mrs. Cecilia returned I would destroy what I had written. In the meantime I tried to tear this writing up but I couldn't; I didn't have the strength, or else I just don't know what happened.

Sunday, July 29

*

I remained in this state until yesterday morning, Sunday, without being able to collect myself; my guardian angel, however, does not leave me: he gives me strength, and I must say that Sunday I had no appetite but he himself ordered me to eat, as he did today also. Every evening he did not fail to bless me, but also to punish me and yell at me.

Today, Sunday, I feel a great need for Jesus but it is already late and I no longer have any hope; I expect to spend the night free and alone.

But Jesus came, you know! How he reproached me because I had not gone to communion. This is how Jesus reproached me: "Why, oh daughter, am I so often deprived of your visits? You know how much I yearn for you to come to me when you are good."

I fell on my knees in front of Jesus and in tears I said: "But how can this be, my Jesus, aren't you tired of putting up with me and all my coldness?" "Daughter," he answered, "see to it that from now on not a day goes by without your coming to me, try to keep your heart pure and adorned with every possible care. Drive all self-love away from your heart and anything else that is not entirely mine, and then come to me without fear."

He blessed me, along with all the members of the Sacro Collegio,[27] and went away; indeed, in the end he advised me to have a little more strength in combating the enemy, telling me to take no account of those words because the devil is a total liar who seeks every means to make me fall, especially about obedience. "Obey, my daughter," he repeated, "obey instantly and cheerfully, and to achieve victory in this beautiful virtue, pray to my Mom, who loves you so much." I would have wanted to tell him that yesterday his Mom didn't wish to come, but he vanished.

Monday, July 30

*

This morning I went to communion. I did not want to: I was not at peace with my conscience; I lingered until 9:00, thinking should I go or not; then Jesus won and I went to communion, but how? With what coldness! I was completely unable to feel Jesus.

Today I was not able to collect myself at all; I was bad, I got angry, but only by myself, no one else saw me: I cried so, so much, because my sister Angelina did not want to leave my room. Yesterday evening, Sunday, for spite, she stayed in my room until 11:00, making fun of me, that she wanted to see me go in ecstasy; today again the same thing. She wrote a letter yesterday to Bagni di S. Giuliano[28] and spoke a lot about me and my experiences. These things, which I should be accepting happily and with thanks to Jesus, instead upset me, and I almost have moments of despair.

While I was in that state, my guardian angel who was watching me, said: "Why are you so upset, my daughter? You have to suffer something, you know, for Jesus." (In truth, what displeased me most were certain words that my sister had said out loud to me), and to this my angel responded: "You are worthy only to be scorned because you have offended Jesus."

Then he calmed me, sat at my side, and said gently, very gently: "Oh daughter, don't you know that you must conform in every way to the life of Jesus? He suffered so much for you, don't you know that you must on every occasion suffer for him? Furthermore, why do you give this displeasure to Jesus, of neglecting to meditate on his Passion every day?" It was true: I recalled that I did a meditation on the Passion only on Fridays and Thursdays. "You must do it every day, remember that." Finally he said to me: "Be brave, be brave! This world is not a place for rest: rest will come after death; for now you must suffer, and suffer all things, to save some soul from eternal death." I begged him urgently to ask my Mom to come to me a little, because I had so many things to tell her, and he said yes. But this evening she did not come.

Tuesday, July 31

We are at Tuesday; I run to communion but in what a state! I promised Jesus to be good and to change my life; I said it, but he didn't answer anything; I also asked that he send his Mom, and also mine, and he responded: "Are you worthy?" I was ashamed, and I said nothing more. Then he added: "Be good and soon she will come with Brother Gabriel."

It's been since Sunday that I have been unable to collect myself; nonetheless I thanked Jesus. When my guardian angel comes, I am awake, and my head does not take off; Jesus, my Mom and sometimes Brother Gabriel make my head take off; but I always stay where I am; I always find myself in the same place, it's just that my head departs. What a great need I have for my Mom! If Jesus would grant me this, afterward I would be better. How am I supposed to stay so long without Mom?

Wednesday and Thursday, August 1 and 2

✳

Wednesday I could not collect myself at all. Nor Thursday; from time to time my guardian angel would say something to me, but I was always awake; indeed, Wednesday evening, inside myself I thought I might be deceived by the devil; my guardian angel calmed me by saying: "Obedience."

Now coming to Thursday. As usual out of obedience I went to bed; I began my prayers and immediately collected myself. For a while I had been feeling ill. I stayed all alone; when I was suffering Jesus wasn't there and I suffered only in my head.

My confessor asked me this morning if I had had the signs, and I said no. They hurt a lot but not compared to my head.

Poor Jesus! He made me stay alone for about an hour but then he came and showed up like this, all bloodied, saying: "I am the Jesus of Father Germano." I did not believe him, you know why? I am always fearful, always. I pronounced these words: "Long live Jesus and Mary" and then I understood. He gave me a bit of strength but internally I was still afraid, and he said: "Do not fear: I am the Jesus of Father Germano." He urged me of his own free will, without my even suggesting it, to pray for Mother Maria Teresa of the Infant Jesus [29] because she is in Purgatory and suffering greatly. Jesus wants her quickly with him, I think.

Friday, August 3

✳

Today I slept a little, then I felt completely collected; after becoming collected I felt my head take off: I was with Jesus. How happy I was! Yes, I suffered so much in my head; I complained a little because he is leaving me alone. I begged him also to tell me when Mother Maria Teresa would be in Heaven. He said: "Not yet; she's still suffering." I commended my poor sinner to him and he blessed me and all the members of the Sacro Collegio and he left me in a happy state.

This evening I felt I could not collect myself; I said a few oral evening prayers and went to bed. To tell the truth, I foresaw a bit of a storm because Jesus had warned me a few days ago, saying: "The enemy will try you with one final battle, but it will be the last because now that's enough." I could not help but thank him for the strength he had always given me, and I prayed that he would want to give me strength for this final test as well, that is to say last night.

I went to bed, you know well, with the intention of sleeping; slumber was not long in coming when almost instantly a tiny, tiny man appeared, all covered in black hair. What a fright! He put his hands on my bed and I thought he wanted to hit me: "No, no," he said, "I am not able to hit you, don't be afraid," and as he said this he lay down on the bed.

I called Jesus to help me but he did not come, but this doesn't mean he abandoned me. As soon as I called his name I felt liberated, but it was sudden.

Other times I had called Jesus but he had never been ready like last night. You should have seen the demon afterward, how angry! He rolled around on the floor, cursing; he made one last effort to take away the cross I had with me but then he instantly fell backward.

How good Jesus was with me last night. The devil, after that last effort, turned toward me and said that since he had not been able to do anything, he wished to torment me the rest of the night. "No," I told him; I called my guardian angel, who opened his wings and alighted next to me; he blessed me and the naughty devil ran away. Jesus be thanked.

This morning I learned that at the very moment the devil was rising in fury, the scapular of Our Lady of Sorrows had been placed on me [by Cecilia Giannini] and I realized that when the devil was trying to take something off of me, it could be nothing but that. My Mom, Our Lady of Sorrows, also be thanked.

Saturday, August 4

✳

Here I am at Saturday: it's the day destined for me to see my Mom, but what should I hope for?

Finally evening has arrived. I set out to recite the Sorrowful Mysteries of the Rosary; at first I abandoned myself, that is to say I placed myself in God's wishes, to spend that Saturday also without seeing Our Lady of Sorrows; but for Jesus this offering was enough of a sacrifice and he fulfilled my wishes. At some point, I'm not sure where in the rosary, I felt completely collected and with self-collection, as usual, quickly my head took off, and without realizing it, I found myself (it seemed to me) in front of Our Lady of Sorrows.

Upon first seeing her, I was a little afraid; I did all I could to assure myself that it was truly Jesus' Mom and she gave me every sign to assure me. After a few moments I felt entirely happy but I was so moved by seeing myself, so little compared to her, and so content, that I could not say a word except to repeat the name Mom.

She stared, really stared, at me, laughing, and approached to caress me, and she said I should calm down. Yes, of course, happiness and emotion grew in me, and she, maybe fearing that it would be bad for me (as happened other times, indeed one time, which I did not tell about, when for the great consolation I felt in seeing Jesus again, my heart started beating with such force that I was obliged, on the orders of my confessor, to tie a tight, tight bandage around that point) left me, saying that I should go and rest. I obeyed promptly, and in one second I was in bed and she did not delay her coming; then I was calm.

I also must say that upon first seeing these things, these figures (that certainly could have been deceptions), I am initially taken with fear; then fear is followed quickly by joy. However that may be, this is what happens to me. I spoke with her about some of my desires, the most important one being that she should bring me with her to Heaven; this I said to her several times. She answered: "Daughter, you must suffer still more." "I will suffer up there," I wanted to say, "in Heaven." "Oh no," was her retort, "in Heaven there is no more suffering; but I will bring you there very soon," she said.

She was near my bed, so beautiful, I contemplated her and could not get enough. I commended my sinner to her; she smiled: that was a good sign . . . I further commended to her various persons who were dear to me, in particular those to whom I have a big debt of gratitude. And this I had to do also on the order of my confessor, who last time beseeched me to commend them fervently to Our Lady of Sorrows, saying that I could do nothing for them but that the Blessed Virgin may ask on my behalf and bestow on them every grace.

I feared that she would leave me at any moment and so I called her repeatedly and said she should take me with her. Her presence made me forget about my protector, Brother Gabriel. I asked about him, why hadn't she brought him along, and she said: "Because Brother Gabriel demands more exact obedience from you." She had something to tell me for Father Germano; to these last words she did not answer.

While we were talking together she constantly held my hand, and then she let go; I did not want her to go and I was about to cry; then she said: "My daughter, that's enough; Jesus wants this sacrifice from you, now it's time for me to leave you." Her words calmed me and I answered with tranquility: "So be it, the sacrifice is done." She left. Who could describe precisely how beautiful, how beloved is the Heavenly Mother? No, for certain there is no comparison. When will I have the good fortune of seeing her again?

Sunday, August 5
❋

Today, Sunday, I prayed my guardian angel to grant me the favor of going to tell Jesus that I would not be able to do a meditation because I did not feel well; I would do it that evening. But that evening I had no desire; I went to bed and made preparations for meditation but collected myself only internally. My head did not take off; I stayed this way an hour. Indeed, I should add that the Sunday meditation is always on the Resurrection, actually on Heaven; but Jesus makes it clearly known to me that he does not wish me to do that meditation just yet, because my mind immediately rushes to some principal point in his Passion. Let his will be done.

Monday, August 6
❋

Here I am at August 6th. The days pass and here I am always in the same worldly abyss.

This evening my guardian angel, while I was saying evening prayers, approached me and tapping me on the shoulder he said: "Gemma, why such disinclination for prayer? This distresses Jesus." "No," I answered, "it's not disinclination: but for two days I have not been feeling well." He responded: "Do your duty with diligence and you shall see that Jesus will love you even more." For a moment he was silent and then he asked: "And Brother Gabriel?" "I don't know." "How long is it that you haven't seen him?" "A long, long, long while." "Then tonight Jesus will send him." "Really? Tonight no, I would be disobeying: at night my confessor is opposed." Oh with how much desire I would have wanted him! but I also wanted to obey. I prayed to send him in the daytime and soon, so that I could write that letter to Father Germano. I urged my guardian angel to go to Jesus and ask permission to spend the night together with me. He immediately disappeared.

I had finished prayers: I went to bed. When he had gotten permission from Jesus to come, he returned; he asked me: "How long has it been since you last prayed for the souls in Purgatory? Oh my daughter, you think of them so little! Mother Maria Teresa is still suffering, you know?" It was since morning that I had not prayed for them. He said he would like me to dedicate every little pain I suffered to the souls in Purgatory. "Every little penance gives them relief; even yesterday and today, if you had offered a little for them." I answered with a bit of astonishment: "My body was hurting; and do bodily pains relieve the souls in Purgatory?" "Yes," he said, "yes, daughter: even the smallest suffering gives relief." So I promised that from that moment onward I would offer everything for them. He added: "How much those souls suffer! Would you like to do something for them tonight? Do you want to suffer?" "Doing what?" I said. "Is it the same suffering Jesus did on Good Friday?" "No," he answered, "these are not Jesus' pains, yours will be bodily pains." I said no, because except for Thursday and Friday Jesus does not want this; the other nights he wants me to sleep. But since the souls in Purgatory, and in particular Mother Maria Teresa, are so dear to my heart, I told him I would gladly suffer for an hour.

These words satisfied him, but he saw clearly that in doing so I would have been disobedient, so he let me sleep.

This morning, when I awoke, he was still beside me; he blessed me and went away.

Tuesday, August 7

During the day yesterday my guardian angel promised me that in the evening I would be able to speak with Brother Gabriel. The long-awaited evening arrived; in the beginning I was sleepy, then an agitation came over me, enough to frighten me. But since Jesus was about to grant me this consolation, either before or after the consolation, he gives me some suffering. Jesus be always blessed.

Still, in undergoing this agitation I saw no one, I mean the devil; it's just that I felt very ill, but it lasted only a short while. Quickly I calmed down; suddenly I felt completely collected and then almost immediately it happened like usual; my head took off and I found myself with Brother Gabriel. What a consolation that was! For obedience I was not allowed to kiss his vestment and I restrained myself. The first thing I did was ask him why he had stayed so long without visiting me. He answered that it was my fault. Of this I was sure because I am very bad.

How many beautiful things he told me about the convent and he said them with such force that it seemed to me his eyes sparkled. On his own, without my asking: "Daughter, within a few months, amidst the exultation of almost all Catholics, the new convent will be founded." "What do you mean, in a few months?" I said, "if there are still 13 months to go." "That's a few," he responded. Then, smiling, he turned to one side and knelt, clasped his hands and said: "Blessed Virgin, look: here on earth is the competition for propagating the new institute; come on, I beg you, make the abundance of celestial gifts and favors shower on all those who take part. Increase their strength, increase their zeal. It will be entirely your gift, oh Blessed Virgin."

He talked as if Our Lady of Sorrows were next to him; I could see nothing, but with such force, with such expression did he say those words that I remained amazed; it seemed like his head also had taken off.

Now I should speak about Father Germano, but my confessor said no, because . . .

I also spoke of my poor sinner; he smiled, always a good sign. Finally he left me, filled with consolation.

Wednesday, August 8

※

Now we come to this morning. A little while after leaving the confessional, a thought came to me; thinking to myself that my confessor made too little of my sins, I was disturbed. To calm me down, my guardian angel approached; I was in church and he pronounced these words out loud: "But tell me, who do you want to believe, your confessor or your head? Your confessor, who has continuous light and assistance, who is highly capable, or else yourself, who has nothing, nothing, nothing of all this? Oh what pride!" he said, "you want to become the teacher, guide, and director of your confessor!" I did not think further; I made an Act of Contrition and went to holy communion.

Thursday, August 9

※

Today also, after having sustained with the help of God a battle with the enemy, a very strong one, my guardian angel came reproaching me, and with great severity said: "Daughter, remember that in failing in any obedience, you always commit a sin. Why are you so reluctant in obeying your confessor? Remember also, there is no shorter or truer path than the one of obedience."

So why all this today? It was my fault. I would deserve even worse, but Jesus always shows me mercy.

Alas, what disgust I experience this evening! Since early morning I have felt so tired, but it's all laziness, bad will; still I want to overcome it, with the help of God.

It is Thursday and therefore I feel very strange; on Thursday evenings

I always feel this way. Yes, suffer, suffer for sinners, and particularly for the poor souls in Purgatory, and in particular for . . . And I know well why this laziness so early in the day. The other evenings it came upon me a few hours later. It was because today my guardian angel told me that tonight Jesus wanted me to suffer a few extra hours, precisely two hours: at 9:00 it would begin, for the souls in Purgatory, and without my confessor's permission; but usually he does not yell at me, indeed he wishes it, and I am free to do it.

Last night, around 9:00, I began to feel a little ill; I was quick to bed but I had been suffering already for a while: my head ached beyond measure and any movement I made caused me terrible distress. I suffered for two hours, as Jesus wished, for Mother Maria Teresa; then with great pain I undressed and got into bed and began to pray. It was very painful but in Jesus' company one would do anything!

Friday, August 10

✳

My guardian angel said the previous evening that I was allowed to keep the thorns in my head until 5:00 in the afternoon on Friday; it was true, because around that time I began to collect myself completely; I hid myself in the Franciscan church and there Jesus came to me again to remove them; I was alone the whole time. How he showed me that he loved me! He encouraged me anew to suffer and he left me in a sea of consolation.

But I must say that many times, in particular on Thursday evenings, I am overcome with such sadness at the thought of having committed so many sins, they all come back to me: I am ashamed of myself, and I feel afflicted, so afflicted. Even last night, a few hours earlier, this shame came over me, this grief, and I find a little peace only in that bit of suffering Jesus sends me, offering it first for sinners, and in particular for me, and then for the souls in Purgatory.

How many consolations Jesus gives me! In how many ways he shows me his love! They are all things of my head; but if I obey, Jesus will not permit me to be deceived. Thursday evening he promised that in these days when Mrs. Cecilia was away, he would not leave me without my guardian angel. He gave me the angel last night and from then on he has not left me for even a moment.

This I have observed many times, and I have not spoken of it even with my confessor, but today I tell all. When I am with other people, my guardian angel never leaves me; however, when I am with her [Cecilia Giannini], the angel immediately leaves me (I mean to say that he does not show himself anymore, except to give me some warnings); the same thing happened today: he never left my side for a minute; if I have to speak, to pray, to do something, he lets me know. May Jesus not allow me to be deceived.

This thing so astounds me that it obliged me to ask of him: "How is it that when Mrs. Cecilia is with me, you never stay around?" He answered like this: "No person, other than she, knows how to take my place. Poor girl," he added, "you are so little that you always need a guide! Fear not, for now I shall do it, but obey, you know, because I could easily . . ."

I went to confession; I told this to my confessor (I had also written to him about it);[30] he explained what I did not understand, so now I understand everything.

Saturday, August 11
✳

It's Saturday; I'm going to holy communion. What shall I do? Whatever, I shall obey. If only I could obtain a little visit from my Mom. But no, I remember the sin I committed last night. It's true that this morning I confessed myself immediately, but alas, the Blessed Virgin does not forgive so easily, especially with me. She wants me to be perfect.

It's Saturday evening, my God! What punishment! It's the biggest punishment you can give me, depriving me of a visit from Most Holy Mary, and it's precisely around Saturday that I always fall into many omissions.

Sunday, August 12
✳

Sunday has arrived. What indifference, what dryness! Still, I do not want to abandon my usual prayers.

Wednesday, August 15, Feast of the Assumption of Mary into Heaven
✳

I remained in this state of dryness and the absence of Jesus until today, Wednesday. Since Friday I've heard nothing. My confessor assures me this is a punishment for my sins or to see if I can stay without Jesus, and to stimulate me to love him more. I have been alone throughout, I mean without Jesus. My guardian angel has not left me for even a second; yet, how many omissions, how many faults even in his presence! My God, have mercy on me! I always went to communion but Jesus was like he wasn't there anymore. But would Jesus wish to leave me alone even today on such a great holy day? I received communion with much more consolation, but without feeling Jesus. I prayed a lot these days, because I want a grace from Jesus.

Today Mother Maria Teresa should go to Heaven; I hope so. But how will I know? I can't collect myself unless I am in a safe place. Today my guardian angel will stand guard at my door.

Here I am at 9:15 of this great day. I feel the usual internal collection; I prayed to my guardian angel to stand guard so that no one should see me; I hid in a room for the nuns.

Oh, not much time passed before collection was followed by rapture. (Whoever reads this should not believe anything, because I could very well be deceived; may Jesus never permit such a thing! I do so for obedience, and I oblige myself to write with great disgust.)

It was around 9:30 and I was reading; all of a sudden I am shaken by a hand resting gently on my left shoulder. I turn in fright; I was afraid and tried to call, but I was held back. I turned and saw a person dressed in white; I recognized it was a woman; I looked and her expression assured me I had nothing to fear: "Gemma," she said after some moments, "do you know me?" I said no, because that was the truth; she responded: "I am Mother Maria Teresa of the Infant Jesus: I thank you so, so much for the great concern you have shown me because soon I shall be able to attain my eternal happiness."

All this happened while I was awake and fully aware of myself.

Then she added: "Continue still, because I still have a few days of suffering." And in so saying she caressed me and then went away.

Her countenance, I must say, inspired much confidence in me. From that hour I redoubled my prayers for her soul, so that soon she should reach her objective; but my prayers are too weak; how I wish that for the souls in Purgatory my prayers should have the strength of the saints'.

From that moment I suffered constantly because until about 11:00 I could not be alone. I felt inside me a certain sense of collection, a desire to go and pray, but how to do it? I couldn't. How many times I had to insist! Finally I had the longed-for permission, and I went with my Mom; although they were only a few moments, they were precious moments!

Because of my bad behavior, Jesus did not permit the Blessed Virgin to come as she always did, smiling, but instead very sad (and I was the cause).

She reproached me a little but cheered up about one thing (that I think here it would be better not to say), and this thing also gave great consolation to Jesus! And in fact it was to reward me for this thing that she came, but as I said, in a serious mood; she said a few words, among them: "Daughter, when I go to Heaven this morning, I shall take your heart with me."

In that moment I felt as if she approached . . . removed it from me, took it with her, in her hands, and said to me: "Fear nothing, be good; I shall keep your heart forever up there with me, always in my hands." She blessed me hurriedly and in going away she pronounced these words as well: "To me you have given your heart, but Jesus wants something else as well." "What does he want?" I asked. "Your will," she answered, and vanished.

I found myself on the ground but I know exactly when that happened; it was when she began to approach me and remove my heart.

Although these things frighten me upon first appearance, still at the finish I always end up being in infinite consolations.

Thursday, August 16

✳

Here I am at Thursday. The usual disgust descends upon me; fear of losing my soul comes over me; the number of my sins and their enormity, all open up before me. What agitation! In these moments my guardian angel suggested in my ear: "But God's mercy is infinite." I calmed down.

Early in the day the pain in my head began; it must have been around 10:00. When I was alone I threw myself on the bed; I suffered some but Jesus was not long in appearing, showing that he also suffered greatly. I reminded him of the sinners for whom he himself urged me to offer all my little aches to the Eternal Father on their behalf.

While I was with Jesus and suffering, and he suffered also, a strong desire came upon me, almost impossible to resist. Jesus realized this, and asked me: "What do you want me to do?" And I immediately: "Jesus, have pity, lighten Mother Maria Teresa's torments." And Jesus: "I have already done so. Do you wish anything else?" he asked. That gave me courage and I said: "Jesus, save her, save her." And Jesus answered like this: "On the third day after the Assumption of my Blessed Mother, she will be released from Purgatory and I will take her with me to Heaven."

Those words filled me with a joy such that I do not know how to express it. Jesus said a number of other things; I also asked why after holy communion he did not allow me to taste the sweetness of Heaven. He answered promptly: "You are not worthy, oh daughter," but he promised that the next morning he would do it.

How could I pass the time until morning? It's true, only a few hours remained but for me they were years; I didn't close my eyes in sleep; I was consumed, I wanted morning to come immediately: in a word, that night seemed like forever to me, but finally morning has come.

Friday, August 17
✳

Jesus, as soon as he arrived on my tongue (the cause so often of so many sins), made himself felt immediately. I was no longer in myself but Jesus was in me; he descended to my breast. (I say breast, because I no longer have a heart; I gave it to Jesus' Mom.) What happy moments I spent with Jesus! How could I return his affections? With what words could I express his love, and for this poor creature? Yet he did deign to come. It's truly impossible, yes, it is impossible not to love Jesus. How many times he asked me if I love him and truly love him. And you still doubt it, my Jesus? So, he unites ever more closely with me, talks to me, says he wants me to be perfect, that he too loves me very much and I should reciprocate.

My God, how can I make myself worthy of so many graces? Where I cannot reach, my beloved guardian angel will take my place. May God never let me deceive myself nor others.

I spent the rest of the day united with Jesus; I suffer a little but no one sees my suffering; only from time to time does some lament come forth but, my God, it is truly involuntary.

Today it took very little, indeed nothing, for me to collect myself: my mind was already with Jesus and I immediately went in spirit as well. How affectionate Jesus showed himself to be today. But how he suffers! I do what I can to diminish the anguish and I would do more if I had permission. He came near today, lifted the crown from my head, and then I did not see him replace it as usual on his head; he held it in his hands, all his wounds were open, but they did not drip blood as usual. They were beautiful.

He usually blesses me before leaving, and in fact he lifted his right hand; from that hand I then saw a ray of light shine forth, much stronger than a lamp. He kept his hand raised; I remained fixed in watching it, I could not get enough of him. Oh if I could make everyone know and see how beautiful is my Jesus. He blessed me with that same hand he had raised, and he left me.

After this happened to me, I wanted to know the meaning of the light that shone from his wounds, in particular from his right hand, the one he blessed me with. My guardian angel said these words to me: "Daughter, on this day Jesus' blessing has showered an abundance of graces upon you."

Now that I am writing he approached me and said: "I urge you, my daughter, always to obey, and in everything. Reveal everything to your confessor; tell him not to neglect you but to keep you hidden." And then he added: "Tell him that Jesus wants him to have much more concern toward you, that he give you more thought, because otherwise you are too inexperienced."

He repeated these things even after I had written them; he said them many times, when I was awake, and I felt as if I actually saw him and heard him speak. Jesus, may your holy will always be done.

But how I suffer for the obligation to write certain things. The disgust I felt initially, instead of diminishing keeps growing enormously, and I am enduring deathly anguish. How many times today I tried to find and burn all my writings. And then? You maybe, oh my God, you would like me to write also about those hidden things, that you let me know out of your goodness, in order always to keep me low and humble me? If you wish, oh Jesus, I'm ready to do even that: make your will known. But these writings, of what benefit are they? For your greater glory, oh Jesus, or to make me fall into more and more sin? You wished me to do so, and I did. You think about it. In the wound of your sacred side, oh Jesus, I hide my every word.

Saturday-Sunday, August 18–19

✳

During holy communion this morning Jesus let me know that tonight at midnight Mother Maria Teresa will fly to Heaven. Nothing else for now.

Jesus promised to give me a sign. Midnight has come, nothing yet; now it's 1:00, still nothing; toward 1:30 it looked to me like the Blessed Virgin would come to give me news, since the hour was approaching.

After a little while in fact I thought I saw that Mother Teresa was coming, dressed as a Passionist, accompanied by her guardian angel and by Jesus. How she had changed since that day I first saw her. Laughing, she approached me and said she was truly happy and was going to enjoy her Jesus in eternity; she thanked me again and added: "Tell Mother Giuseppa that I am happy and set her at ease." She made a sign several times with her hand to say goodbye and together with Jesus and her guardian angel she flew to Heaven around 2:30.

That night I suffered a lot because I too wanted to go to Heaven, but no one thought to take me.

The desire Jesus had nurtured in me for so long finally was satisfied; Mother Teresa is in Heaven; but even from Heaven she promised to return to see me.

Monday, August 20

✳

Yesterday during the day I had to talk with my guardian angel once again; he reproached me above all for my laziness about prayer; he reminded me of many other things: all about the eyes, still, he threatened me severely. Last night in church he reminded me again of what he had said that day, telling me I would have to reckon with Jesus. Finally, before going to bed, as I was asking his blessing, he warned me that today, August 20, Jesus wished me to undergo a demonic assault, this because for several days I had been negligent in prayer. He warned me that the devil would make every effort to prevent me from praying, especially mentally for all of today, and he would also deprive me of his visit (I mean my guardian angel's), but only for today.

I went to holy communion, but who knows in what a state! So distracted—with my mind still on last night—that is, on a bad dream, which I recognized as the work of the devil.

Oh God, the moment of the assault has come; and it was strong, even terrible I would almost say. No sign of the cross, no scapular was enough to halt the most ugly temptation one could imagine; he was so horrifying that I closed my eyes and never opened them again until I was absolutely freed.

My God, if I am without sin, I owe it only to you. You be thanked. What to say in those moments? To look for Jesus and not find him is a greater penance than the temptation itself. What I feel only Jesus knows, who watches secretly and is pleased. At a certain point when it seemed the temptation would take on more force, it came to mind to invoke the holy father of Jesus, and I shouted: "Eternal Father, for the blood of Jesus free me."

I don't know what happened; that good-for-nothing devil gave me such a strong shove that I fell off the bed, causing me to bang my head on the floor with such great force that I felt a sharp pain; I fainted and remained on the ground for a long time before regaining consciousness.

Jesus be thanked, that today also everything turned out in the best way, as he wished.

The rest of the day went splendidly. In the evening, as it happens to me many times, all my grave sins came to mind but with such enormity that I had to make a great effort not to cry out loud: I felt a pain more alive than I had ever undergone before. The number of my sins surpasses by a thousand fold my age and my capacity; but what consoled me is that I endured the greatest pain because of my sins, so that I wished this pain would never be canceled from my mind and never be diminished. My God! to what point my malice has reached!

This evening, to say the truth, I was awaiting Jesus—no way! No one showed up; only my guardian angel does not cease to watch over me, to instruct me and to give me wise counsel. Many times during the day he reveals himself to me and talks to me. Yesterday he kept me company while I ate but he didn't force me like the others do. After I had eaten, I didn't feel at all well so he brought me a cup of coffee so good that I was healed instantly and then he made me rest a little. Many times I make him ask Jesus for permission to stay with me all night; he goes to ask and then he does not leave me until morning, if Jesus approves.

Tuesday, August 21
✳

I may perhaps be wrong, but today I await a little visit from Brother Gabriel and if this is true, I have a lot to talk about with him. Jesus, give light, give light not to me but to Father Germano and to my confessor.

Wednesday, August 22
✳

Yesterday my guardian angel informed me that in the course of the day Jesus would come; he yelled at me, called me conceited, but then we made up quickly. I did not think further about Jesus' visit because I did not believe it; but in getting ready for evening prayers I felt in union with Jesus, who instantly reproached me sweetly, saying: "Gemma, don't you want me any more?" "Oh my God, my God," I answered him, "what do you mean, I don't seek you? I desire you everywhere, I want you, I seek you always, I yearn only for you."

Then right away it came to my mind to ask him: "But Jesus, you came tonight so that means you won't come tomorrow night?" He promised me he would. But my confessor told me that my conscience would be responsible if I suffered and then did not feel well; if I feel well, I may suffer the usual hour with Jesus; if not, let Jesus come anyway but without making me suffer; I may stay with him and have compassion for him and take part with him in the deathly sadness he suffered in the Garden of Olives. Anyway, I shall obey.

Jesus also spoke to me, without my bringing it up, of the holy soul of Mrs. Giuseppina Imperiali. "Oh how dear she is to me!" Jesus repeated. "See," he added, "how much she suffers, without a moment of peace. Happiness to her!" He left me with an ineffable sense of consolation, as usual.

For the grace of Jesus and for his infinite mercy, my guardian angel does not leave me for even a tiny second. Yesterday I saw several angels: mine assisted me continuously and I saw another for another person, and here there certainly is no need to record further all the details; if obedience should require it, I shall be ready, but for now . . . that's enough . . . If necessary, I shall remember.

Thursday, August 23
❋

Alas, evening comes and the usual coldness, the usual repugnance assails me; fatigue would want to win over me, but with a little effort I never want to neglect to do my duty.

Tonight Jesus placed his crown on my head at about 10:00, after I had been collected for a little while. My suffering, which in no way equals Jesus', was very strong: even all my teeth hurt; any movement brought a sharp pain; I thought I could not resist but instead I did, everything went well.

I offered those little penances for sinners and in particular for my poor soul. I begged him to return soon. When he was about to leave, a contest sprang up between me and Jesus: which of us would be the first to visit (and I went first, I mean to holy communion) and together we said and we agreed that I would go to him and he would come to me. He promised me the assistance of my holy angel, and he left me.

Friday, August 24
❋

Later Jesus returned to take back his crown but he came very early, saying I had already done a lot; and since I did not want to, because I did not keep it the requisite number of hours, he answered that I was still little, and this is more than enough.

I suffered continuously for several hours; Jesus caressed me a lot. At a certain point in our discussion I asked enlightenment for my confessor; on that point my guardian angel had tattled on Jesus. The morning before he had told me how Father Germano is enlightened about me and how he cares for me. I mentioned this to Jesus without thinking, and Jesus did not know that my guardian angel had told me this; he made a serious face and told me he did not want my guardian angel to tattle on him.

While he was talking in this way, instead of being speechless, as happens when Jesus becomes serious or severe, I was taken, on the contrary, with more intimacy toward him, and I asked: "Jesus, could you not . . ." I kept quiet, thinking to make myself understood without speaking further, and Jesus did understand instantly and responded: "Do not be afflicted, my daughter: we will make use of Father Germano soon enough. Do you understand?" he asked. "Yes," I answered. And at the end he repeated these words: "Fear not, because soon we will use him." He waved goodbye and disappeared.

Still later I went to church for the usual blessing but I felt tired; in fact I truly was, but it is not, as I've said many times, true tiredness; it is laziness, a lack of desire to pray. My guardian angel whispered in my ear that I should pray even while sitting. At first I could not give in but he insisted a second time and so for obedience I remained sitting. For sure I was pleased about this, since I was unable to stay on my knees.

Last night he also made me understand that when Jesus complains about me because I do not do my meditation, he does not mean Thursday and Friday, he means the other days of the week; in fact it's true, because on those two days I never forget. I promised to be more conscientious, and he ordered me to bed, saying I was tired and I had to sleep. I urged him to stay with me but he made no promise, and in fact he did not stay.

"Now then," I said to him, "run to Jesus and plead with him, because tomorrow evening I must go to confession and I need to see him"; and he instantly responded: "And if Brother Gabriel should come?" "That would be the same," I answered. "Either Jesus or Brother Gabriel, one way or another I need a visit; beg him to concede me this grace, I need it." "Can you tell me?" he asked. "As for you," I responded, "go to Jesus and tell him everything and then return and tell me." He nodded yes.

He had spoken to me a few minutes ago about Brother Gabriel and, as always, even just hearing him remembered made me happy all over, so I could not refrain from exclaiming: "Brother Gabriel, how long I have been awaiting him, how much I desire him!" "Just so, because you have such a strong desire, Jesus does not want to satisfy you." Then, laughing, he instructed me that when Jesus came I should not let him know that I had a yearning to see Brother Gabriel, in which case Jesus would grant my wish easily.

I realized he was kidding, because I know nothing can be hidden from Jesus.

"Show indifference," he repeated, "and you will see that Jesus will send him more often." "I won't be able to do that," I said. "I'll teach you; you have to talk like this to Jesus: If he comes, fine, if not, it's all the same." And in saying this he laughed heartily.

So I also repeated the phrase but I understood that he was having fun. He ordered me to bed, saying I had to stay alone that night, because if he stayed I would never get to sleep, and he left.

It's true, because when he is there I do not sleep: he teaches me so many things about Heaven and the night passes quickly, very quickly. But last night was not like that: he left me alone, and I slept, although I did awaken several times and instantly he said: "Sleep, otherwise I'm going away for real."

I heard loud thunderclaps, very loud, and I was afraid; so he came and made himself visible; he blessed me once again and I went back to sleep.

Saturday, August 25

✳

In communion this morning no consolation; I did everything coldly. Let the holy will of my God be done. What will happen today? Jesus is not coming, and I don't even feel him nearby. I go to bed and I see a guardian angel approaching, whom I recognized to be mine; but I was overtaken with a bit of fear and an internal disquiet.

So many times fear assails me when I see someone appear but little by little this passes and ends in consolation. Yesterday, instead, my disquiet grew until, if someone touched me, I shook: something that never happens to me when it is truly my dear angel. In short, I was uncertain about this when he asked me: "When are you going to confession?" "This evening," I answered. "And why? Why do you go so often? Don't you know that your confessor is a swindler?" Then I understood what was happening here and I made the sign of the cross several times; he struck me so severely that I shook. My angel never speaks to me this way.

The combat lasted in this way for a long while and I promised that in spite of him I would go to confession, and in fact I went. I called Jesus, and my Mom, but what! No one. After a while my real guardian angel appeared, obliging me to confess every detail and he specified two things to tell my confessor.

Distress and fear of the enemy vanished quickly and I calmed down until it was time to go to confession; I didn't want to go for anything. With effort I went but I was able to say very, very little. But I do want to tell everything, so I will write.

Last night my beloved Mom came, but her visit was so short; nevertheless it consoled me greatly. I prayed to her as much as I could on my own behalf, that she take me to Heaven, and I also prayed fervidly for other matters. How she smiled when I repeatedly called her Mom! She came near, caressed me, and left me in the company of my guardian angel, who remained affable and cheerful until morning.

Sunday, August 26

✳

In the morning, after I left my room, he also left. I received holy communion without knowing anything of Jesus; during the morning I felt such a strong wish to cry that I had to hide myself out of the sight of others so they wouldn't notice. My soul felt uneasy and I did not know what to rely on. My God, how shall I begin to describe it! But it's for the best, because if this notebook of mine should fall into people's hands, they will recognize in me nothing other than a disobedient, bad person.

Yesterday, while eating, I raised my eyes and saw my guardian angel looking at me with an expression so severe I was frightened; he did not speak. Later, when I went to bed for a moment, my God! He commanded me to look him in the face; I looked and then almost immediately I lowered my gaze, but he insisted and said: "Aren't you ashamed to commit sins in my presence? You certainly feel ashamed after you commit them!" He insisted I look at him; for more than half an hour he made me stay in his presence looking him in the face; he gave me some very stern looks.

I did nothing but cry. I commended myself to my God, to our Mom, to get me out of there, because I could not resist much longer. Every so often he repeated: "I am ashamed of you." I prayed that others would not see him in that state, because then no one would ever come near me; I don't know if others saw him.

I suffered for an entire day, and whenever I lifted my eyes, he always looked at me sternly; I could not collect myself for even a minute. That evening I said my prayers anyway, and he was always there watching me with the same expression; he let me go to bed, but he did bless me; he never abandoned me: he stayed with me for several hours, without speaking and always stern.

I never did have the courage to speak a word to him; I only said: "My God, what shame if others should see my angel so angry!"

There was no way I could sleep last night; I was awake until after 2:00; I know, because I heard the clock strike. I stayed in bed, not moving, my mind turned to God but without praying. Finally, after the clock struck 3:00, I saw my guardian angel approaching; he placed his hand on my forehead and said these words: *"Sleep, bad girl!"* I saw him no more.

Monday, August 27
✳

This morning I received holy communion: I hardly had the courage to receive it. Jesus seemed to let me know a little about why my guardian angel was acting this way: I had made my last confession badly. Unfortunately, this was true.

Tuesday, August 28
✳

My guardian angel remained very stern until this morning, after I revealed everything to my confessor. Upon my exiting from the confessional, he looked at me laughingly, with an air of kindness: returned from death to life. Later he spoke to me on his own (I did not have the courage to question him): he asked me how I was, because I was not feeling well the night before. I answered that only he could heal me; he came near, caressed me again and again, and said I should be good.

Repeatedly I asked him if he loved me as much as before and if he loved me despite everything; he answered in this way: "Today I am not ashamed of you, yesterday I was." I asked many times for forgiveness and he indicated that I was forgiven for every past action. Finally, I sent him to Jesus for three things: (1) If he was happy with me now? (2) If he had forgiven everything? (3) That he should rid me of this shame so that I could be obedient to my confessor.

He went away instantly and returned very late; he said Jesus was very happy; that he has forgiven me, but for the last time; as to the shame, he said Jesus responded with these exact words: "Tell her to obey perfectly."

Later, then, I went to bed and after a little while I felt some remorse. I was thinking, it's true, on the subject of a meditation on the Passion, but in bed. My guardian angel asked what I was thinking. "About the Passion," I answered, "what will Jesus say about me, who leads such an easy life, praying little, and in bed; in short, all my time in prayer I spend in bed?" Unfortunately, all this is true. He answered by asking what I thought. "It's laziness," I responded. But I promised that from that evening on I would never again pray in bed; except for the day that I was supposed to, for obedience. Last evening and for the whole night he never left me, but with an agreement: I must be quiet and sleep. I did it.

Wednesday, August 29
✳

Today there's one thing I shall do: I want to write a little note to Brother Gabriel; then I'll give it to my guardian angel and await a reply. And we're going to do this without Jesus knowing; he himself said we will not tell Jesus anything.

And I did it: I wrote a very long letter; I spoke of all my experiences without leaving out anything; then I advised my guardian angel that it was ready, and if he wanted to . . . This evening, Wednesday, I placed it under my pillow, and this morning when I got up I didn't think about checking because I had better things in mind: I was going to Jesus.

Thursday, August 30
✳

As soon as I returned I looked, and how odd! The letter wasn't there any more. I say odd because I heard from others that this is a strange happening; but to me it doesn't seem so. My guardian angel then asked me if I needed an answer. I laughed. "What else," I told him, "of course I need one." "All right," he added, "but until Saturday you can't have one." Patience, until Saturday then.

In the meantime, here I am at Thursday evening. Oh God! All my sins are paraded before me. What an enormity! Yes, all of you should know; my life until now has been a continuous series of sins. Always I see their great quantity, and the malicious intent with which I committed them, especially when Thursday evening approaches; they parade before me in a manner so frightening that I become ashamed and unbearable even to myself.

So, especially that evening, I make resolutions and repent continuously; but then I keep none of them and return to my usual ways. A little strength, a little courage comes to me when I feel Jesus at the hour when he places the crown of thorns on me and makes me suffer until Friday evening, because this I offer for sinful souls, especially my own.

This is how things went yesterday evening, Thursday; I thought Jesus would do like usual that evening: he placed the crown of thorns on my head, the cause of so much pain for my beloved Jesus, and left it there for several hours. It made me suffer a little but when I say suffering I mean taking pleasure. It is a pleasure, that suffering. How he was afflicted! And the cause: for the many sins committed, and the many ungrateful souls whom he assists, only to receive in return exactly the opposite. Of this ingratitude how much I feel guilty myself! For sure, Jesus must have spoken of me.

My guardian angel warned me that the hour allowed to me for obedience had ended; what to do? Jesus would have stayed longer, but he saw clearly the embarrassing situation I found myself in. I reminded myself about obedience, and for obedience I should have sent Jesus away, because the hour was up. "Come on," said Jesus, "give me a sign now that you will always obey." So I exclaimed: "Jesus, you can go away because now I don't want you anymore." And Jesus smiled as he blessed me, along with all the members of the Sacro Collegio, and he commended me to my guardian angel, and left me so happy that I cannot express myself.

As usual, that night I cannot sleep because I am united with Jesus, united more closely than usual, and also because I think my head aches a bit; I kept vigil together with my beloved angel.

Friday, August 31

✳

In the morning I ran to receive holy communion, but I could not say anything; I just stayed in silence; the pain in my head impeded me. My God, how much I lack in this! Jesus held back nothing on my behalf while I instead, in order not to suffer, avoid making even the slightest movement if I can. What would you say, my Jesus, about this laziness and ill will?

All morning I did nothing but rest. Day came and effortlessly I flew to Jesus; he lifted the thorns and asked if I had suffered much. "Oh, my Jesus," I exclaimed, "the suffering begins now because you go away. Yesterday and today, I took much pleasure because I felt close to you; but from now on, until you return, it will truly be constant suffering for me." I implored him:

"Come, my Jesus, come more often: I will be good, I will always obey everyone. Make me happy, Jesus." I suffered as I spoke this way because little by little Jesus was leaving me.

Finally after a short while he left me alone, once again in the usual state of abandonment. Toward evening I went to confession and the confessor, believing I was not feeling well, because I had been suffering some, ordered me to go to bed as soon as I entered my room, and he ordered me to sleep, without speaking with my guardian angel (because sometimes we would talk for hours on end), and that I should sleep.

I went to bed but I could not fall asleep out of the curiosity I had; I wanted to ask my guardian angel so many things, and I waited for him to speak on his own, but no way! All he told me was to go to sleep, several times. Finally I fell asleep.

Saturday, September 1

✳

This morning on his own he awakened me early and said that today I would have an answer. "How?" I asked. "You will see," he said, laughing.

For all of today I stayed without any temptations; toward evening one suddenly came over me, in the ugliest manner. But here I don't think it would be good to tell, because it's too . . .

Who would have imagined that my beloved Mom would come to see me? I wasn't even thinking about it because I believed my bad conduct wouldn't allow it; but she took pity on me and in a short time I felt collected; following this collection, as so often happened, my head took off. I found myself (I thought) with Our Lady of Sorrows. What happiness in those moments. How dear to pronounce the name Mom! What sweetness I felt in my heart in those moments! Let whoever is able to, explain it. It seemed to me, after a few minutes of commotion, that she took me in her lap and made me rest my head on her shoulder, keeping me there a while. My heart in that moment was filled with happiness and contentment; I could desire nothing more. *"You love no one but me?"* she asked from time to time. "Oh no," I answered, "I love someone else more than you." "And who is that?" she asked, pretending not to know. "It's a person who is most dear to me, more than anything else; I love him so much I would give up my life this very instant; because of him I no longer care about my body." "But tell me who he is," she asked impatiently. "If you had come the evening before last, you would have seen him staying with me. But you see, he comes to me very rarely while I go to him every day, and I would go even more often if I could. But do you know, dear Mom," I posed, "why he does this? Because he wants to see whether at so great a distance I might become capable of not loving him anymore; instead, the further away he is, the more I feel drawn to him." She repeated: *"Tell me who he is."* "No, I won't tell you," I responded. "You should see, dear Mom, how his beauty resembles yours, your hair is the same color as his." And it seemed my Mom was caressing me as she said, "But, my daughter, who are you talking about?" And I exclaimed loudly: "Don't you understand me? I'm talking about Jesus. About Jesus," I repeated even more loudly. She looked at me, smiling, and she hugged me tightly to her: "Go ahead and love him, love him a lot, but love only him." "Don't be afraid," I said, "no one in the world shall taste my affections, only Jesus."

She hugged me again and it seemed like she kissed me on the forehead; I awoke and found myself on the floor, with the crucifix nearby.

Whoever reads these things, I repeat again, should not believe, because they are all my imagination; nevertheless I agree to describe everything, because I am bound by obedience, otherwise I would do differently. I believed that from day to day the repugnance I experience in writing certain things would finally cease, but instead it always increases: it is a punishment such that I cannot withstand, I almost die from it.

Sunday, September 2

✳

Tonight I slept with my guardian angel by my side; upon awakening I saw him next to me; he asked me where I was going. "To Jesus," I answered.

The rest of the day went very well. But my God, toward evening what happened! My guardian angel got serious and stern; I could not figure out the reason, but he, from whom nothing can be hidden, in a stern tone (at the moment when I started to recite my usual prayers) asked me what I was doing. "I am praying." "Who are you waiting for?" (becoming yet more serious). Without thinking, I said: "Brother Gabriel." Upon hearing me pronounce those words he started to yell at me, saying I was waiting in vain, just as I could wait in vain for the response [to my letter] because . . .

And here I remember two sins I had committed during the day. My God, what sternness! He pronounced these words more than once: "I am ashamed of you. I will end up not coming around anymore, and maybe . . . who knows if even tomorrow."

And he left me in that state. He made me cry so much. I want to ask forgiveness but when he is that angry, there is no way he wants to forgive.

Monday, September 3

✳

I did not see him again that night, nor this morning; today he told me to adore Jesus, who was alone, and then he disappeared again.

This evening it was much better than the evening before; I asked him many times for forgiveness and he seemed willing to forgive me. Tonight he stayed with me constantly: he repeated that I should be good and not give further disgust to our Jesus, and when I am in his presence, I should be better and more good.

CHAPTER FOUR

Ecstasies and Letters ✳ Summer 1902

Our third and final selection from Gemma Galgani's writings moves ahead two years to her last summer and, by giving primacy to her ecstasies, enters into Gemma's deepest intimacies with Jesus. With the exception of a single ecstasy on July 4, 1902, her celestial Mom will not appear, and her friend Brother Gabriel will vanish entirely from her thoughts. There will be only her lover Jesus, now her bridegroom. But before commencing on this part of Gemma's spiritual journey, you may wish to know more about the worldly setting in which she now found herself.[1] Back in the summer of 1899, when Monsignor Volpi and the Salesian mother superior had agreed on the ruse of requiring four medical certificates before they would consider admitting Gemma to the convent, they had left this vulnerable young woman with few options. Clearly she was not very welcome in her natal home, presided over by her aunts who had always preferred the other children. The family was destitute and twenty-one-year-old Gemma no longer did anything to support herself, much less help out with the domestic economy.

Several of the surviving Galganis had little sympathy for Gemma's spiritual longings. Indeed, according to a letter of November 1899 from Gemma to Monsignor Volpi, one evening her aunt had charged into her room in a fury, shouting that since little Giulia was not around as a shield, now was the time to end all this nonsense about bleeding stigmata. Maybe a beating would do the trick, the aunt screamed, as she grabbed her niece in a choke hold and began to rip away her dress so she might see the wounds for herself. The sudden arrival of Gemma's other aunt ended this threat, but only momentarily. As Gemma was about to fall asleep, the evil aunt returned, fulminating that she was not as easily deceived as Monsignor Volpi and insisting that Gemma tell her where the bleeding came from and why. Amidst uncontrollable wailing, the terrified girl answered that her brother's blasphemy was the cause. "What, blasphemy causes you to start bleeding?" "Yes," Gemma responded, "I see how much Jesus suffers from blasphemy, and I suffer with him, and my heart suffers, and blood comes out." The aunt regained enough calm to continue her interrogation: "Is it only your brother's blasphemies that cause you harm, or everyone's?" Answer: "Everyone's, but with a big difference—his make me suffer much more!" The next morning the chagrined aunt asked only that Gemma keep the incident quiet, in which case she could stay with Cecilia Giannini if she wished, just that she come home on Sundays.[2]

Two pious Lucchese acquaintances, Palmira Valentini and Cecilia Giannini, ultimately rescued Gemma from her plight. Mutual affection among the three women deepened after their first encounter in June 1899, apparently along with a corresponding deterioration of familial rapport, as Gemma revealed in another letter of November 1899 to Monsignor Volpi:

> There are my aunts who I think are becoming very bad because they say I like Palmira and Mrs. Cecilia more than them; last night when I was brought home, one of my aunts took me by the throat and put me in front of the cross and wanted me to swear that it was I who told Palmira all of what had happened to me. I responded truthfully, that I would suffer whatever rather than tell them anything because when they had been with me in church I sometimes would drift off and they abandoned me, or else they awakened me with a rap on the head, saying they were afraid I was out of my mind.[3]

To say the least, life at home was not good. Another time, Aunt Elisa complained about having to scrub blood stains on the floor in Gemma's room. When the girl told her aunt to mind her own business and not bother to come in for cleanup, she starting smacking Gemma on the head, in public no less, as they walked down the street.[4]

In the past, sometimes alone and on other occasions with her sister Giulia, Gemma had visited Palmira every day during this good woman's lengthy illness, just one of the saint-to-be's many charitable acts. Upon her recovery, Palmira, who was twenty-six years older, regularly accompanied Gemma to church and for confession with Monsignor Volpi, thus relieving the Galganis of a chore they complained about. (As may be seen in the map of Gemma Galgani's world, there were other confessionals much closer to home.) Most opportunely, Palmira introduced Gemma to Cecilia Giannini and to Father

Gaetano, the two individuals primarily responsible for the path her spirituality took in the difficult summer and fall of 1899, when she lost the confidence of Monsignor Volpi and had not yet found Father Germano. Palmira was a working-class woman, too poor and without sufficient living quarters to offer lodging to Gemma, but such was not the case with Mrs. Cecilia.

Gemma mistakenly recalled in her autobiographical confession that Father Gaetano introduced her to Mrs. Cecilia, but Cecilia Giannini's niece Eufemia correctly testified that they had met even earlier, in June, after the prayers to the Sacred Heart of Jesus, before Gemma attended the Holy Missions where she first encountered the Passionists. One evening, upon leaving church, Eufemia and her Aunt Cecilia encountered Palmira with Gemma; they stopped and Palmira said: "Mrs. Cecilia, would you like to meet the little girl of the miracle?" Eufemia recalled that her aunt was in a rush that evening but said: "Yes, bring her to our house, that way she can better recount everything." Two or three days later Palmira and Gemma returned to tell of her miraculous healing, with Palmira doing most of the talking because Gemma was timid and ashamed to be the object of such attention. Cecilia Giannini, who had a wide reputation in Lucca for assisting spiritually-minded young women, took an immediate liking to such a good girl, and urged her to return some time.

After the Holy Missions ended, they met frequently; Cecilia Giannini wanted Gemma nearby and "was almost unable to stay without her, so good was it to be with her!" Gemma's aunts gave permission only for her to stay during the day, so the kind lady went to fetch Gemma every morning and brought her home each evening (a little over a mile, round-trip). A friend of the Giannini family, Don Nicola Giannoni, during the canonization proceedings at Lucca, no doubt in response to unfriendly gossip about which the official record is otherwise silent, offered the reassuring testimony that Gemma "certainly did not go as a servant but as a member of the family." However that may be, when the other members of the Giannini household went on their usual August vacation, perhaps in 1899 or in 1900 or both, Gemma slept over to keep Mrs. Cecilia company.

Giulia, now a teenager, was heartbroken and went to implore Gemma to come home, invoking memories of their dead mother and of happy days gone by. But Gemma was firm and told her sister: "Don't think of the past. Try to forget!" Even in the summer of 1901, when meddling by Monsignor Volpi put a severe strain on Gemma's relations with the Giannini family, she dismissed Giulia's renewed pleas to return home as an insidious diabolic trick and invoked Father Germano's aid by reminding him that her brother surely would call in a doctor to examine her at the first sign of illness, something the Passionist priest wanted to avoid at all cost given the fiasco caused by the previous medical visit.[5]

In fact, the Galgani household had declined to a sorry state. Once a family of substantial means, with a lifestyle appropriate for a successful pharmacist, Gemma's father had been forced to sell the country home and then even their city place in order to meet the expenses that arose during his wife's long battle with tuberculosis. Eventually, even their household furnishings had been seized for nonpayment of debts, leaving the children to sleep on the bare floor, and they had been forced to ask a waiver of the monthly fees for Gemma's schooling with the nuns. For a time, before her own health gave way, Gemma took a job at a local sewing school.

Upon her father's death from throat cancer in 1897, the situation became hopeless. At some point her eldest brother Ettore left for Brazil, determined to return to Lucca a rich man or not at all, and Gemma never saw him again. Her brother Guido was too late with too little in trying to take up his father's profession of pharmacist. Her favorite brother, Gino, already was dead and her next brother, Antonio, had one foot in the grave, afflicted as he was with the same pulmonary tuberculosis that had taken their mother. Her sisters were two opposites. The youngest, beloved Giulia, was distinctly malnourished and would die from an unspecified heart condition in August 1902. Angelina, three years younger than Gemma, already was reputed to live a wicked life. After being expelled from school, she had gone off on her own and her bad reputation caused Gemma much preoccupation. Even before that break, Angelina had ridiculed her goody-goody sister, calling her friends over to observe and mock Gemma's ecstasies. Gemma's diary entry of Monday, July 30, reveals how deeply this hurt her, and one may recall also her letter to Monsignor Volpi with a similar lament. Even though Angelina later married and presumably became a more responsible person, her testimony at Pisa in 1922 nonetheless was unanimously rejected as "dubious and useless" by the ecclesiastical tribunal that reviewed the cause for her sister's canonization. And even during her participation at ceremonies to honor Gemma Galgani's elevation to the status of blessed and then of saint, commentators remarked that Angelina's demeanor was less than exemplary. For years, she supported herself in part by demanding money from miracle-seekers beseeching her for some "relic" from her now-sainted sister's childhood, an abuse noted by no less than Cardinal Pietro Maffi, who headed the apostolic canonization proceedings at Pisa.

Things were better by far in the Giannini household, where the Passionist fathers habitually stayed as guests when they preached or had business in
town, since the order as yet had no foundation near Lucca. Cecilia Giannini
and her group of women-friends already had taken Gemma under their pro-
tection, so Father Gaetano's request to meet with Gemma at the Giannini
home a few days hence was welcomed. By the time Gemma arrived the following afternoon, Cecilia Giannini's brother, Cavalier Matteo Giannini, also
joined in: "Tell her to come again and have her stay for dinner!" He added
that the house was always full anyway, with more than twenty at table every
day. And when Cecilia seemed so anguished at the thought of Gemma having to return home after the August holidays, Matteo took her in for good:
"We have eleven children in the house, what's one more?" When this arrangement became permanent is unclear, for Gemma's diary entry of July 28,
1900, states that she was still at her natal home during this time. It is likely
that the final move did not occur until the fall of 1900, despite Cecilia Giannini's recollection of an earlier date.[6]

Further evidence that the transition from her birth household to her new
family did not go as smoothly as Cecilia Giannini later mis-remembered may
be found in the testimony of Sister Maria Giulia di San Giuseppe, who reported during the canonization investigation that Gemma stayed at the Mantellata monastery as an external guest from August 1899 until April 1900, the
expenses being paid by Mrs. Cecilia, who felt she could not bring Gemma immediately into the Giannini home, as it was already filled with her brother's
children. The reason for this temporary arrangement was that Monsignor
Volpi anxiously wanted to remove Gemma from prying secular eyes at the
Galgani house (her brother Guido and her sister Angelina), again according
to Sister Maria Giulia. Unlike the Salesian convent to which Gemma had
been denied entry, where the nuns were uniformly of well-to-do origin and
brought impressive dowries upon their admission, the Mantellata sisters ca-
tered to women of humble origin, often impoverished widows. Although
they provided a temporary refuge for Gemma, the order's mission made it inappropriate for them to take in a young virgin as a regular member. (And vice
versa, but as Gemma reportedly said: "It's better than nothing.") In addition,
there was more trouble when the monastery's regular physician refused to
give Gemma a certificate of good health, even though she had just received
such a document from her family doctor since birth, Lorenzo Del Prete.[7]

The Giannini house, a large three-story structure in the well-to-do south-
eastern section of town, already served as the residence one priest, Don
Lorenzo Agrimonti, and as a guesthouse for visiting preachers. Room would

be found for the spiritually blessed Gemma, who brought Aunt Cecilia such comfort. Initially as a daily visitor and after several months as a permanent resident, everyone in the extended family loved Gemma, and she them. The eleven children ranged from the eldest, Anna, who at nineteen was two years younger than Gemma, down to a one-year-old, and soon Matteo's wife Giustina would become pregnant with her twelfth and last child, born on September 30, 1900.

Gemma's affections also reached out to the household servants and employees: the laundress Zeffra Pracchia; the candle-maker Basilio Morelli, who alone she allowed to lift her from bed during her final illness; the elderly Leopoldo (Poldo) Lucchesi, who with his extravagant words of humility could make even Gemma laugh; the babysitter and chambermaid Caterina Morelli (no relationship to Basilio), known for her sharp tongue; and her favorite, the cook Bartolomea (Mea) Francioni, whose leg sores Gemma patiently cleansed and medicated. These and other humble acquaintances would play an important role in Gemma's canonization, for their unpretentious testimonies assured the high prelates who judged the matter that folks who had not been corrupted by scientific learning might well be the most reliable witnesses about what was holy and what was hysterical. Take as an example Zeffra Pracchia, who saw Gemma regularly in her room when she came to fetch the wash: "I found her taciturn and of few words, and I know nothing else," hardly the demeanor of a hysteric.[8]

Then there were the Giannini children, eleven and soon to be twelve, who uniformly welcomed Gemma as a "gift from Heaven." Certainly they treated her with far greater compassion than she had received in her own home, at least since her brother Gino's death. Five of the seven daughters would become nuns and one of these, Eufemia (Sister Maria Gemma Maddalena in religion), who was six years younger than Gemma, is the main source for what is known firsthand about the saint's daily routines during the final years of her life. Other recollections are from Eufemia's brother Mariano, age ten or eleven when Gemma moved in for good in the fall of 1900. According to these two witnesses, although Gemma was two years older than the eldest natal child in the Giannini household, she always obeyed everyone, never put on airs, and never gave a hint of feigning. She did not care whether she was believed or not. She was kind to everyone but without affectation and sometimes she absent-mindedly neglected to say a "thank you!" She was always thinking about Jesus. When others at dinner started talking about business or worldly things, she would engage in chitchat with the youngest ones at the foot of the long rectangular table, or gaze intently at the huge cross that dominated the dining room wall. At meals she seemed embarrassed and would try to hide behind Aunt Cecilia, especially if some guest of honor was present.

According to matriarch Giustina Giannini, in the presence of others Gemma would disappear like a pet cat. Generally, she excused herself as soon as possible, either to play with the little ones in the garden or to retire to the attic. In the evening she would remove herself to the next room and sit in the dark waiting for her Mom Cecilia, so they could go to bed together. When Don Agrimonti was present he would accompany her and on each step going upstairs they would alternately say prayers. Gemma would undress quickly, hiding behind a window curtain, and she was always in bed facing the wall well before Cecilia Giannini and the eldest child Anna, affectionately called Annetta, who also slept in the room, arrived. An hour or two later, they would hear Gemma saying "Jesus, Jesus!" But if they arose and lit a lamp, Gemma always seemed to be sleeping.

In their "books of memory," Eufemia and her younger brother Mariano then recount how the pious girl accompanied their Aunt Cecilia on vacations to the mountains and the sea, indeed, wherever she went. At the beach, Gemma enjoyed watching everyone swim but she herself never participated, they reported. She was always natural, simple, and restrained in her acts, without ostentation, very serious and reserved, but gentle and good to everyone. She spoke very little but without ever giving a sense of being taciturn or sulky. She always sought out the worst garment and the last place. Never one to show off about her labors, she quietly took charge of keeping all the family's socks in order, mending old ones and making sure each person had a pair, all kept numbered in perfect order in a drawer. They recalled singing songs in the family, but Gemma never joined in, not even on the hymns. She never prayed with the family or gave long discourses, so as not to give the appearance of being a teacher or a presumptuously holy person.

Suddenly Eufemia's testimony turns defensive: "Saint Gemma in our house assisted the two servants, just as we all did because that is what our mother wished, but she was not our domestic, as someone falsely wrote. She lived with us like a beloved sister and was considered one of the family; she ate at the table with us and, as I said above, she only helped the women make the beds, prepare the children in the morning for school, and peel potatoes and wash vegetables in the kitchen; when these chores did not need doing, she stayed in the work room and knitted stockings." She helped everyone, but without attaching any importance to it.

The same document reveals how Gemma's ecstasies came to be recorded.

The person testifying is again Sister Maria Gemma Maddalena (Eufemia Giannini).

> In the morning, before going to church she never spoke; upon her return she drank a little water, then had breakfast like the rest of us, and after helping with making the beds or with kitchen chores, she went to the workroom to knit stockings. Often, reflecting on communion and thanking Jesus, she would feel the internal concentration that preceded ecstasy; then, since she knew she would be enraptured, she retired to her room, where she thought no one would see her. But we older ones, who knew, would follow her, enter the room, call her, and if she did not respond we would go near and find her already in ecstasy, sometimes seated on her bed, or on a chair, or kneeling at Aunt Cecilia's bed, with her hands folded and her eyes nearly closed, talking with Jesus, her guardian angel, or the Blessed Virgin. We would find whatever piece of paper came to hand and with a pencil start writing, even abbreviating the words she said. But many of these ecstasies have been lost because we did not have time to write, others because they occurred in church or other places where it was not possible to write. When she became silent we went away; and she, returning to her senses, found herself alone and believed that no one had seen her. This always happened, so that not even once did she realize our presence.[9]

Given these circumstances, with Eufemia Giannini and her assistant scribes sneaking in when they thought Gemma was thoroughly in ecstasy and slipping out as she regained awareness of her surroundings, questions may be raised about Gemma's "authorship" of her ecstasies. People in trance-like states generally speak softly and in fragmentary ways; they may have some awareness of their surroundings and may even respond to human questions posed to them. Visions do not usually start and stop at precise instants. While Gemma may not have acknowledged the presence of scribes, the statement that "not even once did she realize our presence" may well be untrue. This in turn raises issues of dissemblance, suggestion, and self-deception—on her part and that of her amanuenses. The historical record does not allow satisfactory resolution of these matters, and, for good reason, the mystic's experience is traditionally regarded as ineffable. I have taken a more mundane approach, looking to what is answerable, and have prepared a chronology of the extant ecstasies, where the dates are known, to see what ebb and flow they may have. And I also counted the ecstasies by the days of the week on which they occurred. (See tables 2 and 3.)

Ecstasies were first recorded in September 1899, when Gemma began spending her days at the Giannini household, where potential scribes were

TABLE 2. *Gemma Galgani's Recorded Ecstasies—By Year and Month*

Year	Jan	Feb	Mar	Apr	May	Jun	Jul	Aug	Sep	Oct	Nov	Dec
1899									7			
1900	3		4	13	9	1	3	5	2	1		1
1901		1	1	2	1	1				2	4	8
1902	10	3	1	4	2	10	8	18	2	6	4	
1903	2											

TABLE 3. *Gemma Galgani's Recorded Ecstasies—By Year and Day of the Week*

Year	Sun	Mon	Tue	Wed	Thu	Fri	Sat
1899			3			2	
1900	3	2	6	2	7	8	8
1901	4		2	3	2	3	2
1902	8	6	9	8	10	12	7
1903		1					1

present. In these early mystical experiences Gemma voices freely her consternation over the results of Dr. Pfanner's visit. A period of intense spiritual activity in the spring of 1900, much of it troubled and all duly reported to Monsignor Volpi by Cecilia Giannini, is reflected in the second cluster of recorded ecstasies. Doubts about these secondhand versions may have been what led him to order Gemma to write down for herself whatever she experienced while in rapture, resulting in the diary translated in the preceding chapter. Another concentration is evident in the winter of 1901–2. Here the words are less anguished, the consolations sweeter, although there is not yet the assured tranquility of the final flurry in the summer of 1902, from June through August.[10] The thirty-six ecstasies of this period are distributed quite evenly across the days of the week. According to table 3, this is also true of the oeuvre for all of 1902, a progression in spiritual immersion from the somewhat more limited frequency and daily pattern of the earlier years. All ecstasies from the summer of 1902 are provided in full in the selection that follows.

The twelve letters Gemma wrote during the same months of June, July, and August are also included—to provide some sense of how her words in ecstasy may relate to her conscious writings. To obtain a chronological rough-and-ready guide concerning the epistolary oeuvre, I also tallied letters to her two principal recipients, 71 to Monsignor Volpi, her ordinary confessor, and 132 to Father Germano, the spiritual director extraordinary who came to her rescue beginning late in 1899 and who took over as her primary guide from September 1900 until her death in the spring of 1903.[11] (See tables 4 and 5.)

Overall, the patterns offer few surprises. Fall 1899's thick correspondence with Monsignor Volpi is a direct consequence of his visit in the company of Dr. Pfanner, and the subsequent suspicions that Gemma might be a hysteric or a fake. The next cluster, from August until October 1900, parallels the diary entries and reflects Monsignor Volpi's continued recognition that he was unable to provide the guidance this young woman sought. Once he consigned Gemma to the care of Father Germano in the fall of 1900, the monsignor had little more to do with her outside his confessional, nor she with him except to beg for permission to enter various local convents, which he always denied. The absence of correspondence between them reflects this break. Her last two letters to him, in February and March 1903, are incoherent and reveal only that disease had diminished her mental capacities, at least according to Father Germano.

Letters from Gemma to Father Germano, whose duties elsewhere made it difficult for him to stay long in Lucca, and who feared for his own reputation should he initiate or approve actions that might bring her to a convent nearer his own location, took up where correspondence with the monsignor had left off. The initial letter of January 29, 1900, innocently reveals

TABLE 4. *Letters to Monsignor Volpi—By Year and Month*

Year	Jan	Feb	Mar	Apr	May	Jun	Jul	Aug	Sep	Oct	Nov	Dec
1899					I		I	I	6	4	4	4
1900	3	2	2	2	2	4	I	4	7	4	I	2
1901			2	4	I		3					
1902		I					I			2		
1903		I	I									

TABLE 5. Letters to Father Germano—By Year and Month

Year	Jan	Feb	Mar	Apr	May	Jun	Jul	Aug	Sep	Oct	Nov	Dec
1899												
1900	I	I	2		I	2	2	2	5	9	7	7
1901	3	8	4	5	5	5	5	3	6	7	2	4
1902	4	5	3	2	I	2	3	2	I	3	2	2
1903	3	2	I									

that Gemma for months had wished to write, only to be refused by Monsignor Volpi. Perhaps lack of permission reduced the frequency of their correspondence over the next few months as well. However that may be, from the fall of 1900 and for the next year and more, the stream of missives swelled, overwhelmingly from Gemma to her spiritual Dad. Indeed, an editorial note to her letter to him of June 26, 1902, indicates that he had not written directly to her in more than a year, preferring to communicate through Cecilia Giannini.

Gemma's letters reveal an arduous, lengthy, careful, halting process of spiritual maturation on her part, sometimes nurtured by Father Germano and other times seemingly despite his guidance. For example, already in February 1901 she voluntarily and successfully asked Jesus to remove her external signs of stigmata while increasing her internal suffering. And shortly thereafter she began writing her autobiographical confession, also in response to Father Germano's suggestion. But when he directly thwarted her spiritual desires, or simply refused to write to her at all except through Cecilia Giannini, as happened for the whole year preceding the summer of 1902, she chose instead to obey Jesus.

Recovery and growth took nearly two years. The path away from the violent alternations of tribulation and triumph recorded in Gemma's diary for the summer of 1900 had been fraught with difficulties, trials she no doubt saw as essential to her ultimate salvation. But this long period of travail finally ended on the Feast of Pentecost in May 1902, when she came to understand that Jesus had accepted her offer to take onto her own body an expiation for sins committed by the Church's priests. For the next sixty days she experienced total lack of appetite and could retain no food. Accompanying this physical disability were supernatural graces such as Gemma achieved at no other time in her life—a fitting accomplishment for this young bride of Christ whose emergence from darkness to light had come only after fierce battles, initially against Monsignor Volpi and in the end even against her beloved spiritual Dad. Father Germano saw Gemma alive for the last time in mid-June 1902, and on the 16th of that month she felt inspired to make a set of resolves, much as she had done several times in years gone by. Her adult, carefully numbered list of promises about what she must try harder to do illustrates, I believe, exactly what she did not do, not as a child and not now:

1. No longer hide anything from my Spiritual Father . . .
2. No longer do anything by my own head . . .
3. Tell everything with sincerity, without being begged.
4. Reveal everything that happens internally.
5. Obey in everything, without laments.
6. Always be content with whatever my Father does, because I know with certainty that he is guided and illuminated by God.
7. Tell about every temptation, however embarrassing it may be; and in my way of behaving in those ugly moments, I will obey what has been ordered for me; I will no longer do as in the past.
8. To tie all this together, I resolve before God to no longer have a will of my own.
9. Whatever temptation comes over me, especially about my Father, I will no longer put faith in it and I will no longer believe it, because the devil cannot do other than tell lies.[12]

But obedience to her confessor was a transitory, earthly problem, and Gemma knew that. Loftier challenges lay ahead. By the summer of 1902 Gemma has developed into a woman who knows she is loved by Jesus, with a love that will bring her salvation, a place in Heaven.

Technical notes pertaining to the translation of the ecstasies and letters that follow:

The source is Galgani, *Estasi, Diario, Autobiografia, Scritti vari, Versi,* 116–49, for the ecstasies, and Galgani, *Lettere,* 259–81, 393–94, and 429–32, for the letters. All ellipses (. . .) are as in these sources.

Spelling out of abbreviations is as for the autobiography.

Ecstasies are conveyed in italic type as a reminder that a scribe took down Gemma's words while she was in ecstasy. In the letters, italic type indicates underlining in the handwritten original.

✳ ✳ ✳

Tuesday, June 10 [1902]

＊

My God, open your heart to me. Oh Jesus, open your sacred breast to me, so I may place all my affections there. And you, oh Jesus, you said many times you would welcome me generously: is that true my Jesus?

How much I love you, oh Jesus. I thank you; but why do you behave so lovingly while I offend you with such ingratitude? This thought alone should make me become a flame of love, if I could understand it well . . . I love you, oh Jesus. What a fine love is mine, loving someone who does not get angry with those who offend him . . . Oh Jesus, oh Jesus, if I were to consider attentively the great cares you show me, how I ought to excel in so many virtues! It's true, yes, I excel, oh Jesus, but in what? . . . In sins. Forgive me, oh Jesus, my great negligence; forgive my huge ignorance.

My God! Oh Jesus, my love, uncreated good! What would have become of me, oh Jesus, if your solicitude had not led me to you? . . . Open your heart to me, oh Jesus; open your sacred breast to me . . . I open mine to you . . . Enter, oh your divine fire . . . burn me, oh Jesus, consume me . . . I feel a fire in me, oh Jesus . . . May it be pleasing to you, oh Jesus, if I went up in a blaze! . . .

June 15 or 16, Letter to Mother Maria Giuseppa, Passionist

＊

Reverend Mother,[13]

Long live Jesus! May Jesus be thanked! Be happy, Mother, because my soul is no longer in danger; my Dad has come, with his words he has enlightened me, and I live once again in the grace of God. Without realizing it, I walked for so long in darkness and I found myself bound in the devil's snares; but now I am walking, with his help, in the holy light of God.

Mother, good Jesus had made you understand everything, right? And with your help and with your prayers, which I felt continuously, I revealed everything, everything. How good I feel! I had completely lost all faith in my Dad. My enemy, that good-for-nothing devil, full of infinite tricks, showed me so clearly that Father Germano wanted me to lose my soul, I nearly believed it; even he himself had a hard time convincing me this was not so. Jesus enlightened me, so I understood myself and my state of mind. But I realize that the devil still works tirelessly for my fall; I beg you to ask Jesus to make the devil flee and to get rid of him before he devours me. Do it for always, and I will do for you whatever you wish. Pray also that the devil will never have consolation from me but always pain, and that Jesus will always be glorified.

I have need for one very special prayer. I must show myself grateful to everyone and I don't know how. I want to be healed of the illness of ingratitude, which so displeases Jesus. For Jesus and for my good Dad, who dug me out of Hell, what will I ever do for them? If I am alive right now, I realize it is only by the mercy of Jesus.

I find myself so happy and at peace that I cannot show it fully. Long live Jesus. Jesus is truth, I instead am a liar; Jesus is perfect, I am utterly imperfect: Jesus is pure, I am impure, always mired in slime; Jesus is saintliness itself, whereas I am the fruit of sin; and with all this, how am I to deal with Jesus? If the angels tremble when they find themselves before Jesus, what should I do, full of sins, when I find myself before him? My God! . . .

I told everything, everything, to my Dad, nothing is left; but I made him go through a bit of effort, he sweated a lot, and he even felt ill; but now I see him happy, he's not upset at having worked so hard. Today he departs again and leaves me entirely with Jesus. *God, may your holy will be done.* Bless me also, like my Dad does, in every moment. I will write again soon, and I am your poor

Gemma

Tuesday, June 17

✳

My Jesus, I am consumed . . . I die . . . I die for you . . . Jesus, food of strong souls, fortify me, purify me, make me divine. Great God . . . God of every sacrifice, Jesus help me . . . My redeemer, God from God, come to my aid. Your eyes, oh Jesus, watch continuously over me. I thirst for you, oh Jesus. Do you not see how I suffer in the morning before I feed on you? . . . After I have fed on you, let me at least remain full! . . .

Around Friday, June 20

✳

Where are you, my God? I feel instantly restored as soon as I can raise my voice in praise of you; but since the joy is brief my soul instantly falls back in its abyss . . . Live in tranquility; you shall see that darkness will pass and light will follow; be happy, hope in Jesus, only in Jesus. . . .

Sunday, June 22

✳

Oh Jesus, you are the magnet of all my affections. If your greatness, oh Jesus, can reach down to the most vile of all creatures such as I am, well then, help me to repair all the damages I have done with my sins. My Jesus! . . .

Oh, I am not frightened, because I live under the providence of a Heaven filled with compassion . . .

Dear Jesus, I love you so much! . . . I shall work always to love you; I shall live to love you . . . I shall die to love you. Dear Jesus, Dear Jesus!

I too, oh Jesus, have a great desire to love you back.

Yes, you who have given me so much! I shall do everything for you; everything you ask of me. But what can you expect, oh Jesus, from a creature of slime, able only to offend you? . . .

I long for Heaven . . . When will I pass, oh Jesus, from darkness to light, from death to life? . . . from fear of losing you to certainty I possess you? . . . When will I be entirely satiated in your divine beauty? . . . When will I be entirely lost in your divine light? . . . But what light? . . . A light that is immense, inextinguishable, in-corporeal . . . Oh Jesus, when, oh Jesus? . . .

Why then, oh my God, do you see me suffer so much? . . . Is it because, Jesus, you dislike this desire in me? . . . Who else put it in my heart if not you? . . .

Come, come, oh Jesus, come to take me, come restore me a little . . .

June 22, Letter to Father Germano

✳

My good Dad,

After you had departed, I was not able to confess myself to Monsignor [Volpi]; this morning I felt myself unable to receive communion so I went to Father Vallini for confession.

My dear Dad, it's only a few days since you left and already I feel the need to speak with you again. *Long live Jesus!*

I find myself continuously in a sweetness of spirit that I can truly say lets me forget I am still on this earth; indeed, this morning we went to mass, received holy communion and then, then I don't know . . . I found myself at home and it took all my concentration to figure out how I had gotten there. Still, the enemy does not fail to put himself next to me from time to time; once again he wants to come and disturb the peace you have given me, but Jesus helps me and he was not able to do anything. It is enough, dear Dad, that I make a sign, a prayer, the beginning of a thought of you together with Jesus, and instantly that good-for-nothing makes me think . . . "What? You care about him! . . . He's a loafer, a windbag . . . etc., etc., etc." But do not fear, dear Dad: Jesus is very strong and with his help I resolve not to give in to even the tiniest doubts.

Continue to stay so united with me, which I feel is so good for me; increase the prayers you offer for me because every day my need increases. Only one desire remains in me, to arrive at the salvation of my soul and to arrive there I am ready for everything; and if death should put a stop to so much faithlessness and so many dangers, my dear Dad, let me die, because I desire to unite with my God, who with such strong love holds me together here on earth.

Be happy, dear Dad; I will give you no further displeasures, I shall always be obedient, always docile. You pay attention to Jesus and Jesus has promised me that he will not be long in manifesting himself. As soon as you had left, Jesus inspired several resolves in me; I hope to fulfill them, if you give me a lot of help with your prayers.

That little book of Meditations you left behind, for now I shall keep it, all right? It does me good, too.

Dear Dad, what of Jesus? Wherever I go he never leaves me, never moves from my side because for sure I realized that I cannot live without him, and sometimes I think and I say: "But what, my God, have you forgotten all your other duties? Have you nothing else to do than watch over me?" And instantly a light goes off in my head: the immutable light of Jesus' divine vision does not grow in watching only one person, me alone, nor does it diminish in watching many creatures.

My heart is always united with Jesus, and Jesus continues to consume me. My dear God, I want to melt completely in your flames. Yesterday morning, Dad, I truly believed that my heart wanted to burst out of my chest. My dear Dad, do you think I do not truly feel the need to be grateful toward Jesus? Or do you think maybe I don't want to reciprocate God . . . a God who has bestowed so much on me? Help me do it, by not offending him again, never, never again.

How happy Jesus would be if he should find my heart returning his boundless love! But how can I do what I do not know how to do? If I love Jesus a little, this is not my own doing or my own strength but entirely his mercy. Time to stop, dear Dad; write soon, tell me many things, pray a lot for me. I do so continuously for you, *do you understand? Continuously.* Listen to Jesus, dear Dad. *Long live the will of Jesus!*

Bless me with all your strength. Your poor

Gemma

[P.S.] Thursday morning, my dear Dad, from my bed I drank the chalice of Jesus with you, and I was obliged to say: "How is it, Jesus, that to my Dad, who is good, you give the chalice of bitterness, of penance, of sacrifices to drink; but to me, who has so offended you, you give the chalice of relief and comfort to drink?"

Around Thursday, June 26

*

Your love, oh God, has truly passed all limits. Yes, toward me it passes all limits. What do you want, Jesus? To a creature, oh my God, who in idolizing pleasure turned her back on you so many times, you do this? . . . You always make me stay under the weight of your divine mercy, instead of making me stay under the weight of your divine . . .

I always seek you, oh Jesus; I seek always to promote your glory, to love nothing but your love. Answer me, oh Jesus; why this silence? . . . My God, why do you not answer? . . . Say something to me. If you wanted something in return from me, you should have granted me these favors little by little, not all in a hurry as you have done.

Oh Jesus, oh light, where are you? . . . Illuminate my eyes; don't make me live any longer in the darkness, oh my God . . . So when will I see you again, oh Jesus? What . . . did you say maybe I would not see you again? . . . I don't remember your saying that.

Give me wings, oh Jesus, so I can fly to your throne . . . But there are too many things, oh Jesus, that prevent this soul from flying to you . . . You issue a command, oh Jesus; you'll see that everyone will obey. You alone stay, oh Jesus, in my soul, and you will see that no one will dare to molest it.

But I don't see you . . . Really, I don't see you . . . When I was little, I was told that you were always present, but I don't see you . . . Where are you? . . . Where have you gone? . . . And without even saying goodbye! . . .

Around June 26, Letter to Father Germano

*

My good Dad,

How happy I am now that you've decided once again to write directly to me!

If I pray for you, if I am good, and if I obey and am always docile, you will always write directly to me, right? That way I understand better. I will never stop praying for you, if Jesus helps me; his help is too necessary for me. Woe to my soul if you had not come to my aid! (You know what I mean.) I would have fallen into Hell, and not just once but who knows how many times! Watch out because the devil has not given up; he continues for one reason or another to make doubts arise in me (about you). But Jesus makes me strong and I can assure you that I have not given in again.

Jesus continues with his usual sweetness. I live on the earth but on this earth I feel I am like a lost soul because my thoughts never, never stray from my Jesus. There will still be a time as you say, when these consolations will change into punishments, afflictions, dryness, etc.? May God's will be done! But I am afraid, dear Dad, I am afraid for my soul. Assist me, and if you see my soul in danger, have no respect for my human self, do whatever Jesus wants.

I will not hide anything, anything, no more, no more.

Things are going normally, like when you were here; is that all right? Oh Dad, pray for me; will things go well, does that ugly good-for-nothing have any part in all this? I'm ready for anything.

With regard to your order that I stay healthy, I have one thing to say. Jesus, I hope, will allow me to carry out your order; indeed, I am certain that by the end of the month I will no longer throw up any food. But now, dear Dad, for quite some time I feel Jesus has been inspiring me to ask a favor of you. Don't get mad, my dear Dad; I'll do what you say but you will see: it will do no harm to grant me this. Sure, you'll have many excuses to offer: that I am too thin, that it is not necessary; but these are worthless. Listen: *are you happy if I ask Jesus the grace of not letting me sense any taste in any food, for as long as I live?* My dear Dad, I need this grace. I hope Jesus will tell you to grant it to me; in any case . . . I am happy. You think about it.

Whether my good Mom [Mrs. Cecilia] is pleased with my behavior I do not know, but she must not be. I will do everything to please her, dear Dad, something you already know, and she also knows; I will try to obey you and hold back nothing.

I no longer remember anything from all the notes I've thrown away, but for the most part they dealt with conversations with Jesus, others with temptations, etc. (all regarding you). Long live Jesus. Here's something for you to judge. Early this morning, before *two,* I awakened; all of a sudden a multitude of thoughts about my soul came to disturb me. Thoughts like this: And if I am deceived? And if everything that happens to me should bring me to my fall? And if Father Germano is deceived? In this combat I stayed until . . . Do you know how long, my dear Dad? Until 5:00. I don't know where Jesus went; he didn't say even one word to me. In the end he was moved to a little compassion, and taking me for a bit out of my senses, he let me hear (I thought) these words: "Daughter, do not fear. It is I who works in you. I shall never leave you, live happily." Dad, ask Jesus if it was him, or else who said these words? Whatever, the happiness I felt at these words was infinite and I am inclined to believe them. Dad, on this tell me many things; but do not write unless you are certain.

How great is the magnitude of Jesus' sweetness!

I have various permissions to ask of you, my dear Dad. Do not get upset, but I want another permission from you. My Dad is so good that if Jesus inspires him just a little, he'll grant it instantly. I want to make a promise to Jesus, to not seek ever again, ever, comfort in anything. And do not doubt, my dear Dad: I can handle it, you know; do not think I will fall into excesses. But understand me clearly: no comfort in anything, *nothing* (I intend this to include everything).

Summed up, then, these are two little things I ask, and there is no harm in granting them.[14] Either way I am happy. Pray a lot for me, for I fear being unfaithful to Jesus; pray especially about this and I will always think of your soul.

I do not know if I have responded to every point, and if I have pleased you, but if I have not done what you want, when you write, number the points you make, so I can better respond to them.

That usual laziness about oral prayer still lingers; what will happen, dear Dad?

Jesus promised to let me keep down a bit of food, so even if my body continues wasting away (as I feel it doing) by keeping down food, it will consume more slowly.

It had been many days since I had last felt pain for my sins but last night Jesus wanted to give me again that grace; if you do not assist me, you will quickly see me reduced to ashes, the ashes of sin.

For now I'll stop, dear Dad. Soon you are going to Rome and you'll surely see Serafina.[15] Have her pray a lot for me, go ahead and reveal to her all my sins: I am happy; tell them to everyone: I want to be known for what I am.

Bless me with strength, my dear Dad, pray for me. I am your poor
Gemma

[P.S.] If Serafina says she wants to come to Lucca, you won't prohibit her, because don't you think Jesus wishes it?

Friday, June 27

*

To you the saints, oh Jesus, and the humble of heart; not me, oh Lord. To you all the spirits and souls of all the just; not me, oh Lord. To you all the inhabitants of Heaven, not me . . . May they all give you infinite praise and thanks. But me too, me too, oh Jesus . . . Yes, I a vile and unworthy sinner desire to love you, with a unique love. Help me, you who are my strength. Fire, fire in my heart: this morning it's burning! . . . Words in my mouth . . . May I be able day and night to meditate on your glory and love you continuously. Impure are my lips, impure my entire body. I need you: that you cleanse me of every stain. Sanctify me, oh Jesus. May your memory, your sweetness keep my soul always united with you. Make me pass from the visible to the invisible, from earthly things to the celestial.

Oh my God, my Jesus! . . . What are you saying, oh Jesus . . . Oh true charity, you are my God because toward you I feel I am always moving, toward you I feel I am always carried, toward you I hope always to reach. When I deal with you I feel revived, but when you leave me I feel lost, fallen . . .

Faith teaches me this, the faith you have placed in my heart to illuminate my way . . . Allow, oh my God, that whoever knows you, knows truth, knows eternity. You, for as long as I live in this fragile body . . .

These are the words that my Dad has taught me: who resembles you, oh my God? . . . Who resembles you, oh my God? . . . Who? . . . You are God omnipotent. My Jesus, true charity, you are my God . . .

Saturday, June 28

*

Lord, if you wish, you can save me; but the number of the sins I carry with me is great, and it is infinite. Remember, oh Jesus, your mercy . . .

I hoped, oh Jesus, as I confessed so many times before you, to be self-sufficient in something; I hoped in my own strength . . . But when I began to act on my own, that was when I fell and lost all you had allowed me to gain. But soon after, oh Jesus, you illuminated me, and then I understood that what I thought I could be self-sufficient in was exactly what I never could have done on my own. I had the will but I lacked strength; I had the strength but lacked the will . . .

Before you I have absolutely nothing to boast about! . . . You loved me, oh Jesus . . . You preferred me to so many creatures. I am proud of your favors but I understand more and more my own sinfulness . . . Expect nothing from me . . . What can you expect from a bit of slime, able only to offend you? . . .

I would give you love but I have none left because I no longer have a heart! . . . Anyway, oh Jesus, do not ask love of me, because I owe it to you for gratitude . . . Oh, if I could make you happy in the same way you make me happy! . . .

My God, my help . . . my strength . . . my support . . . my light! . . . Enlighten my steps . . .

Where have you gone, my love? . . . Where are you hiding? . . . Why don't you let me see you anymore? . . . If I can't see you, because I am alive, then let me die, as I desire. I wish to die, so I can come to you alone.

Where have you gone, my Jesus? . . . Infinite beauty, where are you concealed? . . . Where should I look for you, oh Jesus? . . . Make yourself seen at least one time . . . Maybe, oh Jesus, you said I would not see you again on this earth? . . . I don't remember. I so much want to see you, oh Jesus . . . But I hear you and that should be enough . . . When I was little, I was told you were always present . . . Why is it that I don't see you? . . . Release this body, oh Jesus . . . break these chains . . . I shall not be happy until my soul is free and flies to you alone. When can I rejoice completely in you?

Oh love of sweetness! . . . oh sweetness of love! . . .

Sunday, June 29, at 9 A.M.
✳

I burn, Jesus . . . I open my heart to you this morning . . . You are divine: lighten this darkness . . . lift the darkness entirely until with a flame you give all of yourself. I love you, but if it is too little, make me love you more . . . You are immense, my God! . . .

Sunday, June 29, at 10:30 A.M.
✳

Who will give me the feathers of an eagle; who will give me the feathers of a dove so I may fly to you? . . . You should give me, oh Jesus, the wings of contemplation. How am I going to fly to you? So many things to go through! . . . Go through all creation; break these chains that prevent me from flying to you . . .

There are many other things, oh Jesus, that nourish my soul when I contemplate them . . . but in none of them do I remain satiated, in none do I find repose. Only in you, oh Jesus, only in you does this soul of mine find repose.

Sunday, June 29, at 4 P.M.
✳

Oh Jesus, how are you doing in the narrow cell of my heart? Are you all right? Dilate my chest, because it is no longer enough to contain you . . . Jesus, allow me to pour out my affections with you . . .

Monday, June 30
✱

Lord my Jesus, when my lips near yours to kiss you, let me feel your gall. When my shoulders rest on yours, let me feel your scourges. When your flesh communicates with mine, let me feel your Passion. When my head nears yours, let me feel your crown of thorns. When my side touches yours, let me feel the lance.

Oh! What shall I ever give you for all the gifts you have given me, for having loved and comforted me? . . . And you, what can you not expect from me, a vile creature? . . . I shall give you all you have given me . . .

My soul, bless Jesus! . . . Never forget the many gifts he has given you. You see, my soul: at every moment, at every instant, I think of you, and I find you and I see you among so many gifts, in such sweetness, yet I find you always . . .

Love that God who loves you so; lift yourself to him, who has stooped so low for you. Do you not see how vigilant he is? . . . And you, oh my soul, behave like he behaves with you; be spotless . . . be pure . . . Love your Jesus, who has rescued you from such wretchedness . . . Love your God . . . Bless your Lord . . .

June-July
✱

Let me embrace you, celestial bridegroom, source of all my consolations. Who am I, to speak so boldly with you? It's true, I am your creature, but I am bad; it's true that I was made by your hands, and those very hands, oh Jesus, I pierced with nails . . . I got going too late, Jesus, in coming to you . . . I found you, Jesus; I found you, Jesus. I call you, I invoke you, because I am sure.

But where are you, where are you hiding? I can smell your presence. Give me wings, Jesus, to fly to your house in Heaven . . .

Tuesday, July 1
✱

Here I am before you, oh Jesus. Before you I show my soul: this soul, oh Jesus, that you created not from your substance but by means of the word . . . with no other primary material. This spiritual soul that you created, that lives forever, that you have sanctified and purified in your holy bath.

Now I am satisfied and I have nothing more to desire . . . because if inside myself I should wish for something more, it would be clear that you are not here. If in this world goodness in itself gives delight, what delight would you not bring, you who are the king of all good? . . . The happiness experienced down here on earth, of things created, is totally different from what is experienced in you, who are the creator. You see, oh Jesus: when a creature desires something, she dies with desire to have it, but even when she manages to get it, she is not happy, she is never satisfied. You alone give satisfaction, you alone give purity, you alone make immaculate all those who in you . . .

I found your dwelling, oh Jesus. You live in that soul you created in your image, not in the one that prefers earthly things over you.

Oh! my soul, although poor, has understood the riches of your love. My soul is too vile, oh Jesus, to be your dwelling, too vile . . . Oh my God, if I could be certain even for a little while that I never offended you! . . . Oh, I don't deny it, I am a sinner, but for this I do not want to despair because should I despair, I would be denying your mercy. My Jesus, I love you, but if I love you too little, let me love you more . . . I don't know, I really don't know, how much I can do . . . I don't know how much I can do . . . to what extent it is enough . . .

Oh Jesus, how are you doing in my heart? . . . In the narrow cell of my chest in love with you, tell me, oh Jesus, how are you doing there?

Establish your permanent abode, oh Jesus . . . establish it from this morning, from this very moment, this very instant . . .

My Jesus, we shall never separate again. However great, however magnanimous the human heart, it must surrender before the force of your love, it must give in. My God . . . my Jesus . . . my father . . . my bridegroom . . . my sweetness . . . my consolation . . . consolation of all creatures . . . love . . . love who sustains me!

Oh fire always burning, without ever dying down, if only you would let all of me go up in flames? Would you let this fire perfect me? Oh Jesus! . . . Oh love! . . . My life, my sustenance, my strength! . . .

Wednesday, July 2, around 9 A.M.

✳

It is an easy love, oh Jesus, to love someone who never gets angry with those who offend him. Indeed, many times I have seen, oh Jesus, that while justice demands that I be punished, you take steps to prevent this punishment, even to have it withdrawn. I have found a Jesus so infatuated with my heart that he knows not how to embitter it . . .

He wants everything for himself in atonement for my sins. It's almost a lucky break for me to have been born a sinner, because the veins of my Lord are always open, full of that sacramental blood!

Oh my God! . . . What would you wish to do, compassionate Jesus? . . . Would you wish to make all your merits mine, appropriate to me everything that is yours? . . . And can there be a heart that will not let itself be taken over by so much charity? Can there be a soul that will not let itself be won over? Can there be a volition that will not let itself be ravished by you?

Oh my soul, how much longer do you wish to be so stingy with Jesus? . . . Why so negligent toward Jesus, who made you? Why so lazy toward Jesus, who redeemed you? Who do you want to love, if you do not want to love Jesus? Oh my God! . . .

Wednesday, July 2, 11 A.M.

✳

Jesus, sacred host, to you I consecrate all my tenderness. I realized, oh Jesus, that your affection was seeking me out, and I ran to you; your charity was calling me and I came immediately.

Oh Heaven, Heaven! . . . Let me be, oh Jesus; leave me to think of Heaven. Oh, if only your divine goodness, after receiving a sharp pain for my sins, like the least of your daughters . . . Oh Heaven! Is it so much that I . . . who will ever be able to tell you? . . .

A desire that never torments enough, that never becomes boring! How those souls must be! . . . How is it that close to you, who are all light, they have become so luminous? . . . How is it that in the midst of your immutable eternity, mutable that they were, they have now become immutable?

What joy, oh Jesus, to live in your Heaven. Is it not you, oh Jesus, who has put this desire in me? . . .

Yes, my Jesus, to do nothing other than your will! . . . Jesus while I live, Jesus after I live, Jesus for eternity! My Jesus, my love! . . .

Thursday, July 3, around 9 A.M.

✳

Oh Jesus, I see you greater that all the treasures of earth. Yes, my sweetest God, my most lovable Jesus: to my eyes you are greater than the greatest treasures on earth. How gladly I would unite with your angels! How gladly I would be consumed in your praises! How gladly I would remain always before you!

But what do I say when I speak of you? . . . I say what I can, never what I ought. And if I do not know how . . . will I stay silent? No, because my Jesus must be loved, honored by everyone! . . . Do not look at what I say with my mind, look inside me . . .

My every secret is manifest to you, oh Jesus . . . So are you certain that I love you more than the sky and the earth? Indeed, all earthly things worthy of being loved exist only to glorify your heart . . .

I have loved you, oh Jesus. Grant me to love you yet more, so that my thought turns only to you, all day, and all night, even while sleeping . . . I wish my spirit to talk always with you, my soul to converse always with you. I wish further that my heart should always be enlightened with your holy light; that you should be my love, my guide . . . I wish to fly from virtue to virtue . . . if not, then I shall be unable to come to Heaven to see you; it's been so long since I last saw you. But to come to Heaven requires purity of heart; give it to me, my Jesus . . . Yes, I so desire purity of heart! . . .

Thursday, July 3, 11 A.M.
*

Who am I to start talking to Jesus like this, every minute? . . . Oh Heaven, oh Heaven, let me think of you! . . . At least when I shall be up there, I shall no longer suffer, I shall no longer endure the sufferings and the pains down here. Oh Heaven! in you there will no longer be nights, nor darkness, nor changes, nor time . . . Oh Heaven! in you there will no longer be . . . Only God of God, light of light, sun of justice, who enlightens; his immaculate heart will give you sunshine . . . precisely because consolation is to contemplate God, the king of kings at the center of Heaven. How great! . . .

What consolation, my soul, to be surrounded by the angels, by his favorites! Everyone's merits are not equal, but each has its happiness. Oh my soul! . . . Oh Heaven! . . . You will see, when I am with you I shall be satiated, I will no longer have need, not of . . .

Oh God . . . let me be engulfed in the charity of your love . . . Oh Heaven! . . . Will I be deemed worthy to see your holy walls? . . . Will I be deemed worthy to see your foundations, your inhabitants, your king? . . . I commend myself to you, holy angels, to you my guardian angel: open the door . . . let me in . . .

Friday, July 4
*

. . . Adored Jesus, word uncreated! . . . Oh Mom, oh Mom! if you are a compassionate mother to me, why do you abandon this daughter, who loves you so? Without you, who will hear my prayers? Who will fulfill my vows? Without you I am like a sinner . . . like a pauper with no aid. Dear Mother, why do you leave me? Bring me also to Heaven. Oh Mom, dear Mother, you are a pure flower that blooms like a white lily. Queen of Heaven . . . you who take from every creature the most

noble part of their love, you took it from me as well, and now you do not give it back to me, so that under your embraces it is no longer earthly, but heavenly. Give it back to me! Eh! Dear Mom, you don't want to give it back because you're jealous that I will give it to my love. All right, give it yourself to my Jesus, then.

Yes, Jesus loves me so much, because my every breath is his, my every desire is his, my every affection is his.

Before you leave me, how about it, dear Mom, carry me to Heaven with you . . .

Saturday, July 5
✴

Why so afflicted, my soul? . . . You are offending your love, if you do not embrace the cross wholeheartedly. You do not care about Heaven if you do not direct your thoughts to Calvary. Do not be afflicted, my soul: you are wed with Jesus for eternity, together with his pains, and you are obliged to live crucified.

Oh Jesus, oh Jesus, Jesus my love! . . . I am hungry for your bread of life, I am thirsty for your sacramental blood.

You know, my soul, why I want you to embrace the cross? . . . Because if the rod of the cross does not knock you down a little, you are in danger.

Oh Jesus . . . I know that the cross is dear to you, and in the cross you have placed all your tenderness, all your affections . . . Do not let your love deny me the cross out of jealousy, I beg you. Either crucify my soul or let me die. My Jesus . . . my adored love, how I love you!

And I understand you, I understand you, my Jesus; I understood you well this morning. My God, I love you, I love you . . . My affections should shout out; my senses, all should shout out: Who resembles you, my God? Who resembles you among the gods?

Wednesday, July 9, Letter to Father Germano
✴

My good Dad,

Long live Jesus! Do not fear: if Jesus helps me, I no longer want to hide anything, no matter what it is. That ugly devil continues to torment me, but now with temptations that Jesus permits to be only brief flashes; as soon as they arrive, they instantly disappear; other times with some dream, etc., etc.

You know why I asked you when the time for punishment would come, for which Jesus is preparing me? Because I asked Jesus one morning after communion and he answered: "As soon as you set foot in the monastery."

That's why I wanted to know if you would give me the same answer. Is it possible that what I thought could come from Jesus?

This morning I made a pact with Jesus about food. Everything is all right, my dear Dad; I will no longer feel a sense of taste but Jesus will make me keep food down, but only the tiniest amounts, I realize, because if I eat a lot I will throw up, if I eat a little, I don't. This morning with Jesus we then talked about my health and in your name, dear Dad, I asked that he make me feel well and gain a little weight. Listen to the response: *"Tell your Dad that I will allow it this time only, but for a very short while."* I don't get it. Tell me what you think. My dear Dad, how calm I feel since Jesus' words! I feel full of confidence in you, such as I have never, never felt, not even when we first met.

About the other permission . . . Long live Jesus! How I awaited your letter to begin! but . . . Rest assured, I won't do anything. Indeed, a while ago I had asked the same permission from Monsignor Volpi. He too had denied me; but Friday he himself gave me license to try it for one month, saying he would judge during this period whether I could continue. I left the confessional and ran to Jesus and prayed him to give me a little light about which of my two directors I should obey. (Your letter had not yet arrived; and in me I felt a strong desire to have this permission.) And Jesus, my good Jesus, made me understand clearly to do nothing, that permission had to come from you. In this I struggled a lot, you know, dear Dad. To feel the desire . . . Monsignor gave me permission . . . but Jesus, how quick he is! . . . I am calm; I await your decision. I would go down very fast, dear Dad, if when you are far away I did not have Jesus.

Needless to say, no vocal prayers; the exclamations, the thoughts toward Jesus are continuous, you know, dear Dad. A few days ago I committed a huge omission, enough that God might have struck me with lightning. Merciful Jesus! Mr. Lorenzo [16] ordered me to do a bill and maybe I gave it too much attention so that I left the presence of God; but it was only for a minute and then I returned instantly within myself; I asked God's forgiveness and he immediately forgave me.

Yes, yes, I do know how to translate Saint Augustine. [17] Listen, Chapter 1, page 5: *"My Jesus, make my heart desire you; desiring you, let it seek you; seeking you, let it find you; finding you, let it love you; loving you, grant it the forgiveness of sins; and obtaining that, let it not commit them again."* Oh dear Dad, a few minutes ago I felt overwhelmed with a strong pain for my sins, enough to die. My God! look first to your son, begotten by you, then take a look at this creature you have redeemed! Afterward, remaining a while like this . . . I don't know how to say it . . . I lost myself and thought of my soul as a huge mountain with Jesus holding it up so it wouldn't fall down. Yes, exactly like that, dear Dad: if Jesus did not support my soul, it would fall . . . Oh my God, since you have cleansed my soul of sin, which is its destroyer, do take it as its guardian!

And do you not feel, my dear Dad, how every moment I pray for you? Indeed, I often say: "My Jesus!" And then I add: "My dear Dad, where are you? Where have you left me? Why don't you return quickly, since I am dying, and dying for love of Jesus? Do you not see that my heart and my body are being consumed and will become ashes? Do you not see that I am a victim of love and soon I will die of love? Do you not see that all worldly things weary me, I long for nothing, only *love, love, love?*" All this, dear Dad, does not bring a lament in my heart, but resignation.

I speak of you with no one.[18] Friday Monsignor asked me: "Did Father Germano give you any permission for external penances?" "No," I answered. "And are you happy with this?" "Yes, it's all the same." "But if you want to do a few, go ahead, because I give you permission, little ones though . . . ," and he listed a few, but I did none of them, none: I feel Jesus does not want it. Then he questioned me some about the mystery of the Holy Trinity; I found myself very confused, dear Dad, because the monsignor uses different ways than yours; but Jesus, how well he knew to blow the trumpet in my ears! So we both remained confounded and humiliated before the majesty of God!

Have no fear for your soul, dear Dad; do you not realize that with Jesus I deal with your soul as if it were my own? You should do as I do. Don't you think it is almost good luck that I was born a sinner? Because Jesus' veins, filled with sacramental blood, are always open to sinners. Long live Jesus!

I will write again soon because I have so many other things to say but this morning I cannot continue because I do not feel well. Bless me strongly, very strongly. I am your poor

Gemma

[P.S.] The Latin I explained hastily; if you want something more extensive, I shall do so; I do not know how to do it literally, but every thought, every word gives me so much to say. You take it as is, right Dad? Indeed, if you think it necessary, I'll do so; otherwise, let's drop it, since I don't do so willingly.

(Thank you very much for the permission you granted me. You will see what Jesus will give you.)

Saturday, July 12, 8:30 A.M.

✻

Saintly soul, assist me; dear Mother, come to my aid . . . Mother Giuseppa, saintly soul, I need you. Chosen soul, you enjoy the most beautiful part of Jesus, being the bride of his heart: you have made him your beloved . . . I turn to you this morning in particular: say some prayer to Jesus for me.

Saintly soul, use a little portion of your great fervor to beseech for my soul, unhappy and needy, that pardon which I have not been able to deserve . . .

More, more . . . I want more. Interpose, saintly soul, your pure love with Jesus on my behalf, so that he will deny you nothing . . .

More, more . . . Apply, saintly soul, the merit of your charity, through which everything is possible with Jesus . . .

Do you see, dear soul, how much I want from you? If you do not want to do this for me, do it in homage to God, the sole object of all your concerns . . . Mother Giuseppa, tell me, will you do it? Yes, right?

But how will you do it if I place obstacles? I deformed my spirit, the living image of Jesus' uncreated beauty. Generous Jesus! . . .

Toward Sunday, July 20, Letter to Father Germano

✻

My good Dad,

Here I am before you. How many things you will hear! Pray a lot, my dear Dad, that Jesus may enlighten you with a true light. I shall withhold nothing, I will do as you say, I will be good, I will be docile; help me, the need for your aid grows daily. Now that you're in Rome, ask Serafina to pray for me.

My dear Dad, is Jesus pleased with my soul? I stay always united with him. Beloved Jesus! my all in this miserable world! What gives me a little pause is that while I receive communion continuously, the angelic bread has not communicated internally to me all those benefits it grants with abundance to so many other souls. And I know the reason why: it is because my few virtues are weak and I come to Jesus with no merit. Help, help, my dear Dad! Today I could have arrived at higher levels of merit but instead I went backward, to the detriment of my wretched soul. This tepidity I encountered this morning; I will try to repent.

Sometimes, can you believe it, dear Dad, I tremble and turn bright red when I think of how impure I am when I receive Jesus, who is the essence of purity. And surely it is for this that beside the fire of Jesus I am colder and colder.

But Jesus, my dear Jesus, loves me even this way, and continuously makes himself felt to my soul. I have only one good thing, dear Dad and it is good intentions; those at least I think I feel. And since Jesus tells me this greatly helps one who is weak and poor like I am, so I hope it will be pleasing to one who is strong and great like Jesus.

Now it is time to begin to recount a few little things. Listen, dear Dad, let me understand what comes from God; do all you can so that the enemy will have no part in anything. The morning of the 12th, it was around 8:45, all of a sudden I felt collected and I thought I heard her, Mother Giuseppa, calling me. For a few moments I was distracted but when certain things befall me, I have to give in. I found myself in a few minutes before Jesus, together with Mother Giuseppa. Finding myself near such a saintly soul, I fully understood my wretchedness and my weakness, I knew my nothingness before God, and turning to her, Mother Giuseppa, I begged like this: "Oh chosen soul, you who take pleasure in your Jesus, being his bride, you have made him your heart's beloved; I turn to your mercy, that you may aid me with Jesus. Offer some prayers to him for me."

My Dad, I thought that saintly soul asked me what I would like to say to Jesus. And I . . . "Use, oh dear Mother, a little of your great fervor to beseech for my soul, the unhappiest and neediest of souls, the forgiveness of sins; beseech that pardon which my soul does not know how to deserve; interpose your pure love, and you will see that nothing is denied you; apply the merit of your charity, by which you will be able to obtain everything for me. If you do not wish to do these things for me, do them in homage to God, whose honor is the sole object of all your concerns."

We passed a few minutes in silence; then I heard Mother Giuseppa truly praying for me. Then I continued: "What do you say, saintly soul, will you pray for me, will you do all these things for me? But to what end since I place obstacles to this grace? . . ."

That soul promised me everything. Oh if she could truly obtain for me from God the pardon of so many sins! Sins, sins, flee from me! You will no longer have a place in the heart you profaned for so long with your abominations! Beloved Jesus, I want to amend my ways, have compassion for me, forgive me.

I suffered so much in these days, Dad; pains enough to die, but now they calmed down. Long live Jesus. The devil, that good-for-nothing, is giving me trouble, he wants to . . . but Jesus makes me so calm with his words that the enemy with all his efforts cannot take away my confidence in God, my faith in you, not even for a moment.

You know where the devil also approached? On that permission I asked for and that you denied me. He suggested as follows: "How Jesus would be pleased if you no longer indulged in any comforts! You think you are progressing this way? Your life is too easy. If you do not make penance to pay for your sins, you will have to stay a long time in Purgatory, if you're lucky! Hell is always open for the lazy, etc. etc." Oh Dad, notwithstanding all this chatter I am calm, at peace; my faith is in you, and I would go straight to Hell rather than disobey. Answer me clearly. And Serafina, have you seen her? . . . What does Jesus say? . . . *Fiat voluntas tua* for always, beloved Jesus. Oh dear Dad, think of my soul; I shall think of yours.

You already know, it's true, that for two straight days, the 14th and the 15th, I had a little visit from my beloved angel. Who would have guessed? He came upon me unexpectedly; I was resting with Jesus. Seeing him disturbed me a little, and I was overcome with fear. I said: "If you have been sent by God, come and I shall receive you but if you are sent by the devil, I'll spit in your face." He then smiled and gave adoration to the majesty of God, then he made a salute to the Holy Trinity. Dear Dad, how I am left when such visits happen! I am left . . . I don't know how to express it. In his presence I was ashamed to have shown no reverence toward him, no devotion; I summoned my courage and asked his forgiveness, saying he should pardon me because in his presence I had sinned, because to his tender love I had preferred love of myself. How many times he had suggested that I change my life, and I never listened! How many times he had suggested that I not offend the infinite goodness, who wished to communicate with my soul, and instead I continued! Oh God! In the presence of my good angel I made almost a full confession (so to speak). How much love he showed me! He looked at me so affectionately! . . . And when he was about to leave (which I realized because he came near and kissed me on the forehead), I begged him not to leave me quite yet, and he said: "I have to go." "Be on your way," I said, "say hello to Jesus." He gave me one last look, saying: "I do not want you to engage in conversations with people: when you want to talk, talk with Jesus and with your angel."

The next day, at the same hour, without my thinking, there he was again. My God! Give light to my Dad and I will believe only in him. He came near, caressed me, and something made me say with all my affection: "My angel, how much I love you!" "And why do you love me?" he asked me. "I love you because you teach me humility and because you keep internal peace in my heart. If on occasion I am bad, beloved angel, do not get angry; I want to be grateful, you know, first to Jesus and then to you." "Yes . . ." he continued, "I shall be your sure guide; I shall be your inseparable companion. Do you not know," he asked, "who gave you to me in custody?" "Yes," I responded, "my merciful Jesus." And here both of us stayed with Jesus. Oh if you had been there, my dear Dad! Dad, Dad, pray for me. Call my angel, and you will see what he says.

Now you think I'm finished, but slow down . . . I want a tiny little permission this time. You will see, Jesus will say yes right away when you ask him. It is necessary. I pray you, reflect on it and write.

You see, dear Dad, you will think that I am one of those who talk very little, right? Just the opposite. I hear a conversation and I say my part; I hear something bad said about a person, and I need to say my part, and a hundred other things; the worst is when I invent (no, not invent), when I initiate conversations. How many sins, how much gossip, and who knows how many slanders. Do you want me to avoid them, my dear Dad? Make me promise Jesus to keep a rigorous silence, not to speak unless I am asked and then only for necessity. Oh, the devil will wage war on me, but Jesus will help me.

Now you must be saying to yourself: "Look how silly that Gemma is! Who put this in her head? Certain things are not for her; they will only be the occasions for greater sins because I who know well how fragile she is, I know she cannot observe them." Oh Dad, you are right, but I hope in Jesus. He will help me, because for me this thing is necessary. I don't ask lightly about certain permissions, you know? Don't you know that before asking I test them? I fall, I fall and fall again, but Jesus is with me.

Bless me strongly, very strongly, dear Dad, at every moment. Write to me, I need so much advice about the path to follow.

Did you see Serafina? Have her pray for me. Hold me tightly. My dear Father, if you feel me stray, hold on to me. My body continues to consume me, but since I eat a little, it's going more slowly.

Goodbye, my dear Dad, bless your poor

Gemma

[P.S.] The angel gave me a few drops of a white liquid in a golden goblet to drink, saying this was the medicine a doctor in Heaven used to heal infirmities.

Sunday, July 27, Letter to Father Germano
✳

My dear Dad,

Long live Jesus! Here I am again, as usual. Yesterday when I was about to leave the confessional, Monsignor gave me a certain order . . . He said: "When you return to Lucca [from vacationing in Viareggio], as soon as you arrive, tell Mrs. Cecilia to call the family doctor to visit you, because you are sick."

For obedience I did so; whatever Mrs. Cecilia does, I submit gladly. Dad, my Dad . . . my everything after Jesus. My good angel will tell you the rest . . .

We returned yesterday from Viareggio and found your letter. About me, my experiences, my permissions you say nothing? . . . If Jesus wishes and if you have time, I'm waiting; if not, it's all the same.

Dear Dad, Jesus continues, even increases, his sweetnesses toward this vile creature: each day instead of offering me a chalice of grief he offers me a chalice of relief, of comfort, of joy, and of love.

The last two days have been a bit topsy-turvy. I looked at the others in the house, for example Annetta and Eufemia and I thought: how I would like to live as they live, without anything extraordinary and a thousand strange ideas.

Jesus, right at suppertime, returned my peace with these words: "Daughter, are you not pleased to do my will?" My calm returned and I dwelt on it no further.

My health goes . . . as Jesus wishes: I retain food well, I eat what is necessary for me, but my body is not yet fully healed. Dad, the monsignor, seeing me so thin, seeks a doctor; but this time it is for bad ends . . . He wants me to undergo a complete examination; they either fear I will die, or else . . .

According to Jesus, this is the time I feel well and the time will be very brief. What will follow, when? . . . Quickly, quickly, my God! Quickly, Dad!

In the morning, after communion, let me know from Jesus if you wish me to send a note with my good angel. I have one thing to say: if he tells you, then there is no need to write but if he does not, then let me know, so I can send my angel with a letter. Jesus will let me know.[19]

Bless me strongly, very strongly. I am your poor
Gemma

[P.S.] The monsignor fears even his angel; but I have lived a life of deception, dear Dad, it's true. Jesus would not let it be known to the monsignor.

Help me, dear Dad. Where I fail, warn me; I want to obey. I no longer want to deceive anyone.

    Gemma

Dad, if the monsignor says it is so, that is a sign he had the light of God; I commend myself to you; pray, pray so, so, so much for me.

    Gemma

Dear Dad, come soon. Don't you know that Jesus wishes it? Hurrah! I do not wish to live deceived and to deceive others any longer.

July, Letter to Monsignor Volpi

✳

Monsignor,

Very well, here I am, poor Gemma, recovered fully; but listen: it seems to me Jesus at this moment is saying this is the last command. Do you not know that for more than a year Jesus has been waiting to have his way with me? I told you the other night. I am the victim, Jesus is and must be my sacrificer. Do you not realize that Jesus cannot wait any longer? I think not. You should have heard how much I took pleasure and pain at the same time from Friday until now! Certain pangs seized me (I say it like that because I don't know how to say it), but so strong; I thought my soul would leave my body, and three or four times, I'm surprised that my heart stayed in place and did not come off. After all this happened I felt like I was being consumed, slowly, very slowly; in those pangs there was pain but when I felt consumed, it was happiness. You should have felt what sweetness I felt in that moment! I don't know how to explain it.

Listen, I think Jesus is giving me this warning for the last time, but for you: put me in hiding soon, because I think Jesus cannot wait any longer.

How I showed myself silly and weak! I expect all sorts of scoldings from Jesus for this.

Bless me, and pray a lot for your poor

    Gemma

[P.S.] Whatever happens, I am happy. You will permit me, right, when Mrs. Cecilia allows it, to visit Sister Maria?

I am happy whatever happens and if Jesus truly wants the sacrifice of my life, I will do it instantly; if he wants other sacrifices, I am ready; it is enough for me to be his victim, but soon, to repay my innumerable sins and those of the entire world (if I am able).

How many complaints, in less than three days! You should have seen how much work! I was afraid to even be alone.

If you allow it, could I let Father Germano know he should come get me?

Wednesday, August 6, around 9 A.M.

✳

Dear Jesus, paradise of charity, wonder of love! I am confused by so many graces, oh Lord, and if you do not help me I shall become ever more ignorant; in the abundance of so many favors I shall become yet worse and worse . . .

What would I like? I would like, oh Lord, you to assist me . . . yes, I would not want to come in such poor condition to receive you. Make me worthy of you, at least a little more deserving . . .

By what means, oh Jesus? . . . With the infinite merit of your most precious blood.

Tell me, oh Jesus, do you find pleasure in being with me? I truly find everything in this. The more I think of you the more I realize that you are sweet and lovable.

Well, beloved Jesus, what do you demand of me, what do you demand? . . .

I love you because you are my benefactor, my creator, my guardian . . . You consume my soul and make it divine. And because you are the bridegroom of my soul . . . I always seek you, seek your affection, your friendship, your glory . . . If you help me, I will never fail, because . . .

Wednesday, August 6, around 11 A.M.

✳

Did you see this morning, oh Jesus? After I received you I began to think about the great battles I won over the devil, with your help. I counted so many! . . . Is it possible, oh Lord, to win such fierce battles without your divine help? Who knows how many times, had you not helped me, my faith would have been shaken! If you had not helped me, my hope and my charity . . . My intellect would have been obscured, if you, eternal sun . . . My love, oh Jesus, how many times it would have been weakened if you had not come to strengthen it with your caresses! And in willpower, which above all is necessary, how many times there was laziness! But you inflamed it with your fire. I admit it: it was all the work of your love, all victories of your infinite love. Now, oh Lord, should I not be grateful?

Do you not see that I can do nothing? You should at least be satisfied that I dedicate myself to you with all my senses, both internal and external . . .

One other very pleasing thing I promise you, oh Jesus: in the morning when I have stuffed myself on holy communion . . .

For sure, the power of your love can do a lot, it can do everything! . . .

Oh, I've told you so many times! I know you would be offended if I preferred my will to yours.

What do you want me to ask, when I see that you give me more than I ask, that you give me more than I request? . . . Always, always I see you interested in me.

Nothing, nothing, oh Lord, of what you do not want. I started this morning . . . I shall strive to serve you more faithfully, generous Jesus!

Thursday, August 7, around 9 A.M.

✳

I would like to have in this instant, oh Eternal Father, the heart of all the angels, the heart of all the saints, of all the elect, even of my celestial Mother; indeed, I would like that of your son, to offer them all in your glory and honor. ′

Beloved Jesus . . . Let's pretend, oh Lord, that you are me and I am Jesus . . .

What do you mean, what would I do? I would stop being me, so that you could be, oh God.

Why, oh Lord do you light up all of myself with your divine fire, with the fire of your love? I would like to inflame all the creatures of the earth . . .

Oh yes, I could do it! . . . You see, my Jesus, I have such great confidence in you that even if I saw the gates of Hell open and found myself at the edge of the abyss, I would not despair. And even if I saw Heaven and Hell against me, still I would not mistrust your mercy, because I would put my faith in you. You are so compassionate, so merciful! . . .

I have offended you, I have offended you greatly . . . You say it is a cruelty to offend any creature; oh, what cruelty must mine be, that has offended a God . . . a creator . . . . a celestial goodness! . . . You granted me so many graces, so many favors; you saved me in a marvelous way, and yet my heart does not melt! . . . How can you, my heart, see the only son of the Eternal Father on the cross and not die? . . .

Thursday, August 7, around 11 A.M.

✳

Oh Jesus, Jesus! Is it you again? . . .

Yes, I want you at every hour, at every moment. Yes! . . . My soul, be firm in your resolves. My soul, do you see Jesus? . . .

I am yours, I am yours, Jesus . . .

But by so much graciousness, by so much love, what power would not be conquered, what willfulness not swept away?

Oh Jesus, you would have reason to complain about me, yes, because I offended you . . . Worthless that I am, I should return to the altar so many stolen hosts, so much blood . . . But I promise to amend; as long as you continue the flow of your favors . . . Why are you raising me to Heaven from the slime where I am? . . .

Rather than let me lack faith and love for you, make me die . . . Better to live in suffering than to live as a sinner . . .

What do you want? What do you want, oh Jesus? . . . That my love should be inalterable? I shall nourish it every day with your body and your blood; and after I am stuffed with your blood . . .

Friday, August 8, around 9 A.M.

✳

When, oh Lord, will I give in completely to your sweet calls? . . . When will I completely? . . .

And what do you get out of my ingratitude? . . . Maybe I am united with you in body, but in heart? . . . No, no, my heart is yours. You see, oh Jesus: you are a strong king, generous, who wages battles and then always wants victories. Allow me the grace to surrender to all your calls, to love you with the tenderness of affection.

My beloved Jesus . . . how poor you have become! . . . Why do you need me so much? . . . And even if you were poor for real, how could I assist you? . . . Here it is, oh Lord, my body which is a fistful of dust, and my soul, which instead my Lord makes great . . . Oh my soul! . . .

My Jesus! . . . With what love, oh Jesus, can I reciprocate? . . . Come on, Jesus, let's leave! . . . Let's go, let's go . . . to your Heaven!

Ah! . . . but no, no departure yet, Jesus, no; because I am afraid, I fear . . . Did you not say, oh Lord, that Heaven is for those who live in the world but have no worldly concerns? . . . Did you not say that Heaven is for the innocents? . . . And me? . . .

With me, what will you do? . . . What will you do with me, oh Lord? . . . Perhaps, oh Lord, you alone know why you keep me on earth . . . Why do you not deign to tell someone? . . .

Saturday, August 9, 9 A.M.

✳

To what I said and promised this morning in holy communion, you must contribute, so that with your precious blood I could be purified . . .

Yes . . . you will do it . . . yes! . . . I realized you wanted that prayer and I took your earnest solicitude upon myself, to your advantage . . . And because my need is extreme, oh Lord, and the moment is right, I pray you to come right away, beloved Jesus. Help me to quicken this desire . . . Give me a hand in this task. And when you have made me pure and clean, then yes, I will do everything; I will say my own prayer, and at every hour, at every moment . . .

I would not want my pupils to be further blinded by the radiance of this most august sacrament . . . You always give yourself to me and I become worse and worse. This thought so gets me down! . . .

But then, aren't you coming in the sacrament? . . . In it is a force that purifies, a virtue that destroys all sins. Oh yes, come, come, sacramental Jesus . . .

Saturday, August 9, around 10 A.M.

✳

Beloved Jesus! . . . When I see the good souls come, oh Lord, to enjoy the delights of your Heaven in communion, I feel compassion; but when you accept bad souls like me, then . . .

Oh Lord, you come to me entirely as love and I come to you as a sinner, one so lazy. Oh Lord, let me say it . . . perhaps in giving me things you debase them too much . . . or else you want a total change in my life . . . What shall I do to be pleasing to you? Do you want me, oh Lord, to change your crown of thorns into a crown of lilies? . . .

To whom should I turn? . . . To all your saints? . . . But if I pay you with the merits of others, my debt always remains open . . . I always remain aware of the many favors you grant me . . . I am a sinner . . . a soul provided for only by you! . . .

Stop with your gifts; if not, give me the grace to take pleasure in all of them. Hear me, oh Lord; if not, put a limit on your generosity . . .

Saturday, August 9, 11:30 A.M.

✳

. . . In the sacramental word, open up to me . . .

Rather than remain deprived of the bread of life . . . A passionate lover, oh Lord, does not need so much pleading: at the first request, he understands immediately . . .

Sunday, August 10, the Feast of Saint Lawrence, around 9 A.M.

✳

I understood your graciousness, my creator. Nothing is left for me but to humiliate my soul before your majesty, which I intend to do right now.

My dear Jesus, what confusion this morning! . . . You wanted me to turn my mind toward Saint Lawrence, oh Lord, but what did you do? . . . To one of your most beloved followers, always in the midst of sufferings, and I with my ungrateful heart . . . I am confused, what with thinking about him in the midst of pain and me with the host enjoying all the sweetness of Heaven. Oh heart of my Jesus, heart too sweet! If you wish to give me a similar part, always in the midst of pain, oh Lord, go right ahead; if then you want me to enjoy greater rewards, go right ahead: just be sure that I always come to you with fear of offending you.

I put together two souls: that of a saint and that of a sinner . . . What else but confusion could I find this way? I wanted by means of this same saint to offer myself, because if I did not, I believed I would be negligent in my duty; I am afraid, I am afraid because before you I know my soul to be guilty toward you. I want you to see my soul as beautiful, as your hands gave it to me. Impossible! . . . I no longer can! . . . Look, my soul is all bound with chains, and when you gave it to me, it was bound with roses. When you gave it to me, it was resplendent like the sun, and now? See how it is totally deformed! . . . Oh dear! . . . It deserves . . .

What were you saying about me? . . .

Dear Jesus, dear Jesus! . . . Is it you who speaks to me this way? . . . Is it you? . . .

Repeat it to me . . . let me hear it more clearly . . .

Say it to me again . . . anew . . . anew . . . once more . . .

May you be blessed! . . .

And this morning you found in me . . .

Sunday, August 10, around 10 A.M.

✳

. . . My Jesus! . . . Yes, my Jesus . . . my affectionate Lord! . . . Jesus who keeps me bound with such force of love . . . Jesus who loves me, who feels only compassion for my wretchedness . . . He is the true Jesus . . . You see, my God: if you gave so many graces, so many gifts, so many favors to a soul who could compensate you with a good store of virtues, your good offices would be well compensated, but if you give them the way you give them to me, only in the name of your mercy . . .

No, there's no harm in it, oh Lord: what you do is well done . . . But at least give me the grace to be able to please you . . .

But I love you too . . . I do not love you only for your gifts, you know! I love you because you are my Jesus . . . I love you because you are the only one worthy to be loved by me . . . I love you because you are good . . . I love you because you promised, you swore, not to abandon me . . . I love you for all purposes, oh Lord . . .

Monday, August 11, around 9 A.M.

✳

Oh love, oh infinite love! . . . Strip me of this flesh; either tear me out of this body or stop, because I cannot go on . . . My body, oh Lord, can no longer stand being continually consumed, so, either remove me from this earth or stop . . .

Oh love, oh infinite love! . . . Of your love I shall never, never be dispossessed! . . . Oh love! . . . Oh pleasure of love! . . . Oh love that so delights me . . . that never torments me! . . . Oh love, your love, oh Jesus . . . I shall never share you with anyone! . . . This bit of love I possess, I shall not share even with the saints in Heaven, nor with earthly creatures. To you, saints in Heaven, to you, earthly creatures, all the virtues; but this bit of love is mine. I want no one ahead of me in the love of Jesus.

Oh love, oh infinite love! . . . See: your love, oh Lord, your love penetrates even to my body, with too much fury. When, when will I unite with you, oh Lord, who with such forceful love keep me in union here on earth? . . . Do it, do it! . . . Let me die, and die of love! . . . What a beautiful death, oh Lord, to die a victim of love . . . a victim for you!

Calm down, calm down oh Jesus; if not, your love will end up burning me to ashes! . . . Oh love, oh infinite love! . . . Oh love of my Jesus! . . . Let your love penetrate my all; from you I want nothing else. My God, my God, I love you. Perhaps I love you too little, oh Jesus? . . . Are you not happy? . . .

But this needs to come from you, if you want me to love you more. Indeed, I should love you with a unique love.

Oh! I have told you so many times, oh Lord: if my life does not end in seeing the suffering of someone who loves me so much, what other pain do you think could bring about my death? . . .

I told you it's enough, oh Lord, what you have suffered for me and for sinners. Yes, enough! . . . My shoulders shall replace yours in bearing the cross! . . .

Tuesday, August 12, 9 A.M.

✳

Let us adore and pray to Jesus . . . We adore God: immense, immortal, infinite. We adore the infinite majesty of our God. Praise to you, oh Father, who saved us; to you, son, who redeemed us; to you, oh Holy Spirit, who sanctified us . . .

And what grace do you wish me to ask of my Jesus, beyond the one he freely gives me and that is so beneficial to me? . . . the increase of his holy love . . . Oh love, oh infinite love of my Jesus! . . .

If you have been sent by God, let me embrace you; if you have been sent by the devil, come close so I can spit in your face . . .

Jesus sent you? . . .[20] *And what did I do to deserve so much?*

Yes, I see Jesus who loves me and seems in love with me, but I don't know either the purpose or the cause of this. I feel he has taken my heart; I feel he has adorned it with his precious blood, but I don't know the purpose of this, either . . .

He is the Lord, the boss . . . let him do everything.

But how can I? . . .

No, I do not want . . . I do not want to prefer my will to that of Jesus.

Yes, I truly wish to be obedient, but if Jesus wished otherwise? . . .

Yes, about keeping down and tolerating a little food, just a little.

I cannot, because my stomach does not wish it.

No, don't touch me, because my Dad wants no one to touch me . . .

But you have the appearance of a man! . . . No, I do not want you to touch me! Say just one word and I will believe you.

Will you conform to what Jesus wants? . . .

Be blessed, my Jesus, infinite love, however you behave. I will never be dispossessed of your love; I will never give in to anyone. Oh love, oh infinite love! . . .

Angel . . . angel! . . . My Jesus loves me, right? . . .

I too love him . . . Tell him I thank him for what he does for me . . .

I see you . . . I see you . . . Don't leave me! . . . If you love me, do not leave me . . . do not leave me . . . do not leave me! . . .

Goodbye, goodbye, yes! Until Heaven! . . .

Friday, August 15, around 9 A.M.

*

. . . Do I receive communion well, or do I steal your hosts from so many other souls? . . . Perhaps I receive communion badly, so I do not cry, I am not confounded and I don't even think about it? . . . Lift this weight from me, reassure me about how I receive communion . . . reassure me . . .

To whom should I turn? . . . Do you not see to what a deplorable state I am reduced? . . . My hope is too weak . . . Do you not see, oh Lord? And after having been favored by you with so many of your gifts . . .

Dear angel, watch over me . . . By this time you have already returned to Heaven . . . Use your influential words on Jesus, come often to my aid, you . . .

Friday, August 15, around 10 A.M.

✳

Oh God, purify me, purify me with your charity . . . inflame me with the fire of your ardor . . . I . . . I love you, I adore you, I kneel before you, I submit to you.

But is it possible that all creatures, all souls do not love you after they have received you even just once? . . . Is it possible they do not love you when they have seen you there, where you reside? . . .

Oh my soul, oh my soul . . . you say so much, it is true, but reflect a bit on yourself; frequency of communion . . . union with the angelic bread, has not conferred on your inner self what it has conferred on so many other souls . . . You receive communion, it is true, but where are the fruits? Maybe you do not know why, but I feel this is what your Jesus is telling you, Jesus who is with you right now . . . You approach him with too little merit . . . too little perseverance . . . And then when you do approach Jesus, how do you approach him? . . . You take communion, it is true, with his person, but with an inclination toward sin . . . Do you not see that every morning he shows you his open veins so that you might touch the rivers of beatitude? And you instead? . . . He approaches you with his lips . . . and you with your filthy ones . . .

I thank you, oh Lord, that this morning you gave me light to know my iniquities. I promise to renounce everything that is not your wish, and all those works not centered on your heart and not aimed toward your divine will.

Monday, August 18, around 9 A.M.

✳

Oh God . . . my God! . . . Do not be offended if in the morning I come as I am. You see, my soul is full of sins, better yet, it is a dwelling filled with every kind of beast. And you, a lily of purity, a fountain of beauty, how can you live in such confusion? . . . You nourish and sustain me, and me, what nourishment do I give you? . . . You graze among the lilies but in my heart there are not these flowers . . . And what do you find? . . . Tell me . . . Thorns! . . . Still, oh Lord, in my soul there is no purer part than . . . The enemy, you see, the devil, deprived me of everything. So what seat can I give you, oh Lord, in my heart? . . . Your bed is of ebony, your columns of gold, your steps are covered in purple; but in my heart these colors do not exist.

I am afraid, I am afraid! In this condition I throw myself too much, too much, into the arms of my celestial bridegroom . . . I know too well my unworthiness but I also know your mercy . . .

What food shall I give you today, oh Lord? . . . Ask me . . . ask me, and then come back! . . .

Monday, August 18, around 10 A.M.

✳

Jesus . . . give me a little strength . . . Dear Jesus! . . .

Is it better to receive you than to see you? Truly it is better . . . yes, yes! . . .

I am afflicted, oh Lord, because I think . . . that even if for years and years like the angels I should prepare myself, still I would never be worthy to receive you . . . And then, you see it, how ill-disposed I come! . . .

So tell me: what is the bed . . . where you sleep so well in my heart?

But is there such peace in my heart? Is there this tranquility in my soul? . . .

No, I do not wish reassurance, I want to live in your holy fear.

Something else afflicts me . . . Do you remember, oh Lord? There was a time when I had completely forgotten your infinite beauty and I preferred the dust of the earth.

Oh Jesus, answer my questions . . . It is sweet to confess my wretchedness before you. You know it better than I; you know well that I indulged my eyes in everything and for whatever reason, and that I never deprived my heart of anything . . . Help me, oh Lord! . . . Let me throw myself at your feet again! . . . I still love faith, and I repeat a thousand times and will repeat forever: better to receive you than to see you . . . But tell me, oh Lord, with what food should I nourish you? . . . Communicate your clear light to me, communicate your divine ardor . . . Oh my God, how can I reciprocate? With the strength of love? . . . It would be necessary to love you with faithful love, with real love . . .

Do you remember, oh Lord, that time when you told me my heart was a muddle of affections, which did not please you? . . .

I find myself more timid in the matters of my affections. Oh my Jesus, oh my Jesus! . . . How much you would be worthy to be loved! . . . The angels are right never to be satiated in singing that beautiful hymn to you! . . . That is what I should do, and what all earthly creatures should do; instead . . .

I shall love you, I shall love you always: when day breaks, when evening turns into night, at every hour, at every moment; I shall love you always, always, always.

Friday, August 29, Letter to Father Germano

✳

My dear Dad,

Do not be angry at me; as soon as I read your letter and realized that my inability to write derived from Chiappino,[21] I got up and instantly seized a pen. I believe it really did come from him but believe me, and I say this with

Jesus truly in my heart, I no longer have those thoughts about you. I feel calm and peaceful, with complete faith in you; the only reason I did not write, dear Dad is because I am so weak that if I put my head down, when I raise it up I feel faint, but I will make an effort. Oh my God! . . . Oh my Dad! . . .

I was at Controne and up there Jesus did not fail to have my good angel pay me a little visit; I was so consoled. After making all my protestations, I started talking with him. My dear Dad, Jesus continues to let me taste such sweetness in prayer. Yes, if Jesus is sweetness, he spreads it all out in the holy sacrament.

But how can it be that such a great majesty tolerates being with such a vile creature? How is this? Maybe he does not see the ingratitude of my soul? Does he not see my heart without devotion? And yet, nevertheless, Jesus puts up with me, loves me; and if Jesus loves me, poor as I am, how shall I not love him, rich and strong? Dad, help me! . . .

Listen to this strange thing . . . Monsignor had allowed me to confess myself with Father Paolo, the apostolic preacher.[22] I confessed thoroughly and he advised me among other things to pray for sinners, which I promised to do. Without thinking further about it, an hour or two after confession, the devil (whom I recognized clearly) said to me: "As long as you are acting on your own behalf, do as you wish, but don't you dare do anything for sinners because you will pay for it!" My dear Dad, advise me on this. Help me, because only God knows the number of sins I have committed and still commit; how much my nature resents every word! how imperfect I am in bearing with this little illness that God sends me! how many times I give people the opportunity to gossip about me and how I cause such disquiet in this household! And yet merciful Jesus caresses me and loves me: why?

It has been thirteen days now that my stomach retains only a little broth; before that it also retained a little milk, but not anymore.

I beg you, Dad, on my knees, to think about making an absolute command to my good Mom not to force me to eat. Listen: at Controne she ordered me to eat; I ate and then in throwing up I also spit up clots of blood and you could see that it was too much effort; blood even came from my nose.

Think about making this command once and for all, begging her never to forget it. I pray continuously to good Jesus to make me well, but how can I do this when Jesus permits these things? Let's hope for the best.

Tell Mother Giuseppa to pray for my soul and soon I will send her a little letter for the feast of the Blessed Virgin. Giulia, dear Dad, is dead; pray so, so much for her.[23] Jesus is strength, he is courage, and he did not fail to give me some. Long live Jesus!

Bless me strongly, very strongly, dear Dad. I will be good, help me. Your poor

Gemma

Saturday, August 30, Letter to Father Germano

✳

My good Dad,

Jesus still has not let you know about the ingratitude of my soul? Oh dear Dad, help me, do not leave me; I will be sincere, obedient, and not with-hold anything.

I would be quite calm, but receiving communion makes me a little afraid; I fear doing it wrong, not preparing properly (even though to this I usually devote most of the night); while I give thanks afterward Jesus holds me to himself; but I do things without rhyme or reason, so Jesus cannot be pleased, no way; so what should I do? I await from you, my dear Dad, a help-ing hand, some counsel. The devil makes great efforts to deprive me of this good; you can imagine, not a night passes that I do not dream of drinking or eating, and it seems so real to me that after, if I did not make sure I was in bed and what I dreamt could not have happened, I would go who knows where rather than to communion; nevertheless, I am not agitated. The monsignor assures me that in dreaming one commits no sin, so I go forward as Jesus likes, but I feel very badly about this, believe me, my dear Dad.

So much up to today, August 30.

Today, September 3, I take up the pen again; I have a fever, since yester-day after dinner. Long live Jesus!

I have to communicate something to you, Dad. For about eight days I have been feeling a mysterious fire where my heart is, I do not understand. The first few days I made nothing of it because it gave me little if any trouble but today is the third day that this fire is growing rapidly, almost to the point that I cannot bear it; I would need some ice to extinguish it; it is very an-noying, prevents me from sleeping, eating, etc. etc. It's a mysterious fire, Dad, that extends to the outside of me as well, and on the skin it leaves a burn mark; it is a fire that does not torment me, you know, it gives me plea-sure, but it destroys me, it consumes me. Jesus will make you understand everything tomorrow morning, indeed, he will already have made you understand everything. Great God, I love you! I want to love you so much!

Dear Dad, in this condition how can I remedy things with the monsignor? I am fully ready to reveal everything to him and to undergo a medical visit, to do everything he wants. I await an indication about what to do from my good Dad.

I'll stop, because with my fever I cannot go on. Jesus and my good angel will tell all.

Bless me with your strength and your heart. Goodbye, my dear Dad, your poor

Gemma[24]

[P.S.] Pray for my soul, in danger of falling. Oh God, I will do anything, do not permit it.

Sunday, August 31, Letter to Mother Maria Giuseppa

✳

Reverend Mother,

Long live Jesus! Long live merciful Jesus! For how long, dear Mother, Jesus has nourished me with his holy sacrament alone! For how long he has guided my life with such affection! And for how long he has placed persons in his stead to help me, bear with me, love me.

Poor Jesus! How does he put up with and suffer such thanklessness and ingratitude from me? Jesus, Jesus who cannot bear the smallest fault in his souls, how does he put up with me, who affronts him every hour, every moment? Often I hear him cry, I feel him afflicted, and he tells me he does this for sinners. But, my God, do not cry for sinners; cry, cry for me . . . No, no, Jesus, do not cry for me either; I will cry, I will make amends, I will become good, obedient. There are so many souls who pray for me; you will see, they will succeed in changing me; save my soul.

Finally this soul, so proud in seeing Jesus so humble, will be ashamed, ashamed even to raise its head. Why such difficulty in yielding to obedience, remembering the admirable obedience of Jesus? Dear Mother, pray for me, for I need it badly; continue as you are doing, as I feel almost continuously your prayers directed to God on my behalf; indeed, increase them because the need increases, and I fear . . . I fear for my soul. Tell me, dear Mother: the continual frequency of holy communion, the repeated banquets at the celestial table, the food of the angels—why do these things not do my soul as much good as they do so abundantly in so many souls? . . . I fear, I fear receiving communion badly, and who knows how many times I would have abandoned it had Jesus' repeated invitations not made me know clearly that it was truly he who called me.

Do I perhaps receive communion well? Then why do I see no fruit? Do I perhaps receive communion badly? Oh God . . . make me die rather than receiving communion badly and living in sacrilege, no, no . . . Dear Mother, pray for me, for this, for all of me. If good Jesus granted us the grace of being together, how I would consider myself fortunate! How I want to listen to your counsels! How I want to make you happy. How I want never to make you cry, as I have made my poor Dad cry so many times . . . but he already has forgiven me. Poor Dad! A few days ago I feared that the enemy once more would torment me with his dirty tricks . . . unfortunately, it must be true that my inability to write derived from him; nevertheless my thoughts were free from his influence. As soon as I got Father Germano's letter, where he warned me, I got up and took a pen and in fifteen minutes I did everything. And I could not wait until my Dad would receive that letter, containing little sense it is true, but at least reassuring him that the devil was not tormenting me by undermining my faith in him. Long live Jesus! Dear Mother, we want to belong entirely to Jesus alone, to that good Father, to that loving Lord, to that generous benefactor, to that sweet consoler, to that passionate lover . . . to Jesus, that's it.

It would be a great charity if you would commend to God the soul of one of my little sisters. She was an angel, you know, but still I feel I should ask for prayers for her. She is happy, Jesus has taken her! One more prayer, dear Mother, that Jesus give me the grace to be, at least in this family, a good example and not a scandal. If in the past I was a scandal, and I caused damage with my bad example, let this be the moment to terminate my scandals, the holy beginning of edification, of an exemplary and virtuous life, where in the past I was a bad example.

Now, dear Mother, let us leave each other, but to find ourselves in a little while with Jesus. I pray for your blessing, for your prayers, and never forget poor

Gemma

August, exact day unknown

✳

At the pretend Academy of Heaven, one must learn only to love. The school is at supper, the teacher is Jesus, the doctrines to learn are his flesh and his blood.

I realize that to me you have given riches neither transitory nor fragile; instead, I have been given true riches, that is the nourishment of the eucharistic word. What would I become if I did not dedicate all my affection to the sacred host? The spirit of the word, who reigns in the fertile breast of the parent uncreated, will depart and come to let me taste his affections.

Oh yes, Lord, I realize that to make me worthy of Heaven in the other world, you give me communion here on earth.

Toward the end of August

✳

Love of my love, Jesus, my delight, my comfort! Sometimes, Jesus, your severity frightens me, but I am consoled by your pleasing ways. You will always be my father and I will always be your faithful daughter and, if you like, I will be your lover . . .

Make me a little place in your ciborium, my solitude, my repose. Most Holy Trinity, so as not to be so ungrateful to my Jesus, I offer you my intellect, may the Holy Spirit enrich me with virtue and grace. I am at fault for not falling in love with you, oh Jesus . . . What a beautiful love yours is, Jesus! Let it never be offended . . . Do not allow, Jesus, that with my ingratitude your infinite wisdom should be discredited. Oh stop, stop with all these gifts. Jesus, listen to me, as well . . .

What shall I do, Jesus, to hide my heart from your fire? Come, Jesus, I open my breast, put in your divine fire. You are flame, Jesus, and you would like my heart to transform itself into flame.

But why does my spirit not make every effort to be pleasing to you? Why does my pride not wish to lower itself before the greatness of so many favors? . . . Lovable Jesus, my solitude, my sleep, my repose! Give me a small place, Jesus, in some tiny niche of your ciborium.

PART TWO

Our Readings: Gemma Galgani's Afterlife

CHAPTER FIVE / *Rudolph M. Bell*

Canonization

A force beyond the historian's gaze—she called Him God—infused Gemma Galgani with deep piety from her earliest days on earth, but after her death it was men of the world who would make her Saint Gemma. Their successful effort to construct, model, and elaborate her reputation for sanctity is the subject of this essay. The endeavor began during her lifetime, not openly or brazenly to be sure, but nonetheless with utmost attention to the details. Making a saint is men's work—necessarily so—since male celibate clerics control all possible outcomes and take it upon themselves to know God's will. Women may have voice as witnesses who observed the holy candidate in life, especially if she lived in a convent, or they may be the recipients of her post-mortem favors, but in accordance with male-made rules, they are denied the right to interpret, understand, or explain the significance of what they have seen and felt. All writings and recorded utterances by the holy woman are subject to painstakingly careful theological examination by male prelates, less for the wisdom or inspiration they may contain than for signs of embarrassing lapses into error or even heresy. The deeds of her entire life span—innocent premonitions at her birth, seemingly trivial pranks in childhood, missteps and doubts of adolescence, and finally mature acts of fully considered self-abnegation, charity, and compassion—also receive detailed scrutiny.

After the pious woman's death, a cult must arise spontaneously among the faithful, comprising people who believe she is with God and who pray for her supernatural help on their behalf. At the time of Gemma's recognition as a blessed, at least two miraculous intercessions were required to bear witness to her place in Heaven, and two more had to follow before canonization as a saint became possible. The requirement of miraculous intercession subsequently was cut to one for each step, but the type of miracle reported remains constant: recovery from illnesses declared by secular physicians to be incurable, documented to have occurred following prayer to the putative saint, either directly by the ill persons or on their behalf by others.

While celestial graces reported during the putative saint's lifetime—such as the wounds of stigmata Gemma Galgani received—may have fired popular imaginations since they first appeared in Saint Francis nearly eight centuries ago, they are not relevant except as they may provide an occasion for heroic suffering, whether from the physical pain or from humiliation by doubters. Miracles performed by the holy person during her lifetime, central though they have been in the popular mind from the earliest Christian saints to those of our own time, also carry no weight in the official judgment.[1]

Even this quick survey of criteria for canonization suggests that the case of Gemma Galgani was by no means an easy one. Seen in a negative light, her story, much of it told by herself, reveals an emotionally immature, orphaned girl, sickly and in need of affection. In her early twenties, possibly as a way of attracting attention to her plight, she may have inflicted skin-puncture wounds on her hands, feet, side, and forehead. At that point her local confessor, who also happened to be an auxiliary bishop, lost what little faith he had in her when his friend, Dr. Pietro Pfanner, washed the blood from her wounds, spied a telltale needle on the floor, and authoritatively diagnosed the girl as hysterical.

Monsignor Volpi preferred scientific truths. As the informative proceedings for Gemma's canonization opened at Lucca in 1907, he felt obliged to warn promoters of her cause, including his friend Professor Giuseppe Ferrari, the metropolitan canon of theology, in no uncertain terms: "Watch out, because she was a silly little thing, indeed, a half-wit."[2] An understandable coldness to any project proposed by Father Germano may have been behind this disparagement, along with a certain degree of hostility toward the Passionists in general, who were, after all, outsiders to Lucca. But there is as well the revealing coincidence that the order's other saint-to-be, Brother Gabriel, also a cause championed by Father Germano, had been derided as "that stupid one, a little short on brains."[3] Childish innocence as an antidote to the excesses of modern rationality emerges as one, but only one, important subtext in the making of both these saints.

Gemma's supporters were hardly much better, maybe worse. Letting his pride get the best of him, none other than Father Germano, unquestionably the key man in the case, alienated several high prelates with his boastful remark that "he could bring even Garibaldi to the honors of the altar." [4] Little wonder, then, that in life, whenever her "head took off," Gemma had been ready to trust the words of her Jesus over the commands of her spiritual directors, either of them: "I would prefer to disgust my confessor than to displease Jesus." [5] But canonization was an entirely different matter, done by thoroughly mortal men, not by God.

The nuns who had known Gemma were not terribly helpful either. During her student days, the teachers at Santa Zita had declined to admit her as a "probationary." Already she was perceived as a special soul, but potentially a source of trouble, one who, if placed together with Sister Giulia Sestini (the nun who introduced Gemma to the Holy Hour), would be like piling "misery upon misery." [6] Over the next few years, one convent after another slammed its doors, for a history of physical illnesses made Gemma a likely burden and her emotional state threatened to prove yet more disruptive. And after death, at the Lucca proceedings, Salesian nun Maria Maddalena Zoli's devastatingly ingenuous testimony, duly captured in the promoter of the faith's subsequent official doubts, threatened to destroy Gemma's eternal reputation.

According to Gemma's version of her May 1899 stay at their convent, as recorded in her autobiographical confession, it was she who had found the daily routine too soft. Sister Maria Maddalena, instead, remembered rather defensively that all the nuns watched Gemma with pious curiosity as she wandered about toting her meager little bundle of earthly belongings and a mattress roll. Not content with the regimen meant for the usual course of spiritual exercises, she invited herself to the refectory, joined in recess, and attended quietly while the sisters sang prayers in the choir. But "a few days were enough to see that, although she was a good girl, she was not meant for us, because she had not been fully healed and in accord with what we had heard, *we judged her to be a hysteric.*" She kept insisting that she be admitted, and when this failed, "*in the name of Jesus she prophesied punishments on our mother superior and our community, if we did not open our doors to her. These remained closed anyway, and the threatened punishments, thank God, did not arrive. The superior got tired of all these pretensions, and had her informed not to come to the parlor and not to write, because one and the other were a waste of time.* Thus did our relations with her come to an end." [7]

Also from the canonization proceedings, Giustina Giannini's testimony reveals that when her two elder daughters, Annetta and Eufemia, accompanied by her sister-in-law Cecilia, went for spiritual exercises to the Passionist convent at Corneto (home to Gemma's beloved letter-writing companion,

Mother Maria Giuseppa), they had wished to take Gemma with them. It was not to be; "the Gianninis are welcome, but absolutely do not bring Gemma" was the response. Apparently the current head of the monastery, Mother Vittoria Bruschi Falgari, had strong reservations, based on reports she had received from Gemma's trusted visiting Passionist confessor, Father Gaetano, not only about Gemma's health but also about her reported spiritual phenomena. The matriarch Giustina Giannini then recalled the prescient bitterness of Gemma's reply: "They didn't want me alive, but they will take me dead."[8] Gemma's earlier written plea to Father Germano that she be admitted to his order, while more considered, had been no less plaintive:

> A while back a Passionist said that in October the Passionist nuns would open the novitiate; can I hope that the last place be for the most humble daughter of Saint Paul [the order's founder]? I shall be good, you know, I shall always obey; tell the nuns to take me to serve them; I will be the servant. I know how to do it, you know. I know how to sweep, wash dishes, draw water, and also to sew; I will be obedient to everyone in everything. Will you tell them to take me?[9]

Locked out and shunned by nuns from several orders, near and far, Gemma ended up finding refuge locally in the Giannini household, a place with fewer formal rules about admission. In retrospect, the move had been very simple. The well-to-do Cecilia Giannini found comfort in the young woman's presence, patriarch Matteo waived his approval, and everyone else happily agreed. But that haven, like all the props and supporting characters in Gemma Galgani's story, is preserved for the historical record only because an orphaned girl was made a saint.

WHILE GEMMA LIVED

As Gemma Galgani of Lucca makes way for Saint Gemma of the Catholic Church, our attention shifts more fully to Father Germano. His intervention, beginning in early 1900, was crucial. He took on a young woman who lived hundreds of miles away, had lost the confidence of her local confessor, was adrift and under assault by demonic visitations, and seemed hopelessly quagmired in spiritual darkness and even despair. By a variety of means that may seem strange or at times plainly cruel, he helped her focus and nurture her spiritual aspirations into a self-supporting, self-fulfilling religious experience. His initial commands upon meeting the penitent for the first time, on September 4, 1900, employed the timeless strategy of a teacher who meets a new pupil (or an inquisitor when he confronts a potential heretic): Gemma must respond, in writing, to seven questions aimed at revealing exactly what she saw and heard when she saw and heard Jesus, how she saw and heard him, what she said to Jesus and what he responded on each occasion when "your head took off," how she meditated on the eternal verities, how she saw the Holy Trinity in the Word, how she understood that Jesus is fullness, and finally, what about that business of the devil at San Michele. In my introduction to Gemma's diary in part 1, I quoted fully her answer to the seventh question, about the devil who wore Monsignor Volpi's miter. As to her other six responses, they were models of unassuming, untutored piety, a promising and safe benchmark from which an experienced spiritual director like Father Germano might confidently proceed.[10]

But there were other formidable challenges. Like so many of the mystics she admired and emulated, Gemma wanted to die. Notwithstanding diabolic torments accusing her of being suicidal and warnings by both her confessors that her longings and her proposed deals were sacrilegious, Gemma saw death as a release from the prison of worldly existence into the paradise of unity with God. Her desire for Heaven, as she told the world in her autobiography, had begun early in her childhood, when a mysterious voice commanded that she willingly give up her Mom. And when in the summer of 1894 her beloved brother Gino lay dying, also of tuberculosis, she had donned his clothes in the hope that she might share his fate. Three years later, when she was nineteen, Gemma chose to sleep in the bed whereupon her father had just died of throat cancer. Were these merely the impetuous acts of a grief-stricken daughter, or were they signs of holiness bearing unmistakable similarities to incidents recorded in the childhoods of saints such as Benvenuta Bojanni, Catherine of Siena, Margaret Mary Alacoque, and Veronica Giuliani, signs that abound in the annals of Catholic hagiology? The male prelates would decide.

And then, what would they make of the adult Gemma's trading in death? In a letter to Father Germano dated September 15, 1900, she offered to exchange the seven years she somehow had decided were left to her life on behalf of her friend, Serafina Imperiali. Initially she had wished to give away all seven years; alternatively, Gemma proposed three for Serafina and four for herself. But only three months later a new need arose, for now Giustina Giannini was very ill and might die, leaving behind eleven helpless children. Gemma recounted how she had proposed to Monsignor Volpi during confession that she would give two years to Giustina Giannini and two to Serafina, even more if necessary, keeping only the remainder for herself.

The monsignor, once he got over his anger and stopped yelling at her, told Gemma to ask Father Germano for permission, which she did instantly. Father Germano replied instead to his confidante, Cecilia Giannini, telling her to inform Gemma that he would never answer directly to letters written in such a presumptuous tone. Furthermore, Jesus had no need to make deals with her if he wanted to grant more earthly time to one of the souls under his care, and in any event, Giustina Gianinni would get better on her own.[11]

Earlier on, when faced with a person of such perplexing religiosity, Monsignor Volpi had come to recognize his need for assistance in guiding his recalcitrant penitent, and already in the spring of 1900 he had sought to talk in person with Father Germano in Rome to discuss the case. Although the effort to meet failed, correspondence between them reveals a regular, although often strained, collaboration. In a letter dated June 3, 1900, Father Germano humbly urged Monsignor Volpi to continue as Gemma's ordinary confessor, while offering very specific reasons for his judgment that Gemma was in the grace of God, notwithstanding the diabolic torments that continuously assaulted her:

> I think that the infernal enemy works very hard to molest the poor girl in soul and body; but I hold that her spirit is excellent and that most of the phenomena which are manifested in her come from God; and I make this judgment on the basis of her ingenuous simplicity, her calm sweetness, and the absence of self-seeking in her and the presence of a profound humility. There is also something, unless I am deceived, that is the result of fantastic impressions such as girls of her type who are supernaturally influenced have.[12]

Father Germano went on to counsel in favor of exorcisms; he also advised prohibitions against keeping night vigils, using harsh penitential instruments, and immersion in contemplative thought. Order the penitent to flee from all extraordinary signs and to keep busy with manual labor, he added. Above all, warned the meek yet firm priest in a stunningly direct rebuke, keep her "away from doctors, however holy they may be, for here the medical art has nothing to find out."

"Therefore, Your Excellency, you must treasure her as a jewel," was Father Germano's closing plea. Gemma's letters and ecstasies show that even when her relationships with other clerics improved and she felt less need to offset their orders with countermands from Jesus, her interactions with Monsignor Volpi remained filled with tension and mutual distrust. Father Germano was well aware of the difficulty and continued to exert whatever influence he dared. He carefully explained to the monsignor that in ordering Gemma to desist from keeping a diary he had been "spurred by the thought of hiding Gemma from the eyes of Gemma,"[13] crafting this strategic aspersion regarding Gemma in a way meant to save face for her soon-to-be "ex" spiritual director. The command also eliminated further output of potentially embarrassing and theologically dubious writings should the young woman's piety ever merit close scrutiny, a possibility that in my judgment resided somewhere in the back of Father Germano's mind from the very moment he learned of her unusual spiritual experiences and her devotion to Christ's crucifixion, both of which made her such a splendid cause to be championed by his Passionist Order.

At other times Father Germano pushed well beyond the limits of the decorum one might expect in interactions between a subordinate and his superior. In a letter to Monsignor Volpi dated November 1, 1900, he wrote: "It seems an impertinence for me to speak. I dare only to say that as things stand at present, it seems to me that it would be better to proceed with greater ease and tranquility, avoiding, in your direction, all that could cause oppressiveness and embarrassment to the spirit of the girl."[14]

Given the monsignor's high status and many obligations, not to mention his suspicions, it is little wonder that Father Germano designated someone else, Cecilia Giannini, as his primary on-the-scene confidante in monitoring Gemma's spiritual experiences. They exchanged letters regularly, with Cecilia reporting all that she saw and Father Germano trying to assuage her anxieties and keep matters quiet. His hostility to physicians ran deep, and with Cecilia he had no need for diplomatic niceties: "Please do not repeat the mistake of calling in the doctor. What would a doctor understand? He would say, 'Hysteria, hysteria' and that is all, and a stupid laugh directed toward those who believe in the supernatural. And this ridicule Catholic doctors know how to make even better that the unbelievers and freemasons. Therefore, absolutely no doctors! Tell Monsignor this in my name."[15]

At this time, the fall of 1900, the stigmata which had first appeared fifteen months earlier still renewed themselves regularly in Gemma. She also experienced swooning, ecstasy, convulsions, and vomiting of blood, all of which made Father Germano most apprehensive about recommending her to a convent, as she so desired. He feared for the scandal that would fall upon himself for having shown interest in a hysteric; "the convent would be turned upside down, and so would the brains of the nuns."[16] They would call in medical doctors and inevitably create situations contrary to God's grand design. Both through Cecilia and in communications addressed directly to his young charge, Father Germano worked carefully over the

following months to encourage Gemma herself to seek from Jesus a cessa-
tion of these painful, even alarming manifestations, in favor of other more
interior graces. There were setbacks, as when she experienced the beatings
on her own body of Christ's flagellation, and also the time that she allowed
her guardian angel to place the crown of thorns on her head, whereupon the
signs of blood and the bruises remained for days.[17] But gradually, mental visions came to supplement and at least partially to supplant her corporeal experiences. In a letter to Father Germano dated February 9, 1901, she conveyed Jesus' intention on the following Tuesday to remove from her all
external signs, including the troubling stigmata, to be replaced with more
intense manifestations in a new phase of her spiritual growth.[18]

Aspects of this progress already are evident in her letters to Father Germano around Christmas of 1900.[19] Childish deals with Jesus to gain healthy
time for her dear ones still abound but are interspersed with different un-
derstandings. Once taught as a disciplinary measure that to see a child suffer
causes the parents equal grief ("this hurts me more than you" is a phrase as
old as child-beating itself), Gemma turned the lesson into compassion on
her part for Mary's anguish in watching Jesus from the foot of the cross, thus
encouraging an amelioration of her fixation on the most physical aspects of
Jesus' Passion. Whereas earlier her desire had been for suffering, always more
suffering, she now accepted the invitation to stay with him at Calvary as an
assurance of redemption. The pain was still there, but more in the sense of
Mary's affliction than as a direct physical re-enactment of crucifixion upon
her own body. Finding solace in roles traditionally assigned by the Church
to women came only fitfully for Gemma, but it did come eventually. In a
significant break with the closing words of all twenty-three of her ecstasies
recorded during the preceding three months, which in every instance concluded with the name of Jesus on her lips, her January 31, 1902, spiritual col-
loquy ended with this plea: "Oh Mom, Mom, why don't you stay more at
my side? . . . How much less I would fear! . . ."[20] The Virgin Mary had not
lamented God's will, and so neither would Gemma. And if she was not to
gain admission to a convent, so be it.

Monsignor Volpi showed little understanding of the change, and interrogated Gemma as follows: "How is this, first Jesus constantly says to put you
in a convent and suddenly no?" Gemma reported to Father Germano how
she tried to reason with the monsignor, parsing her words with admirable
skill and triumphantly concluding that only a Passionist convent now would
do for her, of which she knew full well there were none in his Lucca juris-

diction. In the days that followed, Monsignor Volpi continued his tests of whether Gemma was "a strong woman" or just a "baby," and in his view she failed every time, but at least she agonized less over being "always little." She also fought back, revealing to Father Germano that Monsignor Volpi had grown very suspicious, calling her deluded and full of fantasies. "He also said the devil is working hard, very hard in me; that made me cry." [21]

Sometimes Gemma literally had nowhere to turn, as even her very name became a source of contention, and for good reason she became terribly confused and even disobedient. When, upon Monsignor Volpi's order, she humbly declined to continue adding "di Gesù" to her signature, as all the members of Father Germano's Sacro Collegio did when they wrote to him, Father Germano scolded her and demanded to know when she would cease acting like such a baby, wanting this and that, even crying to get her way. Instead, she must behave like the dead people do, indifferent about whether they are stepped upon or caressed, praised or cursed, viewed well or badly. Faced with the impossibility of resolving these conflicting orders, in her next few letters Gemma tried variously: "G.G.," "Gemma, *Viva Gesù!,*" "la povera Gemma," "Gemma di Gesù solo," and "Gemma di Gesù," before finally settling, after May 1901, with only rare exceptions, on just plain "Gemma." [22]

Achievements and setbacks came in rapid alternation. At midnight mass on Christmas Eve of 1900, Gemma felt herself enter into mystical marriage with Jesus, presented personally by him, as the fruit of his Passion, to his mother Mary. [23] But a week later she wrote to Father Germano to tattle about how the monsignor had started repeating his usual story that he might die and so she should find another confessor right away, maybe Father Vallini. Gemma's diary entry of July 20, 1900, documented her deep aversion to this particular confessor, something Monsignor Volpi must have known. [24] Moreover, she was well aware of Father Germano's wish to shield her from prying questions by unknown, unpredictable clerics; even men of the cloth might inadvertently subvert his overall efforts, either by creating confusion in the present or by providing authoritative contrary testimony in the future. The known challenge of Monsignor Volpi's skepticism was easier to surmount, or at least to manage.

Whenever there were difficulties, it was always Gemma who paid the price. It was she, not Father Germano, who had to put up with being called "liar, liar just like the devil" when she revealed her inner thoughts during confession. It was she who suffered when Monsignor Volpi threatened to deny her communion, she from whom the privilege of writing might be taken, she who had to listen when he called her beloved Dad the devil's dupe, and she who felt shamed when even her adopted Giannini family gave credence to his suspicions.[25]

Nor did the prelate limit his tests and torments to the confessional. Consider, for example, Gemma's letter to Father Germano of March 1, 1901, with its opening plea: "What a bad Dad I have! He leaves me here alone and does not help me." The same paragraph reveals that Monsignor Volpi, after saying he would come in person to see how Giustina Giannini was doing, instead sent his secretary, Don Bernardino Farnocchia, who never even looked in on the family matriarch but instead went straight to Gemma's room. Finding her in ecstasy, he began examining her arms, while telling her he had seen her in his dreams. Then he spoke in Hebrew and insisted that she say she believed him to be a professor of Hebrew, Greek, and French. According to Gemma, this last affront was too much for Jesus, who whispered in her heart to tell the man he might be a teacher of these languages but he was no professor!

She then relates that Jesus became even more displeased when the secretary stopped on his way out and got Cecilia Giannini to babble all about her other spiritual experiences, planting yet more doubts and suspicions in his head and leading him to the idea of making a return visit. About her own concerns Gemma feigned indifference, but she felt obliged to let her distant Dad know how much the monsignor and his secretary had upset Jesus. Three days later Father Germano sent what for him must have been a blistering letter of castigation to Monsignor Volpi, telling him in no uncertain terms to "send NO ONE" and "speak to NO ONE" further about Gemma. "Judge things for yourself how, when, and as much as you wish, but do not make use of other intermediaries," he added. The letter went on and on with tirades against modernity, physicians, and diagnoses of hysteria, before closing with a repetition of the order (plea) to send "no priests, no seculars, no extraordinary confessors, and no PHYSICIANS." On March 7, 1901, Monsignor Volpi shot back with his own missive, expressing full confidence in his secretary and pointedly warning Father Germano that "the works of God do not fear the light of day." Not only did he offer no apology for his doubts, he reaffirmed the need for unrestricted examinations by priests and physicians before he could have confidence in the girl.[26] Privately, Father Germano must have been beside himself. He concluded a letter to Cecilia dated July 1, 1901, by asserting that: "I know what I am saying. I know that that *holy man* [Volpi] *with his little head and with the insinuations of his famous Secretary may be my ruin.*"[27]

Her mother, Aurelia

Her aunt, Elisa

Her father, Enrico

Her brother in Brazil, Ettore

Her brother the pharmacist, Guido

The Giannini Family
from left to right: back row—Eufemia, Giuseppe, Dina, Mariano;
middle row—Cecilia, Giustina, Annetta, Prisca, Martino;
front row—Guglielma, Carlo, Gabriele, Matteo, Elena, Maria

Giustina Giannini, family matriarch

*Cecilia Giannini, Gemma's second Mom,
and confidante of Father Germano*

Matteo Giannini, family patriarch

*Zeffira Pracchia, laundress in the
Giannini household*

*Palmira Valentini, working-class woman Gemma
befriended and nursed*

*Bartolomea Francioni, domestic in the
Giannini household*

Dr. Pietro Pfanner, physician who diagnosed
Gemma as "hysteric"

Dr. Lorenzo Del Prete, Galgani family physician

Sister Giulia Sestini, Gemma's favorite teacher

Mother Maria Giuseppa, with whom
Gemma corresponded frequently

Monsignor Giovanni Volpi, Gemma's primary confessor

*Father Germano, Gemma's later spiritual director
and biographer*

Gemma as a child; image used on prayer cards invoking her intercession

Gemma as a child (same image) shown with her younger sister Angelina; the photo has been cropped for the prayer card at left, although not with great care, since Angelina's hand clutching Gemma's is still visible.

Gemma at age twenty-two or so;
the most authentic photo of her as an adult

Gemma as portrayed on most prayer
cards, and on books by and about her

Gemma as portrayed on many prayer
cards, as well as on the Internet

The charred pages of Gemma's autobiography

Gemma's mantle, and around it her instruments of flagellation

Gemma's black straw hat and other objects she used in life,
now preserved for the faithful to venerate

The crowd of devotees assembled at St. Peter's Square in Rome
to witness the ceremonies for her beatification in 1933

Father Germano's fears were well founded, even if in the end he triumphed. The secretary in question, Don Farnocchia, testified at the Lucca inquiry that in his opinion the case for Gemma's sanctity was entirely a fabrication by Father Germano and his collaborators in the Giannini family, who wished to see her canonized by whatever means necessary. Then, well after Monsignor Volpi had chosen a course of silence, at the Pisa proceedings more than a decade later, Don Farnocchia unabashedly stated his belief that Father Germano's death in 1909 had been "a disposition from God *to truncate any possibility of Canonization.*" Shortly thereafter, the secretary made a partial retraction—when he became aware of Pope Pius X's public statements in support of Gemma's cause—but it was too late. Cardinal Pietro Maffi, who headed the apostolic proceedings, declared that Don Farnocchia's testimony had no credibility; it had been wavering, verbose, and incoherent—a prelude to his recent decline into insanity and imbecility. His unrelenting doubts about Gemma Galgani's sanctity, concluded the cardinal, constituted "malevolent turpitude." [28]

Strained relations among the clerics who directed Gemma persisted for many months, indeed, to her dying day. In June 1901 there was the charge by Gemma that Cecilia Giannini had intercepted her letter to Father Germano and secretly brought it to Monsignor Volpi, a matter much confused by the fact that Gemma customarily left her missives to be collected and delivered by her guardian angel, rather than entrusting them to the Italian postal system.[29] As it turns out, the charge was true; moreover, Cecilia had been acting upon the monsignor's explicit order. In response, Gemma started writing secretly to her "Dad," excusing herself for violating his command to let Mrs. Cecilia see everything first and suggesting somewhat defiantly that if he was too upset with her disobedience, he could simply refuse to read what she had written. Yet later, according to the results of an investigation by Father Germano and Mrs. Cecilia, even the devil got into the act, first writing the father a spurious letter and later sending a postcard to the provincial general, telling this high official not to get involved with Gemma's case, because the anonymous writer "already has enough light from Jesus to guide Gemma." [30]

A year later, relations between Gemma and the confessor to whom she revealed her sins virtually every morning were no better. Sometimes she felt completely unable to tell him anything, so much so that she overcame her aversion and went instead to examine her conscience with Father Vallini, as she reported in her letter to Father Germano of June 22, 1902. At other times she returned to Monsignor Volpi, only to receive scant consolation.

Even on the morning she died, reportedly a death of heroic acceptance following months of physical isolation, diabolic apparitions, and spiritual despair,[31] his doubts surfaced. Accompanied dutifully by a second priest (Don Farnocchia?) as he blessed Gemma for the last time, the monsignor was overheard by Cecilia Giannini to remark: "They say it was all fantasy, that they were not battles with the devil."[32]

It was in this difficult context that Father Germano's spiritual direction of a pious woman whispered about only in the environs of provincial Lucca continued hand-in-hand with his shaping of a putative saint. The canonization process requires a detailed investigation into the entire life of a proposed candidate, and for a person of relatively modest origins such as the orphaned Gemma, what better way to capture precious details than an autobiography? His reservations about the diary Gemma had kept at Monsignor Volpi's order the previous summer were much assuaged now that the pious young woman had become less despondent. He decided to read carefully not only her answers to his seven recently posed questions but all her writings, which he found "filled with celestial knowledge and particulars of the utmost importance," a proper basis upon which to compose, "should it ever be necessary, a most edifying biography."[33] Now he wanted more.

Reflection on her life in preparation for a confessional autobiography might enhance Gemma's appreciation of more subtle yet equally sublime expressions of Jesus' love for her, he reasoned. Furthermore, she would be writing not a theologically dangerous account of her turbulent nights but a factual record of memories from early childhood, surely a safer, more controlled terrain. Since Father Germano knew nothing of these years, the exercise also might give him a better understanding of his reserved penitent. In the first edition of his biography (but not in the second through fourth editions, in which he dropped matters he thought might cause disapproval among modern rationalists) the confident saint-maker told readers openly about how he had relied on Gemma's innocence ("sure as I was of the infantile simplicity of the good Gemma") to trap her into doing what he wished.[34]

Thus did Father Germano come to possess two substantial works that could serve well in a future canonization process: an autobiographical confession covering the period from early childhood until the fall of 1899, and a diary kept at Monsignor's Volpi's orders for the summer of 1900. Gemma's many letters also provided a spiritual record of considerable value—at least potentially—to be assembled, selected, annotated, and published in due course. Never a man to overlook the details, Father Germano determined to add yet another source to this oeuvre, one with a revered place in the mystical tradition. The ecstatic thoughts of Angela of Foligno and Catherine of Siena, along with many great mystics, Italian and otherwise, come to us, as they do for Gemma, through amanuenses. By encouraging the devout young Eufemia and her Aunt Cecilia to sneak in on Gemma when "her head took off," Father Germano believed he was doing God's work: capturing the very words of Jesus, Mary, her guardian angel, and the heavenly host. At the same time, the procedure inevitably gave him considerable authorial control in fashioning a mystical persona for Gemma. Exactly how he redacted the scraps sent to him by his two collaborators is hard to say, but the parallels between them and Gemma's conscious letters to him for the same time period suggest that Father Germano did not weave the ecstasies from whole cloth. Maybe he added a little here and maybe he dropped a lot there, but I believe the essence remained hers. It was Gemma Galgani, not merely Father Germano's fashioned Saint Gemma, who by the summer of 1902 had achieved inner peace and an assured sense of salvation.

At least some of the inspiration for these ecstasies came from Gemma's own initiative in reading selections from Saint Augustine, something she apparently did without informing her confessors and while the Giannini family members must not have been watching, since in later canonization proceedings they dismissed her as not being interested in books. But in a letter dated June 22, 1902, Gemma had asked permission to keep a volume containing Augustinian *Meditations* that Father Germano had left behind, and in another of July 9, 1902, she engaged in a lively contest with her mentor about how well she could read Latin (both letters are translated in chapter 4 above). Many decades later, the Jesuit scholar Carlos Maria Staehlin examined the evidence closely and found that an ecstasy dated May 8, 1902, already reveals unmistakable signs of coming in substantial part directly from the 41st chapter of the *Meditations* and that Augustine's influence continues to be seen at many points in ecstasies from the months that follow.[35] He suggests convincingly that Gemma had an Italian version of the *Meditations* long before she asked to keep Father Germano's Latin version. Surely her knowledge through reading contributes to the greater maturity, tranquility, even elegance in Gemma's writings for the summer of 1902 in comparison with her earlier autobiography and diary. And her autonomy in choosing books and incorporating their message as her own complicates nicely the issue of what was Gemma's and what was not in the corpus of her writings submitted for clerical review of their theological correctness.

AFTER GEMMA DIED

Forging a pious girl from Lucca into the future Saint Gemma had required a good measure of Father Germano's prodigious talent and experience. During her lifetime, his efforts as her extraordinary director and confessor had guided Gemma's spiritual quest on a classic pathway to re-living the Passion, directly after the model enacted by Saints Maria Maddalena de' Pazzi, Margaret Mary Alacoque, and Veronica Giuliani. He had kept Gemma away from potential nay-sayers and carefully introduced her to people whose religiosity he could trust. He had negotiated as gingerly as possible his pivotal participation in the awkward triangle formed by Gemma, himself, and her primary confessor. His skills as an archivist and editor also had produced a substantial body of doctrinally correct writings appropriate for canonization: an autobiography, a diary, letters, ecstasies, and prayers. And now that Gemma was dead, his work in making her a saint might proceed yet more openly and unabashedly.

During the preceding ten years, Father Germano had played a key role in preparing the cause of Brother Gabriel (Francis Possenti), whose supernatural visits Gemma so eagerly recalled in her autobiography and diary. Initially he had served as an assistant to his fellow Passionist, Father Norberto di Santa Maria (author of the earliest biography of the saint-to-be, written by March 27, 1862, within a month of his death), and then, when Father Norberto pleaded the infirmities of advanced age, he had assumed the role of an energetic colleague eager to provide detailed explanations on proper canonical procedures. Father Germano also made suggestions on how the material should be arranged, procured special quality paper on which to transcribe various documents to be placed in evidence, and bolstered Father Norberto with assurances that a little repetition in the depositions, which "after all are not a history," would do no harm. As the case proceeded over the remainder of the decade, the two clerics continued to write mutually supportive letters about particular points in the *vita* being constructed for canonization.[36] On the public front, Father Germano did much more, at a critical juncture writing a popular biography of Brother Gabriel that went through several editions, as well as editing a collection of Possenti's writings.[37] By the time Gemma died in 1903, Gabriel's cause was already well on its way to the successful conclusion it reached on May 31, 1908, when he became the only Passionist other than the order's founder to be beatified. Thus, Father Germano was fully ready and able to apply the skills he had acquired from that endeavor to bringing his beloved protégée Gemma to the highest honors of the altar.

First, he arranged for a post-mortem visit, specifically intended to find any supernatural signs, such as those long associated with miracle-working saints, and with resounding success: the autopsy revealed (to everyone except Dr. Tadini) that Gemma's corpse contained an enlarged, fresh, rubicund heart. He knew full well that such phenomena had no standing in the official process, but he also understood their enormous power in creating an aura of sanctity sure to fire popular imagination. The finding also was likely to obfuscate any debate over hysteria and self-inflicted wounds, since even the most skeptical observers would not claim that girlish neurosis might affect the decomposition of her dead body. Therefore, upon arriving at Lucca twelve days after her death, Father Germano explicitly violated Gemma's last request—"I do not want my body to be touched by anyone; let the Sisters who have assisted me dress me, and have Giuseppe Giannini and Basilio [Morelli] put me in the casket." Instead, he ordered her body exhumed, her heart excised, and her corpse re-clothed in a brown habit such as the Passionists wear, with the order's symbolic heart placed on her breast.[38]

Nor was this Father Germano's first involvement in the exhumation and re-vestiture of a holy corpse. According to Luigi Possenti, brother of saint-to-be Gabriel, it had been none other than Father Germano who had taken care of all the civil and ecclesiastical bureaucratic forms necessary to allow for the translation of Brother Gabriel's remains from the sanctuary at Isola del Gran Sasso d'Italia to another resting place. The priest had hoped to do the actual transfer of the relics in total secrecy, only to be thwarted by crowds of people from immediately surrounding towns who gathered to interfere with his plans. Notwithstanding this healthy sign of spontaneous affection for the deceased holy man, the exhumation proceeded only when it was agreed that delegates from each village might be present to see with their own eyes that all the remains were dispensed appropriately; each of them also received a handful of wonderworking dust from the tomb. As to Father Germano, among the items he extracted was a belt worn by Brother Gabriel (the same one Gemma's diary reports was so effective in warding off the devil), which he then used as a relic to restore fully to health a child who had been suffering from phthisis for four years and had been declared incurable by her physicians, a miracle duly approved for Brother Gabriel's beatification.[39]

Father Germano turned next to a more scholarly endeavor, writing the biography of Gemma Galgani, still available today in an only slightly revised form, amounting to over 400 pages, and seeing to its distribution through Passionist networks reaching around the world. The book became something of a bestseller, with 23,000 copies of five editions printed in the first two years, more than twice that number by 1913, and an estimated 160,000 by 1929. Translations into English (1913) and Spanish (1914) followed, along with an abbreviated Italian version (1911). For devotees who wanted more, a selected edition of Gemma's letters and ecstasies, published in 1909, circulated in 8,200 copies. And for those with other needs, over one million images, in the forms of postcards, bookmarks, intercession cards, and a variety of devotional paraphernalia made their way into convents and homes of the faithful.[40]

Anticipating future objections to the best of his ability, Father Germano undertook the academic research on hysteria he felt would successfully confound probable positivist critics on their own turf, thus providing a scholarly refuge for the promoter of the faith and other high prelates willing to support canonization only if no embarrassment would befall them. Thus did he labor tirelessly during the six years from Gemma's death to his own in 1909, when at the age of fifty-nine the exhausted priest suffered a cerebral hemorrhage as he worked into the night correcting page proofs for a revised edition of his biography of Gemma. At his specific request, he was buried adjacent to his spiritual daughter, a symbolic, defiant, eternal response to the forces of modernity that nearly half a century earlier, in 1870, had driven him from his native land. A contemporary scholar of Italian Catholicism, Lucetta Scaraffia, develops a tripartite typology of modern female sainthood in which the second model aptly captures Father Germano's choice for his final resting place: "symbolic saints, whose bodies were a figure of the Church's body martyred by secularization."[41] But while I agree with Scaraffia that Gemma Galgani was an anti-modern saint, one of considerable political and psychological value to her promoters, this categorization by no means adequately describes the full richness of her piety.

Even Father Germano could not do everything single-handedly, especially given the continued disbelief of Monsignor Volpi, in whose bailiwick the investigation into Gemma's sanctity necessarily took place. He needed a network of credible persons beyond himself to make the case, a process he began even while Gemma lived. Little could be expected from the Galgani family, most of whom were dead. Aunt Elisa would have to play a part, because she knew best about how Gemma's devout mother had so piously reared her special infant. She might also provide solid evidence on the family's harsh change of circumstances when her brother Enrico died of cancer during Gemma's teenage years, an appropriate background for displaying Gemma's fortitude in the face of adversity. Once the questioning got to Gemma's stigmata and other supernatural signs, however, Aunt Elisa's skepticism at the time—whatever she later came to believe—made her a problematic witness.

Supportive testimony also might be sought from Gemma's brother Guido. He had achieved some success as a pharmacist, although his peddling of magical health pills probably raised a few eyebrows. Ultimately called upon as lead witness despite his reputed secularism, he managed to say all the right things about Gemma's childhood and to skip over any doubts he may have entertained about her adolescent behavior. However, his tendency to answer the questions before they were asked compromised his testimony, suggesting there had been undue coaching of the witness. In fact, he had been reading from a prepared set of questions. Moreover, it became clear that he did not even understand the theological meaning of several of the heroic virtues, nor the difference between the material church as a temple and the holy church of the faithful. These deficiencies were resolved favorably only with a stroke of admirable clerical logic by Cardinal Maffi, who concluded the apostolic review at Pisa in 1922 by acknowledging the coaching but excusing its impropriety on the grounds that Guido had been struck with fatal cancer of the liver (from which he died within weeks of giving testimony, after a vision assuring him he would see Gemma in Heaven).[42]

Guido's wife Assunta was another matter; when Gemma had appeared at their wedding in her usual garb (old black straw hat, oversized black mantel, drab smock, no stockings, probably her hair parted zig-zag as usual, since she never looked at herself in a mirror) the new bride told her loudly "not to come again" and called her a "sciapitella" (nitwit).[43] The surviving members of the Galgani family—a long-lost brother in Brazil, a reputedly wicked sister, and an uncomprehending aunt—also could be bypassed or at best channeled into offering no testimony that would undermine the portrait of Gemma's heroic virtue so carefully crafted in Father Germano's biography.

More would be needed. The female members of the Giannini household knew a lot, but their reputation for pious excesses and irregularities could not be set aside entirely. My reading of the record suggests that Eufemia (who testified under her name in religion, Maria Gemma Maddalena di Gesù), with her training as a nun, had learned thoroughly what to say and what not to say, but Cecilia Giannini predictably turned out to be more of a problem, tending to drift into potentially heretical claims of sanctity and to cast doubts on the Magisterium that must have made male clerics wince at shades of Jansenism. The family patriarch, Matteo, ultimately proved to be a splendid witness, as did his son Giuseppe, a lawyer, but those strokes of good fortune could not have been anticipated with certainty during Gemma's years on earth.

Even presumably safe witnesses might spring unwanted surprises. Father Germano thought it best not to invite Sister Elena Guerra (beatified in 1959) to testify, despite her status as former headmistress at Santa Zita, probably because she was currently being ostracized by the other nuns for some unknown fault. Clearly he had greater confidence in Sister Giulia Sestini, although this judgment also seems problematic in retrospect. She was one of Gemma's "good teachers" at the same convent school, and had visited Gemma during her paralyzing illness and introduced her to Blessed Margaret Mary Alacoque's practice of the Holy Hour. But at the hearings, Sister Giulia somehow drifted into other matters, and recalled that Gemma had not always received a perfect "ten" on her report card because on occasion she had engaged in disputes with the nuns, and one time Sisters Gesualda Petroni and Elisa Pieri had said: "Gemma *has a derisive way about her, sardonic, an insincere smirk*—and we cannot give her a ten."

Then there was Mantellata Sister Maria Giulia di San Giuseppe, who remembered an incident when Gemma had wanted to linger at the convent to adore the sacred host, only to be called away by Cecilia Giannini, who in turn cited the need to obey Monsignor Volpi's order that they return home. The sister overheard Gemma to respond: *"Just tell him we did,"* which Mrs. Cecilia declined to accept. Then Gemma shot back, *"What's the matter? We'll confess it."* Sister Maria Giulia immediately explained to her interrogators that Gemma must have been kidding, because she had great confidence in Mrs. Cecilia. Nevertheless, in his brief raising doubts about Gemma's heroic virtue, the promoter of the faith cited each of these telltale incidents.[44]

Looking beyond Lucca, Father Germano turned primarily to trusted members of his own Passionist Order, assembling a team of experts who had supported Gemma Galgani in life and who after her death would join him in providing safe, convincing testimony documenting her sanctity. First among these was Father Pietro Paolo dell'Immacolata, who provided a detailed eyewitness account of how Gemma suffered as she wore Jesus' crown of thorns. Equally of value was his shift in emphasis away from purely physical description and onto Gemma's profound humility expressed within a life of heroic virtue, exactly what the expert judges needed to learn about. In 1909, as the Lucca proceedings were winding down, Pope Pius X elevated him to the rank of Archbishop of Camerino, a grade above Monsignor Volpi's current status, hardly a coincidence; rather, according to subsequent editors of Gemma's biography, it was a ringing affirmation of the veracity of his testimony. Another key witness was Father Andrea della Madonna del Buon Consiglio, who in his recollections emphasized Gemma's ingenuousness, with the clear implication that she was incapable of the dissimulation some suspected.

Among women, there was Mother Maria Giuseppa del Sacro Cuore, the Passionist mother superior at distant Corneto who became for Gemma, the child rejected by every convent, an inspiring yet unattainable female role model. At Father Germano's suggestion Mother Maria Giuseppa kept up a regular correspondence with Gemma beginning in January 1901, with an exchange of twenty-eight known letters between them. The two letters Gemma wrote to her in the summer of 1902 (translated in chapter 4 above) are typical of the full epistolary oeuvre, which along with Mother Maria Giuseppa's testimony, gave authoritative and detailed confirmation of Gemma's sanctity by someone with considerable expertise in how such matters are best conveyed. Because Gemma remained a layperson until her death, the approbation of her cause by this highly placed prioress counted heavily.

Several Passionists who had known Gemma in life did not testify at the canonization inquiry, Father Gaetano di Gesù Bambino and Father Ignazio di S. Teresa being the stand-outs. They were the first priests other than Monsignor Volpi with whom Gemma had confessed, in circumstances vividly recalled in her autobiography as she innocently told of her initial inability to reveal herself to Father Ignazio. It was to him, at a time when he had become consultant general of the Passionist Order, that Gemma wrote one of her many unsuccessful appeals to be admitted to a convent, any convent, replete with the damaging admissions that she was an impoverished orphan, considered by some to be hysterical, and so possessed only of great desire. Why he did not testify I have been unable to determine with certainty, but my strong suspicion is that he doubted the authenticity of Gemma's supernatural phenomena and chose to say nothing.[45] Father Gaetano's failure to appear, by contrast, is easily ascribed to the years of spiritual aridity and instability he experienced at this time, but his falling out with Gemma had already begun in the autumn of 1900.[46]

Apart from these two individuals, other Passionists must have been less than fully committed to the cause, and when Father Germano died unexpectedly on December 11, 1909, the order's next curial meeting decided "to wash their hands" of the whole matter. And in fact, it did languish for several years until Father Luigi Besi, postulator from 1914 to 1921, "definitively unblocked the process." Achieving the formal introduction of the cause in apostolic proceedings, which at the insistence of skeptical members of the Curia took place in Pisa, deemed a safe distance from Lucca, where Gemma had lived and where the preliminary hearings had been held beginning in 1907, filled Father Besi with pride: "Who would have said it!" "Truly a miracle!" is how he reported his unexpected success.[47]

Beyond the Passionists, there were Gemma's lay friends, all women. Among them, her beloved Giuseppina Imperiali (Serafina) came first. Although her death precluded direct testimony at Lucca, nine extant letters to Serafina constituted ample evidence of how Gemma's love for her friend reflected heroically virtuous charity toward a fellow human being. So also with Palmira Valentini, whose humble status seemed to enhance the veracity of her testimony about Gemma's prodigious charity, fortitude, and temperance. Responses and recollections from servants and other workers employed in the Giannini household, along with a deposition by Don Lorenzo Agrimonti (died March 29, 1906), rounded out and confirmed the picture intended by Father Germano: a short life filled with perpetual devotion, selflessness, cheerfulness, and angelic simplicity. Finally, local priests, nuns, and a few lay people added what they could about Gemma's innocent childhood.

Table 6 lists people who testified in person or by acceptance of a deposition at one or more of the hearings held to investigate the cause for Gemma Galgani's canonization: the Ordinary Proceedings at Lucca (1907–10), the Apostolic Proceedings at Pisa (1922), the special session at Gaeta (1922) to take testimony from Eufemia Giannini (in religion Sister Maria Gemma Maddalena), and at Rome (1922 and 1925), essentially on questions of her cult.

There are striking overall symmetries in the list. Although I would not judge them to be entirely planned, I believe they do reflect the careful and ultimately successful effort of Father Germano and some of his fellow Passionists (but pointedly not Father Ignazio, who may have sided with Monsignor Volpi) to make Gemma a saint. Looking first at the column labeled Sex, a quick tally finds that exactly half the sixty-two witnesses were female. Another obvious divide emerges in the column Status, where secular versus

TABLE 6. *Witnesses at Canonization Proceedings for Gemma Galgani*

Name	Sex	Status	Family	Focus of Testimony
Agnese, Maria	F	prioress	Mantellata	adult spirituality
Agrimonti, Lorenzo	M	priest	Giannini	adult spirituality
Andrea della Madonna Buon Consiglio	M	priest	Passionist	cult/healing
Andreuccetti, Roberto	M	priest	Giannini	adult spirituality
Angeli, Giuseppe	M	priest		adult spirituality
Armellini, Maria Giuseppa	F	prioress	Passionist	adult spirituality
Balsuani-Maggi, Alessandra	F	domestic		childhood
Bargellini, Olga	F			cult/healing
Bartelloni, Luigi	M	cousin	Galgani	childhood
Bartoloni, Andrea	M	priest		childhood
Bastiani, Isabella	F	teacher		childhood
Bertini, Cecilia	F	nun		childhood
Bertuccelli, Letizia	F	domestic	Galgani	childhood
Bianchini, Maria Anna	F	domestic	Giannini Mantellata	adult spirituality
Bini, Cleophes	F			cult/healing
Canterini-Bini, Filomena	F			cult/healing
Cianetti, Raffaele	M	priest		childhood
Del Prete, Lorenzo	M	physician		medical
Famiano del Sacro Cuore di Gesù	M	monk	Passionist	adult spirituality
Farnocchia, Bernardino	M	priest		adult spirituality
Figlia di Maria	F	nun	Mantellata	adult spirituality
Galgani, Elisa	F	aunt	Galgani	childhood
Galgani, Guido	M	pharmacist	Galgani	childhood
Germano [Ruoppolo], di San Stanislao	M	confessor	Passionist	adult spirituality
Ghilardi, Federico	M	priest	Giannini	childhood
Ghiselli, Maria Angela	F	nun		childhood
Giannini, Anna	F		Giannini	adult spirituality
Giannini, Cecilia	F		Giannini	adult spirituality
Giannini, Giuseppe	M	lawyer	Giannini	adult spirituality
Giannini, Giustina	F		Giannini	adult spirituality
Giannini, Maria Gemma Maddalena	F	nun	Giannnni Passionist	adult spirituality

(cont.)

TABLE 6. *(Continued)*

Name	Sex	Status	Family	Focus of Testimony
Giannini, Matteo	M		Giannini	adult spirituality
Giannoni, Nicola	M	priest	Giannini	adult spirituality
Giorgetti, Erminia	F	domestic		childhood
Giulia, Maria Giulia di San Giuseppe	F	nun	Mantellata	adult spirituality
Giustino a Sacro Corde di Gesù	M	priest	Passionist	cult/healing
Grotta, Angelo	M	official		medical
Morelli, Basilio	M	candle-maker	Giannini	adult spirituality
Natali, Tecla	F			childhood
Nerici, Ugo	M	physician		medical
Pacini, Samuel	M	priest		childhood
Pardini, Gentile	M	priest		adult spirituality
Pasquinelli, Angelo	M	priest	Giannini	adult spirituality
Peruzzo, Giovanni Battista	M	bishop	Passionist	cult/healing
Petrucci, Giuseppina	F		Giannini	adult spirituality
Petrucci, Sofia	F		Giannini	adult spirituality
Pfanner, Pietro	M	physician		medical
Pietro Paolo	M	bishop	Passionist	adult spirituality
Pracchia, Zeffra	F	domestic	Giannini	adult spirituality
Puccinelli, Carola	F		Giannini	adult spirituality
Rose, Ethel Marion	F	secretary		adult spirituality
Serafini, Isolina	F	domestic		childhood
Sestini, Giulia	F	nun		childhood
Stazzuglia, Camilla	F	nun		medical
Tadini, Giulio	M	physician		medical
Tei, Paolo	M	bishop		adult spirituality
Tiburtius a San Pietro	M	priest	Passionist	cult/healing
Tommasi, Jacopo	M	physician		medical
Tonetti, Maria Antonietta	F	nun		childhood
Valentini, Palmira	F	seamstress		childhood
Volpi, Giovanni	M	confessor		childhood
Zoli, Maria Maddalena	F	nun		childhood

religious vocations split once again at precisely thirty-one each. Further cross-tabulation reveals that eleven of the women had taken religious vows whereas twenty were laypeople, while for men the proportion is just the reverse. Among the laywomen were eight of working-class status, whereas only one man, the candle-maker Basilio Morelli, clearly belongs in this category. (Perhaps the domestic workers, meeting in Rome in the 1930s, who declared Blessed Gemma to be an exemplar of their profession, if not yet its patron saint, did not quite deserve the umbrage they received from Gemma's adopted niece, who fulminated against their "lack of truthfulness, delicacy, and tact" in so characterizing a holy relative of two pharmacists, father and son Enrico and Guido Galgani.)[48] The tabular data show no readily apparent occupation for many laywomen, and for these the circumstances suggest that they were matrons and widows from among Lucca's bourgeoisie.

In the next column, I have identified thirty persons as belonging to a family, using the term broadly as a reminder that members of a religious order are also a "family." The Giannini household, with sixteen members testifying, and the Passionist Order, with nine members, plus Sister Maria Gemma who fully deserves to be counted in each family, loom large numerically, just as these two groups in fact dominated the actual hearings, consuming far more pages and offering much weightier testimony than everyone else combined.

Two other family names—Galgani and Mantellata—also mattered. The secondary but still significant contributions of the Galganis concentrated on details of Gemma's childhood innocence. While such behavior is not required for canonization—the dissolute youth of Saint Francis of Assisi being only the most obvious example among dozens that might be cited—in a case such as Gemma's, which lacked a dramatic conversion to holiness that might transfix the public imagination, any defects would have counted heavily, nor would the licentiousness excused in boys have been allowed as easily in a girl. Furthermore, the defense against charges of hysteria would include evidence that hysterics generally come from unstable families and show signs of mental turbulence from the earliest years, making her brother Guido Galgani's testimony about Gemma's placid youth doubly significant—even if he did not understand exactly which heroic virtues were shown in what he said.

The supportive testimony of the three Mantellata Order sisters was important in a different way, as a counterweight to the actively negative reports from Sister Maria Maddalena Zoli about Gemma's rejection by the Salesians and the inadvertently ambiguous recollections of Sister Giulia

Sestini concerning Gemma's schoolwork. Mantellata prioress Maria Agnese remembered vividly, two decades after the fact, how Gemma, when the monastery's regular physician refused to certify her for admission, had pleaded: "Jesus told me that if you put me in the convent I will live until the age of 50, but if you do not put me in the convent, Jesus will take me at 25."[49] This statement might easily have been pounced upon as yet another threatening, defiant remark, but the promoter of the faith apparently decided upon a more charitable interpretation. Instead, Gemma's many refusals to take "no" for an answer were simply stripped of meaning, dismissed as tales told by prattling nuns, now offset by the conflicting memories of other prattling nuns.

Finally, the rightmost column of the table categorizes each witness's main focus of testimony. Only seven persons are assigned to the cult/healing category: four Passionists who had never known Gemma but who told of worldwide spontaneous cult activity on her behalf, and three widows who recounted thankfully Gemma's healing powers in life. The men's testimonies were brief and factual, a necessary part of the record. The women's accounts, also brief, were tangential. Although cures worked during a person's lifetime fascinate the faithful and have accompanied saints' lives for as long as there have been saints, they have no official standing for canonization. Witnesses to the two miraculous intercessions required for beatification and to the additional two necessary for canonization would also fall into the cult/healing category, but I have not included them here since they obviously were not part of the "process" leading to papal approval of Gemma's heroic virtue, the step that must precede any official veneration of the holy person.

The seven people who testified on medical matters include five physicians, with Dr. Pietro Pfanner the key witness in afterlife, just as he had been during Gemma's years on earth. Dr. Tadini, subsequently dismissed by Cardinal Maffi as a positivist, claimed that Gemma's autopsy had revealed a normal heart but he was contradicted by the other two persons whose focus of testimony I have classified as medical, Sister Camilla Stazzuglia and Mr. Angelo Grotta. Contrary to Dr. Tadini, at the autopsy they saw an enlarged, rubicund heart.

Among the other forty-eight witnesses, there is considerable balance between the twenty who told mostly or entirely of Gemma's life before she received stigmata in June 1899 (where I have drawn the distinction between "childhood" and "adult spirituality") and the twenty-eight whose testimony primarily dealt with the four years from then until Gemma's death, the period when she was an object of intense scrutiny and cautious adulation. Testimony about Gemma's childhood focused heavily on her pious mother, on whether her baptismal name of Gemma was too secular, and on how obedient she had been, even though such "obedience" before the age of rational choice is not what the official criteria mean by obedience. I have included Monsignor Volpi in this group because in his testimony he carefully avoided lengthy discussion of his skeptical opinions about Gemma's supernatural graces, and the inquiring clerics apparently knew better than to press him. Among twenty-eight witnesses to Gemma's adult spirituality—after she experienced stigmata—twenty were members of the Passionist Order, the Giannini household, or both, proof if any were needed of how tightly Father Germano had drawn Gemma's circle of acquaintances once he became her extraordinary spiritual director. The other eight included three Mantellata nuns who knew Gemma before Father Germano took over, the reliable and powerful Bishop Tei and his servant, two priests who knew nothing of consequence, and finally Monsignor Volpi's unbelieving secretary, the dangerous Don Farnocchia. His potential for damaging the case must have been great, which in my judgment helps explain the vitriolic quality of Cardinal Maffi's dismissal of his testimony as the words of an insane imbecile.

The original record, taken down during the four proceedings, amounted to nearly 3,000 folios: 1,341 at Lucca, 1,511 at Pisa, 27 at Rome, and 87 at Gaeta. Authenticated copies of these are preserved at the Passionist General Archive in Rome. The evidence then was rearranged and printed in a very limited edition for experts to study before advising the pope on whether the candidate had led a life of heroic virtue. These are the printed volumes I consulted at the Biblioteca di Spiritualità A. Levasti of the Convento San Marco in Florence and have used throughout this essay. In them the evidence is arranged according to the specific heroic virtues on which saints are measured. Following lists of witnesses for each session (with age, status, and occasionally a lively characterization of their demeanor), there is a general biographical section, and then chapters on faith, hope, charity toward God, charity to one's neighbor, prudence, justice, temperance, fortitude and patience, humility, chastity, and obedience. To close out the record, there are sections on ecstasies and stigmata, other supernatural gifts, death, cult, and miraculous intercessions. Reconfigured in this way, Gemma as a person disappears, replaced by formulaic, often repetitive phrases; whether they are read casually or with great concentration, to an ordinary person the printed words constitute an overwhelming endorsement of her goodness.

But the promoter of the faith, or the devil's advocate as he is popularly called, must see through another lens. His task is to go through everything with a magnifying glass, looking here for bits of defiance, there for signs of pride, everywhere for flaws, accentuating not the virtues but the vices, highlighting not the heroic but the craven. Sure, readers of Gemma's autobiography know that she thought herself to be bad indeed, a sinner of the first order, but such is the proper modesty of a would-be saint; the promoter of the faith in any canonization process must locate corroborating witnesses to any such evil doings. In Gemma's case, the promoter's animadversions concerning her heroic virtue were poorly supported in the testimony: a few nun's tales from a Salesian convent too lax to recognize a future saint in its midst, and the opinion of a lone priest unmasked years earlier by Jesus and Gemma as a false professor of Hebrew, and now dismissed by the presiding judge as guilty of malevolent turpitude. The promoter did his duty and raised objections, but not harshly or persuasively. Casting yet more widely for hostile testimony, even had the assembled prelates been allowed to hear from Gemma's reputedly wicked sister Angelina, such a woman's statements would not have counted for much either way. Thus did Gemma Galgani pass the test of heroic virtue. (As with all other cases, had Gemma Galgani failed, she would not have been rejected outright; rather, the cause for her sainthood would have stopped going forward, consigned instead to a pending file without call-up or purge dates. The same practice is true for failure to pass the other tests discussed below.)

The promoter also raised doubts about possible lack of spontaneity in the formation of a cult, especially since so few of Lucca's townspeople actually knew anything of Gemma during her life. Here the strenuous efforts of Father Germano to hide his protégée from the world partially backfired; the list of witnesses presented above, especially considering that Gemma was not a cloistered nun, is frankly rather unimpressive as a measure of "popularity," which for saints does matter a lot. Post-mortem testimonials from as far away as Brazil and the Philippines were fine, but they smacked of excessive promotion by members of the Passionist Order, who were caught in the rule against official veneration prior to declaration of a candidate's heroic virtue. How else but through organized channels could Gemma's fame have bypassed most of Lucca but yet made its way to Buenos Aires, San Francisco, Hunan, and Tokyo? As Canon Regular Giuseppe Angeli so cuttingly expressed the matter during the local 1907 inquiry: "I heard it said that there were persons, both secular and ecclesiastic, who criticized Father Germano for publishing the life."[50]

The sentiment, at least in some quarters, was that for the Lucca proceedings Father Germano had organized a panegyric rather than a historical inquiry. At the apostolic proceedings in Pisa, the always plain-spoken Don Farnocchia used his opportunity to have the next-to-last word by giving the following impression of Gemma's reputation for holiness: "it was all the work of Father Germano and the Giannini family, *especially with writing and propagandizing the vita.*"[51] This particular cleric's views, however, although they may appear reasonable to a secular historian, were dismissed with a vengeance by the prelates in charge. They concluded that zeal in a holy cause might be allowed if circumstances dictated and, on balance, Father Germano had been very wise in working so diligently to publish his book about Gemma just in time to coincide with the 1907 hearings. Indeed, desire to read the biography, and after 1909 a selection of the letters and ecstasies, inspired some correspondents to enroll for lessons in Italian. Even Pope Pius X, when he informally opined that he found Gemma's spirituality to be inspirational, certainly a boost to supporters of her eventual canonization, presumably referred to his reading of printed copies of her writings. So it came to pass that Gemma's cult was deemed to be truly motivated by the faithful.[52] For secular confirmation of this positive assessment by churchmen, one need look no further than the work of anthropologist William A. Christian Jr, who carefully and convincingly documents Gemma Galgani's deep impact, through the Passionist Order to be sure, on Spanish religiosity in the 1920s and 1930s.[53]

The Congregation of Rites ultimately made a similarly affirmative judgment with regard to Gemma Galgani's writings, albeit only after overcoming several reservations. The question of whether preserving and making public her autobiographical account had violated confessional secrecy admitted of no easy answer, especially given all the precedents that, if cited, would have raised doubts about improprieties in many other saints' causes approved over the centuries. Saint Veronica Giuliani had been ordered to write her autobiography five times because her excessive candor displeased her various confessors. Margaret Mary Alacoque's understanding that her writings would be kept secret also offered a threatening precedent, one better avoided since she already had been beatified. But historical digging and accuracy in this instance gave way to practicality since, in any event, the possible breach of decorum or regulation would have been the fault of her spiritual director and not the putative saint.

Once admitted into evidence, Gemma's writings to some seemed a bit simplistic, perhaps displaying excessive familiarity, especially with her guardian angel. Rather embarrassingly, it seems that in addition to letter-carrier duties that suspiciously defrauded the Italian postal system, her guardian angel reportedly brought Gemma her morning coffee, and when asked, helped her into bed and kissed her goodnight. As one may well imagine, Father Luigi Besi, who by this time (1916) had taken over the cause, had to labor mightily *(Questa benedetta Gemma mi fa lavorare assai)* in finding precedents that would allow for such unseemly behavior. But he succeeded when he located similar relations in a *vita* of Saint Francesca Romana (presumably that of her confessor, Giovanni Matteotti, since the seventeenth-century *vitae* are hopelessly embellished). Although he found this information by accident while browsing at a local bookstore, he left little else to chance, and already had assembled a formidable team of dedicated scholars, assigning Passionist nuns in two monasteries to pore over the biographies and writings of all the great mystics looking for passages that might help his cause. From the women at Lucca came the stunningly supportive account about Saint Maria Francesca delle Cinque Piaghe's guardian angel, whose intimacy with her was such that his stature reportedly increased and then diminished with hers, from their first encounter when she was only four years old in 1719 until her death many years later in 1791. With such research assistance, this problem and all others concerning the probity and correctness of Gemma's writings were favorably resolved, eased by the fact that, for the moment at least, no one was claiming her to be a potential Doctor of the Church. Careful examination revealed that her words contained no glaring theological errors, which in the end was the litmus test. Moreover, her letters had a certain beauty of expression about them that might be useful as examples of pious female devotion, and the sensuous quality of her ecstatic words had ample precedent in the works of revered female mystics. All in all, no reason here to canonize but also no need to halt the case further.[54]

Finally, there remained her stigmata, and whether the candidate for the Church's honor was instead a victim of hysteria.[55] The complex, subtle relationship between hysteria and the supernatural, as it was understood at the turn of the century (and still reverberates in our own time), is the subject of Cristina Mazzoni's book, *Saint Hysteria*. The treatment below rests on her analysis of the theoretical issues, including her in-depth study of Gemma Galgani, but highlights instead what went on in the minds of the men who made the official decisions about Gemma, at least insofar as they put their thoughts in writing.

As a purely medical condition, hysteria might exist without disqualifying a potential saint, and Gemma herself pleasingly accepted that she might be a hysteric, as many people who knew her suspected, but two issues absolutely had to be resolved in her favor: no fakery and no diabolic deception.

Supporters convincingly put the question of fakery to rest by appealing to Gemma's thoroughly documented heroic virtue, along with her simplicity. They reasoned that such an innocent, pure girl was not capable of dissimulation, as the testimony of Father Pietro Paolo, now Archbishop Camillo Moreschini, made clear.

The possibility of diabolic deception, manifested as hysteria, needed more attention. In the modern age of Sigmund Freud and scientific rationalism, cavalierly dismissing all skeptics of supernatural causation as materialistic positivists no longer would do. The works of Jean-Martin Charcot, Nestor Charbonnier, Paul Richer, and others had poisoned the popular mind, threatening to expose the Church to ridicule. Father Germano's laborious studies,[56] dutifully received years earlier for the record, were not enough to convince the high prelates assembled at Pisa. Nor were they persuaded by citations of precedents for supernatural phenomena in the lives of mystics from an earlier time, such as Catherine of Siena, Bridget of Sweden, Angela of Foligno, Caterina de' Ricci, Maria Maddalena de' Pazzi, and Rose of Lima.[57] Re-examination of old documents concerning women long revered as saints was the last thing these churchmen wanted, especially since the enemy already had sacrilegiously co-opted no less a personage than Saint Teresa of Avila. After the hearings concluded, they turned instead to Prof. Dr. Joseph Antonelli for a second opinion, one that might include illustrative references to past centuries but that would be based primarily on modern science.

The eminent theologian/scientist had devoted a lifetime to studying mystical phenomena, and he understood fully that the question about stigmata—Gemma's most exquisite and therefore most controversial sign—was not one to be answered with a simple yes or no. Stigmata may have natural origins, and these in turn may be psychological or physical, or some combination of both. Or, stigmata may be of supernatural origin, either divine or diabolic, but never both. To complicate matters, stigmata may result from a synergy of natural and supernatural origins. Technically, stigmata of entirely natural origins counted neither for nor against sanctity, but certainly in the popular mind and even among prelates, such a condition would have been inconsistent with the heroic virtue required of approved saints, especially if the bleeding somehow might be attributed to hysteria. Moving on, a conclusion that the stigmata were of diabolic origin would have meant instant disqualification, something even Gemma's fiercest opponents never suggested. In addition, such a charge, much less such a finding, would have subjected the Church to boundless derision from modern science, without offering any offsetting gains. Thus, Dr. Antonelli's analysis came to a predictable finale: Gemma's stigmata were a divine grace, although purely physical factors may also have been present. Carefully and respectfully, he addressed each doubt raised by the promoter of the faith (who also knew the rules but who was required only to raise possible objections, not to reach a conclusion), dividing his response into sixty-two numbered arguments.[58]

1. Were her ecstasies the result of hypnosis and/or somnambulism, and not in conformity with the theological norms of mystical experience? No, the *incomplete* nature of her insensibility during rapture, allowing her to speak even while she was unaware of the presence of humans in the room, reflected precisely the sort of absorption in God found in Saints Catherine of Siena, Caterina de' Ricci, and Veronica Giuliani.

2–4. Could a person be afflicted by magnetism, hypnotism, somnambulism, or hysteria and still exhibit supernatural graces not caused by these maladies? Yes.

5–8. Did Gemma exhibit any signs of the physical and moral disequilibria that always accompany nervous diseases? No.

9–25. Was Gemma a hysteric? No, virtually all victims of hysteria, whether *parva hysteria* or *magna hysteria,* are morally deficient: inconstant, duplicitous, irritable, loquacious, mendacious, and injudicious. Gemma was none of these. The causes of hysteria are bad parents, unhappy love affairs, alcoholism, uterine problems, fickle lifestyle, rational education, and bodily debility due to frequent childbirth, prolonged lactation, anemia, chlorosis, and sexual activity. Gemma experienced none of these.

26–34. Were Gemma's visions and ecstasies the result of hysteria? No, her moral states before and after all her supernatural experiences were consistent with spiritual health, not physical illness or diabolic deception. So also with the content of what she saw, heard, and felt while in rapture.

35. Was animal magnetism, as described by Francesco Guidi, involved? No, number 23 of the animadversions was wrong, and in any event a decree of April 7, 1856, had placed Guidi's book on the *Indice libror, prohibitor.*[59]

36–37. Did Gemma suffer from epilepsy, as one might suspect from the testimonies by Alessandra Balsuani-Maggi, Sister Maria Giulia di San Giuseppe, and Eufemia Giannini that she thrashed on the floor and foamed at the mouth? No, Dr. Todini's [*sic*] diagnosis of epilepsy had been wrong from the start. Like most physicians, he was a positivist and an atheist, ignorant about mystical experience.

38–40. Were Gemma's experiences a result of diabolic deception? No, the skepticism and careful guidance of both her confessors—Monsignor Volpi and Father Germano—had seen to that.

41–54. Were Gemma's stigmata caused by some sort of auto-suggestion? No, their disappearance without a trace (in the presence of secular examiners, and later at her confessor's command) made this explanation medically impossible. So also for the physical signs from re-living Jesus' flagellation and wearing the crown of thorns.

55–60. Were her other manifestations of divine origin, in particular Gemma's reported sweat and tears of blood? Probably not, since mystics may experience these phenomena in consequence of the profound affliction they feel when they contemplate their sins.

61–62. What of the case of the stigmatic Theresa Neumann and the opinion of Dr. Ooly, moderator of an international institute of metaphysics, that in principle any physical manifestation may have a human explanation? Not proven and in any event not relevant to Gemma.[60]

In the final section of his seventy-seven-page dissertation, Dr. Antonelli reached his admirably brief conclusion. Except for the sweat and tears of blood, *"every extraordinary event in Gemma Galgani is of divine origin, and conceived by God."*

But the trusted senior prelates who advised Pope Pius XI still were not convinced. The Servant of God Gemma Galgani would have to pay a high price to become Saint Gemma. Only after three years of further reflection did the Church move beyond recognition of her heroic virtue to formulate the decree under which the faithful would be allowed to venerate her and pray for the miraculous intercessions that would make her a blessed and then finally a saint. And when at long last that decree came on November 29, 1931, it pointedly disavowed acceptance of Gemma's stigmata, or any of her other supernatural graces in life. Maybe they had happened, and maybe not. Maybe they had come from God, and maybe not. Believers were free to think whatever they wished.[61]

A decision to recognize a woman's sanctity while declining to acknowledge the supernatural manifestations that graced her lifetime had been made at least once before, in the 1839 canonization of Veronica Giuliani, and the churchmen who sat in judgment on Gemma Galgani's case, like dutiful lawyers, specifically cited that precedent. It dictated that in canonization proceedings, supernatural graces should be investigated in a manner sufficient only to show that they derived neither from "machination nor delusion," and that they contained nothing "indecorous or alien to sanctity," without probing more deeply to prove or disprove their veracity, which in any event is not relevant to the issue at hand.[62] Narrowly construed, the resolution here is the same as that made for a proposed saint's writings: none are required, but if they exist, they must not be heretical or otherwise erroneous. Whether they are inspirational does not matter. Perhaps to make certain that everyone knew that their demurral extended beyond Gemma's stigmata and other manifestly physical signs, the clerical experts went on to cite separate precedents for denying approbation for Gemma's visions as well. Page 67 of the *Responsio* refers back to Caterina de' Ricci, who died in 1590 and was canonized in 1746. Initially there had been much political concern over Caterina's consolatory visions of Fra Girolamo Savonarola, who by order of Pope Alexander VI in 1498 had been burned for heresy. But then Pope Benedict XIII ordered that her offensive presentiments simply be ignored. His scholarly successor, Benedict XIV, subsequently turned this narrowly political decision into a doctrine by using that specific precedent to make the more general argument that "when a Servant of God is canonized, her virtues are being canonized, not her visions."[63]

And that is how it would be with Gemma. The obscure, scholarly *Responsio* closes with essentially the same rationale that ultimately came to be adopted in the highly public formal papal decree issued three years later. *"If the holy Church should judge the Servant of God Gemma Galgani worthy of the honors of the altar, it would thereby canonize only her heroic virtues, leaving her visions and revelations to be judged according to the science and prudence of the competent persons."*[64] Presented with this logic, in italics and boldface in the translation here exactly as it was in the original, Pope Pius XI needed only to eliminate some subjunctive grammar and the word "if," which is exactly what he did. He chose the first Sunday of Advent to express "his judgment on the heroic virtue of this innocent and penitent girl, but without pronouncing by the present decree (which in any event is never done) any judgment on the supernatural gifts of the Servant of God."[65] Gemma's followers made what they could of the "which in any event is never done" parenthetical phrase in the pope's decree,[66] but the fact remains that no such caution is stated for any other saint except Veronica Giuliani. Among the thousands who have been canonized, there are only two such official, formal skeptical aversions, both applied to women.

The Church judged that, in life, Gemma Galgani had been a person of extraordinary goodness, a model of heroic virtue in a young woman, and following the painstakingly crafted decree recognizing her virtue, four miraculous intercessions quickly were documented to her credit. Two of them had been fully prepared in advance, one dating back to 1907 and the other to 1919. They were formally approved on February 5, 1933, and two weeks later Pope Pius XI signed a degree of beatification, which was celebrated the following May 14. Subsequent to beatification, the two new healing miracles required by the rules occurred, and on March 26, 1939, Pope Pius XII recognized them. He set May 2, 1940, for the canonization ceremony, and on that day Gemma Galgani became Saint Gemma. The pope's decision is covered by the doctrine of papal infallibility, and so for the faithful she must be so honored. But the liturgy that exalts her makes no mention of Christ's wounds in her body, and a century later there were no public commemorations of June 8, 1899, the day she first experienced stigmata. Indeed, whereas the approved liturgical office for Veronica Giuliani refers to her stigmata, no similar concession was made for Saint Gemma's devotees.[67] Later, Pope Pius XII, while mentioning Gemma's stigmata, carefully stated that she "felt her hands and feet pierced by nails and her side wounded with a lance," the key word being "felt," which of course is far from affirming that she in fact suffered these wounds.[68] And since the Church chose so pointedly to make no judgment on the matter, it is allowed to each of us—Catholic or not, believer or not—to decide for ourselves what to make of Gemma Galgani's stigmata, along with her visions, ecstasies, and crown of thorns.

Long ago, four decades before the bells of St. Peter's pealed to recognize Gemma's canonization—the highest honor the Church may bestow—she had been told. In March 1901, Gemma wrote to Monsignor Volpi, as he had ordered her to do whenever she experienced anything unusual, informing him that Jesus had just visited her in ecstasy and said: "Daughter of mine, the truth you need to know, you already know; as for the monsignor, it is not yet time for him to know, but the time will come when he will know. Assure him that it is I, Jesus, who speaks with you and that in a few years by my doing you will be a saint. You will perform miracles and you will receive the highest honors of the altar."[69] This presentiment did not sit well with Father Germano, who excised the passage from his printed version of Gemma's letters. Upon learning so explicitly from her celestial bridegroom that such a wondrous future awaited her, she may have been far less shocked or chagrined than her confessor proved to be. For less than three months earlier, on December 22, 1900, the Saturday before Christmas, as she slept peacefully, Gemma had been consoled by a dream in which "a bishop, accompanied by almost fifty boys and girls—like little angels, it seemed to me, all with lighted candles in their hands—surrounded my bed in adoration." Influenced no doubt by prior warnings from Father Germano, to whom she wrote of this event, she expressed her fears that the dream might be a diabolic trick meant to feed upon her sinful tendency toward vainglory. Then again, maybe Gemma Galgani knew all along that one day she would become Saint Gemma.[70]

A Saint's Alphabet,
or Learning to Read (with) Gemma Galgani:
Theory, Theology, Feminism

AUTOBIOGRAPHY, BODY, CLOTHES, DAD, EUCHARIST,
FOOD, GUARDIAN ANGEL, HYSTERIA, IMAGINATION,
JESUS, KENOSIS, LAUGHTER, MOM, NUNS, OBEDIENCE,
PASSION, QUESTION(ING), RESEMBLANCE, SAINTHOOD,
TRANSGRESSION, UNION, VIRGINITY, WEDDING,
EXTASY, Y, ZEAL

BEFORE THE ALPHABET, OR THE ROSETTA STONE:
DECIPHERING THE HIEROGLYPHS OF
A TURN-OF-THE-CENTURY WOMAN AT THE
TURN OF THE MILLENNIUM

In what ways, with which voice, does Saint Gemma Galgani of Lucca speak to us today? Is this odd turn-of-the-century saint able to communicate with us, at this other turn of the century—and of the millennium? And are we, for our part, willing to hear Gemma's words and to experience her world—despite and above all through her ungrammatical sentences, her invocations of pain, her bleeding stigmata? What might inspire us to read her writings? And what could Gemma's relationship with feminism, with theology, with critical theory possibly be, given that she was unliberated and unlettered, impetuously, loudly submissive to a society and a church dominated by a patriarchal and often downright misogynist outlook? Is Gemma worth our time, and if yes (and clearly I mean yes or my essay would end right here), then why? Or, in the questioning words of two other writers, "If saints are embodied beings of extraordinary spiritual power, how does that power reach us, in what ways can it travel down to us today?"[1]

I propose in these pages to embark on a pilgrimage to this saint, with this saint: I invite the reader to undertake a metaphorical, alphabetical voyage to an imaginary turn-of-the-century place where we might find access, if we allow ourselves certain freedoms, to an Other, to ourselves, and perhaps even to some of the "secrets" of love. For, as the preface to a 1940 play on Gemma Galgani puts it, "The inspiration of this holy maid's life, however, lies not in the supernatural gifts that were hers but in her untiring struggle with self, that she might prepare a place in her heart for this impetuous Lover."[2] Not all of us might choose, as Gemma Galgani did, Jesus Christ as Lover; but should her particular object choice nullify the value of her experience for those of us who are, or want to be, like her, lovers, good lovers, even? I think not. I hope not.

My primary objective in what follows is to begin to "translate" Gemma Galgani's theology—taking this latter term in its literal meaning of "thinking and talking about God"—into a language that is hopefully more comprehensible, more meaningful to those reading Gemma's writings today. Hence the Rosetta Stone image I selected for the title of my introduction to this chapter: my hope and my work is that the hieroglyph of this holy woman will become more legible once it is turned into an alphabet. I will develop, perhaps weave this "translation" with the aid of two vocabularies that I believe can be of great help in such a mediation: feminist Christian theology and feminist critical theory. And let me state right away that I believe the perceived incompatibility between feminism and Christianity is itself a source of strength rather than dismay, of hope rather than resignation: for in my view it is this type of discomfort that keeps us intellectually, emotionally, and spiritually alive. It is significant, for example, that although feminism is generally perceived as a secular movement, African American feminist thought regularly integrates references to spirituality and religion, and that some illustrious white feminist theorists—such as, most notably perhaps, psychoanalyst Luce Irigaray—are preoccupied with issues of mysticism and transcendence.

The convention of the alphabet has allowed me to cover the subjects I deem most important without giving my own text the illusive quality of narrative continuity that the traditional essay form would inherently provide. The fragmentary appearance of these meditations is designed to invite the reader to make new connections, and to question my own. Thus, I have gladly and self-consciously fallen into the temptation, as Roland Barthes put it, "to adopt the succession of letters in order to link fragments, [which] is to fall back on what constitutes the glory of language: . . . an unmotivated order (an order outside of any imitation), which is not arbitrary (since everyone knows it, recognizes it, and agrees on it). The alphabet is euphoric: no more anguish of 'schema,' no more rhetoric of 'development,' no more twisted logic, no more dissertations! an idea per fragment, a fragment per idea, and as for the succession of these atoms, nothing but the age-old and irrational order of the French letters (which are themselves meaningless objects—deprived of meaning)."[3] Well, obviously the alphabet I have chosen is the English, which contains five more letters than the Italian alphabet, and my fragments have turned out to be quite a bit longer than I anticipated. But still, I find joy in placing my little text, if I may be so bold, in the genealogical line of Barthes's *A Lover's Discourse* and M. F. K. Fisher's *An Alphabet for Gourmets*.[4]

At the same time my explicit self-identification as a Catholic reader, as well as a feminist literary critic, is meant to elucidate the perspective which governs my interpretation—for it is a principle of contemporary hermeneutics and a tenet of feminist epistemology that pure objectivity is not possible, that every interpretation is influenced and even determined by the interpreter's interaction with the object to be interpreted. The best we can hope for, then, in terms of objectivity, is an acknowledgment of the interpreter's own stance. (And by the way, I do realize that "hope" is a recurring theme in these introductory remarks.) My personal and professional position I feel to be an especially visible, even vulnerable one: to be a feminist, and an intellectual, and a Christian today is seen as impossibly contradictory everywhere other than in the context of feminist theology (a marginal place where, furthermore, I find myself only marginally), and that is why I deem this very discourse to be so appropriate for understanding Gemma Galgani without diminishing her writings. Additionally, the position of a Christian feminist seems to me more likely to allow an analysis of Gemma's writings without automatically condemning her to the hopelessly reductive status of victim of a collective illusion.

"A critical liberationist theological perspective," according to Elisabeth Schüssler Fiorenza, "understands feminism as embodied in the visions and movements of those who seek to transform patriarchal/kiriarchal structures of domination and to eliminate the exploitation and marginalization of all women without exception."[5]

Christian feminist theology is not a homogeneous field. Often understood, somewhat inaccurately, as a branch of liberation theology, Christian feminist theology, which is what I refer to when I use through this essay the expression "feminist theology," is characterized by the union of historical

gender studies and liberationist commitments, by the retrieval of marginalized women's voices throughout the centuries, including, but not limited to,
the texts of the Scriptures and of the Christian traditions, and the development of a "hermeneutics of suspicion" (a term drawn from French phenom-
enologist Paul Ricoeur) with respect to all sacred texts: the assumption, that
is, that these texts were probably written by men, giving a patriarchal perspective and deploying a masculinist agenda. Theologian Elisabeth Schüssler
Fiorenza's strategic use of a hermeneutics of suspicion complements literary
theorist Elisabetta Rasy's claim that "in order to avoid prejudices, those who
want to understand the relationship between women and literature need to
have an approach that is different from that of normal literary historians or
critics. They need to privilege clues, traces, details, more than general categories. . . . In speaking of women and literature, it is necessary then not only
to bring to light female bodies that have been eliminated and repressed, but
also what literature itself has eliminated and repressed."[6] What Rasy says
about literature can be extended to religious texts. Feminist theology is indeed linked to feminist theory, including literary theory, in many ways; both,
for example, aim for the reunifications of reason and feeling (mind and body,
or body and soul), of content and form, and of theory and practice.

From a historical perspective, feminist theology and feminist theory work
at redressing the distortions of androcentrism: first, by recognizing, criticiz-
ing, and deconstructing sexism in all aspects of our tradition—be it religious,
literary, cultural, and so on; second, by discovering those hidden themes of
liberation present through the centuries that an androcentric tradition has
kept submerged, forgotten; and finally, by articulating a new vision, be it
secular or religious, in which women and men can share a full humanity. Central to the larger project of feminist theology are African American womanist theology, mujerista theology, and Asian women's theology: as the ethnic
positionalities of these other ways of doing theology, for example, attest,
feminist theology—like feminist theory in general—does not claim to be
preoccupied exclusively with women's issues. Rather, both feminist theology and feminist theory are perspectives from which to view social, cultural,
existential, spiritual, religious questions. As feminist theory is a way of doing theory, rather than a branch of theory, feminist theology is not a branch
of theology but rather a way of doing theology. Finally, and most important
for their own self-definition, feminist theology and feminist theory are not
a new type of authority but rather ways of rethinking authority itself.

I hope to show that Gemma's concerns, in spite of her bleeding, in spite
of her ecstasies, in spite of her anorexia—or rather because and across all of

these things—are not incomprehensible for today's readers, are not utterly discontinuous with our lives as they are, even in the contemporary American or Americanized world of corporate capitalism that is so far removed, in many, many ways, from Gemma Galgani's own turn-of-the-century, provincial Lucca. Throughout these pages, my own intellectual and/as religious struggles, doubts, and convictions will emerge in more or less veiled form. Without wholly embracing an autobiographical approach, without overshadowing Gemma's experience with my own, I also want to reclaim the importance and indeed the duty to assume a personal stake, a risky self-engagement, in theoretical writings—and in writings about religion especially. Thus, I strive in these pages to reunite in my own writing reason and feeling, content and form, theory and experience, even as I keep in mind, painfully, Linda Kauffman's warning that "writing about yourself does not liberate you, it just shows how ingrained the ideology of freedom through self-expression is in our thinking."[7] From a secular perspective, my writing practice aims to reconcile the personal and the political, the public and the private, and to challenge the myth of neutrality in the production of knowledge—the very myth that has relegated Gemma's truth claims, because acquired and communicated through personal experience, to a marginal status. (And Gemma is in this case exemplary of an entire class of marginalized writers and their truth claims.) The more "spiritual" intent of mine, in the choice of this practice, is to avoid both textual narcissism and moral hypocrisy—thus attempting to walk a fine line that Gemma herself struggles with throughout her writings; and to reveal my own spiritual as well as cultural (dis)location as part of the exchange between writer and reader (and mine, the critic's, peculiar status of writer-as-reader of another writer).

And so let me end—or, rather, begin—with a deeply personal wish. The name of my six-year-old daughter is Gemma. Like Gemma Galgani, my Gemma is beautiful and strong-willed, enjoys praising God in prayer and song, speaks of food, worries about what she wears, adores her dad, loves to laugh, obeys her inner sense of truth and justice, and makes me question my assumptions. Also like Gemma Galgani, my Gemma has a vivid imagination, a passionate bent, resembles but also, at times, struggles with her mom. I do not wish for her a life of illness, suffering, and deprivation, of social rejection, family loss, and early death. Of course not. Yet there are so many things I want her, someday, to know and appreciate about the saint after whom she was, more or less, named. I hope in these pages to fulfill that wish and that in reading them, a few years from now, my Gemma will not find the life, joys, and sufferings of another Gemma, one hundred years ago, to have been useless and without meaning.

A: AUTOBIOGRAPHY
— OR, THE TEXT AS THE BODY OF THE SOUL . . .
AND OF THE BODY

Like other women mystics, including great ones such as Angela of Foligno and Catherine of Siena, Gemma does not write spontaneously, but rather she is encouraged, even forced to do so by her confessor. As she explains in her diary, she writes out of OBEDIENCE (even when she writes of her disobedience!), she writes in spite of her repugnance against writing, and above all she writes despite her ever-present doubts of self-deception, of her excessive IMAGINATION: "(Whoever reads this should not believe anything, because I could very well be deceived; may Jesus never permit such a thing! I do so for obedience, and I oblige myself to write with great disgust)" (*Diary*, 92).[8] Later Gemma confirms her initial hesitation: "But how I suffer for the obligation to write certain things. The disgust I felt initially, instead of diminishing keeps growing enormously, and I am enduring deathly anguish" (*Diary*, 95). She repeats this feeling later in her diary, for the "repugnance" Gemma feels in writing increases with every passing day, and she ultimately writes purely out of obedience: "Whoever reads these things, I repeat again, should not believe, because they are all my imagination; nevertheless I agree to describe everything, because I am bound by obedience, otherwise I would do differently" (*Diary*, 106). Gemma also tries to burn her writings, questioning their usefulness and even their appropriateness: do these texts point to God's glory, as she hopes they do, or do they instead misguide her and lead her to an increased sinfulness? Should she believe the devil when he tells her: "Good, good girl! Sure, go and write everything: don't you know that everything there is my work and if you are discovered, think about the scandal! Where will you go to hide?" (*Diary*, 81). She does believe him, in fact, and tries to destroy what she has written but, mysteriously, is not able: "I tried to tear this writing up but I couldn't; I didn't have the strength, or else I just don't know what happened" (*Diary*, 81). So also when it comes to describing her vision of many angels, Gemma brushes off its necessity, protecting her privacy, when she claims: "Here there certainly is no need to record further all the details; if obedience should require it, I shall be ready, but for now . . . that's enough . . . If necessary, I shall remember" (*Diary*, 98). Gemma experiences firsthand, in her writings, the controversial relations between authorship and authority, especially insofar as the latter is a tenuous achievement for her, and her voice, both oral and written, seems at times to reach others as a quiet whisper even when she is, practically, screaming (about her need and desire to enter a convent, above all; see the entries NUNS, QUESTION(ING), ZEAL).

The violations of Gemma's privacy are especially visible when we think of the ways in which the medical gaze accompanies the priestly in repeatedly scrutinizing her—her life, her body, her experiences. After she is diagnosed with HYSTERIA by a physician in September 1899—a diagnosis which Gemma curiously embraces as yet another reason for Jesus to love her—Gemma discovers that her writings will also be shown to the doctor. So, in an ecstasy, she expresses the fear that Jesus will be ridiculed through such a display, and therefore she encourages him—or rather, more imperatively, demands of him—to do with her writings what he had done that very day with her stigmata, which had disappeared when the doctor wiped off the blood: "Watch out, they want to show my writings even to the doctor; make sure that is not the case. Oh Jesus, they are ridiculing you. Do this, Jesus: if they want the writings, do as you did today . . . If they want to see the writings, show them the blank paper."[9] Gemma could not state more clearly, in spite of her avowed disgust for the act of writing, the coincidence between her experiences and her written words, the identification of her text with her body, the realization of her body as a text and of her text as a body; this is almost a trite connection by now among cultural theorists and historians of the body, yet it is one of which this uneducated saint was quite aware *ante litteram.* Her body as her text will not be a spectacle to the penetrating medical gaze, her body and/as her text are meant for the greater glory of God, *ad maiorem Dei gloriam,* the body of her text, the text of her body refuse to be colonized by the imperialism of medical science. So Gemma's authority over her own writings is materialized to the point of being able to make these writings disappear, like her bodily marks, when the gaze under which they might fall risks contaminating them. She writes something similar in her autobiography: "The monsignor thought it best to have a doctor visit me without my knowledge, but Jesus himself informed me of it and said: 'Tell your confessor that in the presence of a doctor I will do nothing of what he desires'" (*Autobiography,* 58). Jesus seems to have obeyed Gemma's command.

She is no less private when it is the church authorities that infringe upon her freedom of loving God. Deftly she uses obedience in order to disobey, TRANSGRESSION in order to escape being confined by priests into too tight a role. Her self-removal from the scene of the medical gaze above has an amusing equivalent that features believing priests rather than unbelieving doctors. As her biographer Father Germano recounts, Gemma used to hide whenever people came to see her, and whenever she was obliged to stay "out of obedience," one could see that she had to make quite an effort; one way out, for her, was to pretend she was a "scimunita"—a nitwit, an imbecile, a fool. So Father Germano remembers a time when a respectable prelate came to see Gemma; since she couldn't escape this visit, Gemma pretended to be supremely interested in the large family cat, for which she had never before shown any predilection whatsoever. She played with the cat in such an absorbed, childish way that the priest, after saying something disparaging about her, promptly departed.[10] Gemma got what she wanted: a break.

"In the passage from life to writing, what strategies have women who 'write [their] own lives' adopted, when confronting their world, to free themselves from the images of role personae and desire encoded in language? How have they moved from silence to speech, engendering through writing alternative motives and myths? And reached that authenticity in the weaving of a text which puts its mark on 'literary' writing?"[11] This quotation is taken from critic Germaine Brée's foreword to an important collection of essays on women's autobiography, significantly entitled *Life/Lines*. Autobiography is indeed a favorite topic of feminist literary criticism, which as a discipline has substantially reshaped its parameters and shifted the ways in which scholars in general engage with life-writings—including the noncanonical ones (diaries and letters, especially) so frequently penned by women. It is at least in part thanks to feminist literary criticism that autobiography can no longer be seen as an unmediated and undistorted view into a writer's life, her/his identity, her/his selfhood.

One practical objective of feminist criticism, as also of this very book on Gemma Galgani, is to read, recover, and interpret women's lives and texts— while also underlining the problematic status of the embodied subject, as Gemma's writings about the self highlight by presenting their author as nonrepresentative, dispersed, utterly displaced. Yet, even as we are engaged in this necessary process of reading and recovering, some uncomfortable, complementary, and perhaps ultimately unanswerable questions arise: How can we speak for another? Are we able to recover Gemma's journey toward God, toward selfhood, so that it may not fall into oblivion, without at the same time boxing her into a discourse which is not hers, without doing violence to her writings if not her memory? And, vice versa: Should I also not admit that in my reading, recovery, and reconfiguration of Gemma Galgani's life-writings, her life has indeed impinged upon my own in a process of intellectual development and, may I say it? spiritual renewal? Indeed, I must acknowledge my indebtedness to this woman whose life-writings Rudolph Bell and I have undertaken to disseminate but which at the same time have, in different and unique ways, changed us, too. It is also thanks to Gemma (through her intercession, I am tempted to say . . .) that I have finally admitted, in ways more than superficially intellectual, the possibility of a contact with the divine while still here on earth.

I am not alone in this woman-to-woman spiritual dialogue, if I may relate the experience of a saint to my more modest one. It is after staying up all night reading the autobiography of Saint Teresa of Avila, in the summer of 1921, that a German-Jewish woman, Edith Stein (born in 1891, just a few years after Gemma), said: "This is the truth." [12] She was baptized in the Catholic Church on New Year's Day 1922, admitted into a Carmelite monastery in 1933 (at forty two, as Teresa Benedicta of the Cross), deported to Auschwitz as a Jew and killed in 1941, controversially canonized by Pope John Paul II in 1998. What I find fascinating in the hagiographic account of Edith Stein's conversion is the vital connection it establishes between two women who lived several centuries apart through a written, autobiographical text; and the fact that what finally prompted the conversion of an intellectual (Edith Stein had received a doctorate in philosophy *summa cum laude* and was chosen by Edmund Husserl as his graduate assistant) was the account of a mystic. It is my hope, my prayer that Gemma Galgani's writings be placed along that genealogical line, that they may enter that intertextual conversation among women.

Let me go back, then, to the questions asked by Germaine Brée in the quotation above, rephrasing them for Gemma Galgani's story: What are the strategies—textual and existential, intellectual and spiritual—deployed in Gemma's writings about the self? Do these writings constitute an autobiography in spite of their scattered nature and their author's intention that they be ephemeral (she repeatedly asks those to whom the texts are addressed to destroy them as soon as possible after reading them)? What does Gemma's autobiography have to contribute to feminism, to theology, to theory, to the history of spirituality? More fundamentally, does Gemma's experience embody a legitimating source for a different aesthetics? If I have devoted so much time and effort to studying Gemma's letters, her autobiography, her diary, her ecstasies, my answer is "yes," but this affirmation, if on the one hand it confirms and is confirmed by Gemma's popularity as saint and her effective canonization, on the other hand it goes against the academic judgment of her writings: "peevish demands for cuddling and caresses, endless whining, moody retorts and whimpering descriptions, seasoned moreover with the dewy and insipid ingredients of devout nineteenth-century trash," we read in a generally sympathetic anthology of Italian women mystics' writings published in 1988.[13]

The above quotation seems to leave little room for the interpretation of Gemma's experience as revelatory in any way, and yet it is not altogether unfounded. Gemma's writing raises many issues, for reasons which include the reproaches made in this pointed critique (reproaches that would doubtless be shared by many if not most literary critics, after reading Gemma's texts). And her work is problematic in many of the ways in which the work of women mystic writers in general is problematic (though I also do not mean to homogenize Gemma with Catherine of Siena or Teresa of Avila): their language is overall not as complex or as rigorously intellectual as the speculations of theology, their writings, usually, not as sublime as the sophisticated rhetoric expected of literary works. An example of this "low language" is Gemma's frequent use of the expression "Viva Gesù," "Long live Jesus," theologically dubious yet deeply grounded in popular piety.[14] Rather persuasively, in fact, Giovanni Pozzi himself argues that these textual or literary reasons play an important part in the psychologization and/or pathologization of women mystics.[15] Yet the issues raised by Gemma's autobiographical writings go deeper than what a stylistic review might reveal, for Gemma is after all claiming not literary expertise but supernatural contact with the divine. Is she mad, or is she right—or both, or neither? For if we claim with feminists that revelation is located in experience, for all its diversity, then we may also wonder, together with many theologians, what experience, whose experience is considered revelatory—with options that might include "women's historical experience of marginalization; women's experience as rooted in the body, imagination, and sexuality; women's friendships; women's mystical experience; women's bonding in circles of celebration, support and activity for justice in Women-Church and/or beyond."[16] Does Gemma have a place in any of these female spaces and traditions? Which? How do/can we know?

The distinction between popular piety and the official stance of the Catholic Church is a prolific one for Catholic feminist theologians, since it allows for a multiplicity of voices often lacking in Vatican-issued statements. But Gemma Galgani, more than by the mouthpieces of popular piety or of official stances, is likely to be censured by scholars—even when they/we ignore her, especially because they/we ignore her. For a reconsideration of traditional aesthetic and ideological expectations, molded by a patriarchal canon, needs to take place before we can appreciate what Gemma has to say and how she must say it. Dale Spender is characteristically blunt about this issue: "Men have been in charge of according value to literature, and they have found the contributions of their own sex immeasurably superior."[17] And Italian philosopher Adriana Cavarero is nothing short of radical on this subject: from the perspective of *pensiero della differenza* (thinking of difference, or difference feminism, which I discuss below) it is necessary "to be suspicious of the purported neutrality of language, of its scientific objectivity, and also of its beauty. So that, in this beauty, being a woman would no longer be the enchantment of a creature who is mute in front of the world."[18]

Teresa of Avila (1515–82) and Catherine of Siena (1347–80), symptomatically the only two women officially invested by the Vatican with the title of Doctors of the Church, are also in a sense relatively easy for feminists to appropriate, because in many ways they incarnate those very values which patriarchal society has taught us to admire: strength of character, independence, willfulness, successful social action. They were tough women, openly chastising men with greater power than they—no less than the pope himself, at times. It is significant for example that Simone de Beauvoir, who rather hastily dismisses mysticism as a "relation with an unreality" in the chapter of her *Second Sex* entitled "The Mystic," nevertheless redeems both Teresa of Avila and Catherine of Siena from her own critique, ironically making the same choices as the Catholic Church: Beauvoir classes Teresa of Avila among men rather than women, and describes both Teresa of Avila and Catherine of Siena as belonging "to the rather masculine type."[19] The admiration for these "masculine" qualities in women is a good thing, no doubt, because it helps us to break gender stereotypes and appreciate, in women, the presence of virtues that we are all too often denied. Women can succeed even within patriarchy, and that is all the more extraordinary given that patriarchal culture has systematically excluded or at least minimized female public achievement. But if Gemma displayed none of these "masculine" attributes, if she remained other to the culture in which she lived, if she obtained no measure of worldly success in her lifetime, if she embodied a suffered yet empowering self-emptying, or KENOSIS, should we not look for her value elsewhere, before discarding her words as the incarnation of peevishness?

In proposing this reading strategy, which informs my "alphabet" at large rather than receiving a simple answer here, I speak from the perspective of Franco-Italian feminism, focused on difference, on that *pensiero della differenza sessuale* which criticizes the homogenization, the homologization of women to men (risked instead by second-wave feminism). For it is only by embracing difference (and thus confronting the reductions operated by essentialism and biologism, as disquieting as such a confrontation must be) that women can escape invisibility and erasure into sameness—into the mask, for example, of gender neutrality. This *pensiero della differenza* is a secular discourse, often a frankly antireligious discourse, and Gemma is an uncomfortable figure in it, too. Yet in all of this there is a place for Gemma if it is in fact intrinsic to *pensiero della differenza* that the difference it celebrates cannot, should not be defined. Just as women's bodies, in *pensiero della differenza,* cannot be distinguished from culture (for instance, there is no conveniently neat distinction in this discourse between biology and culture, nor between sex and gender), so also our reading of Gemma Galgani is authorized to reveal a unity of body and soul, of nature and the supernatural, of human and divine which gives value and meaning to a body of writing fraught with pain—and with stylistic flaws.

B: BODY
—OR, HOW TO HAVE A HEART AND GIVE IT, TOO

Gemma's textual, devotional, existential insistence on her body is constantly moving from surface to interior and back, in a continuous crossing over that forever binds corporeality and spirituality, her body and her soul, her heart and her love. As she tells Jesus about her writings, "In the wound of your sacred side, oh Jesus, I hide my every word" (*Diary,* 95). Such a crossing provokes a parallel, incessant transformation at the level both of her embodied soul/ensouled body and of our reading of it; it brings about a challenge to biological models and, ultimately—through the heart—an integration of elements that appear at first, both to Gemma and to her reader, to be irreconcilable. Let us see how.

"If God had left the choice to me, I would have preferred to free myself from my body and fly to Heaven," Gemma writes in her autobiography (38). An analogous request is made during an ecstasy, when Gemma asks JESUS to "release this body," to "break these chains" so that her freed soul may fly to him (*Ecstasies and Letters,* 128). And in another ecstasy, Gemma seems to really have had enough, when she forcefully demands of Jesus to "strip [her] of this flesh; either tear [her] out of this body or stop, because [she] cannot go on" (*Ecstasies and Letters,* 147). Was Gemma a dualist, then, clearly separating her soul from her body and despising the latter as a worthless shackle to be discarded in order to attain her spiritual objectives? Yes and no—and Gemma's paradoxes mirror those of the Christian tradition itself which, in spite of its official anti-dualist stance, has often been contradictory on this subject, and continues to be so. As I hinted above, it is in the ceaseless meta-morphosis of body into soul, and, at the same time, of spirit into flesh, that mystics often find a livable model, a saving, redeeming paradigm. For the central act of Christianity, the incarnation—of God into human, of spirit into body—proclaims the goodness of the flesh (and an analogous enflesh-ment takes place at every Catholic mass, when Christ moves into and replaces the species of the eucharist). And yet the socio-cultural environment in which Christianity first formulated its theology was deeply committed to a dualism of body and soul, with the superiority of the latter. One of the most crucial contributions of feminist theology to Christian theology at large has been precisely its insistence on the return to a unitive model of the relationship be-tween body and soul—the model proposed by Jesus himself when, after his resurrection, he comes back and cooks a fish dinner for his friends by the lake (John 21:1–14) and eats with them (Luke 24:41–43). And by the way, this unitive model of feminist theology is analogous, in the secular sphere, to the emphasis placed by feminist theory on the inseparability of body and subjec-tivity: the feminist stress on "our bodies, our selves," an early focus of fem-inism renewed in the 1990s, is after all among the most important foundations for the academic fascination with the body in recent years.

The unitive model of body and soul, at the center of feminist theology, represents in fact the "more orthodox" perspective in terms of Christian doctrine, dualism of spirit and flesh having been the result of neoplatonic and gnostic influences in early Christianity. Likewise, feminist theology cel-ebrates embodiment. As theologian Beverly Wildung Harrison writes, "a moral theology must not only be rooted in a worldly spirituality but must aim at overcoming the body/mind split in our intellectual and social life at every level." For, as Harrison reminds us, "all knowledge is rooted in our sen-suality," and "feeling is the basic bodily ingredient that mediates our con-nectedness to the world."[20] Analogously, in spite of her alleged desire to leave her body behind and be a pure soul, Gemma Galgani's spirituality and her theological reflections are irretrievably rooted in her body, in her sensuality, in her feeling—in short, in her desire. This is the very aspect of her theol-ogy that might render it unappetizing to some traditional theologians and interpreters (in many of whom women's spirituality evokes what we might call somatophobia, fear of the body): it is not intellectual enough because it is not sufficiently separated from her bodily experience, from her sensuality, from her pains and from her pleasures, from her PASSION. Without a body, Gemma's reflection on God would not have survived because her mystical experience would not have taken place.

Gemma's relationship with her body is a complicated and difficult one, never resolved toward pleasure or pain, paradoxical in ways that are sometimes reminiscent of medieval women mystics. The body as the site of carnal desires is despised by Gemma as "slime" (see for example *Ecstasies and Letters*, 121, 122, 127, 144), as "impure" (*Ecstasies and Letters*, 121, 127), as "a fistful of dust" (*Ecstasies and Letters*, 144). Sinfulness inspires "repugnance" in Gemma (*Diary*, 98), it is the object of a disgust that we might term, following French-Bulgarian psychoanalyst and theorist Julia Kristeva, "abject." The abject, as Kristeva discusses in her book *Powers of Horror*, is constituted by bodies or bodily processes that fascinate and repel at the same time.[21] The abject elicits disgust because it is neither self nor other, it defies boundaries and definitions, it reminds us of the temporariness of our separation from undesirable objects—it is both other than and yet also part of ourselves. Hence the intensity of the response it evokes: as much as we would like to exclude it, the abject threatens to return, reminding us of our vulnerability and of the permeability of our borders.

The paradoxes of our relation to the abject are mirrored in Gemma's relation to the body, for in spite of her deprecatory stance toward the flesh it is through the body that Gemma attains the conformity to her Lover, her "impetuous Lover," to which she so ardently aspires: her body allows her to unite with her Lover even before, certainly before she dies. It is her injured body that bleeds in painful yet comforting stigmata, those controversial wounds which in turn allow her to mold herself to Jesus and to mitigate his sufferings (more on stigmata in the entry RESEMBLANCE). It is her body that, by suffering, through her passion, alleviates the pain of the community which suffers with her (the souls in Purgatory); and, lest we imagine an ethereal and symbolic rather than a fleshly body, we are told that even Gemma's teeth participate in this pain (*Diary*, 98). It is her body that receives the EUCHARIST, again a physical communion with her Lover, this time carried out through the physical swallowing of the consecrated host that has become, through transubstantiation, nothing less than Christ's body. It is her body that, in an ecstasy dated between June and July, allows Gemma to even "smell" her Lover's presence (*Ecstasies and Letters*, 129). Thus the saint asks Jesus: "Do you not see that I can do nothing? You should at least be satisfied that I dedicate myself to you with all my senses, both internal and external" (*Ecstasies and Letters*, 142). Gemma's body provides for her the means of self-sacrifice, and thus the body is the primary instrument of Gemma's salvation through her imitation of Christ's sacrifice. Most eloquently, Gemma exclaims in an ecstasy that "your love, oh Lord, your love penetrates even to my body, with too much fury" (*Ecstasies and Letters,* 147).

A particular corporeal aspect that is a telling metonymy of Gemma's incessantly metamorphosing body is her emphasis on the heart. Gemma's heart, like the heart of her Lover, suffers physically as well as spiritually, and these two types of pain are forever entwined, enjoying full UNION: "In these instants, my heart and the Heart of Jesus are one single thing."[22] When, in her diary, she tells of the great consolation she feels in seeing her Lover again after a long separation, Gemma's "heart started beating with such force" that she had "to tie a tight, tight bandage" at the order of her confessor (*Diary,* 86). Gemma also experiences, like other women mystics before her (Catherine of Siena and Veronica Giuliani, for example), the mystical rapture of the heart: the Virgin Mary takes Gemma's heart out of her chest and up to Heaven with her (*Diary,* 93). In an ecstasy, Gemma implores Jesus to open his heart to her so that she may deposit all her affections therein. In exchange, she offers to open her own heart in order that divine fire may enter and burn her (*Ecstasies and Letters,* 120). In a later ecstasy, Gemma asks her Lover to dilate her chest so that he may be more comfortably contained therein (*Ecstasies and Letters,* 128). Gemma's heart, like Christ's, stands between body and soul, between pleasure and pain, partaking of all these elements: Jesus is for her "the powerful King of Hearts," object and subject of passion.[23] The heart is a figure (both metonymy and metaphor, both desire and symptom) allowing Gemma Galgani to overcome this very dualism of body and soul, physiological and psychological, material and immaterial, visible and invisible, somatic and semantic. Her heart is the seat and the convergence of erotic and religious passion. As Roland Barthes put it, the word heart "refers to all kinds of movements and desires, but what is constant is that the heart is constituted into a gift object—whether ignored or rejected. . . . The heart is the organ of desire (the heart swells, weakens, etc., like the sexual organs). . . . The heart is what I imagine I give."[24] That the heart Gemma refers to is palpably physical, positively fleshly, a prelinguistic anatomical organ that eludes to some extent language can be discerned by the fact that it has to be physically contained, in its excessive beating, with a bandage. And yet the heart is also a construct of literature, science, theology; it is also an icon of feeling (the symbol of love), of life (blood-pump), of redemption (Christ's self-sacrificial love). The gift of the heart is the gift of the self. French-Algerian writer and critic Hélène Cixous, one of the first theorists of sexual difference, has assigned a peculiar function to the heart: the task to reunite what feminists of difference, including herself, normally separate: the genders. Thus Cixous has declared in an interview that "what the sexes have in common is the heart. There is a common speech, there is a common discourse, there is a universe of emotion that is totally interchangeable and that goes through the organ of the heart. The heart, the most mysterious organ there is, indeed because it is the same for the two sexes. As if the heart were the sex common to the two sexes." [25]

Metaphor of sentiments, metonymy of body, Gemma's heart points to both her past and her future, since her emphatic preference for this most symbolic of internal organs has precedents as well as followers among Christian women. In Gemma's past, the Sacred Heart of Jesus, although revered since early Christianity, was brought into prominence by French Visitation nun Margaret Mary Alacoque (1647–90), a saint whom Gemma frequently invokes and by whom she is even visited while in bed (and although she was only canonized in 1920, well after Gemma's death, Margaret Mary Alacoque had been declared blessed in 1864). The cult of the Sacred Heart came out of the convents and became widespread in the course of the nineteenth century. It is significant that Gemma received the eucharist for the first time on the feast of the Sacred Heart of Jesus, and her stigmata also first appeared on the eve of that same feast (June 8, 1899). As she writes to Father Germano, "the day of the feast of the Sacred Heart of Jesus is also my feast day." [26] The emblem of the Passionist Order, to which Gemma so desperately wanted to belong, is the Sacred Heart of Jesus.

The heart is for Gemma the place of corporeal bleeding and the place of mystical union, the source of pain and the origin of love, of desire, of E X T A S Y . It is the privileged site of relation to Jesus Christ, as it is in contemporary theological appreciations of this organ. For in terms of Gemma's future, our present, the concept of heart is central to the theology of, for example, Rita Nakashima Brock. Her book *Journeys by Heart: A Christology of Erotic Power* establishes the heart as the privileged place for the union of body, spirit, reason, and passion, as the seat of knowledge and of self, as the core of our very being, concluding that "the reclamation of heart is crucial to the redemption of Christ and ourselves." [27] If heart is, powerfully, the seat of our self at its best, heart can also be broken, and its healing requires the acknowledgment of brokenness and the act of reaching out for connections to others —connections which in turn recreate the heart, the self, continuously. Thus, Brock writes, "in exploring the depths of heart we find incarnate in ourselves the divine reality of connection, of love" (17).

Gemma's heart resembles her Lover's, Gemma's heart becomes one with her Lover's, because heart—who we are, our self, our intellect, our feelings—incarnates nothing less than a divine reality: connection, love. Of these the heart is metaphor—through resemblance (love)—as well as metonymy—through contiguity (connection). Heart points to the fundamentally relational character of all human beings (and relationality is also a focus of feminist theory in general; see the entry UNION below). The mystery of the incarnation of God into Christ, the scandal of KENOSIS, through which God contracts into a human being, can be approached through an examination of the heart as a mirror of divine love—love manifested in turn through connection to others: "Searching for connections is the heart's search, the search to heal suffering and brokenness" (Brock, 45). So, to return to the perspective of Catholic theology: the heart represents the incarnation of God into a human being, into a body, into a heart. Christ's resurrection is the ultimate example of the inextricable union between body and soul. As Sara Maitland puts it, "If there is no way of being a self, if there is no personhood without material reality (i.e., a body) . . . then there is no resurrection without the body, because there is nothing to resurrect." [28] In Gemma's writings, the heart foreshadows the human redemption achieved through Christ's resurrection, and also our own resurrection: by breaking the divide between metaphor and metonymy, between body and spirit, between this world and the next (for Gemma's heart travels freely between every dichotomy, across each dualism), the heart incarnates the self as well as the spirit, it connects, through the love it stands for and next to, present and future, human and divine, death and resurrection.

C: CLOTHING
—OR, IF THE HABIT DOES NOT MAKE THE MONK, DOES IT MAKE THE NUN?

"All the belongings she brought with her consisted in a few undergarments, two dresses, and a hat, nor did she ever want to own anything else." "No one ignores how difficult it is for an unmarried young woman to give up the vanity of clothing, not only internally in her heart, but especially with deeds, even while remaining in the world." [29]

In both her diary and her autobiography Gemma Galgani makes repeated mention of clothes and related items such as a cilice and a scapular—we might call them, humorously, "accessories." She also used to wear gloves in order to conceal the wounds on her hands (*Autobiography*, 55). As a child, around the time of her first communion, Gemma displayed a predilection for strolling "always in new dresses," a desire for "more and more new clothes" to show off during her daily *passeggiata*—a whim in which her father, characteristically, indulged her for quite a long time (*Autobiography,* 33). And she admits to getting "tired of dresses and all such things" not because of an inner, spiritual conversion but as a result of external pressures: for her father, after Gemma had been stealing stuff from around the house in order to give it, together with her allowance, to the poor who crowded around her as soon as she stepped outside, finally stopped giving her money, and her confessor forbade her to steal. So, unable to give to the needy, Gemma ended up never leaving home except if it was absolutely necessary (*Autobiography,* 34). And she also, rather predictably, I might add, got tired of clothes—for what is the use of fancy dresses for a young Italian without a *passeggiata* to show them off? Indeed, by 1900 Gemma had nothing to do with fancy dresses: she received out of charity a dress and a pair of shoes, without which she would have been in trouble because her aunts could not have afforded to clothe her.[30]

In all her photographs Gemma wears a striking black outfit: a black dress, a black cloak, and at times a black straw hat. None of her hagiographers seem to be able to resist commenting on her attire: "Her clothing was the simplest: a black wool skirt with a cloak of the same fabric and color, and a straw hat, also black. No cuffs at her wrists, no collar around her neck, no earrings, no brooches on her chest, no flowers or ribbons on her hat. Her relatives complained in vain: this was Gemma's one and only dress while she lived, in winter and in summer, on weekdays and holidays; nor did she ever want another one."[31] Gemma's choice was, to say the least, peculiar (and let us not forget that many people thought she looked and in fact was weird, and she was frequently the object of LAUGHTER),[32] especially when we consider that in turn-of-the-century Italy, women's clothing was rigidly defined by aesthetic as well as socio-cultural rules, aimed at indicating differences such as age, social class, education, civil status, geographical provenance. The shape and color of a woman's dress denoted her age and her respectability. By the age of fourteen, for example, a girl's dress had to cover her feet as well as her ankles.[33] Because, more generally, clothes are placed at the boundary between self and world, they wrap or contain the subject, they are border zones which mark the margin between the self and the non-self—and for Gemma most importantly between her sacred BODY and an impure world. In the words of Hélène Cixous, "clothing is skin. It is adopted skin, adoptive skin."[34] This is the function of the cilice and the scapular, which allow Gemma to define, to construct the sacredness of her body: the latter by protecting her from demonic assaults, the ultimate contamination; the former by more actively working to expel, or at least keep at bay, through willfully self-inflicted pain, all that threatens the autonomy of the self, the abject (more on abjection above, in the entry BODY).

Abjection, the revulsion at the dissolution of the boundaries that define the self, is just what Gemma experiences when she needs to undress in order to undergo a medical examination. Gemma says, and I think she means it, that she would have preferred death than to be seen "undressed," first by one doctor and then by three others: "(my suffering from the illness was nothing in comparison); the pain, the distress was only when I had to stay in their presence almost completely naked . . . My dear Dad . . . how much better to die!" (*Autobiography*, 42). She also significantly equates being seen with being touched (and touch is central to her life, as I discuss in the entry HYSTE-RIA). We might think here as well of one of the two passages eliminated in the Passionist edition of Gemma's autobiography: as a child, Gemma was taken in a closed room and undressed by one of the servants (*Autobiogra-phy*, 31). In this passage, the themes of clothing, unclothing, and unwanted seeing and touching converge to reveal the pain of a child who did not have the opportunity, perhaps, to live as a child. Both seeing and touching con-taminate Gemma's sacredness: she attributes her wish not to be seen and touched, not even by her own eyes and hands, to her observance of the Pauline interpretation of the body as a temple of the Holy Spirit (1 Cor 6:17). Seeing and touching break boundaries, let the abject, the forbidden, in. Clothes, and not just any clothes, are deemed capable by Gemma of insulat-ing the sacred body from the contamination of the world. Accessories do this too, both proactively—through the penitential use of the cilice—and im-mediately—the safeguard constituted by the scapular. Nakedness, on the other hand, like the nakedness before the servant in the closed room, implies the infiltration into the self by the other, for the armor, the carapace is gone.

Furthermore, clothes are associated with the female gender. Like women, clothes are frivolous and flighty—in spite of the fact that it is only since the nineteenth century that women's clothing have become more elaborate and decorative than men's (whose clothes are in turn commonly though inaccu-rately perceived as unchanging and plain). Clothes are the metaphor for an exteriority allegedly inferior to its contents: the emperor falls into the tricky weavers' trap because he is vain and thus susceptible to flattery. Clothes, like the emperor's nonexistent ones in Hans Christian Andersen's tale, point to issues of presence and absence, revelation and concealment, truth and simu-lation: "L'abito non fa il monaco," "The habit does not make the monk," is a popular Italian proverb. By starring a representative of the supernatural, a monk, this is a saying that exacerbates the division between appearances and an inner and spiritual truth. While the spiritual (the monk) is posited as real, the immediate and sensual surface (the habit) is minimized, even downright denigrated as simulation, as a lie. But the monk cannot be so easily separated from his clothes. For a subject is, and not only has, the clothes it wears, as Gemma Galgani's black outfit shows. (And if you are the clothes you wear, it won't be so easy to take them off . . .)

Indeed, "The habit does not make the monk" is a saying of great relevance for understanding Gemma Galgani's vestimentary practices, since we cannot help but note, in the several pictures we have left of her, not only her beauty but also her attire. Although she does not wear a veil—which she replaced with a rather eccentric black straw hat—Gemma's dress looks remarkably like a habit, a religious uniform for NUNS and one of the most clearly recognizable examples of symbolic clothing. After Gemma sees a Passionist preacher, Jesus asks her: "Would you like . . . to be clothed in the same habit?" (*Autobiography*, 57). As a highly symbolic garment, the habit makes an outwardly visible statement about the social and sacred identity of a large group of women: above all, the religious habit proclaims total commitment to an order (i.e., the suppression of individual identity along with the acquisition of social status and more personal freedom than single and married women), and lifelong celibacy (i.e., the suppression of sexuality along with independence from men, marriage, childbearing, and childrearing). "Clothing was a mystical symbol, each item expressing the spirit of penitence. In an age when many women still did not know how to read, a nun's habit conveyed a lesson more powerful than mere words: it expressed the body, its duties, its destiny." [35] Now, we know very well, for it is a recurrent topos in her writings, that Gemma Galgani was never allowed to make her vows and become a woman religious, for both economical and especially medical reasons.

So why does she dress like a nun if she is not a nun? Why does Gemma's corporeal body, through her dress, announce an allegiance to a social and sacred body, the nuns', which she does not have? If clothing is cultural and communicative, if it is a way in which groups construct and proclaim their identity in nonverbal ways, if it is intimately bound up with matters of status and power—and hence with ideology—then what kind of a personal, cultural, ideological statement is Gemma Galgani making with her peculiar sartorial choice? Is she abiding by the rules of the uniform, which could be seen as nullifying the subject, as preventing the establishment of an autonomous identity, or is she in fact subverting those very rules by wearing the uniform of a group to which she does not belong, indeed from which she had been formally excluded? (In so doing she also exploits a different function of the uniform, its effects of differentiation and separation from the world and not only of homogenization to the group—the nuns.) How has this vestimentary challenge Gemma posed been ultimately appropriated by an order—the Passionists—to which she so desperately wanted to belong, which so definitively excluded her from its ranks when she was alive, whose uniform she nevertheless donned, and which finally embraced her as its own after her death? For Gemma Galgani is seen, peculiarly unproblematically, I might add, as a Passionist saint, and she was buried, ironically, with the Passionist habit.

Through her choice of a black habit in which to mask as well as display her body, Gemma is true to her old self—the little girl always wanting new clothes to sport in the daily *passeggiata,* the same girl reprimanded by her guardian angel because instead of paying attention to the mass she kept looking at how two other girls were dressed (*Diary,* 75)—despite her earlier resolution "not to wear and not even to talk about vain things" (*Autobiography,* 38). The habit does make the monk, or better yet the nun (*monaca* as the feminine of *monaco*); you are what you wear, Gemma must have decided. Forget about the emperor's new clothes, she wanted the nun's old habit. So Gemma, prevented from *being* a nun, decided to *look like* a nun. She dressed herself from the inside out. She inscribed her body, her self, as visibly religious, as clearly consecrated, as recognizably untouchable. Her black outfit in this context becomes both an insulating frame, a boundary, and a connective tissue; it is material and disembodying at once. Gemma self-fashioned her body as the body of Christ's bride, as forever spoken for, as utterly unavailable to the hands and to the eyes of other men. The straw hat, according to one of Gemma's hagiographers, was specifically ordered by Gemma at the local milliner's shop: she wanted it with a wide enough brim so as to cover her face, and insisted in this request despite the milliner's suggestion that "such a hat was not really in fashion and was not suited for such a pretty girl as she."[36] Gemma's habit displays as much as it masks, reveals even more, perhaps, than it veils. And ultimately, Gemma's wearing the habit questions the hierarchy of presence over absence, revelation over concealment, truth over simulation, that the saying "The habit does not make the monk" proclaims with altogether too much facility. For not only did Gemma successfully establish herself as a bride of Christ, as *the* bride of Christ in fact, but even many of those around her, her Passionist confessor first and foremost, established her as a Passionist religious woman, if not, as she would have wanted, a Passionist woman religious.

D: DAD
— OR WHAT IS IN THE NAME OF THE FATHER?
(THE DAUGHTER'S SEDUCTION)

Gemma's biological father died in 1897 of a tumor of the larynx. In that instant, Gemma states, God took on for her the role of "Heavenly Father and Earthly Father" (*Autobiography*, 40). Although her father's death may not have been as emotionally devastating for Gemma as her mother's death had been a few years earlier, it entailed greater practical consequences for her and her siblings. For after this second parent's death they were completely destitute, left with nothing, trusting in and totally dependent on the kindness of friends and relatives: even the pockets of Gemma's smock, as the pious legend has it, were emptied of the few coins they contained. And although she did not identify as profoundly with him as much as she did with her sickly mother, Gemma was quite close to her father, judging from her autobiography and her diary. Her father could not resist her demands and obviously favored her among his children (along with her brother Gino, who also died young)— much to Gemma's chagrin, sometimes: "Dad, especially, always gave in to me; he frequently said (and it made me cry so many times): 'I have only two children, Gino and Gemma.' He talked like this in front of everyone else and to tell the truth we were disliked by everyone else in the house" (*Autobiography*, 37). At the same time, Gemma herself did not hesitate in writing about the ruses she employed with her father when she was a little girl in order to manipulate him into doing her will: "But I knew a good trick to bend him into giving me anything, so I put it into effect and immediately got what I wanted. (Every time Dad saw me crying, he did whatever I asked.) I cried, otherwise I got nothing" (*Autobiography*, 31); later, she confirms that "anything I wanted he gave me, and I started once again to take advantage" (*Autobiography*, 37).

This manipulative aspect of Gemma's relationship with her father, understandably little discussed, glossed over by the hagiographers, continues, I believe, during her relationship with her other fathers—her confessor, Father Germano, and God/Jesus himself. Gemma starts writing to Father Germano in January 1900, addressing him as "Very Reverend Father" or "Father Germano." But by mid-September of that same year, immediately after she has met him in person, Gemma's letters to Father Germano more intimately begin with "Babbo mio," "Dear Dad." Her letters begin this way until August of the following year. Then Father Germano orders Gemma, through Cecilia Giannini, to address him as "Reverend Father." But this strangely belated order remains in force for only the space of two letters, and then Gemma goes back to her intimate ways—to "Babbo," that is, "Dad."[37] (Gemma does return to "Reverendo Padre" later, but only very occasionally.)[38] It is this familiar north-central Italian term for dad, "babbo," that Gemma Galgani prefers in order to refer to her confessor. Gemma even uses for her confessor the playfully affectionate term "babbino mio," roughly the equivalent of "dear daddy."[39] In the context of Gemma's total allegiance to the divine at the expense of her OBEDIENCE to anyone else here on earth, her choice of "dad" over "father" and, especially, of the fatherhood of God (her "Eternal Father"; *Diary*, 93) over that of biology make some powerful statements. As I reflect on this choice, I am reminded of Sara Maitland's interpretation of "God the Father" as "a radical critique of patriarchy rather than the affirmation of it," because just as the Gospel tells us to "call no man father," so God is our only authority—through whom women of faith and spirit, such as Gemma herself, have found autonomy and their own authority to defy the patriarchs (let us not forget that the term "patriarchy" derives from father, "pater").[40] Similarly, Anne E. Carr supports the argument, first delineated by Elisabeth Schüssler Fiorenza, "that the fatherhood of God opposes patriarchal structures in the church and that Christ's lordship opposes relations of dominance and submission in the Christian community."[41] Rather than affirming patriarchy as the earthly reflection of a divine order, then, the fatherhood of God, as experienced and conveyed by Gemma and feminist theologians with her, questions the fatherhood of everyone else— fatherhood as the founding institution of patriarchy. Since God is her father, she needs to obey no one but God—not even her confessor, whose status as "Dad" is utterly subordinate to the fatherhood of the divinity.

Divine fatherhood itself assumes more than one form. For although Gemma's relationship with Jesus is primarily a friendly, and, especially, an erotic or bridal one, it must be remembered that she also calls Jesus "Father": "I too was happy, not because I had regained my health but because Jesus had chosen me to be his daughter" (*Autobiography*, 46). Her use of the same relationship, that of fatherhood, in three different contexts, with three different figures (or perhaps four, if we distinguish between God and Jesus), has the textual effect of "contaminating" each relationship with the connotations of the other two. Jesus is a father but he is also, primarily, desire (he is

Gemma's bridegroom and even her lover); Father Germano is a father but he is also, primarily, her director, and thus earthly power, worldly authority (and Gemma's entitlement to its TRANSGRESSION); Enrico Galgani is her biological progenitor but he is also, peculiarly yet quite clearly, Gemma's subordinate in terms of willpower and spiritual authority. What is striking is that clearly for Gemma the model, the paragon of fatherhood among these three is Jesus, the one who least conforms to the patriarchal model of fatherhood. Paternal authority is repeatedly eluded by Gemma, and certainly never internalized as a forming aspect of her religious persona. Obeying her director's orders is for her a constant struggle, one she insistently displays and can never take for granted, and one in which obedience does not always win. Significantly, the biggest temptation that the devil proposes to her, and one to which she temporarily yields, is precisely to disbelieve Father Germano's authority—making her think of him as someone who "wanted me to lose my soul," as "a loafer, a windbag" (*Ecstasies and Letters*, 120, 122).

Yet the reasons why Gemma chooses to call Jesus father, rather than reaffirming the patriarchal order, seem to be grounded in an antipatriarchal view of fatherhood: "Allow me to call you father because no one forgives like you my weaknesses, my thoughtlessness, the way you do . . . You are an abyss of love, Jesus"; "I recognize in Jesus a true father, full of mercy . . . the goodness of Jesus' heart is more than paternal."[42] What Jesus' fatherhood implies is not lordly power but rather kind forgiveness and loving self-giving —attributes we might more readily attach to a mother than to a father, and certainly this would have been true in the nineteenth-century bourgeois Italian context. The same is true of the fatherhood of God, if Gemma can exclaim in an ecstasy that "the spirit of the word . . . reigns in the fertile breast of the parent uncreated" (*Ecstasies and Letters,* 155)—a unique and strikingly nonsexist definition of the Trinity. Desire, rather than authority, is what marks each part that Jesus plays in Gemma's life, for indeed the role of father temporally and spiritually precedes that of lover, as Gemma explains in an ecstasy: "If I experience such consolation in the morning, when you let me call you father, oh, how will it be when I can call you my beloved? Yes, Jesus, console this poor daughter of yours, your future bride."[43] The daughter's seduction, to borrow the title of Jane Gallop's book on feminism and psychoanalysis, is the seduction of the daughter by the father and the seduction by the daughter of the father. But fatherhood and daughterhood, in Gemma's journey, do not simply move in the straightforward itinerary, from connection to separation, from mother's body to father's law, fantasized by classical psychoanalysis. Jesus' fatherhood, with its maternal overtones, embodies a parental-filial relationship which moves back and forth between prenatal union and postnatal separation. It illustrates Jessica Benjamin's contention that a critical psychoanalytic theory shows how "the self does not proceed from oneness to separateness, but evolves by simultaneously differentiating and recognizing the other, by alternating between 'being with' and being distinct."[44] The daughter's position, the daughter's seduction, is an early place in Gemma's journey, it is the "morning," as she calls it, of her itinerary, a stage which is to be followed by complete (if, again, blissfully provisional) UNION through her mystical WEDDING: when the two lovers will move instead, with pleasure, with *godimento,* from separation into oneness: "I am a jealous father and bridegroom; will you be my faithful daughter and bride?" (*Autobiography,* 49).

E: EUCHARIST
— OR, "OF GEMMA'S SINGULAR DEVOTION
TO THE HOLY EUCHARIST"[45]

"Jesus then is *there* we can go, receive Him, *he is our own*—were we to pause and think of this thro' Eternity . . . that *he is There* (oh heavenly theme!) is as certainly true as that Bread naturally taken removes my hunger—so this bread of Angels removes my pain, my cares, warms, cheers, soothes, contents and renews my whole being."[46]

A convert to Catholicism and to the doctrine of the real presence of Christ in the species of the eucharist, Elizabeth Ann Seton (1774–1821) has written moving meditations on this belief that was so at the center of her spirituality. The word "eucharist" is derived from the thanks given by Jesus Christ before breaking the bread and sharing the cup in the Gospel accounts of the Last Supper (Matthew 26:26–27, Mark 14:22–23, Luke 22:19). The eucharist is the central rite of the Roman Catholic religion. Although the term "eucharist" is associated by metonymy with the elements of communion (the host or wafer, especially, but also the wine), it more generally refers to the sacrament itself, the holy eucharist. It is now well-known that eucharistic devotion characterizes the spirituality of women mystics, especially during the medieval period. This subject has been explored at length and in depth by historians of religion, and is related to the subject of FOOD which I discuss below and to some questions tied to the conception of the BODY as delineated above. It is crucial to note about the eucharist that Roman Catholics, like the members of the Orthodox Church, believe in transubstantiation, namely in the miraculous transformation of the bread and wine, at the time of consecration during mass, into the actual body and blood of Christ (a doctrine officially established in the Fourth Lateran Council in 1215). This belief is essentially different from the Protestant interpretation of the eucharist as a symbolic reminder of JESUS' Passover, and even from consubstantiation, an interpretation held by some denominations, according to which the bread and wine are also bread and wine even as they become the body and blood of Christ. For in transubstantiation the bread and wine are no longer present after being consecrated; only the body and blood of Jesus Christ remain—hence Elizabeth Ann Seton's enthusiasm.

Transubstantiation is a radical statement, one that is bound to have considerable faith effects on any believer who dwells on it. Numerous miracles are related to this dogma, and they occurred especially around the time of its official establishment in the medieval period. I clearly remember visiting as a young girl, in the impressive medieval Cathedral of Orvieto in central Italy, the blood-stained cloth still venerated there from the miracle of Bolsena (1263): when a priest was having doubts, during consecration, regarding the truth of transubstantiation, the host began to bleed profusely onto the altar cloth. Needless to say, his doubts were immediately dispelled. But rather than in such macabre details, I find the spirit of transubstantiation and its emphasis on communion and the body best expressed by twentieth-century French mystic and activist Simone Weil (1909–43), who has written: "If I grow thin from labor in the fields, my flesh really becomes wheat. If that wheat is used for the host it becomes Christ's flesh. Anyone who labors with this intention should become a saint." [47] Certainly not an orthodox statement (and Weil never officially entered the Catholic Church), yet it is a suggestive and persuasive one because of the images of corporeal transformation it evokes: if it is impossible to understand how a piece of bread can turn into the body of Christ on the altar (this is after all "*the* mystery of faith," as the celebrant announces after consecration has ended, and a mystery, by definition, cannot be fully understood by reason), it is not as impossible to imagine a corporeal connection between the body who tends to the wheat and the wheat itself, the bond established between this body's decrease and the increase of the growing grains. If we can see how flesh can become bread, then perhaps we may have an intimation of the ways in which bread could, mysteriously, also become flesh.

The eucharist is Gemma Galgani's sacrament of choice, her most prized connection with the supernatural. Gemma anxiously awaits her first communion, especially after she hears a preacher state that "whoever eats of the life of Jesus will live of his life" (*Autobiography*, 32). After hearing this,

Gemma spends "entire nights consumed with desire" to receive communion, for she wants Jesus to live within her (*Autobiography*, 32). Her first communion in 1887 represents a turning point in Gemma's life, for she feels Jesus' presence "forte forte," she has a glimpse of the delights of Heaven, she desires to be continuously united with God, she feels detached from this world, and she receives from Jesus the desire to become a nun. At communion Gemma often "taste[s] great consolations" (*Autobiography*, 33), and starting in 1899 she plans on receiving communion daily—with the mysterious qualification "except a few times because my many sins rendered me unworthy or if my confessor punished me" (*Autobiography*, 46). For the sacraments, Gemma was dependent on a confessor who could withdraw them at his discretion, which we have reason to believe he did given Gemma's pervasive scruples. (If on the one hand this power on Father Germano's part constitutes an intrusion into the mystical relationship of an earthly patriarchal authority, on the other hand as we will see in more detail Gemma's relationship with the divine is hardly interrupted, let alone halted by her confessor's prohibitions.) The heading for this section in her autobiography is significantly entitled "Hunger for the eucharist" (*Autobiography*, 46). In her diary she complains to her Lover because "after holy communion he did not allow [her] to taste the sweetness of Heaven" (*Diary*, 93–94). In an ecstasy, on the other hand, she refers to her state after receiving holy communion as being "pasciuta," literally "stuffed" (*Ecstasies and Letters*, 143).

Eucharistic desire goes hand in hand for Gemma, as for some other women mystics before her, with eucharistic TRANSGRESSION. Sicilian mystic Lucia Mangano (1896–1946) was too poor for her parents to buy her the white dress necessary for a proper celebration of first communion; so, on her way back from an errand, she went into a confessional and the next morning received communion unbeknownst to her family.[48] From Gemma's life, one striking example must suffice. We are in the year 1899. On Good Friday, when it is customary not to consecrate bread and wine into body and blood, Christ nevertheless gives himself to Gemma in communion, without the normally necessary intervention of the priest. (For in the Roman Catholic Church, only men can become priests, and only priests can consecrate bread and wine into the body and blood of Christ, therefore it is impossible for Gemma, as for any woman, to consecrate legitimately.) Gemma writes in her autobiography: "Even though I did not receive the true Jesus from the hands of a priest, because it was impossible, still Jesus came on his own and gave me communion" (*Autobiography*, 49).[49] The language is clear: Gemma received "communion" with Christ, she was given his body to eat, from Christ himself. The effect of this communion was a UNION "so strong" that Gemma "remained like stupid" (*Autobiography,* 49). During the experience recounted in this passage, Gemma bypassed the need for priestly mediation in the eucharist, thus completing even in this forbidden area her direct relationship with Christ already present in every other aspect of her spiritual life. Angela of Foligno, a medieval Italian mystic, had performed a similar action several centuries earlier: after washing a leper's sores, she drank the water used for the washing and a scab that got stuck in her throat tasted to her as if she "had received holy communion."[50] The institutional need for priestly mediation is rendered temporarily null and void, and the power of performing transubstantiation, denied to women, is fully assumed by Angela as well as Gemma (though Angela qualifies her experience with an "as if"). The consecration of the eucharist, for these women, is not the prerogative of the clergy or hierarchy—an issue at the center of the modern debate for the ordination of women. Rather, they are directly and without mediation in touch, literally, with God's will and with God's body.

A contemporary of Gemma, Thérèse of Lisieux (1873–97), was even more direct about her ambivalent relationship with the Church's teaching on the role of priesthood. Like Gemma, Thérèse lost her mother when she was a child, had a complicated relationship with death and the desire for Heaven, and replaced her earthly mother with the Blessed Virgin, whom she called "MOM";[51] she had a vivid IMAGINATION which she at times mistrusted (46), was different from the other children (54), and adored by her DAD; she decided early on that she would become a SAINT, and spoke of this conviction throughout her writings (27, 104, 207, 267, 276); she had a privileged relationship with God (75), the only one she recognized as her director (151, 158), and she called God "dad" (265); experienced UNION with Christ (77), was PASSIONately in love with Jesus (102, 178), who in turn was passionately in love with her (256), so that Thérèse called him the bridegroom of her soul (151, 276); she desired and loved suffering (79) and depended on the EUCHARIST to nourish her spirit (104); she had difficulty with OBEDIENCE to her superiors, even the pope's guards, and had at one time to be forcibly removed by three men from the pope's presence (116, 134–35), but she wrote out of obedience (233); she was opposed in her desire to become a NUN, though in part thanks to her father's help, she, unlike Gemma, succeeded (106–44); like Gemma, Thérèse died in her mid-twenties of tuberculosis. Her photographs, like Gemma's, attest to her beauty. Like Gemma, she did nothing of importance in her life. Well, Thérèse, painted by hagiography as a rather insipid eternal child, remembered for her "little way," powerfully wrote that to be Christ's spouse, and a Carmelite, and a mother of souls did not suffice her, for she felt other vocations as well: of warrior, priest, apostle, doctor, martyr. With the exception of the last, perhaps, they are all traditionally male vocations, really. Particularly, Thérèse writes: "I feel in me the *vocation of* the PRIEST. With what love, O Jesus, I would carry You in my hands when, at my voice, You would come down from heaven. And with what love would I give You to souls! But alas! while desiring to be a *Priest,* I admire and envy the humility of St. Francis of Assisi and I feel the *vocation* of imitating him in refusing the sublime dignity of the *Priesthood"* (192). What does she mean, "refuse"? Who is refusing whom, here? From Thérèse's passage, one might think that the priesthood was a possibility for Thérèse, as it was for Francis, and that she refused it just as he did. And that she could have had it, if she willed it. Long live Thérèse!

F: FOOD
—OR, OF MEATBALLS, COFFEE, CHOCOLATE, AND WINE

"Dear Dad, today finally your dear angel has also appeared. How beautiful he was! . . . Imagine, he came into the kitchen while the servant was making meatballs! I was there watching her make them, and I was thinking. . . ." [52] Being an avid, even obsessed cook, I could not resist quoting the statement above. Medieval mystic Angela of Foligno, after all, also had a powerful spiritual insight while washing lettuce. [53] Although meatballs, lettuce, and spiritual beings seem to have little in common, the sharing of food is considered central in most religious traditions, for this is an activity that unites all living things and that represents for us both need and pleasure; in this it is similar to sex, though food is more inclusive because it can be shared with anyone and everyone. Food is also associated at some levels with women, for it is usually women who prepare it and distribute it in traditional societies.

Food is EUCHARIST, for Gemma, food is the BODY of Christ that becomes part of oneself by being ingested and that in so doing participates us in the mystical body of the Church. In an ecstasy, Gemma tells JESUS that she is thirsty for him, that in the morning she suffers before feeding on him, praying that after feeding on him she may remain full (*Ecstasies and Letters,* 121). With her Lover's beauty, Gemma exclaims in another ecstasy, she wants to "be entirely satiated" (*Ecstasies and Letters,* 122). Later, Gemma tells her Lover that she is "hungry for your bread of life" and "thirsty for your sacramental blood" (*Ecstasies and Letters,* 133). And later yet, Gemma says she will "nourish" her love for Christ with Christ's own body and blood, and she will be "stuffed" ("pasciuta") with his blood (*Ecstasies and Letters,* 144).

At the risk of anachronism, it is useful to remember at this point what religious historian Caroline Walker Bynum has so eloquently explained about medieval holy women, namely that "to religious women food was a way of controlling as well as renouncing both self and environment. But it was more. Food was flesh, and flesh was suffering and fertility. In renouncing ordinary food and directing their being toward the food that is Christ, women moved to God not merely by abandoning their flawed physicality but also by becoming the suffering and feeding humanity of the body on the cross, the food on the altar."[54] To some extent this is true of every Catholic who partakes of the sacrament of communion, for the eucharist participates us in the mystical body of Christ. But what Bynum's more gendered explanation underlines is the food aspect of communion, the sacramental connection between body as food and food as body (and this despite any distasteful intimation of cannibalism). In this perspective, women's particular association with food results not (only) in pathology and/or self-destruction, but most importantly in a heightened experience of communion with others, with the Other—with Christ and with humanity as well, as Christ's body.

Yet I will not deny that food is also for Gemma bodily need and fleshly temptation; as such it is abhorrent to her. Her desire is to ask Jesus, as she reveals in a letter to Father Germano, "the grace of not letting me sense any taste in any food, for as long as I live" (125). So she makes "a pact with Jesus about food": in exchange for keeping down a bit of food ("but only the tiniest amounts"), Gemma "will no longer feel a sense of taste" (134). As much as she would want to eat (or rather, she would *want to want* to eat), she cannot: although she wants to be obedient "about keeping down and tolerating a little food, just a little," still she must recoil, because perhaps that is not Jesus' wish—nor her body's: "I cannot, because my stomach does not wish it"—a passage which again links Gemma's desire (her longings, her needs, her wants), to Jesus' own: "Yes, I truly wish to be obedient, but if Jesus wished otherwise? . . . " (*Ecstasies and Letters,* 148). Her stomach obeys Jesus' potential wants more than anyone else's commands. And when, after eating, she feels unwell, the angel offers Gemma "a cup of coffee so good that I was healed instantly" (*Diary,* 97). For the same reasons, the angel on another occasion gives Gemma a somewhat more mysterious potion, "a few drops of a white liquid in a golden goblet," "the medicine a doctor in Heaven used to heal infirmities" (*Ecstasies and Letters,* 139). Other than the eucharist, these are prominent examples of physically and spiritually healing food. In contrast to the contemporary American disdain of caffeine as of medically questionable value, coffee is still seen as a healing potion by many Italians; as a familiar ad campaign for a prominent brand of espresso claims, "più lo mandi giù, più ti tira su," or "the more you down it, the more it picks you up." Cecilia Giannini's nutritionally therapeutic choices also remind us, in a delightful way, of how culturally relative interpretations of food are: when Gemma is sick, she receives from her "chocolate and a lot of wine."[55]

G: GUARDIAN ANGEL
—OR, IS THERE AN ANGEL IN THE HOUSE?

On the very first page of her autobiography, Gemma Galgani writes briefly to her spiritual director Father Germano first about his angel (who scolds her and predictably incites her to obey her confessor), and then, somewhat more in depth, about her own angel—though still in passing, quite matter-of-factly. For Gemma's angel, the first meeting with whom is recorded, in her texts, to have taken place in 1895, is a normal being always present in her everyday life, someone who at the beginning of the feared composition of this very autobiography promises to help her remember everything (*Autobiography*, 28), someone who is a "teacher and guide" (*Autobiography*, 47) and who "sharply reproached" her (*Autobiography*, 47), gives "warnings" (*Diary*, 75), and makes Gemma take off the penitential cilice she had been wearing without anyone's permission or knowledge (*Autobiography*, 50). The angel is a messenger from and to JESUS who normally visits her frequently, and who leaves her alone or reprimands her harshly if she disobeys Jesus or her confessor. Her angel disciplines Gemma as if she were a child ("castigare," the old Italian equivalent of today's "time-outs," is the verb used by Gemma for his punishments; *Diary*, 79), but is also full of "charity, vigilance, and patience" and assists Gemma both at home and outside the house (*Diary*, 73), and even helps her climb onto her bed when she is too weak and wounded to do it alone, suffering from her bleeding stigmata (*Autobiography*, 55). The angel carries on conversations with Gemma using, like Gemma herself, a simple and almost childlike language, and "opened his wings" to protect her from the devil (*Diary*, 85). Her angel is "affable and cheerful" (*Diary*, 101), "caressed" Gemma "again and again" when she felt sick (*Diary*, 102), talks with her "for hours on end" (*Diary*, 105), sleeps "by [her] side" (*Diary*, 106), and, eventually, never leaves Gemma except when Cecilia Giannini, regarded as the only fit substitute for the angel's presence, is with her. The angel also functions, somewhat improbably yet, it seems, at least as effectively as the

Italian postal system (!), as letter carrier between Gemma and others (*Diary,* 103; the word "angel" derives from the Greek for "messenger"), such as her beloved Brother Gabriel.

Angels are very popular today, and many books, not to mention cards and bumper stickers, have been printed on the subject of their existence and interventions in our daily lives. We have probably all read "I brake for angels" on the car of a neighbor, friend, or stranger (or, more amusingly, "Don't drive faster than your angel can fly"). There are popular television series starring angels of various sorts who have taken up human appearance, and the sites dedicated to angels of all denominations on the Internet are countless. Being part of Judeo-Christian as well as New Age spiritualities (they also appear in the Koran), angels are politically correct religious beings in this nonreligious age, they are figures of the supernatural that do not necessarily identify us as belonging to any sectarian group (as opposed to, for example, the saints that so promptly brand some of us as Roman Catholics). And it would of course be tempting in this context to enter the debate on the sex of angels and therefore discuss the meaning and function of gender in one's daily and supernatural life. (Gemma's angel, by the way, takes on an undoubtedly male appearance, which is important in some of her dealings with him; see the entry HYSTERIA.)

But it is another aspect of Gemma Galgani's angel and their relationship that I wish to discuss here, one that I think represents a microcosm of so many of the questions that Gemma-as-text elicits in today's reader. For what strikes the reader in Gemma's relationship with her guardian angel is the level of intimacy the two have attained, an intimacy most obvious in the language used in their conversations as well as in his reprimands. This childlike language has been employed by some critics, including believers, to underline Gemma's childishness, even peevishness (as I discuss above in the entry AUTOBIOGRAPHY); during the canonization process, Gemma's intimate, too-intimate relationship with her guardian angel, as well as with Jesus and the Virgin Mary, was considered excessive, out of place, just too much.[56] On the other hand, this excessively familiar language could easily be invoked to underscore the illusory nature of the angel's presence in Gemma's life: common sense seems to dictate that an angel cannot possibly speak like an uneducated teenage girl, and therefore no angel was ever really there; he is the product of Gemma's all-too fertile religious IMAGINATION. What is most striking and relevant to me about these two critiques, and what joins together their seemingly opposite worldviews (religious and secular), is their insistence on a certain aesthetics, whereby only a lofty, highly intellectual and cultured language should be the appropriate medium for theology, for thinking and speaking of God. This criticism has been countered in depth both by feminist theology and, mutatis mutandis, by feminist theory more generally.

One of the main thrusts of Christian feminist theology has been and continues to be a redefinition of the language used to talk and write about God. Another related task is to recover and study the experiences and writings of Christian women of the past and of the present in spite of their obfuscation, in defense of which specious reasons have regularly been adduced (often, precisely their "inappropriate" use of language), by a male-dominated tradition. It is after all in this spirit of recovery that this book on Gemma Galgani is being produced. This obfuscation is also the subject of feminist criticism of the literary canon: tradition, this criticism claims, needs to be revised in order to include as part of the significant mainstream canon, female, ethnic, gay and lesbian, and working-class writers, who have been excluded on the basis of a middle-class, male, white, heterosexual aesthetics which they had no part in shaping. Yet this is admittedly a difficult move, the critics themselves point out, since perhaps it is the very notion of canon that needs to be challenged: a canon, any canon, may be intrinsically unable to accommodate diversity, and therefore new canons would not necessarily be less oppressive than the old one. It is possible, perhaps even likely, some say, that we cannot establish aesthetic criteria that would encompass both genders and a wide variety of experiences, values, and traditions.

But then how do we decide what to read, what to write about, what to assign to students, what to anthologize? Are criteria of selection and evaluation inevitably elitist and exclusive? These questions, although of central importance to both literary theory and feminist criticism, have not been adequately answered by either discipline, though they still need to be kept in mind in our discussion of Gemma Galgani. Because, comparably, feminist Christian theology still struggles with issues of language, especially when it comes to speaking of God from within a tradition that has privileged, for example, masculine modes and images of the divinity. How can/does one stay within Christianity without being complicitous with the inability or unwillingness of this very tradition to include the specificity of women, their difference, in its elaboration of full humanity? Why is this tradition so resistant to the incorporation of, for example, female aspects of the divinity within its representational imaginary? Why does it denigrate certain modes of relating to the divinity which are particular to women—such as the daily language which characterizes Gemma's texts and which cannot aspire, it is claimed, to the ranks of theology?

So, we need to return to reading Gemma Galgani's language and her words on and with her beloved angel with these questions in mind. Only my feminist phrasing of them is relatively new. When the angel comes to save her from the ugly little man that is the devil, Gemma begs him to stay with her through the night, to which the angel replies "'But I'm sleepy.' 'But no,' I kept repeating, 'the angels of Jesus don't sleep.' 'But really,' he added, 'I have to rest (then I realized he was kidding); where will you put me?'" (*Diary,* 74). Gemma and her angel "kid around" the way old friends do, and the angel is indeed one of Gemma's best friends (see also the entry LAUGHTER). And if, on the one hand, Gemma interprets the angel's alleged need to sleep as a joke, yet the angel seems to indeed sleep through Gemma's going off to mass, and leaves in her absence: "I fell asleep and this morning he was still there. I left him and when I returned from mass, he was gone" (*Diary,* 75). Gemma's linguistic interactions with her guardian angel are both sublime and informal, instances of that chatter, that prattle, that gabbing, even gossip, *chiacchiera* in Italian, that distinguishes women's language as excess: chatting eludes the rhythms of daily duties. In the words of Elisabetta Rasy, chatting is language that is "only apparently mimetic," it is a "chain of digressions which leads speech to the margins and gives speech over only to what comes from the margins. It does not follow major topics, it does not know highs and lows, thus uniting high and low, it levels, it destroys public and private, while recognizing only externally their difference."[57] Chatting, above all, allows "the infinitely great to coincide with the infinitely small" (Rasy, 66)—in Gemma's case, then, the divine with the human, the sublime with the everyday. Angels and meatballs. Holy coffee.

Could we also, then, interpret Gemma's language from a positive perspective? Is there something valuable in her writing, repetitive and ungrammatical as it is, childish, childlike, that could not be found in a more refined text? Could her language be compared, for example, to the use of the vernacular by medieval mystics, who could not accede to the more lofty, elitist Latin because it was a language reserved to the educated—men, then? To see Gemma's low language as a forced choice, in this perspective, risks producing a reductive reading. For, as Italian philosopher Luisa Muraro puts it, "the choice of those who 'do not have a choice' is a symbolic creation and must be seen as the highest exercise of freedom."[58] Rather than a facile underestimation of Gemma's linguistic competence, we could then see the limits of her language as representing the limits of language as such when it is confronted with the mystical experience. The Greek root of the word mystical, after all, means "hidden," so that the expression "mystical phenomena" is a paradox of sorts: a phenomenon is something directly perceptible to the senses (from a Greek root meaning "to appear, to show"), and not something hidden. And (how) can we speak of what is hidden?

Gemma's ecstasies, her stigmata, her ability to go without food for long stretches of time, are other ways of speaking the unspeakable, of adding to her written texts other texts yet, which cannot be expressed in words. But we can only "read her body" even as we read—carefully, attentively, suspiciously—her writings, her words, or we would end up silencing Gemma— much as Jacques Lacan, the French Freud, reductively interpreted Teresa of Avila's mystical experience as speechless orgasm exclusively on the basis of Gian Lorenzo Bernini's statue of her in Rome.[59] And in this decoding process, we must also recognize our complicitousness, as readers, with the injunctions, issued by Gemma's spiritual directors, to write all that happens to her and to confess everything in the most minute detail. Spirituality needs to be transformed into a legible discourse if it is to be controlled; the hidden must be shown, to Gemma's great disgust. In reading Gemma Galgani's writings we participate in that process of invasion of her privacy; we should therefore approach her with tact and gratitude. And yet could this paradox —Gemma's disgust at writing—be at the basis of our own difficulty with Gemma Galgani's written experience? Does her repugnance at making the invisible visible, at having to proffer the untouchable to human touch, seep from her writing into our reading? And if in this process of transformation the spiritual, mystical experience needs to be adapted, purged, censored, translated of course from one medium to another, from one discourse to another, from one existential dimension to another, how much of it can we expect to have survived?

H: HYSTERIA
—OR, "HYSTERICS SUFFER MAINLY FROM REMINISCENCES"

Anna O.: Her boring and futile daily life leads to a hysteria characterized by an elaborate series of speech disorders, auto-hypnotic absences, and excessive daydreaming (Josef Breuer, *Studies on Hysteria*); Lucy R.: A poor governess in love with her rich employer hysterically hallucinates smelling the burnt pudding and the cigar-smoke she detected when she first realized her love dreams were hopeless (Sigmund Freud, *Studies on Hysteria*); Katharina: At eighteen suffers from hysterical shortness of breath as a result of sexual attempts on the part of her own father (Freud, *Studies on Hysteria*); Rosalie: a singer who loses her voice as a result of her uncle's seduction attempts (Freud, *Studies on Hysteria*); Dora: Experiences hysterical aphonia, or loss of voice, after the husband of her father's mistress attempts to seduce her at the age of fourteen (Freud, *Fragment of an Analysis of a Case of Hysteria*).[60] As Freud says, "hysterics suffer mainly from reminiscences."

Hysteria, the female malady par excellence, is a somatization of psychical conflicts, the symptomatic embodiment of a trauma, its corporeal acting out as opposed to its linguistic articulation. Symptoms included paralyses, seizures, ranting and raving, but also more subtle signs such as those mentioned in the cases described above. What these motley symptoms have in common is that they are functional and lack a concomitant organic pathological change. Psychological pain, that is, turns into physical pain through the process of hysterical conversion, and not as a result of a lesion or an infection or another bodily pathology. Hysteria reached its apex of popularity precisely at the turn of the century, during Gemma Galgani's own lifetime (*Studies in Hysteria,* Sigmund Freud's first book-length study, co-authored with Josef Breuer, was published in 1895; psychoanalysis is seen by many critics as the offspring of hysterical women).[61] Hysteria was an illness easily, all too easily, applicable to Gemma, and in this ease lies the disturbing nature of the diagnosis; for Gemma's life abounded in those phenomena sometimes called by modern scholars of religion "paramystical" and diagnosed by positivist psychology as hysterical symptoms: stigmata (spontaneous, or, worse yet, self-inflicted bleeding) and E X T A S Y (hysterical paralysis, or as Jean-Martin Charcot called it, *attitudes passionnelles*) are the most dramatic examples of these experiences.

I am not about to psychoanalyze Gemma in this entry. Accusations of hysteria abound in the history of her life and canonization proceedings, and this is of course not at all surprising given the historical and cultural background: in nineteenth-century European medicine, for example, women mystics were definitively diagnosed as hysterics. Saint Teresa of Avila is symptomatically chosen by Freud as "the patron saint of hysteria."[62] Yet any connection that I am revealing between this popular turn-of-the-century diagnosis and Gemma's spiritual experience develops for the sake of understanding these two parallel discourses on the BODY (hysteria and mysticism) and not with the objective of medicalizing one into the other. Besides, as I have discussed at length elsewhere, turn-of-the-century diagnoses of hysteria had themselves been deeply affected, if not downright shaped, by the discourse of and around medieval and later mystics. The hysteria diagnosis had been a popular one in the decades immediately preceding Gemma's own birth, though as a diagnosis it existed at least since the time of Hippocratic medicine, when it acquired its name—which derives from the Greek word for uterus. But it is worth remembering that nineteenth-century hysteria affected especially women (linked with the irrational and driven by the vagaries of an unstable reproductive system), especially young women of Gemma's age (hormonal volcanoes, it seemed), especially girls with problematic family backgrounds—like Gemma, orphaned at an early age, impoverished, unwanted. Numerous nonmedical interpretations have been adduced for the popularity of this diagnosis, most from a feminist and/or psychoanalytic perspective.[63] But the primary question in our discussion should be: Can the discourse around hysteria help us understand Gemma's writings and her spiritual experience? If so, how?

I would like to turn to a specific example, to a point of convergence between Gemma, autobiography, and the discourse of hysteria. This juncture, significantly, does not consist for me of her stigmata nor of her ecstasies. Rather, in reading Gemma's texts through a feminist hermeneutics of suspicion, in paying attention that is to the apparently insignificant, to the small details and the telling silences (see the reference to the work of Elisabeth Schüssler Fiorenza and Elisabetta Rasy in the introduction to this alphabet), I have been struck by the more than occasional references to unwanted touching that occur in her writings and those of her biographer, Father Germano. The latter, at the beginning of his biography of the saint, details little Gemma's outraged reactions to her father's caresses and kisses—which he "almost never" succeeded in giving her because of Gemma's innate "modesty": "'DAD,' she would say crying, 'do not touch me.' 'But I am after all your father,' he replied. 'Yes, dad, but I do not want anyone to touch me.' And her father, so as not to sadden her, immediately stopped, and instead of being sorry, he would usually end up mixing his own tears with his daughter's."[64] Why this extreme reaction in such a little girl—or rather, since this is a hagiographic text, why such a focus on it? Should we interpret it as a sign of Gemma's supernatural purity (as her biographer does), as an excessive and pathological mistrust of the flesh, either on the part of Gemma or of Germano the biographer (as psychoanalysis would have us believe), as an instinctively protective reaction against the possibility of incest (as a suspicious feminist hermeneutics might)?

The answer we choose is clearly not without relevance, though it may reveal more about us, the readers, than about Gemma. Freud himself had initially linked the etiology of hysteria with child molestation, thus believing the words of those women who told him they had been sexually abused as children (and Freud, by the way, is considered the first scientist to acknowledge in writing the significance of the sexual abuse of children). "But, unable to accept the possibility of so many perverse fathers," writes Jane Gallop, "he presses on to the discovery of infantile, polymorphous perverse, sexuality. Not fathers but children are perverse: they fantasize seduction by the father."[65] Freud also problematically saw disgust for sexual touching as a hysterical symptom, even when fourteen-year-old Dora was disgusted at a forty-something man fondling her. This diagnostic strategy has been harshly criticized, predictably and justly, by Freud's feminist readers. Furthermore, it is clear that Freud's patients were hurting from memories of touching, of inappropriate, unwanted, or just plain painful touching: Emmy's brother-in-law's and Rosalie's uncle's grabbing, Elisabeth's father's swollen foot on her thigh . . . It is not necessary to resort to psychoanalytic interpretations to identify connections between the various parts of Gemma's texts—especially the more uncomfortable and previously unacknowledged, or even unpublished, parts. And all these accounts suggest a continuity, which I do not think even Gemma would deny, between her earthly story and her supernatural developments. The painful touching of her body binds her text to the interrelated discourses of literature and psychoanalysis, through the rhythms of hysteria.

Let me finally turn to Gemma's text. In her autobiography, when she describes staying at the house of an aunt, Gemma reports that this aunt's fifteen-year-old son "teased me and put his hands on me" (le cousinage est un dangereux voisinage, the French wisely say). Once, when she brought him some clothing as he was horseback riding, he "pinched" her; the Italian term Gemma uses here is "pizzicotto," the one we associate with what happens to women tourists on crowded buses in Italian cities. Interestingly, Gemma's spirited reaction was to shove him so hard that he fell off the horse and hurt his head. As a consequence Gemma's aunt tied her hands behind her back for an entire day: the aunt clearly saw the pinch as legitimate and the shove as inexcusable. Even this punishment, however, did not prevent Gemma from getting mad, answering back, making faces, and vowing to get even (Autobiography, 30). An analogous episode occurs in an altogether different setting. When Gemma is facing, in the course of an ecstasy, a being of whose identity she is unsure—her GUARDIAN ANGEL, most likely—she tells him: "No, don't touch me, because my Dad wants no one to touch me . . . But you have the appearance of a man! . . . No, I do not want you to touch me" (*Ecstasies and Letters,* 148).[66] The devil, at least, is more explicit in his intentions: his touch is a beating, to which Gemma can more easily respond—even when he hits her in unmentionable places: "All of a sudden he began to hit me on my shoulders and even further down" (*Diary,* 74); or, in the shape of a huge black dog, "he put his legs on my shoulders," in the attempt to mount her (*Diary,* 75).

Gemma saw her body as sacred, as the temple of the Holy Spirit (in Saint Paul's definition, 1 Cor. 6:17, *Autobiography,* 41), as untouchable (see the entry CLOTHING). This perhaps is what gave her the strength to resist what other girls her age might not have had the promptness of spirit to push away —the "normal" advances of a teenage boy, the "kind" caresses of a guardian angel, the kisses of a loving father . . . (Though she could do nothing, it seems, about the servant's undressing her in the closed room, as one of the unpublished sections of her autobiography attests.)

Let me end by returning to a more standard definition of hysteria as neurosis and by deferring to the French scholar of mysticism Michel de Certeau. In an encyclopedia article on the definition of mysticism, after noting the dangerous proximity of mysticism and pathology (represented in the case of women by hysteria above all, I would say), de Certeau points out that the ties between madness and truth are enigmatic, and that it is an especially mistaken position to use social conformism, the rules of which are themselves ever changing, as the criterion according to which one judges mysticism. For psychological balance is based precisely on the norms of society, and the mystic repeatedly crosses over these.[67] Just as pointedly, Sara Maitland and Wendy Murford have criticized that reductionistic endeavor to "reduce all marks of holiness to pathology, and all struggles with faith, with interiority and with Otherness to psychological manifestations." It is not that this type of interpretation is necessarily untrue, but it is just not sufficient, not adequate: "If holiness is a liminal state (as we are arguing throughout this book), then it is inherently an unstable one: it is not surprising that many of its manifestations are, or are very similar to, psychopathological conditions. Does this matter? Are heroic lives less interesting, less noble, if lived by the neurotic? Is mystery more explicable?"[68]

Or, in Gemma Galgani's own words, "Let it be as that doctor said, that it is hysteria: precisely for that reason, Jesus loves me more."[69]

I: IMAGINATION
— OR, SEEING IS BELIEVING . . . OTHERWISE

" 'Imagination' is a slippery term, designating a power that penetrates the inner meaning of reality but also a power that creates substitutes for reality; I
am interested in both meanings. In one way or another, imagination has
been for many women the seed of grace, and often the subject as well as the
impetus of their writing." [70] An excessively fervid imagination has been
regarded as an important element in the causation of HYSTERIA—through
its power to create, in literary critic Patricia Meyer Spacks's words quoted
above, "substitutes for reality." The vivid imagination of young women is
often explicitly connected, in medical reports, with the higher incidence of
hysteria among members of this group. Girlish imagination was for many
the cause of the religious visions of another nineteenth-century woman
saint, Bernadette Soubirous of Lourdes. And imagination, or *fantasia,* to
use Gemma's own slippery word, plays an important part in the drama of
Gemma's spiritual experiences and their interpretations. Gemma herself often attributes her supernatural experiences to her own imagination, thus discounting—on a superficial level at least—their objective value. The first
entry of her diary, for example, which discusses Gemma's painful reception,
from JESUS, of his crown of thorns (an experience which I discuss further
below, in the entry on PASSION), is undermined at the end by Gemma's last
sentence: "I suffered greatly with any movement I made: but this was all
my imagination" (*Diary,* 72). Similar phrases abound in Gemma's writings,
as they do in those of other holy women: Gemma's contemporary Benigna
Consolata Ferrero (1885–1916), for example, after she complains in a language strikingly similar to Gemma's that for a long time Jesus "has not made
himself felt," then speculates that her hearing his words "is perhaps the effect
of my imagination" (like Gemma, she uses in Italian the word "fantasia"). [71]
When on a Friday Gemma is asked by her aunt to go fetch some water at the
well, the exhaustion she felt made the crown of thorns which she usually
bore on that day hurt her so much that she writes: "I thought the thorns went
into my brain (but this was all my imagination)"—though the bleeding from
her temple is so visible that Gemma has to tell her aunt she got scratched by
the well-chain (*Diary,* 80). More than undermining her believability, though,
this statement confirms the exceptional nature of Gemma's visions: as we
realize by reading her texts, Gemma is quite sure, however paradoxically,
of the "impossible things" she writes about, she knows that it is God who
appears and speaks to her, so that her questioning the interference of her

imagination only goes to confirm that God has chosen her in spite and because of her head. To refer again to Spacks's dense quotation, Gemma's imagination is both a "power that penetrates the inner meaning of reality" and "a power that creates substitutes for reality," it is "the seed of grace" and the "subject as well as the impetus of [her] writing."

Gemma's position regarding her imagination becomes clearer later in her diary. When she speaks of the consolations bestowed on her by the love of Jesus, Gemma writes: "They are all things of my head; but if I obey, Jesus will not permit me to be deceived" (*Diary,* 90). In her UNION with her Lover, her thoughts (the "things of her head") become in Gemma's view Jesus' own, and since divine love is incompatible with fraud and self-deceit, all of the saint's doubts on this matter are assuaged. In a letter to her confessor Gemma inadvertently makes explicit this essential link between Jesus' will and her own: "I wanted to go on, but it seemed to me that Jesus (namely, my head) did not let me finish."[72] Is Gemma in this sentence discounting what Jesus said as just the fruit of her imagination, or is she on the contrary equating her imagination, her head, with the workings of Jesus—"namely, [her] head"? Is she in fact positing a connection between Jesus and herself to the point that what she calls her imagination could really be seen as an imaginary of sorts (the lack of differentiation, in Lacanian psychoanalysis, between child and mother—between Gemma and Jesus)? For it is clear that as far as Gemma is concerned, OBEDIENCE is due to her visions more than to any human order, and at this point the role played by her own imagination becomes secondary to the experience of God. Gemma seems to be saying, then, that God operates in her and for her even through her own imagination, rather than in spite of it: if she obeys the latter, she will not be deceived—for it connects human and divine. Her imagination, therefore, for all its potential traps, is another way for Jesus to manifest himself to her, another form of mystical union, the imaginary stage. The mother's body must be near. Significantly, then, in an ecstasy, Gemma consecrates her imagination to the Blessed Virgin Mary, her celestial MOM: "Today, Mom, I have to consecrate something to you . . . Accept it. To you I consecrate my imagination. Once it is consecrated to you, I will have nothing to fear . . ."[73]

Yet for some, Gemma's imagination is a reason, if not *the* reason, to discount the truthfulness of her assertions; its ability to create "substitutes for reality" erases its "power to penetrate the inner meaning of reality." As Gemma puts it in one of her first recorded ecstasies, "They don't really believe it is you: they think I am crazy; but I am not at all crazy, right, Jesus?"[74] That very imagination which skeptics might blame for the lack of veracity of her visions and experiences lies at the basis of Gemma's highly and newly meta-phorical language about God. God is for Gemma a father and a mother, a redeemer and a friend, a spouse and a lover. For theologian Sallie McFague, the metaphors of God as mother, as friend, and as lover are precisely three necessary pathways to an improved understanding of the divinity and our re-lationship to God in today's world. As McFague puts it, "How language, any language, applies to God we do not know; what religious and theological lan-guage is at most is metaphorical forays attempting to express experiences of relating to God."[75] Gemma herself is frightened at times by the boldness of her own language, and, more generally, her "lingua troppo lunga," her tongue that is "too long," that causes her much distress (*Diary,* 78). For in spite, or perhaps because, of its lowly, uneducated status, what she says is of-ten new. Even Gemma's occasional mistrust of her own imagination points in this direction. How could her lowly language really be the manifestation of an infinite God? Could the doctors be right about her hysteria, her mad-ness—a needless, pathological prolonging of the imaginary stage, the un-differentiation from the mother's body? Or, is the devil infiltrating himself into her head, turning her imagination into his work?

In her linguistic self-deprecation, embodied in the concept of *fantasia* —a term in turn indissolubly tied to her being perceived as a hysteric— Gemma reminds me once again of the medieval Italian mystic Angela of Foligno, who repeatedly called her own language a "blasphemy"—presum-ably because, like Gemma's imagination, it went beyond commonly accepted parameters of piety and devotion.[76] Marguerite Porete, the French mystic and teacher burned at the stake in 1310, analogously spoke of her language as a "lie." Yet all these suspicious definitions, we could claim, ought to be seen as a realization of the effectiveness of language, rather than of its fail-ure. If mystical language is felt as an effect of blasphemy, of lying, of one's imagination, it is because its power, as well as its fragility, have been realized. If language had remained ineffective, there would have been no need to question its validity through this assortment of (self) accusations and (self) censorships.

Let me end this entry by turning the tables around and address the role of our own imagination in understanding Gemma Galgani. If we are to an-swer some of the questions with which I began this alphabet—concerning our potential connection with a woman saint of another time and another place—then it is helpful to become aware of the role of our own imagina-tion in her "hagiography," that is, in the way we reconstruct (or choose not to reconstruct) Gemma's life as a holy, a saintly life. For the past hundred years or so, Gemma's story has been claimed over and over again by faithful Catholics, and it can be claimed by others, too (be they unfaithful, non-Catholic, or both), as a sustaining narrative of and for the disempowered, of and for the marginal. Indeed Gemma's very location at the margin, dislocated from most dominant paradigms, and yet struggling to get in, can help us perhaps to see differently, to imagine a new perspective, to (dis)locate our own position of (dis)comfort. Thanks to the power of our imagination, that imagination with which Gemma herself lived so uncomfortably, we can interpret her truths, reinvent them, embrace their affective power by reading them, as I propose to do in this piece, antipatriarchally, against the grain of orthodoxy, "otherwise." In diversity (Gemma's, women's, our own—whatever such a difference might consist of) we can find a rich source of creativity rather than just another center from which to create an oppressed margin (though that is always a risk, of course). Just as it is through her imagination that Gemma Galgani has managed to disrupt and explode the restricted social, cultural, religious tradition in which she was brought up, so also it is through the imagination that one may be able to overcome the discomfort, disbelief, mistrust, suspicion, perhaps the threat that the holy, the miraculous, elicit in so many people today.

J: JESUS
— OR, (QUEERING) CHRISTOLOGY

Who is Jesus Christ for Gemma? Despite her attachment to her GUARDIAN ANGEL, her MOM—the Blessed Virgin Mary—and holy people such as Gabriel of Our Lady of Sorrows and Margaret Mary Alacoque, Gemma's spirituality is undoubtedly Christ-centered—or perhaps I should say Jesus-centered, for that is the name that Gemma normally uses to refer to the God-man, her "impetuous Lover." This choice of name stresses the intimacy of their relationship, for Gemma uses Jesus' first name rather than his attribute "Christ," meaning more grandiosely "the anointed one." She uses his human name rather than the one referring to his divinity, his incarnation of God, his KENOSIS. Gemma's Jesus is above all the Jesus of the PASSION, but he is also a singularly familiar Jesus, one who, after sharing with Gemma the pain of bearing the crown of thorns—an experience among the most advanced forms of mystical UNION—prosaically becomes "serious and a little mad" ("arrabbiato," the Italian word Gemma uses, is colloquial) when Gemma tells him (she *tells* him, rather than, significantly, *asking* him) not to send her to confession to a certain priest (*Diary*, 73). Likewise, she speaks to him in a threatening way when she writes about him in her diary: "I told him that if he loved me he should grant me the grace of entering the convent" (*Diary,* 78). Even more vehemently, and at this point she might sound a bit like a peevish child (until one realizes, that is, that she is speaking to God), she exclaims in an ecstasy, about the grace of entering a convent: "I want this grace at all costs. I want it, I want it . . . and don't tell me no, or it's going to end badly. But if you give it to me . . . I am sure you will." [77] And she explicitly threatens Jesus, at the end of this same ecstasy, that he should inform her confessor of all of her needs, "otherwise, I will no longer laugh with you, you know: I will remain very serious and I will not embrace you." [78] She loves him and seeks him and does not always find him, and in their seduction games she calls him and he does not always answer, so that Gemma ends up losing her patience: "I am just about to get mad and tell him that he is rude. O, Dad, why does he make me seek him so? At times I have even called him cruel." [79]

Their games include humor, as when, in a discussion about the relative enlightenment of her confessor regarding her specific needs, Gemma writes: "Jesus did not know that my guardian angel had told me this; he made a serious face and told me he did not want my guardian angel to tattle on him" (*Diary,* 99; "fare le spie," child's language, really, is the expression used here). At times the angel, Jesus, and Gemma play some different mind games: when Gemma asks her angel why Brother Gabriel has not visited her in such a long time, the angel claims that it is because she so wants such a visit that Jesus does not permit it. Therefore, the angel complicitously suggests, next time Gemma sees Jesus she should feign indifference about it, and then Jesus will allow Brother Gabriel to come. But in saying this the angel "laughed heartily," and Gemma comments: "I realized he was kidding, because I know nothing can be hidden from Jesus" (*Diary,* 100).

Gemma's intimacy with Jesus is expressed not only through their mutual familiar language, seductive and playful, but by their common actions as well. Jesus, for example, caresses Gemma on more than one occasion, and Gemma exclaims in an ecstasy, "I am yours, I am yours, Jesus . . ." (*Ecstasies and Letters,* 144). More explicitly, Jesus "approaches [her] with his lips" (*Ecstasies and Letters,* 149). The relationship between Jesus and Gemma, as I discuss below in the entry WEDDING, is an erotically charged one, or at least it is described with the language of eroticism—the one that for Gemma most closely approaches the reality of the mystery, the God-made-man and the man-as-God. That very Jesus who is for Gemma both a historical reality and a symbol is also a being who escapes or exceeds all categories. Jesus is undoubtedly male, and his gender stimulates Gemma into an erotic discourse which alone can express their intimacy, their mutual seduction. But Jesus' maleness is nothing like that of every other male in Gemma's entourage, for the intimacy developed between these two is steeped in a mutuality absent in every other human relationship Gemma entertains; and her relationships with others are quite similar, I would claim, to those of the women represented in other turn-of-the-century secular Italian texts, fictional and nonfictional: she is a dutiful daughter, though subtly manipulative, to a traditional father; she is the admiring sister of a more privileged older brother; the sickly daughter of a sickly mother; the undesirable poor relative to several better-off aunts; the courted, attractive young woman who wants nothing to do with marriage; the pretty cousin unwillingly fondled by a teenage male; the titillatingly undressed female patient of various male doctors . . .

In fact, in spite of many feminists' discomfort with a male incarnation of the divinity, one of the feminist advantages to Jesus having been a man is precisely his disruption of the male paradigmatic style of authority: his compassion, his service to others, and the death to which all of this has led are what women are supposed to do by nature and what males of power in a patriarchal world are simply not involved in. His actions question identity, deconstruct categories such as gender itself, represent subjectivity as fluid, amorphous, provisional. They point to the essential performativity, in Judith Butler's formulation, of all gender identity. As Eleanor McLaughlin writes, "Jesus is the Trickster who peels us open to new depths of humanity, divinity, femaleness, maleness. There might be no telling what boundaries and categories could be dis-mantled as male gender hegemony is disrobed. That is what the Gospel is about, the piercing of categories in the womb/by the dart of love. A merely male Jesus has been and continues to be a violation of the scandal and transgression which is the Gospel."[80] (A "queer Jesus," perhaps—and may parentheses protect me here—if we think of queer as a discursive position rather than an identity: "To be queer in the 1990s is to be passionate about your sexuality and your politics and to adopt an 'in yer face' strategy or lifestyle which makes no concessions to mainstream tastes and sensibilities"[81]—sound familiar? Compare with Roman Catholic theologian Elizabeth Johnson's statement: "Since Jesus the Christ is depicted as divine Sophia, then it is not unthinkable—it is not even unbiblical—to confess Jesus the Christ as the incarnation of God imaged in female symbol.")[82] And this identification of Gemma with Jesus and of Jesus with Gemma, grounded in kenosis and developed in mutuality, leads to the topic of RESEMBLANCE, of *imitatio Christi,* another instance of gender-bending to which I turn below:

gender-bending, (re)turning (to) queer, overcoming and/or blurring one's gender identity are seen as phenomena symptomatic of the postmodern condition, (un)founded as it is on the collapse of the classical notion of identity as a whole. But the collapse of identity, its exhaustion and implosion, is and has for a long time been intrinsic to the mystical project, so it is not surprising that such phenomena should recur, of all places, in Gemma Galgani's work (see also the entry MOM).

K : KENOSIS

— OR, OF GREATNESS AS A DISAPPEARING ACT

Kenosis, or self-emptying, is the term used by Saint Paul in the Christian Scriptures to refer to the contraction, the reduction of God to the human level, or God's self-emptying in the incarnation in Christ. In the human JESUS of Nazareth, God emptied the divine self into time and space: Christ "emptied himself, taking the form of a slave, coming in human likeness" (Philippians 2:7; this is the only reference in the Christian Scriptures to the incarnation as God's self-emptying). Kenosis is often seen as the paradox and even the scandal of Christian revelation, for incarnation goes beyond those mysterious, incomprehensible, transcendental characters attributed to God by much theology and so easily incorporated by an authoritarian conception of religion and the church. The basic metaphors and models of Christianity, Sallie McFague notes, are "triumphalist, monarchical, patriarchal."[83] Still, theology is a thoroughly interpretive enterprise and its models are not descriptions but rather interpretations; they ought not to be understood literally. Indeed, their potential violence needs to be unmasked, their intrinsic hierarchy disrupted, in order for a properly kenotic understanding of God to take place. Thus, since kenosis is opposed to the vision of God as "wholly other," since in kenosis the radical distinction between divine and human is no longer unsurpassable, kenosis is appropriately at the center of much feminist Christian theology. From this perspective, kenosis is seen as the meaning of creation and of redemption, as the continuity between God and the world, as the affirmation of the BODY through the embodiment of God.

And kenosis can itself be seen as a model, the model, even, of human relations. "The cross," Elizabeth Johnson argues, "stands as a poignant symbol of the 'kenosis of patriarchy,' the self-emptying of male dominating power in favor of the new humanity of compassionate service and mutual empowerment."[84] Gemma, in her imitation of Christ, empties herself of the little she had, thus undergoing her own suffered kenosis. Contempt for her body is a necessary part of this process. Her powerlessness, then, paradoxically becomes a source of empowerment through mystical UNION, as we can see in an ecstasy: "You know, Jesus, that this morning I found a way to capture you? By placing myself in my own nothingness."[85] Hélène Cixous makes a similar argument for self-emptying, or self-renouncement, from a secular perspective when she illustrates the way to "get to" love: "To get there, one needs strength, the real strength of abnegation which is renouncement: before all the other renouncements that will follow, in particular the renouncement of the affirmation of an identity. One must open oneself, one must make room for the other. Accept an entirely amazing change in economy that is produced: *less self*."[86] Another practical way in which Gemma strives for self-emptying, for kenosis, is through her embrace of abject poverty: when her father dies, she loses everything, even the coins in her pockets. But Gemma's self-emptying choice is a more radical one, one which finds its genealogy in the quietism of Marguerite Porete and its successor in the writings of Simone Weil. For the most profound way in which the mystic may approach divine kenosis is through the annihilation of the will—even, and this is where Marguerite Porete got in trouble, of the will to do good, the will to do God's will. The point, here, is not to turn to evil, but to let God's will be done *through* us rather than *by* us: "Good will must become indifference (is this the right word? there are no others) toward what is right/wrong, because only this indifference, Marguerite Porete teaches, allows one to operate unconditionally well."[87] Even as a child, Gemma eagerly awaited the EUCHARIST, the day of her first communion, because she realized that "when Jesus will be with me, I will no longer live in me, because Jesus will live in me" (*Autobiography,* 32).

Twentieth-century French mystic and activist Simone Weil is even more radical in her appropriation of the ideal of kenosis, for which she uses the term "decreation"—among the most important concepts in Weil's writings. Rather than seeing creation as an addition to God by God, Weil sees creation as the contraction or self-emptying of God: creation is an effect of divine restraint and renunciation rather than self-expansion, creation is the voluntary absence of God, it is God's abdication. And in this self-emptying of divine power is found the fullest expression of divine love: God withdraws to make room for the world, in an act of love and self-sacrifice that is repeated by Christ on the cross and by all human beings when we express compassion and mercy through self-denial. For it is in self-denial, or in "decreation" of the self, in renunciation, that we humans participate in the creative act. By renouncing the "I," the individual acknowledges oneness with God's part in creation and with Christ's act of willingly dying on the cross. With the ability of ceasing to be, we have the possibility of giving God something in return. So the duty of Christians, and the task of those who choose to be lovers of the world, does not consist so much in a generalized benevolence toward all human beings, but rather in the much more costly availability in service which leaves no room for the superficial interests of the self. This is the practical aspect of that "becoming divine" advocated by some feminist theologians—for divinity, in this kenotic perspective, is not the power to control but the power to refrain from controlling the other, it is not creation but *de*-creation. In abstaining from FOOD, in controlling her BODY, in OBEDIENCE, in VIRGINITY, with ZEAL, always through PASSION, and at times even in the midst of LAUGHTER, Gemma decreases her self (a dangerous choice when it is made by a woman in an oppressive context, to be sure) and in this lies her greatness, her creativity, because of this she is elected to SAINTHOOD—or, more radically yet, through this Gemma "becomes divine."

L: LAUGHTER
—OR, SHE WHO LAUGHS, LASTS

"You only have to look at the Medusa straight on to see her. And she's not deadly. She's beautiful and she's laughing."[88]

Throughout her life, Gemma Galgani is laughed at, derided, scorned by the people who surrounded her in the world. This is part of the reason why she wanted to enter the convent: to be protected from such mocking laughter: "What will I do, when I am sick and everyone will be there? I am ashamed, Dad."[89] But the laughing Medusas of Gemma's world are those very sacred figures that she dares look in the eye. Those figures who, instead of deadly silences, provide her with the words to say it, who give Gemma language rather than ineffability. Those beautiful laughing beings who, like women for Hélène Cixous in the essay from which the above quotation is taken, are figures of otherness, of difference, who are not impenetrably dark, nor, for Gemma, hopelessly beyond representation. Instead, they laugh. Mother M. Teresa, upon going from Purgatory to Heaven, "was laughing loudly";[90] the Virgin Mary laughs when Gemma calls her "MOM" (*Diary,* 86); Brother Gabriel speaks "laughingly" when he teasingly offers Gemma his miraculous belt and then refuses to give it to her until the following Saturday (*Diary,* 77); the guardian angel laughs a lot, as when he encourages Gemma to play mind tricks with Jesus: "In saying this, he laughed heartily . . . I understood that he was having fun" (*Diary,* 100); JESUS himself laughs over and over again, and kids around with Gemma: "'*Your Dad is bad, yes, really really bad,*' but he was kidding."[91]

There is certainly something disruptive about Gemma's perception of these holy characters and its written description, something unexpected and uncomfortable that explosively transforms Gemma's, and perhaps our own, relation to the supernatural—to God and the saints. This is the discovery of the presence of God in the quotidian, in the mundane, in laughter and smiles. It is a laughter that redeems instead of damning, a laughter which, like other aspects of Gemma's spirituality, crosses again and again the intersection of BODY and spirit, rational and irrational, individual and society, sacred and profane, nature and the miraculous—for laughter works to open up connections even as it physically opens up the body to the world, the self to otherness, identity to difference. It is a laughter which cannot be contained much like the holy cannot be contained by the worldly (and must be understood, at times, as madness, as HYSTERIA), much like grace cannot be contained by theological discourse. When the devil cannot hurt her because she is wearing the belt of Saint Gabriel, Gemma repeatedly says that she was laughing as she watched the devil being devoured by rage: "I laughed . . . I stayed happily in bed and laughed . . . In short," she somewhat surprisingly claims, "today I had a lot of fun with him" (*Diary*, 76).

When I lived, for a short while, at the edges of the Bible belt, one of my roommates had a picture hanging on our living-room wall that was entitled "Jesus laughing." Because I grew up in Italy, perhaps, I found the image disturbing: to my knowledge, medieval and Renaissance as well as later religious art, whether high or low, certainly never depicted Jesus that way: mouth open, teeth showing, head thrown back, clearly laughing. When I asked my pious roommate whether the laughter of Jesus was found in any scriptural passage, she replied that Jesus spent a lot of time with children, and she could not imagine how anyone could possibly spend any time with children and not laugh. True enough. But if Lamennais could exclaim "Who could picture Jesus laughing?"[92] and if more recently Umberto Eco could center his best-selling novel *The Name of the Rose* (1980) on the issue of whether or not Jesus ever laughed and, therefore, whether or not laughing should be permissible for Christians, then I am in good company in my disquiet concerning that picture in my former living room.

So I can certainly understand why Gemma's hagiographers felt impelled to add some footnotes claiming that in Gemma's vernacular the verb to laugh, "ridere," really means to smile ("sorridere," in Italian).[93] Laughter is not scriptural; laughter is associated with the body (and it would thus point, rather transgressively or at least inappropriately, to the body of Gemma's spiritual interlocutors); laughter is an inarticulate outburst violating rational thought and orderly speech; laughter is undisciplined; it is incompatible with dignity—hardly appropriate, then, for the saints, and much less for the divinity incarnate. Above all, perhaps, laughter cannot co-exist with the thought of the suffering of Jesus and his death on the cross. So, although many regard laughter today as liberating, rehabilitative, and even therapeutic, Gemma's laughing Jesus, laughing Mary, laughing angel, remain uncomfortable. Yet these laughing figures express a salvific generative power. For their laughter connects body and soul, Jesus and Gemma, Mary and Gemma, the angel and Gemma. In this effect, their laughter is analogous to pain: both pain and laughter prevent as well as transcend language, both pain and laughter open up the body to the other, both pain and laughter are essential components of Gemma's spirituality. So I would claim that the joyful laughter of Gemma's supernatural friends (more disquieting, in the long run, than the mean-spirited laughter of those who mock her) is liberating precisely insofar as it is disturbing for our religious and aesthetic sensibilities. In this disruption we may be empowered to find the ability to break, to productively subvert, the established representational and social structures, the conventions of a religion that would prefer a silent smile to a bellowing laughter. For, as one of her hagiographers simply expressed it, "Gemma, too, loved to laugh."[94]

M: MOM
—OR, THE REPRODUCTION OF MOTHERS

"Nineteenth-century Catholic culture ascribed to the mother the functions of religious formation and moral correction, under the banner of an unlimited spirit of sacrifice."[95] No one could come closer to this model than Gemma Galgani's mother, whose relatively brief maternal relationship with her daughter is posited by the hagiographers and by Gemma herself as the inception of the latter's SAINTHOOD: "Gemma wanted to become a saint at all costs. She sucked this ardent desire along with her mother's milk," provokingly writes Father Germano.[96] We first encounter Gemma Galgani's mother in the saint's own autobiography, right under the heading "First memories—Mom" (*Autobiography,* 28). A morbid mother she was, fond of saying things from which any child psychologist today (and most parents, I like to think) would recoil in horror. Gemma was less than seven years old when her mother would take her in her arms, crying, telling her of her sickness and impending death and asking Gemma if she would go with her. When little Gemma, who "understood very little and cried," asked "where would we go?" her mother answered "To Heaven, with JESUS, with the angels . . . "—to which Gemma agreed (*Autobiography,* 28). It is in fact to her mother that Gemma attributes her desire to go to Heaven. During mass, a voice asked Gemma if she was willing to give up her mother so that she could be brought to Heaven, and although Gemma consented she stayed at her mother's bedside so relentlessly that her father had to send her away from Lucca, to the house of an uncle, for fear that Gemma herself would be infected and die before her mother did. Thus, Gemma was not there when her mother died in September 1886. And "ever since Mom died," Gemma later wrote, "I have not spent a single day without suffering some little thing for Jesus" (*Autobiography,* 39).

In my subtitle to this entry I refer to an influential and controversial book on mothering, written by a feminist object-relations psychoanalyst: Nancy Chodorow's *The Reproduction of Mothering,* first published in 1978. I paraphrased its title in order to refer to the proliferation of mother figures in the life of Saint Gemma: a number of aunts attempted to yet were incapable of filling the emotional gap left by her biological mother's premature death, and, although Gemma called one particular teacher, who used to take her in her arms and caress her "even though I was eleven years old," as Gemma herself admits, "Mom" (*Autobiography,* 35), it is only the Virgin Mary who will provide sufficient maternal affection for Gemma. As Jesus tells Gemma: "'I am your father, your mother will be . . . ' and he pointed to Most Holy Mary, Our Lady of Sorrows" (*Autobiography,* 46). But, although I cannot develop its themes at length here, there is more in Chodorow's book that relates to Gemma's story than just the title (and although I agree with some of the criticism leveled against the book, I believe it provides a useful framework for discussing mothering practices in Western, middle-class society of the past hundred years or so). For example, Chodorow notes that "prolonged symbiosis and narcissistic overidentification are particularly characteristic of early relationships between mothers and daughters" (104), that "girls come to experience themselves as less differentiated than boys, as more continuous with and related to the external object-world and as differently oriented to their inner object-world as well" (167), that "feminine personality comes to include a fundamental definition of self in relationship" (169). Now, these points have also been raised by feminist theology, with its emphasis on relationality, and by studies of mysticism (dominated by women, founded on UNION), as well as by literary criticism.

An intense psychological, emotional, spiritual connection with her mother, sharing her fate of sickness and early death, the painful tension between likeness and unlikeness, being sent away from her mother by her father, loneliness and isolation when this happens . . . these are also elements that recur, to varying degrees, in turn-of-the-century Italian women's lives and writings, such as in the autobiographical as well as fictional works of Sibilla Aleramo, Ada Negri, and Neera, all contemporaries of Gemma Galgani. This recurrence points to the centrality in women's lives of a relationship that, as poet and critic Adrienne Rich lamented in her book *Of Woman Born,* has been strikingly absent from traditional theology, art, sociology, and psychoanalysis (though in recent years, I am glad to say, there has been a proliferation of writings on the actual and potential variations of the mother-daughter bond; still, look at the conspicuous absence/irrelevance of mothers of daughters in Disney's feature-length cartoons!).[97] Intimacy and distance, passion and violence characterize a relationship made of continuity—and interruption—between two alike bodies: "Mothers and daughters have always exchanged with each other—beyond the verbally transmitted lore of female survival—a knowledge that is subliminal, subversive, preverbal: the knowledge flowing between two alike bodies, one of which has spent nine months inside the other."[98] "You look at yourself in the mirror. And already you see your own mother there. And soon your daughter, a mother. Between the two, what are you? What space is yours alone? In what frame must you contain yourself? And how to let your face show through, beyond all the masks?"[99] Based on that subliminal, subversive, preverbal (Julia Kristeva would say semiotic) knowledge, Gemma reconstructs the broken mirror of her mother's motherhood into a figure whom she cannot lose, into a frame that can include her own mask as well as her mother's: Mary of Nazareth, Our Lady of Sorrows, the Mother of her Bridegroom, or, for short, Mom.

The Virgin Mary, and particularly Our Lady of Sorrows ("Mamma Maria Santissima Addolorata," "Mom, Most Holy Mary, Our Lady of Sorrows," as Gemma calls her, in an idiosyncratic mix of official and familiar words, *Diary,* 73), fills the maternal frame Gemma so desperately needs, and she does so completely and successfully. Indeed, Mary is the realization of the daughter's want, as expressed poetically by Luce Irigaray, which in her worldly life Gemma was instead denied: "When the one of us comes into the world, the other goes underground. When the one carries life, the other dies. And what I wanted from you, Mother, was this: that in giving me life, you still remain alive."[100] Mary, "beautiful" and "beloved" (*Diary,* 86), smiles when Gemma calls her "with the sweet name of Mom," inviting Gemma to come and rest on her breast, and kissing her forehead (*Diary*, 74); she caresses Gemma who "could not say a word except to repeat the name Mom" (*Diary*, 85); she takes Gemma on her lap and kisses her, and her hair is the same color as Jesus' (*Diary*, 105–6). In the *Ecstasies*, Mary is for Gemma "Mom" as well as, less often, "Mother," and her relationship with Gemma at times assumes, in a playful tone, the rivalry between mother-in-law and daughter-in-law. For instance, Gemma chides her "Mom" for not returning to Gemma her love, out of jealousy that Gemma will then give it back to Jesus, her own "love" (*Ecstasies and Letters*, 133).

But Gemma goes further in her motherhood imagery, much further. For the ultimate mother for her is not so much the Virgin Mary as Jesus himself, Jesus as mother—a recurrent topos in medieval mystical writings (as I also discuss in the entry RESEMBLANCE), yet one obscured by androcentric tradition and rarely mentioned in theological discourse; it was, not surprisingly, an image especially dear to holy women.[101] But also in the twentieth century Edith Stein wrote to God, of God: "You guide me forward, like a mother's hand."[102] The motherhood of God can after all be talked of more easily than the motherhood of Christ, for in spite of representations of God as an old man with a white beard and a long robe, as "the man upstairs," God is not supposed to have a gender, and everyone, even the stodgiest and most conservative of theologians, will likely concede that point; how God's asexuality is to be represented in our gendered language is another matter: Bible translations, lectionaries, preaching, and teaching all tend to reinforce the implicit assumption that maleness is closer to the divinity. Yet Jesus was undeniably male, a man who could not possibly have been a biological mother, though in an important simile in the Gospels Jesus compares himself to a hen or bird gathering her little ones under her wings (Matthew 23: 37 and Luke 13:34).[103]

Gemma, on the other hand, daringly asks, in an ecstasy: "Do you think that children can stay without their mother? . . . To have a mother as generous as Jesus, a mother as infinite as Jesus!" And in the next ecstasy she tells Jesus: "I am yours, I was born of you."[104] Jesus is the being with whom Gemma once shared a body, and with whose body she will once again be one. Caroline Walker Bynum's statement about medieval women mystics elucidates this position and gives it a context, a genealogy: "The idea of Christ's motherhood becomes either a way of referring to the fact that Christians eat and drink Jesus or a metaphor for Christ's suffering on the cross, which gives birth to the world."[105] An analogous gender TRANSGRESSION is the center of Gemma's last letter to Father Germano, her confessor whom she usually addresses as "Babbo," "Dad." But this last letter, much to the dismay of Gemma's hagiographic editors, starts with "My dear Mom (forgive this word)." The footnotes, anxious to recuperate Gemma within an orthodox tradition, say that Father Germano interpreted this letter as being addressed to the Virgin Mary, though then the editors also have to admit that using the formal "Lei" with the Virgin Mary was unusual for Gemma (while it is the form with which she always addressed her confessor)—and attribute the pronoun confusion to the instability of Gemma's mind during her last days on earth. But then, why does Gemma ask to be forgiven about using the word "Mom" if her addressee is in fact the Virgin Mary, whom she has called "Mom" throughout her writings? Toward the end of the letter, Gemma writes again "Forgive this name (Mom) which I don't know why comes spontaneously to my lips." [106] Clearly Gemma is addressing Father Germano, and she is calling him "Mom," much as she had called Jesus himself "Mom." Language, including language about God, is indeed rooted for Gemma in the maternal BODY. And just as the signifier of the maternal body, for Gemma, is constantly in motion (referring to her biological mother, to the Virgin Mary, to Jesus, to Father Germano), so also her language about God defies, in its perennial displacements, the boundaries of traditional hagiography and theology. Gender metaphors are central to Gemma's journey, but they are not stable ones; rather, these metaphors repeatedly break the illusion of an abiding gendered self; they are guided by an imagination (an imaginary?) which constantly transforms them over and against a fixity (the paternal symbolic?) that would paralyze the female body into a gender-neutral spirit.

N: NUNS
— OR, HABITS OF EXCLUSION

"They did not want me in the convent alive, but they will take me in when I'm dead!" [107]

In 1861, the first census of the newly formed kingdom of Italy revealed that there were in Italy 42,664 women religious (no distinction is made between cloistered and uncloistered sisters), namely 1.95 nuns for every thousand women, while the male clergy constituted a significantly smaller group: 30,632 men. Many, perhaps even most, of these women religious had been obliged to take the veil by their family—unwilling or unable to put up the larger dowry necessary for a good marriage (though a modest dowry was also required in order to enter a convent). [108] But when we think of nuns it is also useful to remember that the convent constituted a respected way of life for women, a valid (and for many, the only) respectable alternative to the domestic role of wife and mother.

Entering a convent was from childhood Gemma's vocation, one that she was never allowed to fulfill: everywhere she knocked she encountered doubts and uncertainties, puzzled reactions and downright rejections—motivated by her bad health as well as her lack of financial means and/or family support. As she writes in her first two letters to Father Germano, "I realized it seemed impossible that I should become a Passionist, because I have absolutely nothing, only a great desire to become one"; "I have absolutely nothing, I am so poor, I only have a great desire to become a Passionist"; and most eloquently: "There are two reasons why my confessor does not let me enter a convent. The first one is because I have an illness called hysteria. . . . The other is a big one: I have absolutely nothing, I have no dad or mom, and I have no money."[109] Nevertheless, Gemma did succeed in spending chunks of time in convents at different periods of her life, with varying results. For example, between 1889 and 1893 she went to school at the Institute of the Zitine nuns (founded by the Lucchese Blessed Elena Guerra), and although she describes this period of her life as being "in Heaven" (*Autobiography*, 30), she also admits that she "got worse and worse" (30) because her only desire was to receive holy communion. Furthermore, Gemma defines herself, among the girls at the Institute, as "the most negligent and the most distracted" (*Autobiography*, 32). Following an illness, her doctor prohibits Gemma from studying and she leaves the Institute in 1895. Still, she claims that "Jesus gave me clear signs that I should become a nun" (*Autobiography*, 38), and she obtains permission to become a nun after healing from an illness diagnosed as both an abscess and as HYSTERIA. When she entered the Salesian Convent on May 1, 1899, Gemma again thought she "was entering Heaven" (*Autobiography*, 51), but she soon came to dislike the regimented schedule which did not allow her the freedom to be alone with her JESUS; furthermore, Gemma felt that life to be too easy and comfortable for the nuns and for herself (*Autobiography*, 52). She nevertheless preferred it to the world, but was not allowed to remain in the convent, ostensibly on account of her ill health, and only spent three weeks there. Still, she says, "my yearning to enter the convent, so I might be ever more united with him, was so strong that I feared someone would be able to take it away" (*Autobiography*, 55). Most decisively, Gemma writes that, in the course of a love conversation, "I told [Jesus] that if he loved me he should grant me the grace of entering the convent" (*Diary*, 78).

Another Italian nineteenth-century saint had a difficult relationship with convents and could only enter one that she herself was to found—barely more successful in this than Gemma, since she died shortly after its foundation. Bartolomea Capitanio, canonized in 1950, was born in 1807 in Lovere, in northern Italy, where she died twenty-six years later. Like Gemma, and at approximately the same age as Gemma, Bartolomea died of tuberculosis. Bartolomea's life and spirituality have much in common with Gemma's: both were beautiful and pious from an early age, both were intimately and unabashedly convinced of their future SAINTHOOD, both consecrated their VIRGINITY in order to be God's brides in mystical WEDDING, both relied on the EUCHARIST to satisfy all their hungers, both were moved by an all-encompassing ZEAL in every act of their short lives. But Bartolomea's familial support, her education, her numerous friendships, and her better (though not much better) health gave her the opportunity to develop more fully the active side of her vocation, to the point of founding a school for impoverished little girls which eventually turned into the "little convent," as Bartolomea called it, of the Sisters of Charity. Life in the existing convent of the Poor Clares, where Bartolomea spent a few years as a student and then as a teacher, "seems to me to be a bit too comfortable," as she wrote to a friend.[110]

But the Poor Clares wanted, even pressured, Bartolomea to join their order. Gemma, on the other hand, was repeatedly rejected, unwanted, both by the order she would have preferred and by those she would have settled for. Her unsuccessful quest for a convent, when understood in the context of her unique spiritual journey, is significant *because* unsuccessful. Gemma was always an outsider to contemporary institutions—be it the family or the convent, those two destinies reserved for women in traditional European societies. Not unlike Simone Weil, who never allowed herself to be baptized a Catholic because her vocation, she repeatedly claimed, was precisely to be a Christian outside the Church, at the margins—even while she was drawn to Catholicism and had a deep desire to partake of the eucharist—Gemma's position outside every form of institutional acceptance provides a powerful model for the many people who do not comfortably fit into any existing community: comfort, indeed, is precisely what Gemma did not like about her convent experiences. Like Simone Weil's impossible desire for the sacraments, Gemma desperately longed for acceptance in the convent, embodying the experience of those who do not belong: what she wants in the convent is not a career but the lowest place, offering to be a servant, to carry out menial tasks such as sweeping, washing dishes, drawing water, and mending. She thus hopes to remove the obstacle of her lack of dowry because if she enters the convent as a servant rather than as a nun the expense would be minimal.[111]

Gemma's inability to enter a convent came from the clergy, Simone Weil's to enter the Church came directly from God. Both, like most disenfranchised outsiders, want to be inside yet they are not allowed to enter. In this, I believe, lies their challenge.

O: OBEDIENCE

— OR, DISOBEDIENCE

"It is difficult . . . for persons to remain sane and mature from a stance of radical rejection of and by the normative culture. . . . It is women acting from a stance of 'radical obedience' rather than dissent who are likely to make the greater impact on their male colleagues, for their claims cannot be so easily rejected."[112]

Obedience, or lack of it, is one of the methods employed by the devil to make Gemma fall into sin, JESUS tells her, inciting her to "obey instantly and cheerfully" (*Diary,* 82). But like other women mystics, Gemma uses the concept of obedience in a personal and idiosyncratic way. What she really means by obedience is something closer, in fact, to disobedience—hence the link between this concept and its seeming opposite, TRANSGRESSION. What constitutes Gemma's absolute, radical obedience to Jesus can easily lead to the infraction of other people's rules—societal rules, for example, as well as the commands of elders and priests. Gemma keeps from her confessor her first strong experience of UNION with Jesus, and is scolded by her GUARDIAN ANGEL for "hiding things from [her] confessor" (*Autobiography,* 49). She promises not to do that again, but a few pages later we read: "With my confessor I was never sincere at all and I was always hiding something" (*Autobiography,* 55). For Gemma as for other holy women throughout Christian history, barred from the priesthood and thus from direct access to the sacraments, the issue of self-authorization, of self-authentication, was a pressing one—and in the case of mystics such as Gemma, visions were instrumental when facing the dilemma of whom to obey. The uncertainty was reinforced for Gemma by the frequent disagreements between her two confessors, Monsignor Volpi and Father Germano: thus Gemma asks Jesus to give her "a little light about which of my two directors I should obey" (*Ecstasies and Letters,* 134). Certainly God comes first, and direct supernatural summons cannot be automatically rejected by church officials, even when they come through an uneducated, impoverished, and sickly girl: "Yes, I truly wish to be obedient, but if Jesus wished otherwise?" she exclaims (*Ecstasies and Letters,* 148). It all comes down to that.

Gemma's idea of obedience is best illustrated in the second entry of her diary, where she cheerfully claims: "Even if this be entirely my imagination, or if it be the work of the devil, I want to obey anyway" (*Diary,* 73). What she obeys, then, is her own calling, her own experience—of her voice, and of Christ's own as it is spoken to her alone even through her IMAGINATION. No one else has access to the commands to which she responds, neither her family, when she still had one, nor her spiritual directors. Indeed, in an ecstasy, Gemma asks Jesus to spare her bleeding because her confessor does not want her to bleed that day; but clearly, if she has to ask, it is because neither Jesus nor her own BODY have automatically obeyed the priest's orders; indeed, she soon thereafter gives herself entirely to Jesus "even in the name of the confessor," not only disobeying, then, but also giving to God a will— the confessor's—that is not her own.[113] In this definition of obedience, Gemma places her experience above all others, at all costs, at the risk of delusion and at the risk, even, of damnation—as she herself admits.

Gemma's ideal of radical obedience is clearly not the passive obedience one so readily associates with religious vows and convent rules, and it is worth reflecting on its consequences, its dictates, and its possible implications for us today. It is a radical obedience that involves for Gemma Galgani many of the issues discussed throughout the entries of this alphabet (and for some of these I repeat the emphasis although it is not their first appearance in this entry). Radical OBEDIENCE, interpreted by some as HYSTERIA, involves the practice of TRANSGRESSION or disregard of the self, of one's own BODY. Radical obedience, to the point of pain, is Gemma's PASSION: as EXTASY and suffering, as LAUGHTER, as VIRGINITY and WEDDING, as RESEMBLANCE to and UNION with her Lover. Gemma even obeys in matters of FOOD and CLOTHING, quotidian trifles that acquire in this context a supernatural aura, a spiritual significance. Gemma's obedience to JESUS and to the EUCHARIST, as well as to their effects on her IMAGINATION, leads to the self-emptying of KENOSIS and consequently—and paradoxically—to an empowering ZEAL and resulting SAINTHOOD. And all this is spoken in the peculiar language of her AUTOBIOGRAPHY, too personal to be included in the ranks of official theology. These issues point to the QUESTIONS, very much alive today in feminism, for example, of self-authorization and self-authentication that are crucial to the ransom of the marginal, the disempowered, the nonhegemonic. This is the message of Catherine of Siena, for example, but also, more recently, of Dorothy Day (1897–1980), that radical Catholic woman who struggled to obey the church while challenging it, a reformer who tested the limits of freedom of mind and spirit in a dogmatic institution: the Church "was founded upon Saint Peter, that rock, who yet thrice denied his Master on the eve of His crucifixion. And Jesus compared the Church to a net cast into the sea and hauled in, filled with fishes, both good and bad. 'Including,' one of my non-Catholic friends used to say, 'some blowfish and quite a few sharks.'"[114] Also, womanist theologians emphasize Jesus' co-suffering as a divine model and as a context in which African American women can experience hope and liberation: obedience to Jesus as solidarity rather than passivity, as healing transformation toward survival and resistance.[115] And resist Gemma does: she openly challenges the theological bases of her confessor's christology, when he repeatedly tells her not to address Jesus so familiarly, not to be so intimate with him. She accuses Father Germano of disagreeing with Jesus himself, warning him that those who do not treat Jesus with familiarity and intimacy sin against Jesus' own goodness. That she immediately afterward says "I don't know, I am speaking randomly, you tell me the truth, and I am certainly wrong. My head is empty," makes effective use of the rhetoric of orthodoxy and the topos of the silly, empty-headed girl—rather than undermining her forceful menaces.[116] Which she propels against Monsignor Volpi as well, again in the context of obedience—obedience to Jesus as he speaks through Gemma's words, rather than through the prelate's: "Obey Jesus," Gemma peremptorily writes to the Monsignor, "place me in a convent."[117]

P: PASSION

— OR, "THE WILD ZONE" ON GETHSEMANE

"Is there a way(s) to speak of suffering without leading women into further denigration, abuse, masochism, and passive martyrdom, and therefore, without adding further justification for the trivialization and oppression of women?"[118] This question haunts every discussion of pain and suffering elaborated from a feminist perspective. Yet no account of mystical experience, and certainly no discussion of Saint Gemma Galgani of Lucca, can escape the confrontation with the meaning of pain. For pain can and does have meaning, and to reject this proposition ultimately means deferring to someone else's definition of the meaning of pain. Since for Gemma pain is inseparable from her project of self-sanctification (see SAINTHOOD), of RESEMBLANCE to JESUS, of becoming divine, we must bear in mind with Grace

Jantzen that "from a feminist perspective, becoming divine is inseparable from solidarity with human suffering."[119] And just as it is difficult to *speak* of suffering, it is also difficult to *hear* of suffering. "Patire," "to suffer," "passion." The Passion of Jesus Christ, the series of events that led to and culminated in his death on the cross, moves the very center of Gemma's spiritual journey, and of much Christian theology as well. Related to the issue of *imitatio Christi,* or imitation of Christ (the resemblance of the human being to the incarnated God), Gemma's focus on the Passion brings to light her complex relationship to the BODY and, more important, the particular bent of her spiritual life.

As a child, Gemma had such a desire "to know [Jesus'] Passion" that she received the highest grades every day in order to obtain the reward of an hour-long lesson on "some aspect of the Passion" (*Autobiography,* 36). Her desire to accompany Jesus during his entire Passion is perhaps most poetically expressed in the ecstasy when Gemma implores Jesus to let her feel the gall ("when my lips near yours to kiss you"), the scourges ("when my shoulders rest on yours"), the Passion ("when your flesh communicates with mine"), the thorns ("when my head nears yours"), the lance ("when my side touches yours"; *Ecstasies and Letters,* 129). In the bodily, even sensuous emphasis of these words, we are faced with the etymological connection between the two meanings of passion as intense feeling, such as erotic love, and passion as suffering—such as, precisely, the suffering and death of Jesus Christ. Gemma is passionately in love with Jesus in and through his Passion, and this is best explained by the fact that, as Sallie McFague has rightly noted, "The bond between the two meanings of passion emerges in the story of Jesus of Nazareth, whose deep feeling for those who believed themselves to be without value brought on his suffering with and for them. Disciples who model themselves on God the lover will inevitably find the same connection to obtain."[120] Gemma's own suffering in love, in passion, that is, takes on meaning through its imitation of the suffering of her Lover as, in turn, the highest expression of a boundless passion for the Other.

So in Gemma's requests for pain we should also keep in mind that "the notion of substituting one's own suffering through illness and starvation for the guilt and destitution of others is not 'symptom'—it is theology."[121] The concept of reparatory suffering has a long history in Christian thought, and it cannot be easily discounted as the product of overzealous masochism. Even more positively, it has been argued that "what we do in our physical bodies and what we suffer in the church also, somehow, completes or participates in the sufferings of Christ."[122] On the basis of Colossians 1:24, that is, we can say that, if Saint Paul's bodily suffering for the sake of his interlocutors completes Christ's own sufferings, then we can also imagine how embracing our present suffering can open us, can open our community, even, to the transforming power of God. If pain broke Jesus open to his divinity, then pain can at the very least open us to our humanity.

Gemma's encounter with pain takes place in the Passion, so ultimately at the cross—without which Christianity cannot be imagined. Feminist theologians have much to say about the cross. "Properly understood, the 'power of the cross' subverts its own nature as harmful and oppressive and becomes instead an intellectual, spiritual, and communal resource for radical change." [123] "The cross in all its dimensions, violence, suffering, and love is the parable that enacts Sophia-God's participation in the suffering of the world." [124] "If Jesus of Nazareth as paradigmatic of God is . . . genuinely revelatory of God, then the mode of the cross, the way of radical identification with all, which will inevitably bring punishment, sometimes to the point of death, becomes a permanent reality. It becomes the way of the destabilizing, inclusive, nonhierarchical vision." [125] It is often in such a spirit—Jesus as the ultimate example of incarnation and human flourishing, of what it means to become divine—rather than in a traditional interpretation of atonement (according to which the final sacrifice of Jesus was required by God in repayment for sin: the cross as the price of reconciliation between God and humanity), that feminist and liberation theologies embrace Christ's death and resurrection.

Certainly the crucifixion is the epitome of Gemma's insistence on the Passion, but other events of the Passion narrative are also important. The first entry in her diary, for example, dated July 19, 1900, discusses the crown of thorns that was placed on Jesus' head as a mockery of his title as King of the Jews. As she lies in bed thinking of Jesus' crucifixion, an ecstasy overcomes Gemma and she "found [herself] with Jesus, who was suffering terrible pains" (*Diary,* 72). This experience brings on the desire to help her Lover by suffering with him, and Jesus grants her "this grace" by taking the crown of thorns off his own head and placing it on Gemma's head. So far so good; this is almost understandable for us: Gemma's desire is to suffer in her Lover's place and thus alleviate his own pain; many of us have wished that we could do that for someone we deeply love (and some of us may even have done it). But things become more difficult to explain when we reach the next passage, in which Gemma looks at her Lover in a way that allows him to understand that she is unhappy with the way things are and doubts his love. Because, as Gemma says, "usually when Jesus wants me to know how much he loves me, he presses the crown firmly down on my head." When Jesus understands and obliges her, Gemma reflects: "They were painful moments, but happy moments" (*Diary,* 72). Later, also on the occasion of her wearing Jesus' crown of thorns, Gemma exclaims: "It made me suffer a little but when I say suffering I mean taking pleasure. It is a pleasure, that suffering" (*Diary,* 104)—where pleasure is referred to with the ambiguous term "godere" (see below).

These perplexing statements lead us to the troubling question: Is Gemma a full-fledged masochist—someone, that is, who derives pleasure (particularly, sexual pleasure) from physical pain? Or is there a powerful push toward finding meaning in the experience of pain and suffering, in Gemma Galgani's story, that is difficult for post-Freudians to accept or even perceive? (And this, despite Freud's own struggles with what takes place "beyond the pleasure principle.") For today pain and pleasure are polar opposites, and the cultivation of pain is inherently pathological: the medicalized worldview which our society embraces sees no other way. And although feminist theory has been rethinking the traditional claims of medical practice to cure and care, feminists are also very skeptical, and rightly so, of any discussion of pain that might lead to romanticize it or, worse, glorify it. Too often such an ideology has been used to silence the battered and bruised bodies and psyches of women (and men) disempowered by ruthless forms of domination. So as a feminist discussing another woman's pain, I am walking in a minefield which I wish I could just ignore. But Gemma is not really letting me do that.

Let me stall at least and state that, in the end, the meaning of pain cannot and should not be pinned down to a neat little formula, for that is precisely what could be turned into the basis for its romanticization and even its glorification. Instead, the multifaceted nature of pain must be recognized, in its paradoxes, its fluidity, its in-process character: "I suffered because I was not able to suffer," writes Gemma to Father Germano in May 1901.[126] Elaine Scarry has discussed at length and in depth the subject of pain in her book *The Body in Pain: The Making and the Unmaking of the World:* physical pain, for the person who experiences it, is "the most vibrant example of what it is 'to have certainty,'" while for the other person it is so elusive that 'hearing about pain' may exist as the primary model of what it is 'to have doubt.'"[127] Much like religious faith, I might add. More could be said on this analogy: Scarry repeatedly notes that physical pain resists language, and that this is essential to it, and not just an accidental attribute. The same is true of mystical experience, although Gemma, unlike many mystics, does not dwell at all on ineffability. Indeed I found as I researched and wrote this entry that a discussion of pain tends to bring up one's faith; so that my presentation from a feminist Christian perspective might seem intolerably remote to those who do not share this position.

"A feminist theology of suffering," Patricia L. Wismer notes, "should state both that suffering can never be justified, *and* that suffering must be accepted as part of life. It should state both that suffering can never be redeemed *and* that meaning can be found in suffering."[128] Dualism here just won't do, in spite of the rather facile distinction made by theologians Carter Heyward and Beverly Wildung Harrison, who state that "it is one thing to accept suffering for the sake of a moral or religious good when confronting unjust power, and another to perceive suffering as itself an intrinsic moral or religious value, the point to which much institutional Christianity came after the collapse of the Roman Imperium."[129] Yes, all of this makes sense, but can such a rational distinction—another dualism, really—always be carried out? Whom does it benefit? And whom does it silence? Later in the essay Heyward and Harrison end up admitting that, in part because the physiological (but also the cultural) line between pleasure and pain is a thin one, "it is one thing to break the ecclesiastical monopoly on the definition of the relation of spiritual pleasure and physical pain, and another to disentangle at the level of personal erotic experience, a clear difference between what hurts and what gives pleasure" (141). It is worth noting at this point that feminist theology often dwells where secular feminist theory barely dares to go: into and within pain and bodily suffering. Because if we are indebted to feminism for bringing the body back in the picture, for reminding us that we *are* our body rather than just *having* an appendix to our self that we call a body, it is also true that we cannot accept and embrace certain aspects of our body and dismiss others. So, along with the *jouissance* so celebrated in feminist theory, pain and suffering also need to be explored. Simone Weil puts pain (epitomized by affliction) into a fruitful perspective of human solidarity and mutual liberation which may appeal to non-Christians as well: "Affliction is by is nature inarticulate. The afflicted silently beseech to be given the words to express themselves."[130]

Q: QUESTION(ING)
— OR, THE QUEST FOR ANSWERS

From one question to more questions: never before, in my own writing, have I penned so many questions in such a (relatively) short space. I became so painfully aware of the questions permeating this piece that it came rather naturally to dedicate an entry to those passages in Gemma's writings that most leave me puzzled and confused, indeed "questioning"—and to leave a place for the reader to pen her own, his own questions. So this is where the other questions throughout the alphabet may find a haven, a resting place, a spot where they are allowed to be asked without being immediately (ever?) framed in a comfortable answer. Gemma, after all, was not one to seek comfort.

Question 1: What is the meaning of Gemma's own confusion, exemplified in that ecstasy when she does not seem to know whether the being she sees is an angel or a devil? "If you have been sent by God, come and I shall receive you but if you are sent by the devil, I'll spit in your face" (*Ecstasies and Letters,* 138). How can Gemma be so sure of "who's who" most of the time, and then be so completely baffled and unable to recognize the identity of her interlocutor? Is she ever to be trusted, then? And is she really going to spit?

Question 2: What does Gemma mean when she cryptically tells Jesus, in an ecstasy: "But then, my Jesus, are you never offended when I do all those bad things? . . . But this morning, Jesus, did you see, Jesus, what I did in the confessional?"[131] What in the world could Gemma have done in the confessional? Was it just a question of not saying everything to the confessor? This seems unlikely, if she is so reluctant to specify a relatively simple sin of omission; besides, she is constantly keeping things from her confessor, so that would not be a novelty to allude to with such shame. But then, did she actually do something that we too would find scandalizing and/or titillating? Might it be something sexual, given Gemma's other allusions to temptations to "holy purity" and such? It is very difficult to know anything about Gemma's actual life and actions, for everything we can know is so filtered by hagiographers—and what her detractors had to say was generally limited to a medicalized and/or patronizing approach to her sanctity. In Gemma's own writings we occasionally encounter an anecdote that illuminates us a bit on her personality, but these are few and far between. This scarcity of detail makes what we have all the more interesting and significant, so I would really like to know what it is that she did that morning in that confessional.

Question 3: Is Gemma's voice to be likened to what French feminists, and especially Hélène Cixous, have termed since 1975 *écriture féminine,* or feminine writing—itself a concept that provides more questions than answers? *Écriture féminine* describes women's language in opposition to masculine language: while the latter is seen as rational and structured, linear and finite, feminine language is playful and fragmentary, fluid and open-ended. The objective of *écriture féminine* is to "write the body," to let the body be heard; although it is a controversial concept, its major corollary—namely the claim that sexual difference extends into the realm of language—is accepted by many if not most feminists. Just as feminist theologians revel in the BODY as the subject of Christ's and our own resurrection, rather than chastising it as inherently inferior to the soul or spirit, feminist theorists celebrate women's association with the body and refuse to subordinate the latter to the mind—as, precisely, in *écriture féminine*. Does it help to see Gemma's writings as an example of *écriture féminine?*

Question 4: What are the "two words written" on JESUS' heart that Gemma "did not understand" (*Diary,* 73)? Jesus' answer, which satisfies Gemma, is "I love you so much because you resemble me so"; this is nice but, even in Latin, it is well over two words. Does the mystery of this passage have anything to do perhaps with the only example we have of Jesus writing, when he cryptically traces letters on the sand while the adulteress is about to be stoned (John 8:6−8)?

Question 5: And what are we to make of Gemma's reticence, her frequent ellipses, her silences? Is she hiding something, is she tired of writing, is she being discreet, polite? For example: "My guardian angel also was happy that I went to bed, because . . ." (*Diary,* 78); her angel says: "Obey, you know, because I could easily . . ." (*Diary,* 91); about Mary, Gemma writes: "She reproached me a little but cheered up about one thing (that I think here it would be better not to say)" (*Diary,* 93); "For all of today I stayed without any temptations; toward evening one suddenly came over me, in the ugliest manner. But here I don't think it would be good to tell, because it's too . . ." (*Diary,* 105). Does she want to let us know, like Edith Stein when asked about her conversion, that "Secretum meum mihi" (my secret is mine)?

Other questions: to be added by the reader.

R: RESEMBLANCE
— OR, OF CHRIST AND CHRISTA

"I must resemble whom I love. I postulate (and it is this which brings about my pleasure) a conformity of essence between the other and myself. Image, imitation: I do as many things as I can in the other's fashion. I want to be the other, I want the other to be me, as if we were united, enclosed within the same sack of skin, the garment being merely the smooth envelope of that coalescent substance out of which my amorous Image-repertoire is made."[132]

Through an image that, as this quotation from Roland Barthes's *A Lover's*

Discourse attests, is both secular and spiritual, erotic and mystical, Gemma stresses her resemblance to her Lover repeatedly in her writings: "Through pain I can become similar to JESUS, show him my love and secure for myself Jesus' love."[133] Although she does not herself use the technical Latin term for this resemblance, numerous predecessors in mystical Christianity have worked to adhere to Jesus' example in what has been called *imitatio Christi,* or the imitation of Christ (also the title of a popular devotional manual of the Middle Ages, written by Thomas à Kempis). Imitatio Christi generally refers to the supple conformity of one's life to Christ's own; as such, all Christians are called to enact it. But in the context of Christian mysticism, the term has come to refer primarily to the physical imitation of Christ's suffering to the point of *becoming* Christ's BODY. Stigmata are perhaps the best-known example of this practice: stigmata mark the body with the signs of the mystic's spiritual power. I believe Caroline Walker Bynum expresses the significance of imitatio Christi for women mystics most eloquently when she writes: "Horrible pain, twisting of the body, bleeding—whether inflicted by God or by oneself—were *not* an effort to destroy the body, *not* a punishment of physicality, *not* primarily an effort to shear away a source of lust, not even primarily and identification with the martyrs. . . . Illness and asceticism were rather imitatio Christi, an effort to plumb the depths of Christ's humanity at the moment of his most insistent and terrifying humanness—the moment of his dying."[134]

Stigmata, or bleeding from one's feet, hands, side, and forehead, in a dramatic imitation of Jesus Christ's Passion wounds, were first displayed by Saint Francis of Assisi in medieval Italy (1224). Significantly, stigmata have affected women considerably more often than men: in fact, Francis of Assisi and the recently beatified Padre Pio (whose stigmata, which started bleeding in 1918, can be viewed on the Internet in startling color photographs), are the only two males known to have received all five visible wounds—at both feet, both hands, and the side. (I cannot escape mentioning the recent Rupert Wainwright movie entitled *Stigmata,* in which rather predictably an uneducated young woman gets them, and a charismatic older man, a handsome priest, interprets them; but unlike the stigmatic in another fairly recent film, *Agnes of God,* this one is not religious—again, however, not a new concept: Georges Bataille has devoted much thought to the atheist's quest for paramystical experiences.)[135]

The very old devotional practice of imitatio Christi and its historical predominance among women is in striking contrast with the stir generated in the mid-1980s by Edwina Sandys' sculpture *Christa* when it was put on display in New York's Episcopal Cathedral of St. John the Divine. This sculpture of the crucified Christ with a female body is at the heart of a moving reflection on women and spirituality by Carter Heyward, as well as lying at the origin of Rita Nakashima Brock's concept of Christ/Community.[136] Heyward and Brock focus on the metaphorical potential of the body of Christa for women today. Yet, if it seems clear on the one hand why the representation of Christ as a woman (as a naked, crucified woman, no less) should be shocking, it helps at the same time to remember that at least since the Middle Ages the flesh of Christ has been symbolically gendered as female: not only because women have traditionally been associated with the flesh (and men with the spirit), but also because Christ's flesh, like women's flesh, bleeds, feeds, and gives birth—by generating redemption through death on the cross. It is not a shockingly contemporary feminist move to (re)claim Christ's body as a female body. Rather, it is a very old tradition which our own secular world has forgotten. It is this tradition which allows Elizabeth Johnson to speak of "the whole Christ" as "*christa* and *christus* alike," and another feminist theologian, Anne Thurston, to poignantly reflect: "Are the battered and bruised bodies of women etched on the body of the crucified Jesus? Perhaps we do not need so much to depict the body of a woman on the cross as to recognize that every raped and beaten female body is the body of Christ. God suffers in the bodies of women."[137]

Gemma Galgani's experience provides a sort of transition between medieval and contemporary representations of Christ's body as female as well as male. Gemma is aware of her resemblance to her Lover throughout her spiritual journey, and in quite a matter-of-fact way. Stigmata are a shocking miracle, of course, they are wholly out of the ordinary. Yet their shock is analogous, mutatis mutandis, to the shock of the incarnation, of God made flesh—and not to the fact that God's incarnation should be reflected on the flesh and blood of a beautiful young woman from Lucca. Body, and not gender, is what is ultimately at stake for Gemma—though significantly there is no body without gender. In the second entry of her diary, Gemma records that Jesus opened his heart to her, and on it she saw two written words (ah, the body as text) which she could not understand; when she interrogated him about their meaning, Jesus replied—presumably interpreting them for her, since he uses well more than two words (though the QUESTION remains open): "I love you so much because you resemble me so." Gemma still did not understand, for she felt so different from him, but it is "in accepting humiliation" that the two are alike according to Jesus himself (*Diary*, 73). KENOSIS. Yes, kenosis, yet this is not kenosis as self-destruction but rather as power of (self) sanctification: these words of resemblance and humiliation come immediately before Gemma's assertion that she is to become a saint (see SAINTHOOD below). In resemblance and humiliation Gemma states: "Finally I understood who I truly am" (*Diary*, 73). Humbled, certainly, but a humbled saint who resembles God.

Resemblance implies connection, relation, mutuality—it is no coincidence then that it is associated with the heart: both human and divine, enfleshed in the body. Resemblance at once rejects, in Gemma's writings, the ideal of women's autonomy touted by that liberal feminism which would make women conform to a traditional masculinist model (one that denies mutual relation); and, at the same time, resemblance establishes Gemma as mutually related to a God who is like her as much as she is like him. Resemblance separates her from a diminishing model of womanhood (the bourgeois stereotype) while proclaiming her UNION with the unfolding divinity. And by the way, this issue of resemblance has practical consequences for many believers today, for physical resemblance with Christ—or lack thereof—is presented as one of the most important reasons why women should not be ordained to the priesthood. As theologian Rosemary Radford Ruether puts it: "Today a Christology which elevates Jesus' maleness to ontologically necessary significance suggests that Jesus' humanity does not represent women at all. Incarnation solely into the male sex does not include women and so women are not redeemed. That is to say, if women cannot represent Christ, then Christ does not represent women, or, as the women's ordination movement has put it, 'either ordain women or stop baptizing them.'"[138]

S: SAINTHOOD
—OR, ON BINDING AND THE ENORMITY OF FEMALE DESIRE

"The *communio sanctorum* is a most relational symbol. From age to age, the same Spirit who vivifies and renews the natural world enters into holy souls, and not so holy ones, and makes them friends of God and prophets. Guided by this core vision, we follow the symbol of the communion of saints into the thought to which its gives rise, seeking to understand the fullness of relationship it means to convey."[139] This eloquent description of the meaning of sainthood from a Catholic perspective, written by Elizabeth Johnson, points to some other issues discussed in this alphabet: relationality and/as UNION, PASSION, and RESEMBLANCE. Along these lines, and in speaking of Saint Teresa of Avila, Italian philosopher Luisa Muraro claims that "her greatness resides in the capacity to bind, her power is the power of binding. Of what with what? In her I see the enormity of female desire binding itself freely to the reality of this world."[140] Gemma's own repeated talk of saint-hood and self-sanctification also points to the "enormity of female desire," though it is a challenge for us to take this enormity seriously if we do not accept, at least provisionally, Johnson's relational symbol of the *communio sanctorum*.

There is now available in English translation the story of seventeenth-century Venetian laywoman Cecilia Ferrazzi, first published in 1990 and edited by historian Anne Jacobson Schutte. Cecilia Ferrazzi was charged and convicted by the Inquisition of "pretense of sanctity": uneducated, of modest social extraction, not a nun, still she "made herself considered a saint" by speaking, for example, of God's bestowal of divine favors upon her.[141] Gemma Galgani's claims are not that dissimilar: "Do you know what I got into my head, Dad? To become a saint at all costs. I made this resolve last night while doing my meditation."[142] It is a shocking aspect of Gemma's story that she claims, as early as July 1900: "Then my God added that in time he would make me a saint." Her subsequent parenthetical disclaimer, "(here I don't say anything because it is impossible that what God said could happen to me)" (*Diary,* 73) does little to abate in the reader the puzzling effect of such a self-assured statement—which gives us a glimpse of that "pride" to which Gemma so often confesses but of which she gives us no other believable examples. On the contrary: she accuses herself of pride after she feels that her confessor regards her sins with too much indulgence; her angel corrects this self-deprecating claim by accusing her of "pride" for thinking she has a better view of her sins than the confessor does (*Diary,* 89). When she states that she will become a saint Gemma does not mean a saint the way we are all called to be part of the communion of saints affirmed in the Apostles' Creed, and perhaps in Johnson's words quoted above, but rather a saint in the most commonly accepted meaning of this word, a saint to be venerated on altars. She reports Jesus' own words to Monsignor Volpi as follows: "Assure him that it is I, Jesus, who speaks with you and that in a few years by my doing you will be a saint. You will perform miracles and you will receive the highest honors of the altar."[143]

So, what does Gemma mean when she says that she will be a saint—a saint who performs miracles and whose image is placed on altars? Does she aspire to being one of those "exemplary women's lives" interpreted as "models of virtue" (doubtful, given her awareness of her own shortcomings) and OBEDIENCE "that support the male-dominated status quo and cast women into submission" (again doubtful, given Gemma's perennial TRANSGRES-SIONS)?[144] Is Gemma more simply hungering for the power, after death, that she was so clearly denied during her life here on earth? What is behind such a shocking self-assurance? "You will see . . . what I will do for you, Dad, when I am in Heaven," she tells her confessor, "I will drag you there with me at all costs."[145] Is she feeling what her contemporary Thérèse of Lisieux more eloquently wrote? "[God] made me understand my own *glory* would not be evident to the eyes of mortals, that is would consist in becoming a great *saint*. This desire could certainly appear daring if one were to consider how weak and imperfect I was, and . . . still am. . . . I always feel, however, the same bold confidence of becoming a great saint because I don't count on my merits since I have *none,* but I trust in Him who is Virtue and Holiness. God alone, content with my weak efforts, will raise me to Himself and make me a *saint.*"[146] Is the claim to sainthood self-aggrandizing, hubris, or is it self-annihilation, KENOSIS? Is it grace or is it a disciplined, ZEALOUS practice, that which impels twentieth-century Italian mystic Angela Gavazzi (1907–75) to state that she desires "ever more ardently to make good use of illness as a means of sanctification"?[147]

I think it is important to start by taking a basic, commonsense approach in order to realize to what extent the aspiration to sainthood would have carried great potential for a turn-of-the-century teenage girl—its ability to contain, better than other life options, Gemma's "enormous desire." In the Catholic tradition, as Elisabeth Schüssler Fiorenza reminds us, "everyone is called to *sainthood.* Even the vocation to the priesthood is superseded by the call to become a saint. Any Catholic girl who grows up reading the 'lives of the saints' might internalize all kinds of sexual hangups, but she would not think that her only vocation and her genuine Christian call consist in becoming married and having children."[148] If the life choices of women saints might be seen as limited and conforming to male stereotypes, they nevertheless went beyond and even contradicted the much more limiting view of woman as reproductive machine, as MOM (especially constricting during Gemma's lifetime): think of Blessed Angela of Foligno, who prays for the death of her family (mother, husband, children) so that she may become free to follow God![149] So the saint paradigm does offer Gemma a place that secular pursuits could not grant her. Her sickness and abject poverty, her lack of family and of worldly support, are not an obstacle in her pursuit of holiness: rather, she zealously constructs them, like many orderly cobblestones, as the very path to her self-sanctification.

It is nevertheless not an easy road to sainthood, and Gemma's right to such a pursuit is questioned by human as well as supernatural powers. Saint-hood is represented as an illusion by none other than the devil himself, who in one of his frequent nighttime visits tests Gemma's zeal and tells her that all her writings are his works, that her sainthood is the fruit of her IMAGI-NATION, and that she will suffer unimaginable shame once she is discovered: "I pass you off as a saint, but you are deluded" (*Diary,* 81). So also in an ec-stasy Gemma excludes herself from the company of "the saints" and "the humble of heart" who deserve to praise and thank God (*Ecstasies and Letters,* 127), and she later refuses the intercession of the saints because, she says, "if I pay you with the merits of others, my debt always remains open" (*Ecstasies and Letters,* 145). Only her own self-sanctification through resemblance can bring her close to her Lover, bind them together, and repay his love for her—the debt of desire, the "enormous female desire," in Muraro's words, that she owes him. This rivalry between Gemma and the saints is repeated when she affirms: "To you, saints in Heaven, to you, earthly creatures, all the virtues; but this bit of love is mine. I want no one ahead of me in the love of Jesus" (*Ecstasies and Letters,* 147). With a tone similar to the one she uses when talking of obedience at all costs, a tone which gives us a better glimpse into this saint's personality than any hagiography ever could, Gemma estab-lishes herself, in spite of all her shortcomings, or because of her shortcom-ings, even, as first in Jesus' affections. She is absolutely certain of this posi-tion of hers, and this faith is what keeps her plowing through the dark nights of the soul and the BODY, through the pain and suffering that pave her pas-sionate pilgrimage toward union, toward becoming, that is, nothing less than divine.

T: TRANSGRESSION
— OR, THE MYSTIC AND THE CYBORG

"Certainly mysticism always collides with a refusal. It is in its nature to be-long to transgression."[150] Mystic language is a transgression against theolog-ical discourse, for it speaks, at length and in often unorthodox ways, of the unspeakable. Mystic speech is a transgression against the laws of language, for it breaks them willingly and repeatedly. Mystic behavior is a transgression against common sense, for it obeys forces which have little to do with social convention. Gemma often speaks of her own disOBEDIENCE and naughti-ness, as well as of her lies: still a child, she tries out penances without ever obtaining permission from her confessor (*Autobiography,* 57); when she does not want to return to an acquaintance the biography of Brother Gabriel which the woman had lent her and to which Gemma was so attached, she tells her that she had not finished reading it yet (although she had read it many times), and she gets to keep the book.[151] At least this is what she writes to her confessor. In her autobiography, this same story is different, which doubles Gemma's lie: when Gemma returns the book to the lady, she cries, so that the lady, moved, lets her keep it a while longer (*Autobiography*, 43); she invents "big lies" for which her angel reproaches her (*Diary*, 79), and soon after that says three more lies (*Diary*, 80). Even Gemma's insistence on obedience often hides some kind of transgression that she sneaks in when she finds it necessary. So when her GUARDIAN ANGEL asks her to suffer some physical pain for the benefit of the souls in Purgatory, Gemma first says that JESUS does not want her to suffer except on Thursday and Friday, then she concedes that since she takes very much to heart the souls of Purgatory, she would "gladly suffer for an hour" (*Diary*, 88), thus contravening Jesus' rules, not to mention her confessor's. So also a few pages later she suffers for the souls in Purgatory "without my confessor's permission," though she also peculiarly continues, "but usually he does not yell at me, indeed he wishes it, and I am free to do it" (*Diary*, 90). Conversely, when Monsignor Volpi gives her permission to do external penances, of which he even lists a few, Gemma asserts to Father Germano: "I did none of them, none: I feel Jesus does not want it" (*Ecstasies and Letters*, 135). She writes to Brother Gabriel "without Jesus knowing," and this with the angel's complicity (*Diary*, 103)—presumably because in previous occasions Jesus has prevented Brother Gabriel from visiting Gemma. And indeed earlier, before Brother Gabriel's visit, the angel had reminded her that she needed to be silent in order to obey her confessor; Gemma says, "Yes, yes, I will obey; have him come," but then she "couldn't resist saying" something to Brother Gabriel, and neither the angel nor Brother Gabriel seems to have a problem with this; indeed, Brother Gabriel laughs and promises Gemma a gift (*Diary*, 77).[152]

But why the reference in my subtitle to Donna Haraway's figure of the cyborg, that ironic speculation of the half-organic, half-machine body, imagined in her 1985 essay "A Cyborg Manifesto"? "A cyborg is a cybernetic organism, a hybrid of machine and organism, a creature of social reality as well as a creature of fiction," writes Haraway; and she continues: "By the late twentieth century, our time, a mythic time, we are all chimeras, theorized and fabricated hybrids of machine and organism; in short, we are cyborgs."[153] I sense a subtle affinity between Haraway's theory of the cyborg and mystical practice such as Gemma's. Perhaps because the cyborg disperses the normative BODY like mysticism also does, like Gemma certainly wants to do; or maybe because the cyborg, like the mystic, is irreverent, committed to partiality, oppositional. Or, most likely, because in this figuration, as in mysticism, the body is forever morphing into new and uncategorizable forms, and thus the determinism of biological constraints can be escaped, and corporeality transgressed—through LAUGHTER, lying, the self-emptying of KENOSIS, self-CLOTHING in stolen uniforms, PASSIONate self-modification in RESEMBLANCE to one's Lover. At the same time, and nowhere is this clearer than in mystical discourse and experience, every transgression conserves or confirms that which it exceeds—bodily boundaries, unified subjectivities. Gemma's transgressions are bodily and sacramental as well as spiritual and linguistic, conserving the body even as she denies it, confirming the spirit beyond which she goes. From a feminist perspective, we could say that Gemma's relationship with her body transgresses those disciplining practices that produce a body that is recognizably feminine—in its general configuration, its repertoire of gestures and movements, its display as ornamented surface. But Gemma's morphological transgressions, because of the mystical discourse which constitutes her place and context, go beyond all this—beyond the cyborg, as well. They do not just question the female body, but the body, any body, *tout court*. And the soul, too. Body and soul, material and immaterial, are concepts, limits, which Gemma repeatedly crosses over. And if the language of transgression confronts and interrogates limits, then transgression becomes the place where meaning itself must be confronted. It is the beyond, perhaps, that geography of otherness which, through EXTASY, Gemma explores. In Michel Foucault's words, "Transgression is not related to the limit as black to white, the prohibited to the lawful, the outside to the inside, or as the open area of a building to its enclosed space. Rather, their relationship takes the form of a spiral which no simple infraction can exhaust." [154]

U: UNION
—OR, ON BECOMING DIVINE

"If material life structures consciousness, women's relationally defined existence, bodily experience of boundary challenges, and activity of transforming both physical objects and human beings must be expected to result in a worldview to which dichotomies are foreign. Women experience others and themselves along a continuum." [155] This continuum which Nancy Hartsock posits from a feminist Marxist perspective can be tied to Nancy Chodorow's arguments on mothering delineated above (in the entry MOM), to the Catholic theology of the communion of saints (see SAINTHOOD), to the practice of imitatio Christi (or RESEMBLANCE), and, especially, to the mystical grace of union. For Gemma's spiritual graces, like those of the great mystics, do not just "happen" to her from another dimension but rather they concretely proceed from her work, from a project of prayer, meditation, contemplation, sacrament, that is not unrelated to Hartsock's Marxist belief that "material life structures consciousness." "Yesterday [Friday] around 4:00 a desire came upon me to unite a little more with Jesus; I tried and immediately united with him" (*Diary,* 72). So also union with her "impetuous Lover"—the elimination of boundaries between self and other—is operated by Gemma in several ways. Union can be metonymic, the part for the whole, as in the EUCHARIST: spiritual communion proceeds from physical ingestion, as bodily experience challenges spiritual boundaries. Imitatio Christi, whereby Gemma conforms herself, soul and body, to the example of JESUS, is a representational medium of union: Gemma is united with Jesus by transforming herself into him: resemblance. Yet another medium, one based on geographical displacement, is the rapture of her heart; in this case, the heart is a metonymy of the BODY. The heart is offered to the Other as gift and taken to Heaven, to that Other place where her Lover is found. Still what is described as mystical union is something that can arise out of the previous experiences, yet goes beyond them. For Gemma, mystical union is always, relentlessly one might even say, bodily and spiritual. No such dichotomy, indeed, exists.

In the summer of 1900 that she records in her diary, for example, Gemma describes her Lover's arrival "on [her] tongue," and her consequent removal of herself from herself in order to make room for Jesus who descends within her breast—now empty of her heart, carried to that elsewhere inhabited by her loved ones. As they exchange assurances of mutual love, "He unites ever more closely with me," a union which lasts the remainder of the day (*Diary,* 94). Even in this, the highest stage of mystical ascent, Gemma maintains her quotidian language as she communicates with her Lover: as a union ends and Jesus is about to leave her, "a contest sprang up between me and Jesus: which of us would be the first to visit"—a contest Gemma says she won by going to receive communion before Jesus' next visit to her (*Diary,* 98). The desire for union is nevertheless reciprocated, since Jesus tells her: "I am burning with desire to unite with you" (*Autobiography,* 49). It is also in simple language that Gemma describes her desire for the highest mystical union: "Let's pretend, oh Lord, that you are me and I am Jesus . . . What do you mean, what would I do? I would stop being me, so that you could be, oh God"

(*Ecstasies and Letters,* 143). Gemma imitates Jesus not just in his pain and suffering, in his PASSION, but, more profoundly, in that radical self-emptying that is KENOSIS: she displaces herself out of herself so as to let the divine in, even as Jesus displaced his divinity so as to make room for a full humanity. In Simone Weil's words, this is "decreation."

Echoing Hartsock's appeal to "the female construction of self in relation to others" (158)—against the dualism which, "along with the dominance of one side of the dichotomy over the other, marks phallocentric society and social theory" (157)—Beverly Wildung Harrison writes that "above all else a feminist moral theology insists that relationality is at the heart of all things." [156] Relationality and the attendant insistence on continuity is a key concept not only in feminist theology but in feminist theory at large. Psychoanalytic thinker Luce Irigaray insists on this issue in her theorization of the mother-daughter relationship, which she considers indispensable if women are to have access to language and thus to society and culture (see the entry MOM). Even more pertinent to this discussion is Irigaray's theorization of religion and her references to women mystics. Her hyperbolic assertion in her book *Speculum of the Other Woman* is often quoted by scholars of mysticism: mystical discourse is for Irigaray "the only place in Western history where woman speaks and acts in such a public way." [157] For Irigaray this is not simply a historical accident, of course. Mysticism is founded on union, a union predicated on the disappearance of the opposition between subject and object—on the loss of subjecthood, then. In this loss of difference between self and other, paradoxically (and paradox is intrinsic to mysticism) the woman mystic may discover herself, her EXTASY, perhaps her *jouissance:* that joy, that pleasure, that delight, that is both sexual and nonsexual, bodily and spiritual at once. Similarly, in the essay "Divine Women," contained in her collection *Sexes and Genealogies,* Irigaray claims that "the love of God has often been a haven for women. They are the guardians of the religious tradition. Certain women mystics have been among those rare women to achieve real social influence, notably in politics." [158]

More than such descriptive statements, it is fruitful to explore some of Irigaray's prescriptive injunctions, theoretical statements she makes with the objective of striving for a truly inclusive society and culture—a symbolic realm to which both women and men would have access, in which women's subjectivity would not be silenced. Unlike other, more secularly inclined post-structuralist critics, Luce Irigaray sees the religious dimension as essential for the full inclusion of women in the social contract: religion cannot be just ignored, for without the wisdom of becoming divine, women and men

in the postmodern world cannot survive. God is our horizon for becoming, God is a goal of human endeavor, God is a standard against which our
thoughts and our actions must be measured. Thus Irigaray states that "as
long as woman lacks a divine made in her image she cannot establish her
subjectivity or achieve a goal of her own"; "if she is to become woman, if
she is to accomplish her female subjectivity, woman needs a god who is a figure for the perfection of *her* subjectivity." [159] "Woman has no mirror where-
with to become a woman. Having a God and becoming one's gender go
hand in hand. God is the other that we cannot absolutely be without. In order to *become,* we need some shadowy perception of achievement." [160] In
short, in order to become fully human, we need a divinity to aspire to. I do
not wish at this point to argue against Irigaray as to whether it is true that
God has served as horizon for male becoming alone. Still, Irigaray's development of the concept of the divinity as the horizon of becoming, and her
insistence on the need for women to become divine touches at many points
the mystical journey of Gemma Galgani.

Irigaray's discourse develops in a context of post-structuralist feminism
and psychoanalysis and lacks the context of feminist theology that makes it
its task, as should be clear to my reader by now, to address precisely the questions that Irigaray so poignantly asks. Significantly, these theological questions that she eloquently articulates are not frequently addressed in critical
readings of her work, maybe because the context in which she is placed, the
scholars by whom she is read, tend to be antireligious, or perhaps closeted
in their/our religious belief. Through the intermediary of Christian feminist theology, however, Irigaray's questions on religion can face Gemma
Galgani's own religious quest. For Gemma, in one of the most sublime moments of her spiritual journey as she recorded it, demands of God: "Make
me divine" ("divinizzami"; *Ecstasies and Letters,* 121), and, even more directly,
"You consume my soul and make it divine" (*Ecstasies and Letters,* 142).[161]
(Now these are the statements with which I ought to probably conclude, yet
we are not there yet. And it is significant, even imperative, *not* to end with
the exuberance of this statement, *not* to place it at the beginning, or at the
center, or at the end of this discussion. Gemma's chosen marginality has
guided perhaps this off-center placement.) Distasteful, maybe, morally and
religiously, is Gemma's demand: how can becoming divine be a task for
women and men? How does it fit in with the first of the Ten Command-
ments, or more generally with the classical sin of hubris? Do we risk falling
into the gaping mouth of pantheism, the undifferentiated—the abject? Still
the incarnation of God into Jesus of Nazareth took place so that we may be-

come like Christ even as God became like us: I vividly remember singing, as a child, "God made himself like us, so as to make us like him" ("Dio si è fatto come noi, per farci come lui"). Or, in more nuanced terms, "as Jesus, a flesh-and-blood man, was said to be the living manifestation of God for all to follow, so it is laid upon each of us, in our flesh-and-blood sexuate existence, to become divine, to incarnate the divine ideals as (differently) gendered subjects."[162] Union, ultimately, consists of this. Or rather becoming divine, Gemma's divinization, is something like—and only approximations will do here—mystical union: the work, the practice, the labor which structure Gemma's consciousness, Gemma's body, Gemma's spirit and soul, work to disrupt boundaries of all sorts between the self and the Other, effect the transformation of desire into an ever-moving connection with her Lover, with her God.

V: VIRGINITY
—OR, AIN'T I A WOMAN?

"Why? Why should the Church *honor* anything so idiotic? Why is 'virginity' regarded as a 'virtue' at all since it lacks all the normal qualities: it can be stolen from someone without consent; it can be destroyed by accident, by horseback riding, by normal bodily functions; the failure to maintain it cannot be fully repented of; it cannot be prayed for, deepened or restored through grace?"[163]

After much insistence, Gemma is finally allowed to make a vow of virginity in 1899: "The vow of virginity that [Monsignor Volpi] never had been willing to let me make, that same evening we made together in perpetuity" (*Autobiography*, 44). For Gemma, this was a necessary step toward self-sanctification, perhaps one more step toward the convent, too. Still, through the work of the devil, the temptations against "holy purity" continue, as Gemma attests in her diary (77). So much so that when Gemma claims that the devil has submitted her to "the most ugly temptation one could imagine" (*Diary,* 96) we are led to believe that it is a sexual one. The "usual little man," whether "black, very black" (*Diary,* 76) or "all covered in black hair" (*Diary,* 85), tries to "climb on top" of her (*Diary,* 76), lies down in bed with her (*Diary,* 85), in the shape of a "huge black dog . . . put his legs on [her] shoulders" (*Diary,* 75). What could the meaning of virginity be for Gemma, why was vowing perpetual virginity so important to this young woman— even, by her own avowal, before she knew what the word meant? (Not surprisingly, given that, as historian Michela De Giorgio explains about the turn of the century, "at exactly the same time as the triumph of physiologic realism of the *scientia sexualis,* Italian Catholic treatises avoid naming virginity in its concise bodily definition.")[164] Is virginity for Gemma a sign of wholeness or of lack, something to give up or something that will be "added on to her"? Does virginity tame her beauty or does it, on the contrary, make it a threat? Or is virginity, more simply, another word for celibacy, the privileged channel to holiness, the quasi-magical attribute, in Roman Catholicism as well as other religions, of a sacramental elite?

These questions acquire an increased importance if we consider in our reflection on Gemma another Italian turn-of-the-century sainted girl, Maria Goretti (1890–1902), a contemporary of Gemma whose claims to canonization (1950) were that she preferred to be stabbed to death rather than to lose her virginity, and that she forgave her killer even to the point of actively intervening in his conversion (she repeatedly appeared to him during his years in prison). Among Italian Catholics throughout much of the twentieth century, Maria Goretti was the most popular icon of virginity after the Virgin Mary herself. On the one hand, Maria Goretti's canonization can be seen, appallingly, as a statement on the part of church and society that a woman is better dead than defiled; on the other hand, however, Maria Goretti's act of obedience—her right to her God-given bodily integrity—unto death resulted in grace and redemption even as it painfully indicted and continues to indict a world in which girls are targets, in which the vulnerable are oppressed: like Gemma, Maria Goretti was very poor and had no family to protect her—her father was dead, her mother was gone working long hours in the fields; she too was almost homeless and had to share a rented house with the killer and his father. In this perspective, Maria Goretti can perhaps be seen as a Christ figure, and certainly as a martyr to violence, to a world in which women are sex objects, in which girls are expendable: once raped, Maria Goretti would have been an outcast, a loose woman, no longer marriageable except, maybe, by the rapist himself.[165]

During the second half of the nineteenth century and at least as late as through the Fascist era in Italy, reproduction was exalted as every woman's ultimate goal: "Maternity is woman's first and essential mission," wrote a popular and influential scientist of Gemma's own time, Paolo Mantegazza.[166] Indeed, as historian Michela De Giorgio pithily put it in her book on Italian women from the late nineteenth century to today, "Italy is the country that has turned the cult of motherhood into a national devotion."[167] So Gemma's vow of virginity even as she remained outside the convent was striking in many ways, most visibly perhaps because of her exceptional beauty (she is called by a journalist "the prettiest among all the saints of the calendar").[168] As Joann Wolski Conn notes, "Virginity, as an ideal, had a double effect: renunciation of sex as a sacramental way to experience God, along with freedom to renounce the social conventions that restricted women to marriages arranged for the sake of property and family status."[169] What Gemma gives up is a complicated role, for motherhood represented in the nineteenth century both social fulfillment and personal annihilation; it was at once the loftiest of middle-class ideals for women and their primary cause of mortality, if they were in childbearing age.[170] Furthermore, in the increasingly secular state of nascent Italy (political unification was achieved only in 1861, and it was still incomplete), when convents were being shut down by anti-clerical politicians, virginity was a complicated choice. Sexual abstinence was downright pathologized in medical texts and novels alike, and connected to—surprise, surprise—HYSTERIA. Mothering, at that time, was more than ever the core of femininity, with its duties of emotion work, self-erasure, silence, and complications of separation and autonomy (see also the entry MOM).

Generally, virginity has had and continues to have powerful social and psychological determinants, and it is the site of many contradictions: it is admired as well as feared, it is both protective and destructive, it is a gift and a prize but also a barrier and a taboo. In a Catholic context, one's first point of reference in matters of virginity is the Virgin Mary: conceived without sin, ever virgin, assumed into Heaven as completely perfect in soul and body. Mary is a contested figure, one of the great dogmatic divides between Catholics and Protestants, a stumbling block for many feminist Christians, and a subject of discussion among Catholics as well: Is her virginity part of the historical data of Scripture or is it instead a symbolic statement indicating a different truth, of an order beyond the anatomical? Is all this theological reflection really about a hymen? Mary's perpetual virginity—before, during, and after her son's birth—has been interpreted as demeaning to women's sexuality for it describes its imperfection: female sexuality needs to be corrected, purified of its bodily element, if the incarnation is to take place.[171] But Mary Aquin O'Neill, for example, is concerned instead with "the way in which Mary, who clearly engaged in what is sexual experience—namely giving birth and breastfeeding—has been pictured in the theological tradition as being somehow preserved from what is considered to be the taint of sexual experience because she never had intercourse."[172] Analogously, Sara Maitland claims that the virginity of Mary "is not about biology, but about meaning, about symbol and metaphor," and she suspects sexism behind the aversion to Mary's virginity—because Jesus was in fact born like everyone else, "the only difference being that maleness was made redundant in this myth." [173] As former slave Sojourner Truth puts it in her much-quoted speech "Ain't I a Woman?" "Den dat little man in black dar, he say women can't have as much rights as men, 'cause Christ wasn't a woman! What did your Christ come from? . . . What did your Christ come from? From God and a woman! Man had nothin' to do wid Him." [174] After all, it is striking that the Gospel of Matthew, so concerned with paternal genealogy, should suddenly present Jesus as conceived without a father. Elizabeth Johnson has said something similar about the virgin martyrs of early Christianity, who through virginity and the refusal of marriage escaped societal controls over women and their fertility: "In this context, these young women, deeply attracted by the word of God, presume to have a life, a body, an identity apart from the patriarchal state's definitions of what constitutes their humanity." [175]

So, in returning to Gemma Galgani after this discussion, we can see the difficulty of renouncing sexuality (Gemma does have temptations on this matter, after all), the spiritual authority she derived from such renunciation, the societal attempts to turn her into a wife and mother (evidenced in the marriage proposals she received and rejected),[176] the spiritual freedom arising from not having a husband and children: in evading the hold of marriage, she can devote most of her waking hours to God; her ill health, by the way, also helps her to achieve this by freeing her from those household chores expected of healthy women. Adrienne Rich put it well in her essay "When We Dead Awaken: Writing as Re-Vision": "To be a female human being trying to fulfill traditional female functions in a traditional way *is* in direct conflict with the subversive function of the imagination." [177] But what makes Gemma's virginity particularly threatening is its occurrence in the world, as opposed to the convent. Gemma is after all not a NUN. So her virginity functions much like her CLOTHING, her peculiar black outfit: it marks her as different, as untouched and untouchable, in spite of her place in the world, or rather in spite of her placelessness. She inhabits the paradox of virginity, its wholeness and its lack, in a double way, for paradoxically she is not where virgins are found. Her virginity has a specific end, Gemma is saving herself for her Lover, as she writes to Monsignor Volpi: "Do you not know that for more than a year Jesus has been waiting to have his way with me?" (*Ecstasies and Letters*, 141). For her virginity, metaphor of her sacrifice, encapsulates some of the most important aspects of her spirituality: the center place held by the BODY, emptied out in its virginity through a movement of KENOSIS which makes room for the annunciation, the arrival of and the encounter with the Other—the GUARDIAN ANGEL, and JESUS himself. Gemma's virginity is also her empty/emptied life, her relatively uneventful biography which is perhaps a long waiting, in tune with others, for the Other.

w : wedding

— or, of matches made in heaven

"When you are in the convent, then we will be wedded; you must tell your confessor to hasten the time of our wedding," JESUS tells Gemma in November 1899.[178] The theme of mystical marriage or wedding is a recurrent one in the history of Christian spirituality, and it is not surprising, given the masculine bent of divine imagery in this tradition, that it should hold a particular importance for women mystics. Mystical marriage finds a scriptural basis in the Song of Songs, the brief book of the Hebrew Bible which celebrates the relationship between God/Christ and God's people, or God/Christ and the soul, with an allegory of explicitly sexual, nuptial language between a bride and her bridegroom. It begins: "Let him kiss me with kisses of his mouth! More delightful is your love than wine!" and continues with a similar tone: "Your lips drip honey, my bride, sweetmeats and milk are under your tongue. . . . I eat my honey and my sweetmeats, I drink my wine and my milk." Although its theology has been developed by important men of the Church such as Origen of Alexandria in the third century and Saint Bernard of Clairvaux in the twelfth, the theme of the wedding between God and the soul was especially popular among medieval holy women: obviously, it was less of an imaginative leap for women than for men to take the place of Christ's bride. Furthermore, there is a liberating potential inherent in the mystical wedding, for it implies an extraordinary bond with God that can go beyond the very limited social roles available to women in a traditional society. Rather than reenacting a heterosexist household code, mystical wedding allowed holy women an unparalleled freedom and authority in their exchange with God and with men.

The mystical wedding between Gemma and Jesus is celebrated throughout the text of her *Ecstasies*. The ecstasy of June–July, for example, opens with Gemma's ardent invocation: "Let me embrace you, celestial bridegroom, source of all my consolations" (*Ecstasies and Letters,* 129). The subsequent ecstasies also contain exclamations such as the following: "My Jesus . . . my father . . . my bridegroom . . . my sweetness . . . my consolation . . . (130); "My Jesus, my love!" (131); "you are the bridegroom of my soul" (142); "In this condition I throw myself too much, too much, into the arms of my celestial bridegroom" (149). In an earlier ecstasy, Gemma had exclaimed even more explicitly—though evidently not without a struggle to come to terms with her multiple, paradoxical roles: "Oh Jesus, but always daughter? . . . nothing more? I would like to be, I would like . . . Always daughter, oh Jesus, always daughter? . . . I would like to be, I would like . . . oh . . . Jesus, I would like . . . Oh, Jesus, I would like . . . Yes, it would be too much, too much, Jesus, for me . . . Do you know what is the thing that I desire? . . . I would like, Jesus . . . I would like to be, oh Jesus, your . . . bride, oh Jesus . . . Yes, your bride, oh Jesus! . . ."[179]

These exclamations, very much in the tradition of *Brautmystik,* or bridal mysticism, are literal renditions of the topos of the mystical marriage. Yet the invocation of the bond of marriage between Gemma and Jesus certainly oversteps the boundaries of the institution of marriage, even in its understanding as sacrament. Throughout Gemma's writings we encounter her love for Jesus as a PASSIONate love, rather than a contractual relationship. The cry "Mio Gesù, io ti amo," "My Jesus, I love you" ("amare" in Italian is used more often for passionate love rather than, say, filial, parental, friendly love, for which "volere bene" is more commonly employed), well expresses the feelings of Gemma for her God, especially as she describes in the next paragraph her "petto innamorato," her "chest in love with you" (*Ecstasies and Letters,* 130). "In love," then, and not simply "loving." This is the language of the Song of Songs, it is the language of a passion that can be described as erotic—hence my choice of the word "wedding" rather than "marriage." Gemma is a bride, not a wife. Her relationship with Jesus is a honeymoon, not a routine cohabitation. In the next ecstasy Gemma finds her passion to be reciprocated, for she finds "a Jesus so infatuated with my heart that he knows not how to embitter it" (*Ecstasies and Letters,* 130). Indeed, in a later ecstasy Gemma says that she sees Jesus and that he "loves me and seems in love with me" (*Ecstasies and Letters,* 148), again using the term "innamorato" that she had used for her own chest earlier. Yet this erotic passion is never completely separable from the Passion of Christ as his suffering and death on the cross. As Gemma tells her own soul, "you are wed with Jesus for eternity, together with his pains, and you are obliged to live crucified" (*Ecstasies and Letters,* 133).

Beyond calling herself bride of God, however, Gemma also defines her relationship with Jesus in even more passionately erotic terms which eventually bypass marriage altogether. In an ecstasy we eavesdrop on Gemma, who sounds like a young woman in love who converses on the telephone with her boyfriend: "Am I enough for you, Jesus? Am I your delight, Jesus? . . . What do you mean! Jesus, you are all mine? . . . I am enough for

Jesus? . . . Say it again to me, say it again to me, Jesus."[180] So she refers to God as "a passionate lover" (*Ecstasies and Letters,* 145). And in an important ecstasy, Gemma exclaims: "You will always be my father and I will always be your faithful daughter and, if you like, I will be your lover . . ." (*Ecstasies and Letters,* 155). Gemma is the only Italian mystic known to have called herself God's lover, God's "amante."[181]

Interestingly, "God as lover" is also one of the three ways of relating to God which Sallie McFague proposes in her book *Models of God* (the other two are God as mother and God as friend). McFague rightly notes that, with the model of God as lover, eroticism must be openly considered—as Gemma certainly does—yet our tendency is to see passion, desire, eroticism in God's love as contaminating, for we assume a pure love of the divine to be "untainted" by bodily intrusions. McFague is very critical of this tradition: "Are we not saying that the most intimate and important kind of human love is inappropriate for expressing some aspects of the God-world relationship? The love of parents to children and perhaps friend to friend is allowed but not lover to beloved. But why not? What is wrong with desire, with passion? Or more positively, what is good, appropriate, and right about it as a model of God's relationship with the world?" (126). Beyond lust, sex, and desire, the crux of being in love, according to McFague, is the value one finds in the other just for being who he is, who she is: "Being found valuable in this way is the most complete affirmation possible" (128). Gemma finds this affirmation in her love affair with Jesus, who reciprocates her feeling, her commitment. God's touch is not only a spiritual touch, eroticism is not only genital contact. Gemma can be wholly virgin and wholly bride. In this paradox thrives her joy.

X: EXTASY
—OR, HOW TO BE A VIRGIN
AND HAVE YOUR PLEASURE, TOO

Pardon the spelling, but the entry for the letter "E" was taken: and without the eucharist, there would have been, for Gemma Galgani, no ecstasy. Yet ecstasy is so central to Gemma's spiritual journey that one of the texts associated with her experience is entitled, precisely, *Ecstasies.* These were not penned by Gemma's own hand but rather they constitute the notes taken by members of the Giannini family who wrote down what she said on the numerous occasions when she "lost her head." For in addition to the more literal "raccogliermi" ("gather myself"), Gemma uses the expressions "andare via la testa" or "andare via il capo" ("my head goes away"), "portare via la testa" ("my head is taken away"), "la testa parte" ("my head takes off"), to refer to these experiences—thus explicitly linking the spiritual encounter and the appearance of insanity, and underscoring the fact that the contact with the divine has a maddening quality and that her experience belongs to the mystical tradition of the "madness of the cross." So Gemma explains in a letter to her confessor that he shouldn't believe that her head "really takes off," but rather that her "brain does take off from the inside," though "her body stays as she leaves it"—most of the time, at least.[182]

But what is ecstasy for this saint? Is it, as etymology would have it, a standing beside oneself, exiting one's normal state in order to access another dimension? "Ecstasy," in the words of Italian psychoanalyst Silvia Vegetti Finzi, "comprises a coming out of the self, a loss of awareness, a dispersal of the mind which leaves the body at its own mercy."[183] It is usually associated with pleasure, or more accurately with what one branch of psychoanalysis, and much feminist criticism, would call *jouissance,* akin to the Italian "godimento." But this is not a word that can be easily translated or even paraphrased: "enjoyment," "bliss," "pleasure," "orgasm," are all painfully partial options. Gemma's ecstasy, like *jouissance,* is an experience beyond experience itself, beyond BODY, beyond physical and spiritual endurance, beyond all reason and meaning (and Georges Bataille has explored all this in great, if difficult, detail). The embrace of *jouissance* implies TRANSGRESSION of the human law, hence its connection, via transgression, to mysticism. *Jouissance,* transgression, mysticism cannot be encased within discourse, because they demarcate the very limits of language: in their excess, they consume meaning itself.

Thus also for Gemma, ecstasy, linked with *jouissance,* transgression, and mysticism in complex ways, is a paradoxical experience of which we necessarily only have vague and untrustworthy traces—and then, through the mediated record of Gemma's ecstasies kept by members of the Giannini household. We can perceive how ecstasy exceeds articulate speech, how it surpasses understanding, goes beyond comprehension in the way it crosses, for example, the experience of pain and/as pleasure, cry and/as LAUGHTER. In the mystical language of paradox, in the paradoxical experience of ecstasy, these apparent opposites no longer stand as such and even come to coincide.

Ecstasy is a touchy topic for Gemma, an experience that fills her with joy and pleasure but also makes her uncomfortable and at times ashamed in front of others—whose response is often laughter. When her sister wants to upset and tease her, she remains in Gemma's room, "making fun of me, that she wanted to see me go in ecstasy" (*Diary,* 83); "Come," the sister says to her schoolmates, "let's go see Gemma go in ecstasy"—words that she repeats constantly and loudly, "even at the portico in the evening";[184] this same sister stuffs Gemma's key hole so she cannot lock herself in order to pray and invite God's presence (*Diary,* 81). Far from having "a room of her own," Gemma is a spectacle in different ways to different people—from family members and friends or benefactors to doctors and priests. She therefore occasionally has to renounce ecstasy, her preferred access to God and divine will, if she does not have privacy: "I can't collect myself unless I am in a safe place," Gemma writes, so she has to go and hide and ask the GUARDIAN ANGEL to "stand guard" at her door (*Diary,* 92). Later, her angel tells Gemma to tell her confessor "not to neglect [her] but to keep [her] hidden" (*Diary,* 95).

Like other aspects of Gemma's journey—such as, for example, FOOD practices, erotic images and penitential extremes, her BODY-centered PASSION—ecstasy is an experience that, in the history of Christian spirituality, has been more prominent among women than among men.[185] Many reasons have been adduced for this connection. Luce Irigaray, for example, claims an intrinsic link between women and ecstasy by focusing on the etymology of this word: displacement (from the Greek "ex," outside, and "histemi," place). Women have a privileged access to ecstasy because they are already outside representation, they are always "displaced," "ecstatic," then: "The poorest in science and the most ignorant were the most eloquent and the richest in revelations. Historically therefore women. Or at least the 'feminine.'"[186] The link between Gemma's displacement (one of her biographies is appropriately entitled *Ritratto di un'espropriata*) and her ecstatic journey places her almost too comfortably within Irigaray's diagnosis. Yet all comfort is dispelled by the proximity, in ecstasy, of pleasure and pain: the mystic for Irigaray, like Gemma for us, perhaps, can elude her own exile, her own "expropriation," and can find a place for herself by entering the divine space within which her own pleasure can unfold. But this space can open up for her only through the imitation of Christ (see the entry RESEMBLANCE), whose incarnation as "the most feminine of all men"[187] undoes masculine patriarchal logic (what Irigaray calls "specular rationality") by finding victory in the abyss and life in the vilest of deaths.

For Gemma as for medieval and later women mystics, ecstatic union is often connected to the reception of the eucharist—to the pleasure of food as feasting in the bodily connection, "communion," with the beloved Christ. In turn, ecstasy is often expressed through that same vocabulary used by poets to sing of erotic love: in an ecstasy, right after describing her body as slime that God should not allow to rebel against divine will, Gemma is overtaken by an intense pleasure—*jouissance* is the term that would be used today to critically describe this experience—and exclaims: "What is, Jesus, this fire that comes all over me? I am in pleasure, Jesus . . . I am in pleasure, Jesus . . . I am in pleasure, Jesus. I would like to be like this for all eternity . . . My God . . . If you make us so happy on earth, what will it be like in Heaven, dear Jesus?"[188] It must be noted that the verb used by Gemma, "godo," refers to orgasm as well as to enjoyment. The Italian dictionary definition of the intransitive form of the verb "godere," used furthermore without a preposition, is "to be profoundly happy" and "to experience pleasure with one's senses"; in sexual slang, it means "to come"—though it does not sound vulgar in Italian as it may sound in English.[189] Indeed the way in which Gemma uses "godere" here—in the first person and without a direct object—most likely refers to something akin to orgasm. When she says "godo" Gemma is also (though not only) saying "I am coming," to put it bluntly. (This translation problem, by the way, is not unique to Gemma Galgani's experience and it has been repeatedly noted in literary theory, especially spurred by Roland Barthes's distinction between texts of pleasure and texts of *jouissance;* thus we can say about "godere" what Barthes's translator Richard Howard says about *jouissance,* that it belongs to "a vocabulary of eroticism," unavailable in English, a vocabulary "which smells neither of the laboratory nor of the sewer, which just—attentively, scrupulously— puts the facts.")[190]

Clearly, we cannot simply say that Gemma is having a sexual orgasm, but the intense bodily pleasure she experiences must be acknowledged and reflected on if we are to make sense of her dark night of the soul, of her physical pain and bleeding wounds. For both eroticism and ecstasy partake of the pleasure enhanced by the tension between Self and Other, between identity and difference, as well as of transcendence as "the power to cross over from self to other"[191]—that power of connection and relationality already discussed above in the context of SAINTHOOD. Furthermore, even if we believe that mysticism embodies an absolute universal reality (as some comparative studies of mysticism claim), each case must be discussed within a particular cultural and historical situation. Gemma Galgani is Freud's contemporary, and she stands between Charcot's hysterics and Bataille's *jouissance*. If Charcot is also responsible for an extensive psychiatrization of the mystic, Bataille is the writer who most explicitly explored mysticism from a godless perspective.[192]

Y

— OR, OF YAKS AND YO-YOS

In my children's alphabet books (and, more improbably, this is the case also in M. F. K. Fisher's *An Alphabet for Gourmets*), the letter "y" is almost invariably represented by a "yak," a sort of bisonish bovine that lives in cold climes; in some cases, in order to stress the use of the letter "y," the yak somewhat miraculously plays with a "yo-yo." In this alphabet of mine, on the other hand, I could not come up with a convincing example for the letter "y" in relation to the experience of Saint Gemma Galgani. Colleagues have suggested "yearning" and "you," but they just did not click. It also needs to be said that the Italian alphabet does not contain the letter "y," which—like the letters "j," "k," "w," and "x"—is primarily used to spell foreign words (thus, the Italian alphabet has only twenty-one letters). Rather than despair about such lack as I did at first, questioning the very viability of the alphabet form of this essay, I have come to realize the theoretical importance of such an absence, a lack of yak, so to speak. Lack is after all a central concept in psychoanalytic accounts of women's subjectivity, as well as of subjectivity in general. Ultimately, there is so much we cannot expect to recover, to know, to understand about Gemma Galgani as about so many women of past times: the experience of lack is intrinsic to feminist historiography, to the postlapsarian condition of women and men, to everyone's entry into full subjecthood. There is no "yak," real or imaginary, to fill the holes of signification (historical, religious, theoretical) that become particularly striking as one goes deeper into this saint's story. I therefore found it more honest and useful to accept this lack than to try to fill it with a meaning that for me is not there. If the entry QUESTION(ING) provided a space for issues I was unable to answer, this entry is an imaginary, a fantasized place for those questions I could not even ask.

I could end this pseudo-entry, then, with an invitation to the reader: What is most conspicuously absent, for you, from Gemma Galgani's life— what would make it, in your view, whole? Or, which is perhaps the same, what would make it holy?

Z: ZEAL
— OR, GEMMA SAYS, JESUS IS WAITING FOR YOU LAZY BUMS TO GET MOVING!

Zeal is that discipline by which Gemma trained her love for God, her holiness. It is the thread holding together the three paths to the love of God: praise, reverence, service. It is the way in which the saint's personal experiences of God (in visions and contemplative prayer, for example) were impelled, through OBEDIENCE and at times across TRANSGRESSION, to realize themselves in words and actions. Zeal includes, then, that life of prayers, penance, poverty, and sacrifice which characterizes Gemma's existence and which is intended as a model for all of us. But zeal is also her unwavering support and work toward what she believed was God's will—even to the point of justified anger. When Jesus chases the merchants away from the temple, he is described in the Gospels as being consumed by zeal for the House of God, thus actually fulfilling the Scriptures (John 2:17). Similarly, through another instance of RESEMBLANCE to Christ, of imitatio Christi, Gemma is consumed by her zeal to found and be part of another House of God, the convent for Passionist NUNS that she succeeded in establishing only after her death (a few months later, more precisely, in October 1903, by the decision of Pope Pius X; the first Passionist nuns arrived in March 1905). In one of their encounters recorded in her diary, Brother Gabriel asks Mary, about those who must build the Passionist convent, to "increase their strength, increase their zeal" (*Diary*, 89). Gemma sounds almost threatening when she speaks of this matter to her confessor: "Why don't you obey? Do not oppose the will of Jesus, as Monsignor has done until now; it is not I who says this, you know? So many times Jesus told me, it seems. Forgive all these talks, and if they anger you do not read them. The angel is commanding me to do this; what can I do?"[193] Her words are, once again, authorized by the divinity, even as they verge on transgression: "Write to me immediately and tell me something about the convent. Jesus is waiting for you *lazy bums* to get moving" ("poltroni" is underlined in the original).[194] And about this same subject she continues, calling upon the authority of her highest Father in order to chastise her earthly Dad: "My Heavenly Father is greatly angered."[195] And again, in reporting Jesus' thoughts and words about the pressing need to found a convent, Gemma writes: "if they resist my will— Jesus added—I will take care of the matter."[196] The Passionist convent is the only place on earth where Gemma can be safe. Her safety is a recurring theme in her conversations with her angel about her confessors' insufficient zeal for her: her angel repeats "many times" to Gemma: "Reveal everything to your confessor; tell him not to neglect you but to keep you hidden. . . . Tell him that Jesus wants him to have much more concern toward you" (*Diary*, 95). On the same matter Gemma prays: "Jesus, give light, give light not to me but to Father Germano and to my confessor" (*Diary*, 97). And she not so subtly reminds the priests around her that her own connection with Jesus is closer, more intimate and reliable than theirs: "If Serafina says she wants to come to Lucca, you won't prohibit her, because don't you think Jesus wishes it?" (*Ecstasies and Letters*, 126); "Thank you very much for the permission you granted me. You will see what Jesus will give you" (*Ecstasies and Letters*, 135); "Dear Dad, come soon. Don't you know that Jesus wishes it?" (*Ecstasies and Letters*, 141).

Gemma complements her ideals and threats with much practical advice —a side of her that we rarely see. For example, in order to solve the question of the building for her proposed Passionist convent, she researches and finds available convents; she communicates all this to Father Germano, so that he may be "God's spokesman"—since, as Gemma painfully knows well, "nobody listens to me." [197] Not surprisingly, I might add: for, in turn-of-the-century provincial Italy (or, for that matter, here and now), who is going to listen to an uneducated and impoverished, homeless and nomad, orphaned, sickly girl who wants to found a convent? Gemma Galgani's zeal, ultimately, can only be understood in light of her complete disenfranchisement. Her offering of pain is Gemma's only gift, her one way of returning another's love. So she poignantly writes: "Oh my God, and what could I give you, when I have nothing? Look at me, look at me: here I am. Look at me from head to toes: I have nothing, I am all ruined, I really have nothing to give you. Enlighten me, if you want me to give. Ah! now I know. This life which you have given me and preserved with such force of love, this life is what I sacrifice to you. Well, oh Lord, I have nothing else to give you." [198] In KENOSIS she fulfills her zeal, finds an outlet for her PASSION, and attains that SAINTHOOD she so ardently desired.

Contemporary common sense and instinct of preservation recoil at some of the penitential practices that Gemma carried out—reminiscent more of early Christian and medieval ascetes than of the materialistic, bourgeois ideals prevalent during Gemma's own lifetime and exasperated in our own. So again it is useful to remember what Caroline Walker Bynum has to say about the complex meanings of the penitential body: "Medieval efforts to discipline and manipulate the body should be interpreted more as elaborate changes rung upon the *possibilities* provided by fleshliness rather than as flights from physicality."[199] Or, in Laurie Finke's words, "The discourse of the female mystic was constructed out of disciplines designed to regulate the female body, and it is, paradoxically, through these disciplines that the mystic consolidated her power."[200] In this perspective, Gemma's penitential choices, in spite of their gruesome effects on us, can be seen and understood not only as aids in reaching a greater level of refinement in the spiritual life but also, rather simply, as gift and, thus, power: the reverse power of kenosis, self-abdication, decreation. Christ encourages us to give up all we have and follow him, if we want to learn how to love. What did Gemma have? No money, no status, no home, no family . . . How could her zeal be expressed? How could she attain the resemblance with JESUS necessary, in the Catholic worldview, for salvation? In other words, what could she offer up as a gift to her Lover? FOOD. Health. Life. What other sacrifice could match, or at least somewhat approach, or even barely attempt to imitate, Christ's own? Self-giving is empowerment—to imitate Christ, to learn love, to live passionately.

Without self-immolation there can be no freedom, as Simone Weil claims like Gemma—though with an intellectual's language informed by the existential climate that is her background and that allows Weil to speak to us in ways Gemma could not: "We possess nothing in this world—for chance may deprive us of everything—except the power to say 'I.' It is that which has to be offered up to God, that is to say, destroyed. The destruction of the 'I' is the one and only free act that lies open to us."[201] To the words of this mystic I would like to add those of an Italian feminist philosopher who, through different paths (and "the paths of the Lord are infinite," Italians are fond of saying), has reached an analogous and surprising conclusion—or perhaps, more than a conclusion, an opening: of the worldly to the sacred, of philosophy to mysticism. Luisa Muraro, at the end of her essay "La nostra comune capacità d'infinito" (Our common capacity for infinity), invites scholars to study the mystical tradition as part of philosophical thought: because of the dominance of women among the mystics and their scarcity among the philosophers, but especially because philosophy, like psychoanalysis, is struggling with the death of the I, with the irreducibility of thought to the *cogito,* "I think." And for the mystic—for Gemma Galgani, for Simone Weil—the "I" *needs* to die in order to attain true knowledge, effective will. For the mystic, in Muraro's own words, "the death of the I is the mediator in the coincidence between being and thought. The death of the I leads to the knowability and the modification of reality by reality itself."[202] Exactly.

ONE MORE LETTER

"I feel that I love, but I don't know, I don't understand whom it is that I love. . . . Still in my great ignorance I feel that there is an immense Good, a great Good."[203]

So, my dear Gemma Galgani, this long (too long?) essay, these twenty-six letters are what I, in turn, can offer you. Like you I have written, like you I have wanted time and again to tear it all up. Burn it and go on with the business of life instead: there is cooking and cleaning (and never again will I be able to make meatballs and coffee without thinking of your angel!), there is diapering and bathing, there is teaching and chatting with friends, there is praying, there is lovemaking . . . Yet unlike you I do find consolation in words, for I don't receive the visits that so consoled your own soul. Mine are words of listening, words, I hope, of compassion and comfort. I have strived to hear you, Gemma, through our differences rather than in spite of them— and there are so many, too many perhaps. Still what I had the privilege of seeing, though in gleams and flashes, never as a comfortable and straight-forward story, was neither a bleeding freak nor a glittered goddess, but rather a young woman of strength and defiance, uneducated yet unafraid, shaken but not broken by the assaults of all that is death-dealing. A person yearn-ing and fighting for that fullness of life which so few of us have the courage to experience here on earth. I pray that my vision of your vision be not too far from your joy, and that the readers of my reading will get to see, through the crooked lines of my writing, the straight signs of the harmo-nious love, the immense Good, the great Good, with whom you once co-wrote your life.

NOTES

INTRODUCTION

1. Enrico Zoffoli, "Gemma Galgani," in *Bibliotheca Sanctorum* 4:107. In addition to formal reports as the canonization process proceeded, which may be found in the *Acta Congregationis a SS. Cruce et Passione D. N. J. C.* and the *Bollettino della Congregazione della SS. Croce e Passione di N. S. G. C.* from as early as July 1920 and continuing through the final celebration of canonization in May 1940, clusters of popular articles appeared on the occasions of beatification and canonization.

Around beatification, and focusing on the Anglo-American scene, see Atun M. Evneb, "Gemma Galgani," *The Sign* 12 (May 1933): 585–89; "Beatification of Gemma Galgani," *The Tablet* 161 (May 20, 1933): 634; and Gabriel Francis Powers, "The Gem of Christ," *The Sign* 12 (July 1933): 713–15. And at the time of canonization, see Mary Fabyan Windeatt, "Lily of Lucca," *The Sign* 19 (May 1940): 586–88; Gabriel Francis Powers, "Two New Saints: An Account of the Solemn Ceremony of Canonization of St. Euphrasia Pelletier and St. Gemma Galgani," *The Sign* 19 (July 1940): 749–51; and E. Beyer, "Gemma Galgani: Saint and Mystic," *Ave Maria* 55 (April 18, 1942): 495–98; also see notices in *America* (May 4, 1940), *Commonweal* (May 17, 1940), and *Catholic World* (June 1940).

Full, front-page coverage of the beatification ceremonies, with supplementary feature articles on pages 2 and 3, may be found in *L'osservatore romano*, May 14, 1933. For similar coverage of the canonization, see *L'osservatore romano*, May 2 and 3, 1940. The canonization itself was a dual ceremony honoring as well Euphrasia Pelletier (1796–1868), a French mother superior and reformer whose life shared little in common with Gemma's. Combined events of this kind are not at all unusual.

2. We cite Gemma Galgani's writings as follows: translated items as *Autobiography, Diary,* or *Ecstasies,* followed by page number of our translation; untranslated ecstasies as *Estasi,* followed by the date; untranslated letters as *Lettere,* followed by the addressee, and then the date; and untranslated miscellaneous items by their full title and page number in Gemma Galgani, *Estasi, Diario, Autobiografia, Scritti vari, Versi,* edited by the Postulazione dei PP. Passionisti (Rome, 1958; reprint 1979).

3. On the motor boat, see *Acta Congregationis* 22 (October 1963): 12. The Gemma League advertisements ran in *The Sign,* a Passionist magazine distributed throughout the United States. For more on the Passionist Order's missionary activities, see Caspar Caulfield, *Only a Beginning: The Passionists in China, 1921–1931* (Union City, N.J., 1990). On the church in Detroit and the popularity of the name "Gemma," see the letter of Sebastian MacDonald, C.P., Provincial Superior, to Thomas Heitjan, May 7, 1987. For permission to consult this unpublished letter as well as a range of published materials, Bell is grateful to Roger Mercurio, C.P., who, as archivist of the Passionist Library and Research Center in Chicago, kindly assisted him with his work there.

4. Also see the special centennial edition, *S. Gemma e il suo santuario* (March 1979). The Internet searches were done on December 20, 2001, using Google's "I'm Feeling Lucky" search engine.

5. B. M. Hagspiel, "New Hospital Patroness: St. Gemma Galgani," *Hospital Progress* 21 (March 1940): 97–98; also see Alphonse M. Schwitalla, "Patron Saints of Catholic Hospitals," *Hospital Progress* 39 (April 1958): 80–82, which identifies Gemma Galgani and Catherine of Siena as the co-patrons of hospitals. Saint Gemma's associations as protector of pharmacists and of orphans derive directly from her biography: daughter of a pharmacist whose parents both died during her childhood, her mother when Gemma was eight and her father before she reached age nineteen. On October 29, 1962, Pope John XXIII also designated her as celestial patron of the diocese of Dodomaënsi in Tanganyika (Tanzania). Less officially, according to Luigi Alunno, C.P., "S. Gemma nella religiosità popolare italiana," in *Mistica e misticismo oggi: Settimana di studio di Lucca 8–13 settembre 1978* (Rome, 1979), 747, she is known as the patron of parachutists (for reasons that elude us), of the Italian League against Blasphemy, and of the Pious Union for the Conversion of Sinners; the latter two have connections with her life that will become apparent as our narrative unfolds.

6. Anon., "Gemma and Mary . . . Two Women Who Followed St. Paul," *The Passionist Orbit* (winter 1966), 15, shows clearly how linking Gemma Galgani to the simplified lesson contained in Maria Goretti's story obscures what the former was about. The "lesson" of Maria Goretti, as stated by Pope John Paul II in a letter dated October 16, 1990, to Passionist Superior General José Augustin Orbegozo, was that she "resisted every temptation and preferred to die rather than lose her virginity." Copy obtained courtesy of Father Mercurio at the Passionist Research Center in Chicago. On Maria Goretti, see especially Monica Turi, "Il 'brutto peccato'. Adolescenza e controllo sessuale nel modello agiografico di Maria Goretti," in Anna Benvenuti Papi and Elena Giannarelli, *Bambini santi: rappresentazioni dell'infanzia e modelli agiografici* (Turin, 1990), 119–46.

   On the rise and fall of Saint Gemma's popularity more generally in Italy, see Alunno, "S. Gemma," 738–50. On the United States, see Jude Mead, C.P., "S. Gemma Galgani nel culto e nella religiosità popolare degli USA," in *Mistica e misticismo oggi,* 760–67; but a recent, specialized work makes no mention of Saint Gemma: Joseph Varacalli, Salvatore Primeggia, Salvatore LaGumina, and Donald D'Elia, eds., *The Saints in the Lives of Italian-Americans: An Interdisciplinary Investigation* (Stony Brook, N.Y., 1999). For the North Dakota relic, see http://www.fcsn.k12.nd.us/Shanley/broanth/gemma.htm as of December 20, 2001. On Latin America, see Miguel Gonzalez R., C.P., "Santa Gemma in Cile e in America Latina," in *Mistica e misticismo oggi,* 768–78.

7. Also published by the University of Chicago Press, 1985.

8. Gabriella Zarri, *Le sante vive: Cultura e religiosità femminile nella prima età moderna* (Turin, 1990), 108–11, vividly captures the sense of "living saints."

9. Cristina Mazzoni, *Saint Hysteria: Neurosis, Mysticism, and Gender in European Culture* (Ithaca, N.Y., 1996), 159–77 and passim; Cristina Mazzoni, "Visions of the Mystic/ Mystical Visions: Interpretations and Self-Interpretations of Gemma Galgani," *Annali d'Italianistica* 13 (1995): 371–86.

10. The Passionist Order was founded by Saint Paul (Danei) of the Cross (1694–1775) to seek the intertwined goals of missionary activity and of re-living the Passion. The order is a relatively small one, numbering a total of just 12,803 men in the 250 years of its existence from its foundation in 1741 until 1991. Of these men, about half are or were priests (and 48 became bishops) while the other half are or were brothers or students. While full admission to the order is restricted by rule to men, there is for women a Passionist-supported convent, initiated at Corneto in 1770 by the Benedictine nun Mary of Jesus Crucified (Faustina Gertrude Constantini), with the direct encouragement of the order's founder, and another at Lucca, dedicated to Gemma Galgani. Outside of Italy, Passionist organizations for women have come (and sometimes gone) in England (starting with a refuge for factory workers in Manchester), France (at Lourdes, now defunct), Ireland, Scotland, Spain, and more recently in Brazil, Chile, and the United States.

CHAPTER ONE

1. For the first printed edition of "Lezioni di Harvard," see Gaetano Salvemini, *Opere,* vol. 6, *Scritti sul fascismo,* pt. 1, edited by Roberto Vivarelli (Milan, 1961), 419–23. See also the background information provided in Salvemini, *Le origini del fascismo in Italia: Lezioni di Harvard,* edited by Roberto Vivarelli (Milan, 1966), 5–7, and for the same text, 156–62. For an English edition based on a 1942 mimeographed copy left by Salvemini at Harvard's Widener Library, see Salvemini, *The Origins of Fascism in Italy,* edited and with an introduction by Vivarelli (New York, 1973), 151–59, for the text from which the above quotations are taken. For an expanded version of the analysis of Italian Catholicism presented in the "Harvard Lessons," including a correction of the number of Italian Jews to 34,000, see Salvemini, *Opere,* vol. 2, *Scritti di storia moderna e contemporanea,* pt. 3, edited by Elio Conti (Milan, 1969), 113–25. Salvemini's admiration for the mystic tradition remains firm in this version. It provides a persuasive starting point for the related work of Arnaldo Nesti, *Gesù socialista: Una tradizione popolare italiana (1880–1920)* (Turin, 1974), 5–7.

2. For biographical background on Gemma's family, see Enrico Zoffoli, C.P., *La povera Gemma: Saggi critici storico-teologici,* 2d ed. (Naples, 1957), 3–5 and 142–48; the quotation is found on page 5. Less reliable, but useful in other ways, is Germano [Ruoppolo] di San Stanislao, *Biografia di Gemma Galgani: Vergine lucchese,* 3d ed. (Rome, 1908), 15–22. Five editions appeared between 1907 and 1909, all prepared directly by Father Germano. Later editions of this work, beginning with the sixth (Rome, 1910), all posthumous and prepared by the Postulazione dei PP. Passionisti at Rome, are built on Father Germano's revision-in-progress which, following upon knowledge gained at the recently concluded canonization inquiry at Lucca, substantially reorganized the chapters into a more chronologically coherent format. While the later revised editions are useful for their correction of a few errors, they lack the fresh zeal of the original. We have

preferred to translate and cite from one of the five original editions (actually, more like reprintings) written directly by Father Germano (while informing our readers of any significant variations in later editions). A recent English translation of the rearranged posthumous edition is available: Germanus of St. Stanislaus, *The Life of St. Gemma Galgani,* translated by A. M. O'Sullivan (Erlanger, Ky., 1999).

References to the canonization proceedings may be found in full in chapter 5 below.

3. Mirena Stanghellini and Ubaldo Tintori, *Storia del movimento cattolico lucchese* (Rome, 1958), 31–34, provides a vivid description of the problem of pauperism in the specific setting of Lucca and its immediate countryside.

4. On emigration generally and specifically on the *figurinai,* see Roland Sarti, *Long Live the Strong: A History of Rural Society in the Apennine Mountains* (Amherst, Mass., 1985), esp. 85ff.

5. Biographical details on Father Germano, given here and elsewhere, are drawn from the account of his life printed in the sixth edition (first posthumous edition) of his biography of Gemma Galgani (Rome, 1910), 499–532.

6. For a readily available English translation of this document, see Anne Freemantle, ed. *The Papal Encyclicals in their Historical Context: The Teachings of the Popes from Peter to John XXIII* (New York, 1956), 143–55.

7. Nonetheless, Gemma Galgani certainly was aware of their influence, as shown by *Lettere,* Vittorio Buchignani, May 25, 1901, written on behalf of his mother; cited in Maria Luisa Trebiliani, "S. Gemma, la spiritualità del suo tempo, la sua città," *Mistica e misticismo oggi: Settimana di studio di Lucca 8–13 settembre 1978* (Rome, 1979), 601–609, 605 for the citation.

8. For a good introduction in English to the issues, see Frank J. Coppa, *The Modern Papacy since 1789* (London, 1998), 100–134. Readers of Italian may consult Alfredo Canavero, *I cattolici nella società italiana: Dalla metà dell'800 al Concilio Vaticano II* (Brescia, 1991), 45–103, and Maurilio Guasco, *Storia del clero in Italia dall'Ottocento a oggi* (Bari, 1997), 64–155, in addition to the classic Gabriele De Rosa, *Storia del movimento cattolico in Italia: Dalla restaurazione all'età giolittiana* (Bari, 1966). See as well, Michael P. Riccards, *Vicars of Christ: Popes, Power, and Politics in the Modern World* (New York, 1998), 5–54; also still useful is Edward T. Gargan, *Leo XIII and the Modern World* (New York, 1961), esp. 101–24, for the essay by S. William Halperin, "Leo XIII and the Roman Question." For an overview of the historiographical debate, see Fausto Fonzi, "L'età leoniana: La storiografia relativa," in Ettore Passerin d'Entrèves and Konrad Repgen, *Il cattolicesimo politico e sociale in Italia e Germania dal 1870 al 1914* (Bologna, 1977), 15–42.

9. Stanghellini and Tintori, *Storia del movimento cattolico lucchese,* 99–107.

10. Zoffoli, *La povera Gemma,* 34, n. 3. The depth of feeling against Pius IX has not abated completely more than a century after his death, as shown in coverage of his recent beatification in *Corriere della Sera* (September 3, 2000), 7–8.

11. Zoffoli, *La povera Gemma,* 35–36, nn. 23 and 24. On limited public education opportunities for women in late-nineteenth-century Italy, see Lucetta Scaraffia, "'Christianity Has Liberated Her and Placed Her alongside Man in the Family': From 1850 to 1988 (Mulieris Dignitatem)," in Lucetta Scaraffia and Gabriella Zarri, eds., *Women and Faith: Catholic Religious Life in Italy from Late Antiquity to the Present* (Cambridge, Mass., 1999), 251–52.

12. Zoffoli, *La povera Gemma*, 156 and 170, n. 174. The quotation is from Giuseppe Giannini, one of the children in Gemma's adopted family; he went on to become a lawyer, and his testimony at the canonization proceedings carried considerable weight.

13. *Lettere*, Father Germano, August 29, 1902; October 20, 1902; Mother Maria Giuseppa, August 31, 1902.

14. *Lettere*, Monsignor Volpi, August 10, 1900, the first of two letters with that date.

15. See Pietro Scoppola, *Crisi modernista e rinnovamento cattolico in Italia* (Bologna, 1961), esp. 40–41, for Giuseppe Toniolo's influence. Also see Stanghellini and Tintori, *Storia del movimento cattolico lucchese,* 205–29, for the political maneuvering in which Monsignor Volpi was involved.

16. On Bartolomea Capitanio (di Lovere) see Maria Clara Bianchi, ed., *Bartolomea Capitanio. Scritti spirituali: Lettere* (Rome, 1978) and *Il suo cammino spirituale* (Rome, 1979); also see Luigi Ignazio Mazza, *Della vita e dell'Istituto della venerabile Bartolomea Capitanio,* 2 vols. (Modena, 1905), 1:43–49, on imitation of Aloysius Gonzaga (1568–91); and Eugenio Belgeri, *Il profilo di una maestra santa: Santa Bartolomea Capitanio* (Vicenza, 1951). Bartolomea Capitanio was declared venerable on March 8, 1866; beatified on May 30, 1926; and canonized on May 18, 1950.

    For the recollection by Sister Giulia, see Germano di San Stanislao, *Biografia di Gemma Galgani,* 27.

17. For a brief introduction on Elena Guerra, see *Bibliotheca Sanctorum* 7 (Rome, 1966), 452–53. See also, P. Scavizzi, *La beata Elena Guerra apostola dello Spirito Santo* (Rome, 1939) and Anon. [a nun at Santa Zita], *L'apostola dello Spirito Santo: Beata Elena Guerra* (Lucca, 1956).

18. Germano di San Stanislao, *Biografia di Gemma Galgani,* 26–27. For an analysis of Gemma's grades and of her relationship with headmistress Elena Guerra and the other teachers at Santa Zita, see Fabrizio Braccini, "Scuola e santità: Per una introduzione ai rapporti tra S. Gemma Galgani e la B. Elena Guerra," in *Mistica e misticismo oggi,* 610–22, and especially 614 for the rejection of Gemma as a "probationary." Also see Fabrizio Braccini, "A scuola da Elena Guerra," *S. Gemma e il suo santuario* 47 (March 1979): 115–20. On the relationship of Gemma Galgani and Elena Guerra to each other, with emphasis on the texture of spirituality among the Lucchese more generally, see Maria Luisa Trebiliani, "Santità femminile e società a Lucca nell' Ottocento," in Sofia Boesch Gajano and Lucia Sebastiani, eds., *Culto dei santi, istituzioni e classi sociali in età preindustriale* (L'Aquila, 1984), 958–95, reprinted with some amplifications of the endnotes in Maria Luisa Trebiliani, *Studi storici lucchesi* (Lucca, 1992), 109–77.

19. In the original Italian, the seven "subjects" are Studio, Religione, Calligrafia, Condotta, Lavoro, Civiltà, and Precisione.

20. Zoffoli, *La povera Gemma,* 533–37.

21. It was precisely on this day, thirty-four years later in 1933, that the official decree declaring Gemma's Galgani's beatification was issued, but this may be coincidental rather than marking the anniversary of an event deemed significant in her life.

22. Suzanne Kaufman, "Miracles, Medicine and the Spectacle of Lourdes: Popular Religion and Modernity in Fin-de-siècle France" (Ph.D. diss., Rutgers University, 1996), directly shapes my thinking on a variety of issues discussed in this chapter. She reports (183–84) among cures at Lourdes a specific case of recovery from Pott's disease (tuberculosis of

the spine), the very condition Gemma's doctors thought she might be suffering from. Also see Ruth Harris, *Lourdes: Body and Spirit in the Secular Age* (New York, 1999).

23. Recent decades have seen an explosion of scholarly works on Marian (and other) apparitions in modern Europe, so that while Lourdes remains preeminent, much more now is known about the texture of such devotions in a variety of times and places. The following works in English are especially important in revealing the complexities of these phenomena in modern times in specific local contexts: Paolo Apolito, *Apparitions of the Madonna at Oliveto Citra: Local Visions and Cosmic Drama*, tr. William A. Christian Jr (University Park, Penn., 1998); Lucia Chiavola Birnbaum, *Black Madonnas: Feminism, Religion, and Politics in Italy* (Boston, 1993); David Blackbourn, *Marpingen: Apparitions of the Virgin Mary in Nineteenth-Century Germany* (New York, 1994); William A. Christian Jr, *Person and God in a Spanish Valley* (New York, 1972), which is the progenitor of much of the new work; also his *Moving Crucifixes in Modern Spain* (Princeton, N.J., 1992); Thomas A. Kselman, *Miracles and Prophecies in Nineteenth-Century France* (New Brunswick, N.J., 1983); Terry Rey, *Our Lady of Class Struggle: The Cult of the Virgin Mary in Haiti* (Trenton, N.J., 1999); Victor Turner and Edith Turner, *Image and Pilgrimage in Christian Culture: Anthropological Perspectives* (New York, 1978); and Sandra L. Zimdars-Swartz, *Encountering Mary: From La Salette to Medjugorje* (Princeton, N.J., 1991). For an insightful introduction to pre-modern Marian devotion, see Marina Warner, *Alone of All Her Sex: The Myth and the Cult of the Virgin Mary* (London, 1976). And for a brief look at the American scene, see Ann Taves, *The Household of Faith: Roman Catholic Devotions in Mid-Nineteenth-Century America* (Notre Dame, Ind., 1986), 56–69.

24. Lucetta Scaraffia, *La santa degli impossibili: Vicende e significati della devozione a S. Rita* (Turin, 1990), 51–58, provides a rich discussion of Italian Catholic devotion in the late nineteenth century. Rita of Cascia was beatified in 1628 but canonized only in 1900.

25. Sarti, *Long Live the Strong*, 175ff.

26. The best introduction to Margaret Mary Alacoque is her own oeuvre, with the autobiography and most of the letters readily available in several English-language editions, such as *The Autobiography of St. Margaret Mary Alacoque*, translated by the Sisters of the Visitation at Horsham, West Sussex (Rockford, Ill., 1996); and *The Letters of St. Margaret Mary Alacoque*, translated by Clarence A. Herbst, S.J. (Rockford, Ill., 1997). As to published sources about Saint Margaret that might have been known and used by Gemma's teachers, it is worth noting that among the earliest non-French biographies of this saint is the *Vita della venerabile Madre Margherita Maria Alacoque* published in Venice in 1784, a thorough edition of 280 pages based on a translation of a Latin version by Joseph de Galliffet that includes ample selections of her writings and that became the basis of numerous devotional pamphlets to appear in the nineteenth century, especially after mid-century and in its last decade, as the Church actively promoted devotion to the Sacred Heart.

27. See especially Alacoque, *Autobiography*, 63–72, 82, 84, 89, and 101–2. For modern French parallels with Gemma's anorectic experiences, see Jacques Maître, *Anorexies religieuses anorexie mentale: Essai de psychanalyse sociohistorique. De Marie de l'Incarnation à Simone Weil* (Paris, 2000). Yet more explicit in exploring the medieval/modern comparison is Nathalie Fraise, *L'anorexie mentale et le jeûne mystique du Moyen Age: Faim, foi et pouvoir* (Paris, 2000).

28. Galgani, *Estasi, Diario, Autobiografia, Scritti vari, Versi,* 273–80, titled "Relazione sulla guarigione."

29. Further confirmation that Gemma initially ascribed her miraculous cure solely to Blessed Margaret Mary Alacoque may be found in her first letter to Father Germano, *Lettere,* January 29, 1900. See also her early, unambiguous statement in *Lettere,* Sister Felicina Parensi, April 2, 1899.

30. Claudia Carlen, ed., *The Papal Encyclicals, 1878–1903* (Wilmington, N.C., 1981), 2:451–54, provides an English translation of the text. The consecration was remembered even a century later; see *L'osservatore romano,* June 23, 1999, 1.

31. William A. Christian Jr, *Visionaries: The Spanish Republic and the Reign of Christ* (Berkeley, Calif., 1996), 235–37, draws a distinction between the deeper implications of the "more active, optimistic image" of the Sacred Heart and the "contemplative" symbol of Mary, Our Lady of Sorrows, "oriented more toward contrition and penance" preferred by the Passionists.

CHAPTER TWO

1. Enrico Zoffoli, C.P., *La povera Gemma: Saggi critici storico-teologici,* 2d ed. (Naples, 1957), 303–6.

2. *Lettere,* Father Germano, mid-February 1901.

3. Galgani, *Estasi, Diario, Autobiografia, Scritti vari, Versi,* 280.

4. *Lettere,* Father Germano, February 23, 1901, note 5.

5. *Lettere,* Father Germano, February 23, 1901.

6. *Lettere,* Father Germano, July 8, 1901; July 18, 1901, notes; July 27, 1901. Germano di San Stanislao, *S. Gemma Galgani: Vergine lucchese,* 10th ed. (Rome, 1972, reprint), 169–72, tells the story, and also carries Father Germano's explanation that in the second through fourth editions he dropped the episode because he feared that it would create a poor impression among "modern rationalists" reading the book; but in the fifth edition he restored the account in response to popular request. A photograph of one of the pages of the original, burn-marked copybook is included in the photo gallery following page 168. Others may be found in Galgani, *Estasi, Diario, Autobiografia, Scritti vari, Versi,* following 238, 248, 256, and 280.

7. Margaret Mary Alacoque, *The Autobiography of St. Margaret Mary Alacoque,* translated by the Sisters of the Visitation at Horsham, West Sussex (Rockford, Ill., 1996), 9, 13–14.

8. *Autobiography of St. Thérèse of Lisieux,* translated by Ronald Knox (New York, 1958), 36: "If a wild flower could talk, I imagine it would tell us quite candidly about all God has done for it; there would be no point in hushing up his gifts to it, out of mock humility, and pretending that it was ugly, that it had no smell, that the sun had robbed it of its bloom, or the wind broken its stem, knowing that all that wasn't true. Anyhow, this isn't going to be the autobiography of a flower like that. On the contrary, I'm delighted to be able to put them on record, the favours our Lord has shown me, all quite undeserved." Nowhere does Gemma ever express such unrestrained confidence in God's handiwork.

9. Zoffoli, *La povera Gemma,* 444–45, provides recollections by Eufemia Giannini that Gemma "rarely read devotional books because she was very busy and given her culture preferred to elevate her soul to God by concentrating within herself." She was able to recall only one specific volume, which she reported that Gemma read with much con-

solation in her final months, a collection including Psalms, the Gospels, and Alfonso de' Liguori's "Preparation for Death."

10. The published edition of Gemma's confessional autobiography omits two passages, both transcribed for our translation by Cristina Mazzoni from the authenticated copy of the handwritten original located at the Casa Generalizia dei Passionisti in Rome. The original for this first omission is "mi mise perfino, a dormire con un mio fratellino di otto anni (ora è in cielo) per non farmi piangere e non allontanarmi da lei, in quel modo ero contenta. (Veda bene babbo mio, sotto ai 7 anni cominciai a disubbidire, e dormire per capriccio più volte col mio fratello.)"

11. There is confusion in the dates, which may also reveal a conflation in Gemma's memories concerning her mother, and quite probably a forced absence for over a year while her mother still lived. According to the parish register, which surely is correct, Gemma was confirmed on May 26, 1885, when she was seven years old, not in 1888 at the age of ten. More important than this discrepancy, which could be a trivial mis-writing by Gemma of an "8" for a "5," is her recollection at the end of this paragraph that her mother died on September 17th of "that year." What year? We know that Gemma's mother died on September 17, 1886. Gemma's exile for health reasons to her mother's brother's house ended at Christmas 1886, but did it begin in the summer of 1886, a few weeks before her mother's demise, or in the summer of 1885, two months after Gemma's first communion and fourteen months before her mother died? I believe that 1885 is the right year, which means that Gemma's association of her confirmation in 1885 with her mother being taken away is accurate, but that in fact the loss refers in the first instance to her forced separation for over a year from the summer of 1885 until September 1886, while her mother still lived and Gemma was denied her loving care.

   Zoffoli, *La povera Gemma,* 31, n. 21, also reaches the conclusion that Gemma was away from home for more than a year before her mother's death, accepting as I do a chronology determined by the date of first communion rather than by the later (and defective) recollections of Gemma's aunt, Elena Landi.

12. The second omission in the printed version occurs here and is as follows: "Nel tempo che stetti in famiglia devo dire delle cose, Babbo mio; io ho paura che in questo scritto ci sia delle accuse, ma faccio per dire tutto, tra le persone di servizio ve ne trovai una che mi pareva non tanto buona, una sera di notte mi chiamò, prese un lume a olio e un piatto di acqua e . . . non so altro, me ne accusò perchè lo feci io, e mi sembra una cosa cattiva. Altre volte mi ricordo benissimo questa donna mi portava in una camera chiusa e mi scopriva . . . e qui basta . . . avrei potuto accusarla al babbo, ma non lo feci perchè sarebbe stato inutile, gli volevo molto bene, anzi alle volte mi ricordo benissimo che un giorno il mio fratello ed io gli facemmo spia e fummo castigati per bene, e il babbo ci picchiò anche, ma questo accadeva perchè io ero disubbidiente e rispondevo e le facevo dei dispetti."

13. Gemma mis-remembered or mis-wrote the month, which Father Germano corrected as being the 9th or 10th of June. Raffaele Cianetti was the local parish priest.

14. Note the shift to the third person, unusual in Gemma Galgani's writings and perhaps a reflection of her feelings here as a neophyte on her spiritual journey.

15. Father Germano corrected the date to 1896.

16. The printed text adds a note reminding readers that she was almost nineteen at this time. For a reflection on this vow, see the entry for "Virginity" in chapter 6 below.

17. A telling interpretation of Gemma's response to her father's death emerged during the canonization proceedings. *Summarium Super Dubio an Constet de Virtutibus,* part 19 of the *Responsio,* page 145, in making a defense against the charge that Gemma suffered from hysteria, noted her unusually controlled behavior. "When her father died she went to sleep in the same bed where a little while earlier the cadaver had rested, and there she remained throughout the time she suffered the spinal inflammation that began shortly thereafter."

18. The triduum is a cycle of three prayer sessions and the novena of nine, usually done at fixed times on consecutive days or weeks.

19. The reference is to a biography by Father Germano of Gabriel of Our Lady of Sorrows (Francis Possenti), who died of tuberculosis in 1862, before he could be ordained a priest in the Passionist Order; the order strongly supported his beatification, achieved in 1908 and followed by canonization in 1920. See Natale Cavatassi, C.P., and Fabiano Giorgini, C.P., eds., *Fonti storico-biografiche di San Gabriele dell'Addolorata, studente passionista* ([San Gabriele dell'Addolorata/Isola del Gran Sasso d'Italia], 1969), esp. 22–175, for biographical materials, and 13–18 and 492–97, for Father Germano's influential role in the canonization process.

    In the original "Report on her Healing" written on March 9, 1899, only six days after the event, Gemma made no mention of Saint Gabriel of Our Lady of Sorrows—neither of the book about him nor of any role by him in her miraculous cure, and certainly she gave no hint that he might have been her mysterious nighttime visitor.

20. Matins, prime, terce (not mentioned in Gemma's recounting of her day), sext, nones, vespers, and compline are the seven offices (prayers or devotions) prescribed in that order for the canonical hours, although this convent apparently did not adhere rigidly to the clock.

21. Both these Passionist priests will be identified more fully in chapter 5 below.

22. The reference is to Cecilia Giannini, Gemma's substitute Mom and a key personage in the last four years of her life who will be discussed shortly.

CHAPTER THREE

1. *Lettere,* Monsignor Volpi, August-September 1899.

2. This account is from testimony by Pfanner analyzed in *Summarium Super Dubio an Constet de Virtutibus,* parts 10 and 32–34 of the *Animadversiones,* pages 13–14 and 37–40.

3. *Lettere,* Monsignor Volpi, September 8, 1899.

4. *Novissima Positio Super Virtutibus,* part 4 of the *Responsio,* page 9, for Pfanner's softening in his Pisa, 1922 testimony. On Tadini's autopsy findings reported at the 1907 Lucca proceedings, see *Summarium Super Dubio an Constet de Virtutibus,* part 21 of the *Animadversiones,* page 25: "In the heart, once cut open, one noted only *tiny globules of blood, which dissolved in water,* so also were the various valves, containing *a light quantity of slightly bloody liquid.* Therefore, *in the heart to me there resulted nothing extraordinary, nothing supernatural. It was a flaccid heart, enlarged,* as one always verifies in consumptive maladies of long duration." (Italics are as in the original.)

For the discussion of refutations by Antonelli and Ludwig, see the *Summarium Additionale* of 31 printed pages, bound with *Novissima Positio Super Virtutibus.*

5. *Estasi,* September 8, 1899, evening; and September 12, 1899, morning.

6. *Lettere,* Monsignor Volpi, September 8, 12, and 13, 1899.

7. *Lettere,* Father Germano, May 1900.

8. Biographical sketches of Monsignor Volpi in the printed editions of Gemma Galgani's writings are brief and uncontroversial, but Enrico Zoffoli, C.P., *La povera Gemma: Saggi critici storico-teologici,* 2d ed. (Naples, 1957), 270–79, reports that Bishop Volpi was removed from his post at Arezzo in 1919, at the explicit command of Pope Benedict XV, following a "whirlwind of accusations" (unspecified) and transferred to Rome, where he held several posts with impressive titles but much less authority.

9. José Agustín Orbegozo, "We Dedicate Ourselves with Love to the Following of Jesus Crucified," Circular Number 3, May 15, 1991, 6: "We know of the difficulties Paul of the Cross encountered with the Church authorities in his attempt to include the full mystical treasure of his foundational experience into the Constitutions. In the 1736 Rule it is the concept of 'Memory' which spells out our purpose as a Congregation; in fact, even our special vow is described in terms of 'Memory.' Later in the Rule of 1741 the concept of 'Memory' practically disappears, to be replaced by 'devotion,' with the concomitant change in the theological perspective. Whatever happened?"

   Also see James Sweeney, C.P., *The New Religious Order: A Study of the Passionists in Britain and Ireland, 1945–1990 and the Option for the Poor* (London, 1994), 49–52, on what he considers to be important distinctions between the rules of 1736 and 1741, whereas the differences are minimized in Fabiano Giorgini, C.P., *Storia della Congregazione della Passione di Gesù Cristo,* vol. 1, *L'epoca del fondatore* (Pescara, 1981), 279–81 and 557–58.

   More generally on Paul of the Cross and the founding of the Passionist Order, see Enrico Zoffoli, C.P., *S. Paolo della Croce: Storia critica,* 3 vols. (Rome, 1963), and in particular vol. 1, pp. 526–39 on the early Rule. For a popular account, see Gabriele Cingolani, *San Paolo della Croce: Incendiare il mondo d'amore* (Turin, 1993). On his relics used to effect miraculous cures in Brooklyn, New York, and Hoboken, New Jersey, see Ann Taves, *The Household of Faith: Roman Catholic Devotions in Mid-Nineteenth-Century America* (Notre Dame, Ind., 1986), 67–68.

10. Mary Carruthers, *The Book of Memory: A Study of Memory in Medieval Culture* (Cambridge, 1990), 193; David Hume, *An Enquiry Concerning Human Understanding,* section 5, part 1. I am grateful to my colleague, Matt Mattsuda, for these references.

11. My thinking on this point is much influenced by Erich Auerbach's essay "Excursus: *Gloria Passionis*" in his *Literary Language and Its Public in Late Latin Antiquity and in the Middle Ages,* trans. Ralph Manheim (New York, 1965), 67–81.

   Sharing in pain must be carefully distinguished from compassion for the sufferer, even when such compassion inspires social action. On compassion and the origins of modern humanitarianism, which in my judgment is fundamentally distinct from the essence of Passionist religiosity, see Thomas W. Laqueur, "Bodies, Details, and the Human Narrative," in Lynn Hunt, ed., *The New Cultural History* (Berkeley, Calif., 1989), 176–204.

   Scaraffia, "'Christianity Has Liberated Her,'" 256 (cited in chap. 1, n. 11 above), argues that "to interpret illness as an instrument and as a sign of spiritual evolution was something that came from outside the culture of religion: it derived from the romanticism that had made of tuberculosis—the most widespread fatal disease of that period—a metaphor of a sickness of the soul." I agree entirely, and therefore question her secularization of Gemma Galgani's spirituality by citing it as an example of this maudlin cultural trend.

More persuasive is the recent formulation by Edith Wyschogrod, *Saints and Postmodernism: Revisioning Moral Philosophy* (Chicago, 1990), 17, which understands Saint Catherine of Siena's experience of pain in a way directly relevant to what I see in Gemma Galgani. "When the entire body is implicated in saintly experience, the *body as a whole* functions as a sensorium. It does not help to say Saint Catherine *saw* the passion, although visions of the passion are common. Instead, truer to her own account, she entered into the passion, felt it with her whole being. Nothing intervened between herself and it. The lack of distance that informs her encounter is experienced as pain. If sense is to be made of Saint Catherine's perceptual acts, her brand of seeing must be redescribed as the body's seeing."

Along with the response to pain and suffering among saints must be considered the experience of more ordinary Catholics. On this problem I am influenced by the essay of Robert A. Orsi, "Mildred, is it fun to be a cripple? The Culture of Suffering in Mid-Twentieth-Century American Catholicism," in Thomas J. Ferraro, ed., *Catholic Lives, Contemporary America* (Durham, N.C., 1997).

Among specifically Passionist texts, see especially the collection of essays by Maddalena Marcucci, who drew inspiration directly from Gemma Galgani and was among the initial group of novices at the order's new convent in Lucca: Maddalena Marcucci, *La santità è amore: Invito alla santità per la via dell'amore,* edited by Fabiano Giorgini, C.P. (Rome, 1989).

12. *Lettere,* Monsignor Volpi, probably September or October 1899.

13. Germano di San Stanislao, *Biografia di Gemma Galgani,* 212–13 (cited in chap. 1, n. 2 above) for the quotation, and 196–215 for Father Germano's account more generally of the stigmata and other signs.

14. Germano di San Stanislao, *Biografia di Gemma Galgani,* 203, reports that he consulted a *vita* of Venerable Diomira Allegri but does not specify the title. One possibility is that he read Alessandro Ciolli, *Vita della venerabile serva di Dio Maria Margherita Diomira del Verbo Incarnato degli Allegri di Firenzuola* (Florence, 1872) but I suspect he also may have consulted the extremely rare L. Malaspina, *Vita della Ven. Serva di Dio Suor Maria Margherita* (Venice, 1704). Such thorough research was a normal part of properly preparing a case for the canonization process, and Father Germano did his work well in alerting fellow clerics and the public to any and all parallels between Gemma Galgani and predecessors such as Venerable Diomira, who also died of tuberculosis, at the age of twenty-six. Beatification proceedings on Diomira Allegri, begun on January 24, 1731, had come to a halt shortly thereafter and were not re-opened until 1926, long after Father Germano's death, but her cause was well known among devotees of mysticism, as attested to by the 1872 biography. Her writings continue to be of interest; see, for example, Diomira del Verbo Incarnato (Margherita Allegri), *Scritti e detti,* edited by Divo Barsotti (Florence, 1979).

On stigmata in the context of female sanctity more generally, see Gabriella Zarri, *Le sante vive: Cultura e religiosità femminile nella prima età moderna* (Turin, 1990), esp. 108–10.

15. For Gemma's active engagement with the devil, see *Estasi,* April 30, 1900; May 3, 1900; May 5, 1900; May 27, 1900; June 1900; August 25, 1900; also see *Lettere,* Monsignor Volpi, September–October 1899.

16. Galgani, *Estasi, Diario, Autobiografia, Scritti vari, Versi,* 184–85, n. 4, explores this testimony, recorded in the *Summarium Super Virtutibus,* no. 11, 8.

17. Galgani, *Estasi, Diario, Autobiografia, Scritti vari, Versi,* 292–93. Gemma reports a similarly frightening incident in *Lettere,* Monsignor Volpi, June 1900. William A. Christian Jr, *Visionaries,* 150 (cited in chap. 1, n. 31 above), provides the ironic twist that "Evarista," the Spanish visionary from Gabiria, in the spring of 1933 saw the devil in the guise of none other than Gemma Galgani.

18. *Lettere,* Monsignor Volpi, August 1900.

19. Galgani, *Estasi, Diario, Autobiografia, Scritti vari, Versi,* 280–86, collects these entries under the title assigned in 1943, "Appunti di diario."

20. *Lettere,* Monsignor Volpi, October 1899.

21. Sister Saint Michael, S.S.J., *Portrait of Saint Gemma: A Stigmatic* (New York, 1950), 138–40, for Father Germano's letter to Monsignor Volpi.

22. Father Martino Vallini, a Franciscan, is not further identified, and there is no documentation suggesting why Gemma might not have wished to go to him for confession beyond her previously stated and understandable aversion to most new confessors. Her confession with him was followed by renewed diabolic torments.

23. Father Germano noted that in the original diary Gemma wrote this sentence about becoming a saint in the margin at some later time. He speculated that since she was under obligation to reveal everything in the diary to her confessor, Monsignor Volpi, and certainly did not wish to reveal this promise, she kept it back until a more secure moment.

24. For the circumstances surrounding this person, identified only as "a stranger she had known at Lucca" on whose behalf Gemma implored, see Germano di San Stanislao, *Biografia di Gemma Galgani,* 235.

25. Father Norberto di San Giuseppe, a Passionist missionary.

26. Brother Famiano del Sacro Cuore di Gesù, a lay Passionist who testified during the canonization proceedings.

27. The Sacro Collegio di Gesù was an institute established by Father Germano for the study of Christian perfection.

28. The letter must have been written to their brother Guido, now a pharmacist at the nearby town of Bagni di S. Giuliano.

29. In life, a nun at the Passionist convent in Corneto headed by Mother Maria Giuseppa (for further identification about her, see chap. 4, n. 13 below). According to a brief memorial written in December 1899, Gemma had had a presentiment about Mother Maria Teresa's death, and for the next two weeks her diary entries will refer frequently to prayers on behalf of this soul. For the presentiment, see Galgani, *Estasi, Diario, Autobiografia, Scritti vari, Versi,* 286–87.

30. See *Lettere,* Monsignor Volpi, August 10, 1900.

CHAPTER FOUR

1. Much of the material that follows is drawn from Father Germano's biography and from Enrico Zoffoli, C.P., *La povera Gemma: Saggi critici storico-teologici,* 2d ed. (Naples, 1957), which contains a rich collection of photographs of members of the Giannini household and the home itself. (Several of these are included in the photo gallery following page 168.) See especially pages 19–25 on Gemma's arrival there and on her daily life, 190–95 on servants, and 230–51 on family members.

2. *Lettere,* Monsignor Volpi, November 1899. The brother in question is not identified but most likely was not Ettore, who by then probably had emigrated to Brazil, nor Guido, who had established a pharmacy and lived in a nearby town. That would leave Antonio, the "libertine" who would die of tuberculosis in 1902. Whether Aunt Elisa or Aunt Elena was the evil one on this particular occasion Gemma did not specify; both aunts had difficulty from time to time in dealing with Gemma. See, for example, *Lettere,* Monsignor Volpi, June 1900, third and fourth letters; June-July 1900. Gemma did not move permanently to the Giannini household until September 1900, so this report to Monsignor Volpi may be seen as an appeal to get out of her natal home, one way or another.

3. Zoffoli, *La povera Gemma,* 165, n. 60, provides the text that documents this incident, an unpublished letter from Gemma to Monsignor Volpi, located at the General House of the Passionists in Rome, dated November 1899.

4. Zoffoli, *La povera Gemma,* 165, n. 60, again provides the text, from an unpublished letter dated January 28, 1900.

5. *Lettere,* Father Germano, July 8, 1901. On Cecilia Giannini's tormented doubts about Gemma and fears that she was possessed by the devil, see Zoffoli, *La povera Gemma,* 242–51.

6. Confirmation of this later date comes in careful examination of changes in various editions of Father Germano's biography. Whereas the early versions give the clear impression that Gemma moved to the Giannini household in the summer of 1899 (Germano di San Stanislao, *Biografia di Gemma Galgani,* 44ff., cited in chap. 1, n. 2 above), the posthumous editions (p. 105 of the 1972 reprint of the 10th edition in Italian, and p. 98 of the English translation), state, accurately, that her aunts initially "allowed her to go during the day only, but finally, in September 1900, agreed to her living permanently with this good family."

7. *Positio Super Virtutibus,* part 3, pages 91–92. Also see Zoffoli, *La povera Gemma,* 26, 27, 43 n. 171, and 44 n. 184.

8. *Summarium Super Dubio an Constet de Virtutibus,* part 1 of the *Summarium: Catalogus Testium,* page 7, *testis* 25.

9. This narrative is constructed from Zoffoli, *La povera Gemma,* 21–25 and 41–42 nn. 152–157, and also 198 and 256 n. 55, which make extensive use of unpublished "books of memory" by Eufemia and Mariano Giannini, the former located at the Archivio delle Monache Passioniste di Lucca, which did not grant me permission to undertake my own consultation; for the latter no location is specified. Zoffoli, 263 n. 214, mentions his personal communications with Prisca Giannini, in religion Sister Vincenza, a teacher at the Santa Zita school that Gemma had attended, and I suspect that Mariano Giannini's "book of memory" is either there or at the same archive with Eufemia's.

10. Galgani, *Estasi, Diario, Autobiografia, Scritti vari, Versi,* xxxi, explains the summer 1902 concentration of ecstasies as a consequence of Eufemia's presence at home when school

was out, surely true, but not sufficient to account for the absence of recorded ecstasies the previous summer.

11. Zoffoli, *La povera Gemma*, xxi, located seventeen unpublished letters to Father Germano and twenty-one to Monsignor Volpi; I was not able to consult these, but the few references to them in Zoffoli do not suggest that they differ in timing pattern from the published letters. The four unpublished letters from Gemma Galgani to Monsignor Volpi that could be dated from information in Zoffoli are included in table 4. The dates of letters to Monsignor Volpi are approximations made by the Passionists who edited the printed collection: Galgani, *Lettere*, xxvii.

12. Galgani, *Estasi, Diario, Autobiografia, Scritti vari, Versi*, 301–2.

13. Eighteen letters from Mother Maria Giuseppa to Gemma are preserved, and ten from Gemma to her, always to her convent in Corneto, where Gemma hoped in vain to be admitted. See Zoffoli, *La povera Gemma*, 208–21, for a full treatment of their relationship. On Gemma's hopes, see *Lettere*, Mother Maria Giuseppa del Sacro Cuore (Palmira Armellini), April 5, 1902, with its desperate attempt to find favor with Father Germano:

> Tell my dear Dad so many things for me; tell him to put me in the convent with you; I shall always be good, I shall always obey, and not do anything that springs from my head; I will tell you everything and do whatever you want. Tell my dear Dad to make me happy. I am truly not meant for the world, my Mother, wherever I am, even with my good Mom [Cecilia Giannini] who shows such care for me that I forget I am in the world, still I am unwell. Tell my dear Dad to pray a lot, really a lot and then to decide, because before long there will not be time.

14. Father Germano granted permission for Gemma to ask Jesus to extinguish her sense of taste, but on condition that Jesus continue to allow her to retain food. With regard to the request for harsher mortifications (no comforts), Father Germano declined approval until such time as he might talk with her in person.

15. Giuseppina Alessandrini Imperiali, usually referred to by Gemma with the nickname Serafina. Nine letters from Gemma Galgani to her testify to their supportive relationship. For Gemma's explicit and fervid desire to leave the Giannini household and live with Serafina in Rome, see *Lettere*, Father Germano, April 19, 1902. Father Germano and Cecilia Giannini worked actively together to block Gemma's wishes in this matter.

16. The reference here most likely is to Lorenzo Agrimonti, the family priest at the Giannini household.

17. Father Germano had scoffed at Gemma's request in her letter of June 22 to keep a little book of Saint Augustine's *Meditations* he had inadvertently left behind on his last visit, calling her a "bad little girl" who did not know Latin anyway but who would claim she did. So he indicated certain passages and ordered her to read them in the presence of Jesus and her guardian angel and then offer him written commentaries on their meaning. This is her response.

18. This was in keeping with Father Germano's strict command: "Be cautious in talking about me, with *no one*."

19. The context here is that Father Germano scolded Gemma for relying on her guardian angel to deliver her letters, rather than affixing postage to them, even though she used the services of the Italian postal system. He worried that she might be charged with an impropriety, and here Gemma suggests checking out the matter with Jesus.

20. Father Germano added several editorial notes to this ecstasy explaining that the figure Gemma sees and converses with is her guardian angel, certainly a reasonable interpretation, one that makes her refusal to accept the advice that follows about eating yet more significant, especially the way she buttresses her refusal with an appeal to Jesus' wishes.

21. A devil in the guise of a monkey, one of Lucifer's minions.

22. Paolo Tei, a Capuchin friar and future Bishop of Pesaro.

23. Gemma Galgani's youngest sister, Giulia, died August 19, 1902.

24. Father Germano responded to this letter the very next day, September 4, but to Cecilia Giannini rather than to Gemma herself. He wrote: "If in your judgment the burning in her heart is the consequence of and has been caused by her raptures in God, the sweetness of God, and her profound sense of celestial love, then this is a *certain* sign that the matter is supernatural. Natural indispositions of the heart *always* carry with them nausea, melancholy, despondency, and boredom with celestial concerns. What if this is Jesus who works, as she thinks, and she becomes alarmed? However that may be, *I do not want* profane eyes (yours alone excepted) to uncover the immaculate flesh of this angel. As far as eating goes, in the name of charity do not force her, but let her go her own way."

CHAPTER FIVE

1. Kenneth L. Woodward, *Making Saints: How the Catholic Church Determines Who Becomes a Saint, Who Doesn't, and Why* (New York, 1990), notwithstanding its quirky iconoclasm, provides a good insight into several aspects of the contemporary canonization process. For the historical and theological background, see Renée Haynes, *Philosopher King: The Humanist Pope Benedict XIV* (London, 1970), esp. 96–150. See also Mario Rosa, "Prospero Lambertini tra 'regolata devozione' e mistica visionaria," in Gabriella Zarri, ed., *Finzione e santità tra medioevo ed età moderna* (Turin, 1991), 521–51.

2. "*State attenti, perchè era una scioccherella (anzi) scemetta,*" in the original, reported in Enrico Zoffoli C.P., *La povera Gemma: Saggi critici storico-teologici,* 2d ed. (Naples, 1957), 373, and repeated (with substantial acceptance) in Giovanni Pozzi and Claudio Leonardi, eds., *Scrittrici mistiche italiane* (Genoa, 1988), 639. The latter includes a harshly misopedic assessment of Gemma's spirituality. For a diametrically opposed view, see Cornelio Fabro, *Gemma Galgani: Testimone del soprannaturale* (Rome, 1987). A more subtle and direct bit of evidence comes from the canonization record (*Novissima Positio Super Virtutibus,* part 46 of the *Responsio,* page 65), which characterizes Gemma Galgani's writings as having "an extraordinary simplicity and familiarity" but "nothing of the ridiculous or the excessively familiar, just a stupendous familiarity between Jesus and a soul inebriated with His holy love." See also *Positio Super Revisione Scriptorum* (Rome, 1917).

3. Father Norberto di Santa Maria to Father Germano dated March 28, 1895, in Natale Cavatassi and Fabiano Giorgini, eds. *Fonti storico-biografiche di San Gabriele dell'Addolorata* ([San Gabriele dell'Addolorata/Isola del Gran Sasso d'Italia], 1969), 230 ("*quello stupido*

e corto di cervello"). For a more sympathetic and brief portrait of Blessed Gabriel, see Roger Mercurio, C.P., *The Passionists* (Collegeville, Minn., 1992), 67–74.

4. Zoffoli, *La povera Gemma,* 374, reports the remark almost in disbelief, but then manages to document it quite convincingly.

5. *Estasi,* August 25, 1900, second ecstasy. Further expressions of Gemma's difficulties with her confessors, primarily Monsignor Volpi but also Father Germano, are reflected in *Estasi,* April 24, 1900; April 29, 1900; April 30, 1900; May 3, 1900; May 18, 1900; May 27, 1900; June 1900; August 25, 1900, first ecstasy; August 25, 1900, third ecstasy; March 21, 1901; and April 1901.

6. Braccini, "Scuola e santità," 620 (cited in chap. 1, n. 18 above), cites D. Abbrescia, *Elena Guerra: Profetismo e rinnovamento* (Brescia, n.d.), 36.

7. *Summarium Super Dubio an Constet de Virtutibus,* part 12 of the *Animadversiones,* pages 15–16 (italics as in the original). A slightly varied version of the same testimony is recorded in *Nova Positio Super Virtutibus,* part 14 of the *Animadversiones,* pages 12–13.

8. *Positio Super Virtutibus,* part 3, section 87, pages 96–97, for the testimony of Giustina Giannini. The harsh details of this denial may be followed in Zoffoli, *La povera Gemma,* 26–27, 32, and 43–44 nn. 177–80. See also Carmelo Naselli, C.P., "Presenze soprannaturali nella vita di Gemma," in *Mistica e misticismo oggi: Settimana di studio di Lucca 8–13 settembre 1978* (Rome, 1979), 629. According to Cecilia and Eufemia Giannini, it was Father Gaetano who had poisoned things at Corneto for Gemma by alluding to her as a hysteric and as self-deluded.

9. *Lettere,* Father Germano, July-August 1900.

10. Galgani, *Estasi, Diario, Autobiografia, Scritti vari, Versi,* 287–92.

11. *Lettere,* Father Germano, December 20, 1900. For Gemma's desire to die, see especially *Estasi*: April 20, 1900; April 26, 1900; May 1, 1900; July 10, 1900; toward the end of September 1900; October 18, 1900; and early December 1900.

12. Sister Saint Michael, S.S.J., *Portrait of Saint Gemma: A Stigmatic* (New York, 1950), 97–98, provides this letter in translation. For the general context of the relationship between the two men, see Zoffoli, *La povera Gemma,* 345–72.

13. Sister Saint Michael, *Portrait of Saint Gemma,* 139.

14. Ibid., 145–46.

15. Ibid., 149–50.

16. Ibid., 151. For the full context, see *Lettere,* Father Germano, November 15, 1900, n. 4.

17. Galgani, *Estasi, Diario, Autobiografia, Scritti vari, Versi,* 293–94.

18. *Lettere,* Father Germano, February 9, 1901, is very clear, but Gemma apparently continued to have difficulty suppressing all external manifestations; see, for example, *Lettere,* Father Germano, April 28, 1901, on bleeding from her mouth after receiving communion; on continued battles to suppress repetition of stigmata, see *Lettere,* Father Germano, March 8, 1902. Gemma's spiritual growth and how her path relates to mystical tradition is explored fully in Zoffoli, *La povera Gemma,* 795–846.

19. Here I am drawing from *Lettere,* Father Germano, December 17, 20, 24, and 26, 1900.

20. *Estasi,* January 31, 1902. This cluster of ecstasies commenced on October 6, 1901.

21. *Lettere,* Father Germano, December 26, 1900.

22. *Lettere,* Father Germano, February 23, 1901; Galgani, *Lettere,* undated, addressed to Father Germano, page 132, n. 1, and signatures of letters from February through May 1901.

23. Sister Saint Michael, *Portrait of Saint Gemma,* 141–55, explains Gemma's mystical marriage most thoroughly and sympathetically. For a skeptical, even caustic, alternative view, see Pozzi and Leonardi, *Scrittrici mistiche italiane,* 640. The question is complicated, as shown in the treatment in Zoffoli, *La povera Gemma,* 836–40.

24. On Father Vallini see *Lettere,* Father Germano, January 1, 1901.

25. *Lettere,* Father Germano, June 25, 1901.

26. The exchange may be found in editorial notes to *Lettere,* Father Germano, March 1, 1901. See also Father Germano's letter of April 3, 1901, to Monsignor Volpi, translated and printed in Sister Saint Michael, *Portrait of Saint Gemma,* 183–84, with its stinging indictment of Volpi's latest attempt to send a priest to observe and evaluate Gemma. In this letter Father Germano pleaded for consideration of the whole person, praised Gemma's growing inner calm, and dismissed hysteria as "a synonym for madness" and the hysteric as a person who is "voluble, inconstant, fickle, futile, restless, etc."

27. Zoffoli, *La povera Gemma,* 370. Italics in Zoffoli presumably reflect underlining in the original.

28. *Nova Positio Super Virtutibus,* part 21 of the *Animadversiones,* page 19, for the quotation of Don Farnocchia; italics are as in the original. *Novissima Positio Super Virtutibus,* part 3 of the *Responsio,* pages 4–5, for the cardinal's conclusions. Zoffoli, *La povera Gemma,* 311, for the original aspersions on Father Germano's motives and means.

29. Gemma's sending mail via her guardian angel attracted the particular scorn of Don Farnocchia, who testified that no angel had ever provided him with such services; see *Summarium Super Dubio an Constet de Virtutibus,* part 30 of the *Animadversiones,* page 36. Zoffoli, *La povera Gemma,* 870–74, examines the postal question carefully and wisely concludes that, however the letters got to their destination, other issues are weightier. For the origin of Gemma's use of her guardian angel for postal services, see *Lettere,* Father Germano, September 14, 1900, notes.

30. *Lettere,* Father Germano, June 15, 1901; June 16, 1901 (suspected by the recipient to be an imitation written by the devil); June 20, 1901; June 25, 1901; and August 22, 1901; for the falsified postcard, see *Lettere,* Father Germano, August 3, 1901. For more on the devil's letter-writing tricks, and active detective work by Cecilia Giannini, Father Germano, Father Pietro Paolo, and even Monsignor Volpi after he had become Bishop of Arezzo, see Zoffoli, *La povera Gemma,* 918–21. Also see Pietro Schiavone, S.J., "Il discernimento spirituale del 'caso' Gemma Galgani," in *Mistica e misticismo oggi,* 640–72.

31. On Gemma's lament that her exclusion from the Giannini household now left her twice orphaned, see *Lettere,* Father Germano, December 24, 1902 ("Despair wishes to overtake me; but, oh Mom . . . *Mater orphanorum*"); and Father Germano, mid-February 1903, for her resentful letter to him: "Two times an orphan on earth, dear Dad; and then you want to accuse me before Jesus?"

32. *Lettere,* Monsignor Volpi, March 1901, note 5.

33. Germano di San Stanislao, *S. Gemma Galgani,* 169 (cited in chap. 2, n. 6 above).

34. Ibid.

35. Carlos Maria Staehlin, *Apariciones: Ensayo Crítico,* vol. 2 (Madrid, 1954), 116–20, wherein parallel instances of the influence of reading upon ecstatic revelation are given for Margaret Mary Alacoque and Josefa Menéndez, both of whom, along with Gemma

Galgani, were especially devoted to the Sacred Heart. Also see his earlier work, *Apariciones: Con palabaras introductorias de Nicolas E. Navarro* (Caracas, 1949), 58–59, and 110–11 for his doubts about all visionary experiences reported in the preceding 150 years.

36. See Cavatassi and Giorgini, eds., *San Gabriele dell'Addolorata,* 13–17, on the initial collaboration, and 87, 106, 114, 128, 139, and 146–47, for its continuation.

37. Germano di San Stanislao, *Vita del Ven. Servo di Dio Gabriele dell'Addolorata* (Rome, 1897) and Germano di San Stanislao, ed., *Lettere ed altri scritti spirituali del Ven. Servo di Dio Gabriele dell'Addolorata* (Milan, 1896).

38. On Gemma's last wishes, see *Positio Super Virtutibus* (Rome, 1927), part 14, page 630, for Elisa Galgani's testimony. For Father Germano's role, see Athos Carrara, *Gemma Galgani* (Florence, 1977), 163–64. Germano di San Stanislao, *Biografia di Gemma Galgani,* 280–81 (cited in chap. 1, n. 2 above), falsely attributes the decision to autopsy Gemma's heart to unspecified members of the Giannini family. On re-clothing the corpse, see Anon., "Gemma è nostra," *Bollettino della Congregazione dei Passionisti* 1 (August 1920): 246–51.

39. See Cavatassi and Giorgini, eds., *San Gabriele dell'Addolorata,* 278, 399, 422–23, and 427–28, on the exhumation, and 384, for the miraculous cure.

40. Alunno, "S. Gemma," 741 (cited in introduction, n. 5 above); Fernando Pielagos Mediavilla, C.P., "Devozione a S. Gemma Galgani in Spagna," *Mistica e misticismo oggi,* 751; Gonzalez, "Santa Gemma," 768 (cited in introduction, n. 6 above).

41. Scaraffia, "'Christianity Has Liberated Her,'" 258 (cited in chap. 1, n. 11 above).

42. *Novissima Positio Super Virtutibus,* part 4 of the *Responsio,* pages 6–7, and Zoffoli, *La povera Gemma,* 151–53.

43. *Positio Super Virtutibus,* part 3, section 62, page 82, for testimony by Sister Maria Agnese. On hair parting and not using a mirror, see Zoffoli, *La povera Gemma,* 695, and for illustrations of her attire, 421–22. See also Mazzoni's essay below for the entry on "Clothes."

44. *Nova Positio Super Virtutibus,* part 33 of the *Animadversiones,* pages 29–30 (italics as in the original). See also Zoffoli, *La povera Gemma,* 206–7, on Gemma's behavior.

45. See *Lettere,* Reverend Father Ignazio, February 1900, note 1. See also Zoffoli, *La povera Gemma,* 256 n. 56, on Father Ignazio's correspondence with Cecilia Giannini over many years, lasting until 1926, concerning foundation of a Passionist monastery in Lucca.

46. See *Lettere,* Father Germano, January 29, 1900, note 7. Also see Zoffoli, *La povera Gemma,* 198–201 and 258–59.

47. Flavio Di Bernardo, C.P., "Il processo di canonizzazione di S. Gemma Galgani e il P. Luigi Besi, C.P.," in *Mistica e misticismo oggi,* 727–29, 737.

48. Zoffoli, *La povera Gemma,* 115 and 161 n. 1, reports the controversy, and also a petition that Gemma be declared the patron saint of Catholic pharmacists, an ironic commentary on how an unmarried daughter was viewed as her father's possession. The pharmacists won out over the domestics, as shown in Hagspiel, "New Hospital Patroness: St Gemma Galgani," 97–98, and Schwitalla, "Patron Saints," 80–82 (both cited in introduction, n. 5 above).

49. Naselli, "Presenze soprannaturali," 627 n. 24.

50. On the diffusion of Father Germano's biography, see Zoffoli, *La povera Gemma,* 306–16, and especially page 306, testimony by Canon Regular Giuseppe Angeli.

51. Zoffoli, *La povera Gemma,* 311.

52. On issues of the legitimacy of Gemma's cult and on the process of canonization to that point, see *Positio Super Non Cultu* (Rome, 1920) and *Positio Super Validitate Processuum* (Rome, 1924).

53. William A. Christian Jr, *Visionaries,* 86–91, 236–37, and 295–96 (cited in chap. 1, n. 31 above). (I think the picture of "Gemma's nephew" actually portrays one of her adopted Giannini family's offspring, rather than a Galgani nephew.) Also see Mediavilla, "Devozione a S. Gemma Galgani," 751–59.

54. See Di Bernardo, "Il processo di canonizzazione," 732–37, on objections to Gemma's writings and successful responses to the concerns that were raised.

55. Readers who enjoy knowing about an ironic twist of fate may wish to consult Jan Goldstein, *Console and Classify: The French Psychiatric Profession in the Nineteenth Century* (Cambridge, 1987), 322, which cites Aragon and Breton, "Le cinquantenaire de l'hystérie (1878–1928)," *Révolution surréaliste* 4 (March 15, 1928): 20–22. According to this source, in 1928 a group of French surrealists decided to have a party to mark the fiftieth birthday of "Hysteria." By their calculation and celebration, then, "Hysteria" and Gemma Galgani were born in the same year. With or without the fanfare, by the time of Gemma's death in 1903 the diagnosis of hysteria had become ubiquitous in classifying women's mental illnesses. Also see Mark S. Micale, *Approaching Hysteria: Disease and Its Interpretations* (Princeton, N.J., 1995).

56. See Germano di San Stanislao, *Biografia di Gemma Galgani,* 305–63, for the three essays (one each on hysteria, hypnotism, and spiritualism) received as part of the official record. They are not included in editions of the biography after the sixth, nor in the English translation.

57. Di Bernardo, "Il processo di canonizzazione," 736.

58. Joseph Antonelli, *Votum R.mi D.ni Joseph Antonelli, Naturalium Scientiarum Doct. ac Prof.* (Rome, 1928). Italics are as in the original.

59. Francesco Guidi, *Il magnetismo animale considerato secondo le leggi della natura e principalmente diretto alla cura delle malattie* (Milan, 1860) is the edition I checked. Earlier versions date back to at least 1854.

60. There was great interest during the 1920s in this German mystic; see Josef Teodorowicz, *Mystical Phenomena in the Life of Theresa Neumann* (London, 1945). Antonelli (73–74) noted articles in October and November of 1927 in *Il mattino illustrato* and in *L'osservatore romano* on the Neumann case that clearly showed the case was still under consideration; he argued that Ooly's assertion had not been accepted in the matter, and therefore its citation in the animadversions about Gemma Galgani was premature at best.

61. Staehlin, *Apariciones: Con palabaras introductorias de Nicolas E. Navarro,* 192–99, a volume bearing a *Nihil obstat,* an *Imprimi potest,* and an *Imprimatur,* takes up the stigmata issue and concludes that while no simulation of any sort was involved, Gemma Galgani's body may have been abnormally hypersensitive due to a nervous or mental condition and therefore produced in itself the signs of the Passion to which she was so intensely devoted, in essence rejecting the assertion of divine origin allowed in Antonelli's analysis. Also see Staehlin's "Los estigmas pasionarios de Santa Gema Galgani," *Manresa* 22 (1950): 41–72.

62. *Novissima Positio Super Virtutibus,* part 37 of the *Responsio,* pages 53–56. For more on Veronica Giuliani, see Rudolph Bell, *Holy Anorexia* (Chicago, 1985), 54–83.

The relevant precedent, from the April 24, 1796, decree concerning Veronica Giuliani, is analyzed by Cardinal E. Pellegrinetti in his preface to Galgani, *Estasi, Diario, Autobiografia, Scritti vari, Versi,* xxiii.

63. *Novissima Positio Super Virtutibus,* part 48 of the *Responsio,* page 67, cites Benedict XIV [*De Servorum dei Beatificatione et Beatorum Canonizatione*]. On Benedict and visions, see Haynes, *Philosopher King,* 109–14.

64. *Novissima Positio Super Virtutibus,* part 48 of the *Responsio,* 67.

65. *L'osservatore romano,* November 30–December 1, 1931, 3.

66. Galgani, *Estasi, Diario, Autobiografia, Scritti vari, Versi,* xxiii–xxiv, for Cardinal E. Pellegrinetti's defensive treatment of the demurral.

67. Galgani, *Estasi, Diario, Autobiografia, Scritti vari, Versi,* xxiv, on the liturgical office allowed for the Capuchin Order for Veronica Giuliani but denied for the Passionists for Gemma Galgani.

68. Maria Grace, C.P., *The Cross in My Heart: Life of St. Gemma Galgani, Lay-Passionist* (Erlanger, Ky., 1990), 43–44, quotes the decretal letter *Sanctitudinis Culmen* of Pope Pius XII. The language of skeptical distance continues in the next sentences, for example: "It is reported that she saw an apparition of the Lord Jesus himself and of the Blessed Mother." Her manifestations of grace "seem to indicate clearly that there was such a union of mind and heart between this chosen virgin Gemma and Christ."

69. *Lettere,* Monsignor Volpi, March 1901.

70. *Lettere,* Father Germano, December 26, 1900.

CHAPTER SIX

1. Sara Maitland and Wendy Murford, *Virtuous Magic* (New York, 1998), 366.

2. Mary St. Michael, *The White Flower of the Passion. A Drama in Three Acts* (Boston, 1940), 3.

3. *Roland Barthes on Roland Barthes,* trans. Richard Howard (New York, 1977), 147.

4. Roland Barthes, *A Lover's Discourse: Fragments,* trans. Richard Howard (New York, 1978); M. F. K. Fisher, *An Alphabet for Gourmets* (San Francisco, 1989).

5. Elisabeth Schüssler Fiorenza, "Spiritual Movements or Transformation? A Critical Feminist Reflection," in Miriam Therese Winter, Adair Lummis, and Allison Stokes, eds., *Defecting in Place: Women Claiming Responsibility for Their Own Spiritual Lives* (New York, 1994), 221–226, 224.

6. Elisabetta Rasy, *Le donne e la letteratura* (Rome, 1984), 11. Unless otherwise noted, all translations are mine.

7. Linda S. Kauffman, "The Long Goodbye: Against Personal Testimony, or An Infant Grifter Grows Up," in Robyn R. Warhol and Diane Price Herndl, eds., *Feminisms: An Anthology of Literary Theory and Criticism* (New Brunswick, N.J., 1997), 1155–71, 1164.

8. In order to facilitate cross-references, in each entry I have emphasized the most prominent (usually the first) occurrence of a word that is also the name of another entry. Quotations from Gemma's work refer to the Bell and Mazzoni translation published in this volume, and page numbers are given in parentheses after the quotation itself. For passages not translated in this volume I provide my own translation; in these cases, the reference appears in a footnote.

9. *Estasi,* September 8, 1899.

10. Father Germano, *Gemma Galgani,* 93 (cited in chap. 1, n. 2 above).

11. Germaine Brée, "Foreword" in Bella Brodzki and Celeste Schenck, eds., *Life/Lines: Theorizing Women's Autobiography* (Ithaca, N.Y., 1988), ix–xii, ix.

12. This story is often mentioned in biographical accounts of Edith Stein; see for example Waltraud Herbstrith, *Edith Stein: A Biography,* trans. Bernhard Bonowitz (San Francisco, 1985), 30.

13. Giovanni Pozzi and Claudio Leonardi, eds., *Scrittrici mistiche italiane* (Genoa, 1988), 639.

14. Also used by other women mystics, see for example Lucia Mangano in Pozzi and Leonardi, *Scrittrici mistiche italiane,* 661–63.

15. Giovanni Pozzi, "L'alfabeto delle sante," in Pozzi and Leonardi, *Scrittrici mistiche italiane,* 21–57, 23.

16. Mary Catherine Hilkert, "Experience and Tradition: Can the Center Hold?" in Catherine Mowry LaCugna, ed., *Freeing Theology: The Essentials of Theology in Feminist Perspective* (New York, 1993), 59–82, 77.

17. Dale Spender, *The Writing or the Sex? Or Why You Don't Have to Read Women's Writing to Know It's No Good* (New York, 1989), 1.

18. Adriana Cavarero, "Towards a Theory of Sexual Difference," in Sandra Kemp and Paola Bono, eds., *The Lonely Mirror: Italian Perspectives on Feminist Theory* (London, 1993), 189–221, 219.

19. Simone de Beauvoir, *The Second Sex,* trans. H. M. Parshley (New York, 1989), 678, 674.

20. Beverly Wildung Harrison, *Making the Connections: Essays in Feminist Social Ethics,* edited by Carol S. Robb (Boston, 1985), 12, 130.

21. See Julia Kristeva, *Powers of Horror: An Essay on Abjection,* trans. Leon Roudiez (New York, 1982).

22. *Lettere,* Father Germano, April 22, 1901.

23. *Lettere,* Father Germano, May 10, 1901.

24. Barthes, *A Lover's Discourse,* 52.

25. Hélène Cixous and Mireille Calle-Gruber, *Hélène Cixous Rootprints: Memory and Life Writing,* trans. Eric Prenowits (London, 1997), 31.

26. *Lettere,* Father Germano, June 15, 1901.

27. Rita Nakashima Brock, *Journeys by Heart: A Christology of Erotic Power* (New York, 1988), xiv.

28. Sara Maitland, *A Big-Enough God: A Feminist's Search for a Joyful Theology* (New York, 1995), 105

29. Father Germano, *Gemma Galgani,* 47, 65.

30. *Lettere,* Father Germano, December 8, 1900.

31. Father Germano, *Gemma Galgani,* 66; see also Giuliano Agresti, *Gemma Galgani: Diario di una "espropriata"* (Rome, 1986), 17; Enrico Zoffoli, *La povera Gemma: Saggi critici storico-teologici* (Rome, 1957), 420–21.

32. See for example Zoffoli, *La povera Gemma,* 420.

33. Michela De Giorgio, *Le italiane dall'Unità ad oggi: Modelli culturali e comportamenti sociali* (Bari, 1993), 67.

34. Cixous, *Hélène Cixous Rootprints,* 106. See also Dani Cavallaro and Alexandra Warwick, *Fashioning the Frame: Boundaries, Dress and Body* (Oxford, 1998).

35. Yvonne Knibiehler, "Bodies and Hearts," trans. Arthur Goldhammer, in Geneviève Fraisse and Michelle Perrot, eds., *A History of Women in the West,* 5 vols. (Cambridge, Mass., 1993), 4:325–68, 329. On this topic, I am also indebted to Linda B. Arthur, ed., *Religion, Dress and the Body* (Oxford, 1999).

36. Amedeo della M. del Buon Pastore, *La beata Gemma Galgani, vergine lucchese,* edited by Suore Sorelle di S. Gemma (Lucca, n.d.), 67–68.

37. *Lettere,* Father Germano, August 18, 1901, August 22, 1901.

38. See *Lettere,* Father Germano, October 14, 1901 (though she addresses him as "Dad" in the letter itself); November 17, 1901 (written for the Giannini family); October 27, 1902, circa (though, again, Gemma uses "Dad" in the body of the letter); December 24, 1902.

39. *Lettere,* Father Germano, mid-December 1901; January 15, 1902.

40. Maitland, *A Big-Enough God,* 18.

41. Anne E. Carr, "The New Vision of Feminist Theology," in LaCugna, *Freeing Theology,* 5–29, 20. See also Elisabeth Schüssler Fiorenza, *In Memory of Her: A Feminist Historical Reconstruction of Christian Origins* (New York, 1983).

42. *Estasi,* December 13, 1901; *Lettere,* Father Germano, April 22, 1901.

43. *Estasi,* January 9, 1902.

44. Jessica Benjamin, "A Desire of One's Own: Psychoanalytic Feminism and Intersubjective Space," in Teresa de Lauretis, ed., *Feminist Studies/Critical Studies* (Bloomington, Ind., 1986), 78–101, 82.

45. This is the title of chapter 19 of Father Germano's biography (*Gemma Galgani,* 215).

46. *Elizabeth Seton: Selected Writings,* edited by Ellin Kelly and Annabelle Melville (New York, 1987), 70.

47. *The Simone Weil Reader,* edited by George Panichas (New York, 1977), 435.

48. Pozzi and Leonardi, *Scrittrici mistiche italiane,* 658.

49. Something similar is described in a letter: "This morning I could not go to church, and Jesus came to me on his own." *Lettere,* Father Germano, March 1, 1901.

50. Cristina Mazzoni, ed., *Angela of Foligno's Memorial: Translated from Latin with Introduction, Notes and Interpretive Essay,* trans. John Cirignano (Cambridge, 1999), 53.

51. *Story of a Soul: The Autobiography of St. Thérèse of Lisieux,* trans. John Clarke (Washington, D.C., 1975), 17–18, 78, 123.

52. *Lettere,* Father Germano, May 9–13, 1901.

53. Mazzoni, *Angela of Foligno's Memorial,* 56.

54. Caroline Walker Bynum, *Holy Feast and Holy Fast: The Religious Significance of Food to Medieval Women* (Berkeley, Calif., 1987), 5.

55. *Lettere,* Father Germano, December 8, 1900.

56. See Ermenegildo Zecca, *Così lontani, così vicini: Gli angeli nella vita e negli scritti di Gemma Galgani* (Milan, 1998), 70; Father Germano, *Gemma Galgani,* 138–40.

57. Elisabetta Rasy, *La lingua della nutrice: Percorsi e tracce dell'esperienza femminile* (Rome, 1978), 65.

58. Luisa Muraro, *Lingua materna, scienza divina: Scritti sulla filosofia mistica di Margherita Porete* (Naples, 1995), 81.

59. Jacques Lacan, "Dieu et la jouissance de l/a femme," in *Le Séminaire de Jacques Lacan, Livre XX Encore (1972–1973),* edited by Jacques-Alain Miller (Paris, 1975), 61–71. See

my *Saint Hysteria: Neurosis, Mysticism and Gender in European Culture* (Ithaca, N.Y., 1996), 44–49.

60. These stories can be read in their entirety in Josef Breuer and Sigmund Freud, *Studies on Hysteria,* trans. James Strachey (New York, n.d.); Sigmund Freud, *Dora: An Analysis of a Case of Hysteria* (New York, 1963).

61. See for example Elaine Showalter, *The Female Malady: Women, Madness, and English Culture, 1830–1980* (New York, 1985), 147; and the collection *In Dora's Case: Freud-Hysteria-Feminism,* edited by Charles Bernheimer and Claire Kahane (New York, 1985).

62. Breuer and Freud, *Studies on Hysteria,* 232; with a feminist intent, Elisabetta Rasy describes Teresa of Avila as "the most perfect among history's great hysterics" (*La lingua della nutrice,* 124).

63. See, for example, Monique David-Ménard, *Hysteria from Freud to Lacan: Body and Language in Psychoanalysis,* trans. by Catherine Porter (Ithaca, N.Y., 1989); Elaine Showalter, *The Female Malady.*

64. Father Germano, *Gemma Galgani,* 17.

65. Jane Gallop, *The Daughter's Seduction: Feminism and Psychoanalysis* (Ithaca, N.Y., 1982), 143.

66. Gemma describes another mysterious touching by a man, this time a repeated beating (though more is clearly at stake, since Gemma calls him "a strange man"): a former employee of the Galgani household, as Gemma writes, would come over and beat her up. *Lettere,* Father Germano, October 2–3, 1900.

67. Michel de Certeau, "Mystique," in *Encyclopaedia Universalis,* 20 vols. (Paris, 1968), 11:521–26, 525.

68. Maitland and Murford, *Virtuous Magic,* 179.

69. *Lettere,* Monsignor Volpi, September 8, 1899.

70. Patricia Meyer Spacks, *The Female Imagination* (New York, 1975), 6.

71. Pozzi and Leonardi, *Scrittrici mistiche italiane,* 654.

72. *Lettere,* Father Germano, February 17, 1900.

73. *Estasi,* October 6, 1901.

74. *Estasi,* September 12, 1899.

75. Sallie McFague, *Models of God: Theology for an Ecological, Nuclear Age* (Philadelphia, 1987), 39.

76. Mazzoni, *Angela of Foligno's Memorial,* 36, 69, 73–75.

77. *Estasi,* September 12, 1899.

78. *Estasi,* September 12, 1899. The following ecstasy contains a similar exhortation and a similar threat.

79. *Lettere,* Father Germano, May 22, 1901.

80. Eleanor McLaughlin, "Feminist Christologies: Re-Dressing the Tradition," in Maryanne Stevens, ed., *Reconstructing the Christ Symbol: Essays in Feminist Christology* (New York, 1993), 118–49, 142.

81. Jackie Stacey, "Feminist Theory: Capital F, Capital T," in Victoria Robinson and Diane Richardson, eds., *Introducing Women's Studies: Feminist Theory and Practice* (New York, 1997), 54–76, 60.

82. Elizabeth Johnson, *She Who Is: The Mystery of God in Feminist Theological Discourse* (New York, 1992), 99.

83. Sallie McFague, *Models of God,* xi.

84. Johnson, "Redeeming the Name of Christ," in LaCugna, *Freeing Theology,* 115–37, 127.

85. *Estasi,* January 31, 1902.

86. Cixous, *Hélène Cixous Rootprints,* 110.

87. Muraro, *Lingua materna, scienza divina,* 46.

88. Hélène Cixous, "The Laugh of the Medusa," in Elaine Marks and Isabelle de Cour- tivron, eds., *New French Feminisms: An Anthology* (Amherst, Mass., 1980), 245–67, 255.

89. *Lettere,* Father Germano, October 30, 1900.

90. *Lettere,* Monsignor Volpi, August 10, 1900

91. *Lettere,* Father Germano, November 15, 1900.

92. F. R. de Lamennais, *Esquisse d'une philosophie* (Paris, 1940), vol. 3, bk. 9, 371. For a more in-depth discussion of laughter and religion, see Ingrild Saelid Gilhus, *Laughing Gods, Weeping Virgins: Laughter in the History of Religion* (London, 1997).

93. See for example Gemma Galgani, *Diario,* 186 n. 2: "The verb *to laugh,* here as else- where, is used by the saint in the sense of *to smile.*"

94. Zoffoli, *La povera Gemma,* 474.

95. Michela De Giorgio, "The Catholic Model," in Fraisse and Perrot, eds., *A History of Women in the West,* 4:166–97, 196.

96. Father Germano, *Gemma Galgani,* 99.

97. "There is no presently enduring recognition of mother-daughter passion and rapture." Adrienne Rich, *Of Woman Born: Motherhood as Experience and Institution* (New York, 1986; originally published in 1976), 237.

98. Ibid., 220.

99. Luce Irigaray, "And the One Doesn't Stir without the Other," trans. Hélène Vivienne Wenzel, *Signs* 7 (1981): 60–67, 63. Irigaray is usually considered responsible for bring- ing back the mother-daughter relationship into the center of psychoanalytic theoreti- cal considerations.

100. Ibid., 67.

101. See Caroline Walker Bynum, *Jesus as Mother: Studies in the Spirituality of the High Middle Ages* (Berkeley, Calif., 1982).

102. In Herbstrith, *Edith Stein,* 91.

103. God is compared to a mother hen in several psalms: 57:1, 61:4, 91:4.

104. *Estasi,* September-October 1902; October 12, 1902.

105. Caroline Walker Bynum, "'. . . And Woman His Humanity': Female Imagery in the Religious Writings of the Later Middle Ages," in Caroline Walker Bynum, Stevan Har- rell, and Paula Richman, eds., *Gender and Religion: On the Complexity of Symbols* (Bos- ton, 1986), 257–88, 265.

106. *Lettere,* Father Germano, March 18, 1903.

107. Gemma quoted in Zoffoli, *La povera Gemma,* 32, from testimony during the canoniza- tion process.

108. De Giorgio, *Le italiane dall'Unità ad oggi,* 31.

109. *Lettere,* Father Germano, January 29, 1900, February 17, 1900.

110. In Gino Lubich and Piero Lazzarin, *Bartolomea Capitanio: Una possibile compagna di vi- aggio* (Rome, 1982), 161.

111. *Lettere,* Father Germano, July-August 1900; *Lettere,* Monsignor Volpi, August-September 1899.

112. Eleanor McLaughlin and Rosemary Radford Ruether, "Introduction. Women's Leadership in the Jewish and Christian Traditions: Continuity and Change," in *Women of Spirit: Female Leadership in the Jewish and Christian Traditions* (New York, 1979), 15–28, 19.

113. *Estasi,* April 30, 1900.

114. In Robert Coles, *Dorothy Day: A Radical Devotion* (Reading, Mass., 1987), 75.

115. See for example Jacquelyn Grant, *White Women's Christ and Black Women's Jesus: Feminist Christology and Womanist Response* (Atlanta, Ga., 1989).

116. *Lettere,* Father Germano, September 12, 1901.

117. *Lettere,* Monsignor Volpi, November 1899.

118. Kristine Rankka, *Women and the Value of Suffering: An Aw(e)ful Rowing Toward God* (Collegeville, Minn., 1998), 12.

119. Grace M. Jantzen, *Becoming Divine: Towards a Feminist Philosophy of Religion* (Bloomington, Ind., 1999), 263.

120. McFague, *Models of God,* 129.

121. Bynum, *Holy Feast and Holy Fast,* 206. The clearest example of this substitution can be found in Gemma's biography by Father Germano: when Giustina, then a mother of young children in the Giannini household, fell violently sick, Gemma asked of God in prayer to take Giustina's suffering upon herself—which resulted in the immediate healing of Giustina, and in Gemma's contemporaneous "suffering for long months that cruel martyrdom." Father Germano, *Gemma Galgani,* 54.

122. Mary Jo Weaver, "Cancer in the Body of Christ," in Joann Wolski Conn, ed., *Women's Spirituality: Resources for Christian Development,* 2d ed. (New York, 1996), 68–82, 74. Zoffoli also claims that this "completion of Christ's Passion" is what Gemma strove for in her own bodily suffering (*La povera Gemma,* 396).

123. Sally Purvis, *The Power of the Cross: Foundations for a Christian Feminist Ethics of Community* (Nashville, Tenn., 1993), 14.

124. Johnson, "Redeeming the Name of Christ," 125.

125. McFague, *Models of God,* 55.

126. *Lettere,* Father Germano, May 4, 1901.

127. Elaine Scarry, *The Body in Pain: The Making and the Unmaking of the World* (Oxford, 1985), 4.

128. Patricia L. Wismer, "For Women in Pain: A Feminist Theology of Suffering," in Ann O'Hara Graff, ed., *In the Embrace of God: Feminist Approaches to Theological Anthropology* (Maryknoll, N.Y., 1995), 138–58, 148.

129. Beverly Wildung Harrison and Carter Heyward, "Pain and Pleasure: Avoiding the Confusions of Christian Tradition in Feminist Theory," in James B. Nelson and Sandra P. Longfellow, eds., *Sexuality and the Sacred: Sources for Theological Reflection* (Louisville, Ky., 1994), 131–48, 134.

130. *The Simone Weil Reader,* 327.

131. *Estasi,* June 1900.

132. Barthes, *A Lover's Discourse,* 127–28.

133. *Lettere,* Father Germano, February 23, 1901.

134. Bynum, "Women Mystics and Eucharistic Devotion in the Thirteenth Century," *Women's Studies* 11 (1984): 179–214, 189–90.

135. Bataille's most relevant works in this context are *Guilty,* trans. Bruce Boone (Venice, Calif., 1988), and *Inner Experience,* trans. Leslie Ann Boldt (Albany, N.Y., 1988).

136. Carter Heyward, "Body of Christa: Hope of the World," in *Staying Power: Reflections on Gender, Justice, and Compassion* (Cleveland, Ohio, 1995), 121–33; Brock, *Journeys by Heart,* 52–53, 66–72.

137. Johnson, "Redeeming the Name of Christ," 129; Anne Thurston, *Because of Her Testimony: The Word in Female Experience* (New York, 1995), 81.

138. Rosemary Radford Ruether, "The Liberation of Christology from Patriarchy," in Ann Loades, ed., *Feminist Theology: A Reader* (Louisville, Ky., 1990), 138–48, 140.

139. Elizabeth Johnson, *Friends of God and Prophets: A Feminist Theological Reading of the Communion of Saints* (New York, 1998), 219.

140. Luisa Muraro, "La nostra comune capacità d'infinito," in *Diotima. Mettere al mondo il mondo. Oggetto e oggettività alla luce della differenza sessuale* (Milan, 1990), 61–76, 62.

141. Cecilia Ferrazzi, *Autobiography of an Aspiring Saint,* transcribed, translated, and edited by Anne Jacobson Schutte (Chicago, 1996), 14–16.

142. *Lettere,* Father Germano, April 22, 1901.

143. *Lettere,* Monsignor Volpi, March 1901.

144. The quotations are from Johnson, *Friends of God and Prophets,* 27.

145. *Lettere,* Father Germano, January 15, 1903.

146. Thérèse of Lisieux, *Story of a Soul,* 72. Though not referring specifically to sainthood, Lucia Mangano also wrote about herself that "it was Jesus who raised his bride to a highest level, unique in the church, inferior only to that of his own mother." Pozzi and Leonardi, *Scrittrici mistiche italiane,* 663.

147. Pozzi and Leonardi, *Scrittrici mistiche italiane,* 681.

148. Elisabeth Schüssler Fiorenza, "Feminist Spirituality, Christian Identity, and Catholic Vision," in Carol Christ and Judith Plaskow, eds., *Womanspirit Rising: A Feminist Reader in Religion* (San Francisco, 1992), 136–48, 140.

149. Mazzoni, *Angela of Foligno's Memorial,* 27.

150. Guy Rosolato, "Présente mystique," in *Nouvelle revue de psychanalyse* 22 (1980): 5–36, 5.

151. *Lettere,* Father Germano, January 29, 1900.

152. For more examples of transgression, see for example *Autobiography,* 49, 55.

153. Donna Haraway, "A Cyborg Manifesto: Science, Technology, and Socialist Feminism in the Late Twentieth Century," in *Simians, Cyborgs, and Women: The Reinvention of Nature* (New York, 1991), 149–81, 149–50.

154. Michel Foucault, "A Preface to Transgression," in Fred Botting and Scott Wilson, eds., *Bataille: A Critical Reader* (Oxford, 1998), 24–40, 28.

155. Nancy Hartsock, "The Feminist Standpoint: Developing the Ground for a Specifically Feminist Historical Materialism," in Sandra Kemp and Judith Squires, eds., *Feminisms* (Oxford, 1997), 152–60, 158.

156. Beverly Wildung Harrison, *Making the Connections,* 15.

157. Luce Irigaray, *Speculum of the Other Woman,* trans. Gillian Gill (Ithaca, N.Y., 1985), 238.

158. Luce Irigaray, "Divine Women," in *Sexes and Genealogies,* trans. Gillian C. Gill (New York, 1993), 55–72, 63.

159. Ibid., 63–64.

160. Ibid., 67.

161. Gemma's contemporary Lucia Mangano similarly writes: "After these self-collections ["raccoglimenti" is the same term that Gemma uses for ecstatic raptures] it seems to me that I am almost made divine" ["divinizzata," again the same term as Gemma's]; and elsewhere: "all the powers of my soul . . . have been touched by God and have been divinely perfected, even made divine." Pozzi and Leonardi, *Scrittrici mistiche italiane,* 662, 664.

162. Jantzen, *Becoming Divine,* 93.

163. Maitland and Murford, *Virtuous Magic,* 329.

164. De Giorgio, "The Catholic Model," 188.

165. For more on Maria Goretti, see Kathleen Norris, "Maria Goretti—Cipher or Saint?" in Susan Bergman, ed., *Martyrs* (San Francisco, 1996), 299–309, and Eileen J. Stenzel, "Maria Goretti: Rape and the Politics of Sainthood," in Elisabeth Schüssler Fiorenza and M. Shawn Copeland, eds., *Violence Against Women* (London, 1994), 91–98.

166. Paolo Mantegazza, *Fisiologia della donna,* 2 vols. (Turin, 1893), 2:7–8.

167. De Giorgio, *Le italiane dall'Unità a oggi,* 18.

168. Pierre Jovanovic, quoted in Zecca, *Così lontani così vicini,* 15. Zoffoli entitles a chapter of *La povera Gemma* (chapter 4 of section 6, in part 1) "Gemma was beautiful," 419.

169. Joann Wolski Conn, "Toward Spiritual Maturity," in La Cugna, *Freeing Theology,* 235–59, 247.

170. De Giorgio, *Le italiane dall'Unità a oggi,* 39. I discuss this topic at length in my book *Maternal Impressions: Pregnancy and Childbirth in Literature and Theory* (Ithaca, N.Y., 2002).

171. A useful introduction to the debates around Mary can be found in Anthony J. Tambasco, *What Are They Saying About Mary?* (New York, 1984). See also Sarah Jane Boss, *Empress and Handmaid: On Nature and Gender in the Cult of the Virgin Mary* (London, 2000); Jaroslav Pelikan, *Mary Through the Centuries: Her Place in the History of Culture* (New Haven, Conn., 1996); Rosemary Radford Ruether, *Mary: The Feminine Face of the Church* (Philadelphia, 1977).

172. Mary Aquin O'Neill, "The Mystery of Being Human Together," in La Cugna, *Freeing Theology,* 139–60, 152.

173. Maitland, *A Big-Enough God,* 188.

174. Elizabeth Cady Stanton et al., eds., *History of Woman Suffrage,* 6 vols. (Rochester, N.Y., 1889), 1:116.

175. Johnson, *Friends of God and Prophets,* 152–53.

176. Zecca, *Così lontani così vicini,* 37; Zecca, *In croce ma col sorriso* (Milan, 1996), 76–77; Father Germano, *Gemma Galgani,* 41; Amedeo della M. del Buon Pastore, *La beata Gemma Galgani,* 81–84; most specific is Zoffoli, *La povera Gemma,* 11, 421–23. The play *The White Flower of the Passion* also dwells on Gemma's marriage proposals, and it makes Gemma's vow of virginity all the more poignant by depicting her chief suitor, Arnaldo, as utterly in love with Gemma and Gemma herself as, possibly, in love with him—though she chooses to give him up for Christ.

177. In Mary Eagleton, ed., *Feminist Theory: A Reader* (Oxford, 1986), 57–63, 60.

178. *Lettere,* Monsignor Volpi, November 1899.

179. *Estasi,* July 10, 1900.

180. *Estasi,* September 1899.

181. Pozzi and Leonardi, *Scrittrici mistiche italiane,* 40, 642.

182. *Lettere,* Father Germano, May 1900.

183. Silvia Vegetti Finzi, "The Female Animal," in Kemp and Bono, *The Lonely Mirror,* 128–51, 144.

184. *Lettere,* Monsignor Volpi, August 10, 1900.

185. On this subject, see Bynum, *Holy Feast and Holy Fast;* Bell, *Holy Anorexia* (Chicago, 1985).

186. Irigaray, *Speculum of the Other Woman,* 239.

187. Ibid., 249.

188. *Estasi,* March 16, 1900.

189. Nicola Zingarelli, *Vocabolario della lingua italiana* (Bologna, 1970), 762.

190. Richard Howard, "A Note on the Text," in Roland Barthes, *The Pleasure of the Text,* trans. Richard Miller (New York, 1975), v.

191. Harrison and Heyward, "Pain and Pleasure," 143.

192. On Jean-Martin Charcot's treatment of mysticism, see my *Saint Hysteria,* chapter 1; this discussion includes an extended bibliography both of Charcot's works and of secondary material on it.

193. *Lettere,* Father Germano, October 6, 1900.

194. *Lettere,* Father Germano, October 6–7, 1901.

195. *Lettere,* Father Germano, October 13, 1901.

196. *Lettere,* Monsignor Volpi, July-August 1899.

197. *Lettere,* Father Germano, September 22, 1901.

198. *Estasi,* October 14, 1902.

199. Bynum, *Holy Feast and Holy Fast,* 6.

200. Laurie Finke, *Feminist Theory, Women's Writing* (Ithaca, N.Y., 1992), 78.

201. Simone Weil, *The Notebooks of Simone Weil,* trans. Arthur Wills, 2. vols. (London, 1956), 2:337.

202. Luisa Muraro, "La nostra comune capacità d'infinito," 72–73.

203. *Lettere,* Father Germano, May 22, 1901.